TO MOVE THE HEART

TO MOVE THE HEART

PHILIP MELANCHTHON'S RHETORICAL VIEW OF RITE
AND ITS IMPLICATIONS FOR
CONTEMPORARY RITUAL THEORY

BY

MICHAEL B. AUNE

SAN FRANCISCO
CHRISTIAN UNIVERSITIES PRESS
1994

Michael B. Aune is professor of worship at
Pacific Lutheran Theological Seminary and
a member of the Core Doctoral Faculty in the
Graduate Theological Union, Berkeley, California.

Christian Universities Press is an imprint of
International Scholars Publications
P.O. Box 2590, San Francisco, California 94126.

Library of Congress Cataloguing-in-Publication Data

Aune, Michael Bjerknes.
To move the heart : Philip Melanchthon's rhetorical view of rite
and its implications for contemporary ritual theory / Michael B. Aune.
San Francisco: International Scholars Publications, 1994.
p.   cm.

Includes bibliographical references and index

1. Melanchthon, Philipp, 1497–1560.
2. Rhetoric – Religious aspects – Christianity.
3. Liturgical Language.
4. Lutheran Church – Liturgy – History – 16th century. I. Title

BR115. R55. A96 1994   264′.041′0092 – dc20   94-7182

ISBN : 1-883255-35-X (cloth)
ISBN : 1-883255-34-1 (paper)

To my parents

CONTENTS

FOREWORDS

We are entering a new age of discovery in Reformation and Renaissance studies. Scholars using a vast array of novel methodologies and sources now are examining the Sixteenth Century from the perspective of its social settings, its gender struggles, its literary production. They are finding new worlds almost more quickly than presses can turn out their books and other scholars can map what they have encountered.

One such uncharted land is the theologian and scholar, Philip Melanchthon. A person of enormous influence in his own day, Melanchthon has often been neglected or caricatured in our own, overshadowed by the more popular figures of Luther or Erasmus. This oversight, especially in the English-speaking world, is corrected in this important contribution to Melanchthon studies and ritual theory. Imitating Melanchthon by developing a mastery of several fields at once, Mr. Aune has outlined the heart of Melanchthon's theology and method and allowed it to speak to both Melanchthon studies and the contemporary debate over the nature and function of ritual. As a Christian theologian, Mr. Aune uses Melanchthon's own theological contributions to address the modern dilemma of Christian worship. In so doing, he not only restores the reputation of a sixteenth-century figure and grounds that thinker's theology in the then-novel insights of rhetoric, but he also challenges the reader to rethink the nature of ritual for today's church.

"Vitandae sunt in ecclesia ambiguitates" (ambiguities must be avoided in the church). This call of Melanchthon in the *Confessio Saxonica* of 1551 is answered by the scholarship in this book. Here Melanchthon's insights into the link between rhetoric and ritual are bound not only to move the heart but challenge the mind of the modern reader.

TIMOTHY J. WENGERT

Philadelphia, Pennsylvania
Commemoration of Olavus and Laurentius Petri, 1994

Michael Aune's study, *To Move the Heart: Philip Melanchthon's Rhetorical View of Rite and Its Implications for Contemporary Ritual Theory*, makes a valuable contribution to our understanding of ritual. Indeed, it is a study that performs a number of distinctive services and can serve as a model for future work. On the one hand, Aune demonstrates that Melanchthon's appreciation of ritual was rich and nuanced, closely intertwined with the values and arguments of his day, while equally embedded in a deep existential appreciation of the nature of human experience – the way God is apprehended by the lips, the ears, the limbs, and the heart. In this way *To Move the Heart* illustrates the importance of close historical work for understanding how ritual is variously located, constituted, and invoked by persons, communities, and liturgical traditions. On the other hand, Aune does not reduce ritual or Melanchthon's analysis of ritual to the status of mere historical artifacts, of interest only to those mapping the full intricacies of the sixteenth century in Europe. He finds that the historical insights of this person and period in the shaping of liturgical practices, cultural styles, and religious expectations means they can still speak to us today as we ritualize and as we attempt to understand what and how we ritualize.

Like most topics that have been the focus of 19th- and 20th-century European and American social science, the study of ritual emerged dependent upon formulas that attempted to describe and organize the basic mechanisms of all ritual everywhere. While such formulas facilitated a form of comprehensive and comparative scrutiny of practices not otherwise possible, they began to falter in the face of increasingly contextualized ethnographic and historical studies. Now we must learn how to speak about ritual in a new way, without implying that it is essentially always the same type of thing, although we may feel differently about it, and without denying that there are great continuities of culture and human experience that can allow the insights and gestures of a distant place and time to move our hearts. Aune begins to work out the intricacies of this language, and in doing so, he illuminates important aspects of where we are in our own locating, constructing, and questioning of ritual.

CATHERINE BELL

Santa Clara University
April 1994

PREFACE

This book is the result of my long-standing interest in why Philip Melanchthon would have used the expression, "to move the heart," as a way of interpreting Christian ritual's nature and purpose. I think that I can accurately pinpoint its origin: in October 1981, I heard my colleague Robert J. Goeser deliver the Graduate Theological Union's Distinguished Faculty Lecture, entitled "Luther and the Heart's Native Language." In this lecture, Goeser unfolded Luther's practical concern for biblical language and interpretation, especially the Reformer's effort to understand the sort of knowing that scripture and proclamation seek to generate in a reader or a listener. Such a knowing for Luther was not a detached, inhuman knowing divorced from experience but one which, according to Goeser, goes through experience for the sake of radical involvement and engagement in human existence. This emphasis on "the heart's native language," a language of actual human existence, reminded me of Melanchthon's comparable theological claim that Christian ritual "moves the heart to believe and to take hold of faith." Thus was triggered a process of reflection and research that took me to the works of Melanchthon in their original context and to modern theories of ritual, rhetoric, and anthropology, although not necessarily in that order.

I also recall that, several years later, I had a conversation with John J. Gumperz, now *emeritus* Professor of Anthropology at the University of California, Berkeley. After mentioning to him my interest in the question of what "to move the heart" might involve, he suggested that I read Michelle Z. Rosaldo's *Knowledge and Passion*. This work was an interpretive ethnography that endeavored to articulate something about the ways that cultures work by showing how they "mean." A key notion in this book – one that would change how I thought about the particular sort of relationship between "words" and the "world" – was how "knowledge" and "passion" work together in the "heart," thereby enabling people to recognize connections among the things they do, connections that made their cultural activities "intelligible and fraught with sense."

The academic discipline in which I usually work – liturgical studies – has been slow to recognize, even to acknowledge, that what people do in church or synagogue is similarly "intelligible and fraught with sense." But with the challenge to go beyond liturgical texts to study sociocultural contexts of those in worshiping communities, liturgical scholars now seek insights from many disciplines in order to proceed to worshipers and how they might understand the significance of what they do.

As I have explored the potential relevance of Melanchthon's "to move the heart" for a more satisfying way to think about Christian ritual, I have found that he, too, drew on the ideas and attitudes of his time. In interrogating and interpreting his work with regard to the concerns of current ritual practice and theory, I have come to the conviction that what we now hear in our discussions is the same appreciation of knowledge, body, self, and emotion that animated his recasting of the role of religious ritual and its purported power.

As this book has unfolded, a number of people have helped me in terms of specific readings, the larger thesis at hand, and the design of my argument. I am very fortunate and grateful to have benefitted from their help and support. I want especially to thank Professors Timothy J. Wengert (Lutheran Theological Seminary at Philadelphia), Catherine Bell (Santa Clara University), and James J. Murphy (University of California, Davis) for their comments, criticisms, and suggestions for improving both sense and prose. I want to mention especially the lively and intense correspondence that I have had with Professor Wengert, who provided prompt and helpful responses to my requests for clarifying various points of Melanchthon's rhetoric, dialectic, and theology.

Professor Ralph Walter Quere (Wartburg Theological Seminary) and my colleague Ted Peters read an earlier draft of this work and I thank both of them for their encouragement and suggestions. Professor Debora Kuller Shuger (University of California, Los Angeles) read an earlier draft as well. When I was tempted to drop the link between sixteenth-century rhetoric and late twentieth-century ritual theory, she suggested that I keep it.

My gratitude for hard and painstaking editorial work as this project moved along goes to Dr. Rebecca Slough. In fact, I owe her a profound debt along with my thanks for her careful reading and critical feedback along the way. Dr. John Hoffmeyer deserves a "thank you" as well for his assistance with some important translations.

As I entered the final stages of revising and rewriting, my colleague Martha Ellen Stortz graciously and patiently read the manuscript. Her suggestions were enormously helpful to me. She is a much-valued friend, colleague, and conversation-partner. And for assisting me in readying this manuscript for publication, I want to thank Matthew Henry Seeger. I appreciate his diligence and keen attention to detail as well as his good spirit.

To complete this project, both Pacific Lutheran Theological Seminary and the Graduate Theological Union provided most of the needed time and financial resources. My deans – Timothy F. Lull (PLTS) and Judith A. Berling (GTU) – thus have my gratitude as well.

M. B. A.

Berkeley, California
The Commemoration of Hans Nielsen Hauge
March 29, 1994

ABBREVIATIONS OF BOOKS

BC   *The Book of Concord: The Confessions of the Evangelical Lutheran Church*. Edited by Theodore G. Tappert. Philadelphia: Muhlenberg Press, 1959.

BS   *Die Bekenntnisschriften der evangelisch-lutherischen Kirche*. 6th ed. Göttingen: Vandenhoeck and Ruprecht, 1967.

CR   *Philippi Melanthonis Opera quae supersunt omnia*. Edited by Carl Gottlieb Bretschneider and Heinrich Ernest Bindseil. Vols. 1–28 of the *Corpus Reformatorum*. Halle: C. A. Schwetschke and Son, 1834–1860.

LC   Melanchthon's *Loci communes theologici* of 1521. Translated by Lowell J. Satre. In *Melanchthon and Bucer*. The Library of Christian Classics, vol. 19. Philadelphia: Westminster, 1969.

LW   *Luther's Works*. American Edition. 56 vols. Edited by Jaroslav Pelikan and Helmut T. Lehmann. St. Louis: Concordia Publishing House; Philadelphia: Fortress Press, 1955–.

MS   *Melanchthon: Selected Writings*. Translated by Charles L. Hill. Edited by Elmer E. Flack and Lowell J. Satre. Minneapolis: Augsburg Publishing House, 1962.

MW   *Melanchthons Werke in Auswahl*. Edited by Robert Stupperich et al. 6 vols. in 7. Gütersloh: C. Bertelsmann, 1951–1963.

RH   *Renaissance Humanism: Foundations, Forms, Legacy*. Edited by Albert Rabil, Jr. 3 vols. Philadelphia: Univ. of Pennsylvania Press, 1988.

SM   *Supplementa Melanchthoniana: Werke Philipp Melanchthons, die im Corpus reformatorum vermisst werden*. Ed. Melanchthon-Kommission des Vereins für Reformationsgeschichte. 5 vols. Vols. 1, 2, and 5, Leipzig: R. Haupt, 1910–1929. Reprinted Frankfurt : Minerva-Verl., 1968.

WA   *D. Martin Luthers Werke: Kritische Gesamtausgabe*. 61 vols. Weimar, 1883–.

INTRODUCTION

WHAT DOES CHRISTIAN RITUAL DO?

Simultaneously through the Word and the rite God moves the heart to believe and take hold of faith.... As the Word enters the ears to strike the heart [*ut feriat corda*], so the rite itself enters through the eyes to move the heart [*ut moveat corda*].[1]

More than four and a half centuries ago, Philip Melanchthon (1497–1560), chief colleague of Luther and lay theologian of the early Lutheran movement, wrote these words in response to one of the most controversial questions of his day: What does Christian ritual do? In fact, he used this "to move the heart" formulation on at least four occasions during the late 1520s and early 1530s to say that this activity – which he called "Word *and* rite" and which we label "ritual" – has a distinctive way of working. Ear, eye, and heart are addressed and moved simultaneously by God through the Word and the rite. Such a way of working possesses an objectivity and a subjectivity. It is both God's work and and a quite human event – one that is ritually enacted and experienced.

The immediate context for Melanchthon's insight was the great Reformation debate about the meanings, forms, and functions of Christian ritual.[2] Critics of traditional religious practice were fond of labelling external observances and official rituals, including the Mass, as "dumb," "vain," "idle," "superfluous," and "supersti-

---

1 Apology of the Augsburg Confession 13.5 (*BC*, 211–212). The Latin text (*BS*, 292) reads as follows: "Et corda simul per verbum et ritum movet Deus, ut credant et concipiant fidem.... Sicut autem verbum incurrit in aures, ut feriat corda: ita ritus ipse incurrit in oculus, *ut moveat corda*." My emphasis.
2 See Peter Burke, "The repudiation of ritual in early modern modern Europe," in *The Historical Anthropology of Early Modern Italy: Essays on Perception and Communication* (Cambridge: Cambridge Univ. Press, 1987), 223–238; and Burke, "Historians, Anthropologists, and Symbols," *Culture Through Time: Anthropological Approaches,* ed. Emiko Ohnuki-Tierney (Stanford: Stanford Univ. Press, 1990), 268–283. See also Andrew E. Barnes, "Review Essay: Religious Reform and the War Against Ritual," *Journal of Ritual Studies* 4/2 (winter 1990): 127–133, and Jonathan Z. Smith, *To Take Place: Toward Theory in Ritual* (Chicago: Univ. of Chicago Press, 1987), 100ff.

tious."[3] They insisted that there was a dichotomy between "true" and "false" worship. What made this activity "false" was the element of "ritual," understood as the use of visual images and awesome ceremonial display to show the objective presence of the divine, the true body of Christ.

The late-medieval church had claimed to provide both control and access to this sacred presence through ritualizing God's saving grace.[4] Of these displays, the most powerful of all was the Mass, i.e., the form that the eucharistic rite had taken in the churches of the West from about the fifth century on. By the late Middle Ages, the Mass was viewed as embodying the entire essence of the sacramental-magical world, capable of delivering believers from the anxieties and tribulations of this world, assuring them access to the next, and providing them with a wide array of spiritual and mundane benefits.[5] Yet, in an ever growing number of instances, this external religious observance did not always give such assurance, but only intensified and redirected the search for it.[6]

To produce an adequate understanding of why Melanchthon would have used such an expression as "to move the heart" to address the controversial question of what Christian ritual does, we find it necessary to issue three challenges: (a) a challenge to the "war against ritual" assessment of the Reformation's approach to this way of acting; (b) a challenge to what we regard as an inadequate understanding, even an ignoring, of the intellectual and cultural resources that, in Melanchthon's instance, contributed to his rethinking of ritual; and (c) a challenge to a caricature of Melanchthon himself that renders it difficult to understand, much less to appreciate, his theology and method.

(a) Challenge to the "War Against Ritual"

Some scholars have believed that the Reformation's war against ritual eventually produced the idea that such activity was not "real" but was "only" and "merely" symbolic, not essential to the experience of faith.[7] Moreover, they have argued that

---

3 Burke, "The repudiation of ritual," 226.

4 Robert W. Scribner, *The German Reformation* (Atlantic Highlands, N.J.: Humanities Press International, Inc., 1986), 11.

5 See James F. McCue, "Liturgy and Eucharist: West," in *Christian Spirituality II: High Middle Ages and Reformation*, ed. Jill Raitt et al. (New York: Crossroad, 1987), 427–438; and Robert W. Scribner, "The Reformation movements in Germany," in *The New Cambridge Modern History*, 2d ed. (Cambridge: Cambridge Univ. Press, 1990), 2:71.

6 Steven Ozment, *The Age of Reform 1250–1550: An Intellectual and Religious History of Late Medieval and Reformation Europe* (New Haven: Yale Univ. Press, 1980), 209.

7 E.g., Smith, *To Take Place: Toward Theory in Ritual*, 100ff.; and Burke, "Historians, Anthropologists, and Symbols," 268–283.

Protestantism's dissolution of the social and ritual bonds of late-medieval Catholicism led to an increasing emphasis on a more subjective orientation to religious belief and practice.[8] The result was the replacement of the traditional sacramental and ritual community with "the narrow subjective feelings of individuals."[9] Social historians, historical anthropologists, and scholars of comparative religion also claim and lament that the Reformation repudiated ritual as the model of communication between God and mortals, and mortals with each other and replaced it with the model of "classically inspired eloquence" – in short, rhetoric.[10]

These scholars, in romanticizing late-medieval Catholicism on the one hand and caricaturing Protestantism on the other, have assumed that ritual possesses some basic mechanism or universal quality. As such, they stubbornly insist that if one can only determine what this mechanism is, then one will know how ritual works. But such an approach imports and imposes a certain understanding of ritual on the period at hand, thereby [in our instance] distorting what the Reformers, Melanchthon included, sought to accomplish in their reconceptualization and reconstruction of late-medieval Christianity's symbolic order.

Thus, if we are to use a critical term such as "ritual," it needs more pliability and nuance.[11] That is, we shall do better to consider it as a particular "how" or "quality" of activity that is differentiated from other, usually more daily, activities.[12] As such, ritual is a strategic medium of a distinctive sort that seeks to deal practically with some specific circumstance. This specificity means that ritual, whether awesome or austere, is "inherently historical."[13] It assumes different forms and is undertaken for different reasons and effects.[14]

From this perspective, we can no longer view the great debate about the relation between words, images, and rituals, and the spiritual reality they were supposed to symbolize as simply a matter of "subjective" religious emotions enhanced by rhetoric

---

[8] See Steven Ozment's summary of this scholarship in *Protestants: The Birth of a Revolution* (New York: Doubleday, 1992), 34–42.

[9] Ozment, *The Age of Reform*, 210.

[10] E.g., John Bossy, *Christianity in the West 1400–1700* (Oxford: Oxford Univ. Press, 1985), 98.

[11] See Sarah Beckwith's caveat in this regard in her "Ritual, Church and Theatre: Medieval Dramas of the Sacramental Body," in *Culture and History 1350–1600: Essays on English Communities, Identities and Writing*, ed. David Aers (Detroit: Wayne State Univ. Press, 1992), 79–81.

[12] Ronald L. Grimes, *Ritual Criticism: Case Studies in Its Practice, Essays on Its Theory* (Columbia, S.C.: Univ. of South Carolina Press, 1990), 13ff; and Catherine Bell, *Ritual Theory, Ritual Practice* (Oxford: Oxford Univ. Press, 1992), 69–74

[13] John D. Kelly and Martha Kaplan, "History, Structure, and Ritual," *Annual Review of Anthropology* 19 (1990), 119.

[14] See Bell, *Ritual Theory, Ritual Practice*, 81–93.

versus "objective" religious practice enacted in ritual.[15] Nor should we regard the Reformers' attack on ritual as always leading to its replacement or repudiation. Rather, some envisioned their task as one of rethinking the very nature and purpose of this way of acting by incorporating elements from the intellectual climate of the time. Melanchthon, for example, turned to one of the early Lutheran Reformation's most important intellectual and methodological resources – the *theologia rhetorica* or "rhetorical theology" of Renaissance humanism, as indicated by his use of the term *movere*, the *officium* of the grand style of oratory.[16] In Renaissance and Reformation rhetorical theory, this grand style was understood as the best way to powerfully convey the themes and intentions of the Christian message.[17]

(b) Challenge to the Mutual Exclusion of Rhetoric and Ritual

In Melanchthon's time as well as our own, rhetoric and ritual were and are often viewed as mutually exclusive, if not altogether contradictory. The one is a particular use of language; the other is a certain kind of action. Less charitably, rhetoric is "mere rhetoric." It is subrational, emotional, seductive. Ritual is "empty ritual." It is mindless, routine, eccentric, a vestige of "popery." Yet rhetoric and ritual have more than their bad reputation in common. Both are suspected of possessing great power[18] and Melanchthon seemed to sense the connection between them.

In a similar fashion, the recent scholarly recognition and appreciation of the link between ritual and rhetoric have made it possible to rediscover the value and power

---

[15] Ozment, *The Age of Reform*, 210.

[16] The term is Charles Trinkaus's. See his *In Our Image and Likeness: Humanity and Divinity in Italian Humanist Thought*, (London: Constable and Co., 1970), 1:126–28, 141–42, 305–07, etc. *Movere* is one of the Ciceronian *officia oratoris*, or duties of an orator. The two other *officia* are *docere* and *delectare*. Marcus Tullius Cicero (106–43 B.C.) "was the greatest Roman orator and the most important Latin writer on rhetoric" (George A. Kennedy, *Classical Rhetoric and Its Christian and Secular Tradition from Ancient to Modern Times* [Chapel Hill, N.C.: Univ. of North Carolina Press, 1980], 90). His major contribution to rhetorical theory was this concept of the *officia oratoris*. Cicero discusses these "duties" in *De Oratore* and *Orator*. In the latter treatise (p. 357), for example, he wrote, "The man of eloquence...will be the one who is able to speak in court or in deliberative bodies so as to prove [*ut probet*], to please [*ut delectet*] and to sway or persuade [*ut flectat*]." This English translation is by H. M. Hubbell in the Loeb Classical Library volume containing Cicero's *Brutus*, trans. G. L. Hendrickson (Cambridge, Mass.: Harvard Univ. Press, 1962). In *Brutus* (p. 157) we read: "Now there are three things in my opinion which the orator should effect: instruct his listener [*ut doceatur*], give him pleasure [*ut delectetur*], stir his emotions [*ut moveatur*]." This combined action of *teaching – delighting – moving* is "a complex knot that cannot be undone or cut" (Renato Barilli, *Rhetoric*, tr. Giulana Menozzi [Minneapolis: Univ. of Minnesota Press, 1989], 30). These concepts were important in Augustine's discussion of Christian eloquence and, as we shall see in chapter 1, in the "rhetorical theology" of the Renaissance and Reformation. Moreover, they were regarded as belonging to an entire way of life, a worldview "founded on the preeminence of praxis over theory" (Barilli, 26).

[17] Debora Shuger, "The Christian Grand Style in Renaissance Rhetoric," *Viator* 16 (1985): 338–341.

[18] Burke, "The repudiation of ritual," 224.

of both and to explore more fully their similarities. Rhetoric as a way of speaking and ritual as a way of acting are able to explain a social world, to shape and define a community, to generate a certain kind of knowing, to construct a particular kind of person, and to stretch the daily experience of human beings into more grand, noble, and delightful meanings.[19] Thus, and perhaps unwittingly, those who have claimed that the Reformation repudiated ritual and replaced it with rhetoric have alerted us instead to pay closer attention to one of the significant perspectives which were used to rethink what this activity is and does.

(c) Challenge to Melanchthon Scholarship

Melanchthon's own rethinking and recasting of religious ritual from a rhetorical perspective has never been investigated. Instead, he is remembered either for his notion of "adiaphora," i.e., that so-called external ceremonial manifestations do not really matter because it is the underlying theology that is the most important.[20] Or, it is pointed out that he preferred to emphasize the larger, "functional" question of the use and purpose of the Lord's Supper in the life of the believer because he was so uneasy with theological attempts to answer the "how-question" of Christ's presence in the elements of bread and wine.[21]

We suspect, however, that an emphasis on "moving the heart" would be regarded as inconsistent with, even contradictory of the conventional image we have of Melanchthon as the great intellectualizer of the Lutheran Reformation who was more interested in doctrines, formulations, and definitions. Yet recent scholarship has demonstrated his concern with the affective, practical import of scripture and theology for a believer[22] as well as the emotional connotations of his concept of faith as *fiducia*.[23] Would he not also have been interested in how religious ritual works in a comparably affective, practical way?

---

19 E.g., Michael F. Carter, "The Ritual Functions of Epideictic Rhetoric: The Case of Socrates' Funeral Oration," *Rhetorica* 9, no. 3 (summer 1991): 209–232; and Celeste Michelle Condit, "The Functions of Epideictic: The Boston Massacre Orations as Exemplar," *Communication Quarterly* 33 (1985): 284–298.

20 E.g., Clyde Manschreck, *Melanchthon: The Quiet Reformer* (Nashville: Abingdon Press, 1958), ch. 21.

21 E.g., Peter Fraenkel, "Ten Questions Concerning Melanchthon, the Fathers, and the Eucharist," in *Luther and Melanchthon*, ed. Vilmos Vajta (Philadelphia: Muhlenberg Press, 1961), 146–164.

22 Timothy J. Wengert, *Philip Melanchthon's Annotationes in Johannem in Relation to its Predecessors and Contemporaries* (Genève: Librairie Droz, S.A., 1987), 161, 208–212.

23 Debora K. Shuger, *Sacred Rhetoric: The Christian Grand Style in the English Renaissance* (Princeton: Princeton Univ. Press, 1988), 68; Uwe Schnell, *Die homiletische Theorie Philipp Melanchthons*, Arbeiten zur Geschichte und Theologie des Luthertums 20 (Berlin: Lutherisches Verlaghaus, 1968), 89–113.

THE PURPOSE AND PLAN OF THIS BOOK

The primary purpose of this book is to answer this question by investigating Melanchthon's use of "to move the heart" to interpret the distinctive working of religious ritual.[24] But my purpose is also to demonstrate the significance of this interpretation for our own theoretical context in which we ask similar questions about how ritual does what it does. Although written in a very different time, an expression such as "to move the heart" still strikes a responsive chord. Participants in ritual, for example, like to speak of an intensely meaningful experience as "moving." Others may think of John Wesley's "heart strangely warmed" experience of listening to a reading of Luther's preface to the Epistle to the Romans. They then conclude that this is an appropriate way to speak of their own religious experience.

There is also a point of contact between Melanchthon's emphasis on the practical, affective workings of ritual with current scholarly interest in understanding how it is that activity which most moves a people[25] or how it exercises "a particularly persuasive effect on the participants' sense of identity and social reality."[26] To speak of "a persuasive effect" points to one of the *officia* or ends of rhetoric – that of being "moved" (*movere*).[27] Melanchthon's own use of *movere*, as we noted earlier, suggests the rhetorical cast of his thinking about religious ritual (and of his theology more generally). Therefore, our investigation of Melanchthon's use of "to move the heart"

---

[24] Melanchthon first used the expression, "to move the heart," in *Answer to the Anabaptists* (1528). He wrote that "the Sacrament confronts our eyes *to move our hearts* to believe" (*MS*, 106; Latin text, *MW*, 1:277). The second reference is the quotation from the Apology of the Augsburg Confession with which we began. The third reference is in the *Römerbrief-Kommentar* of 1532 (*MW*, 5:137). In his discussion of Romans 4.11 (*Signum accepit circumcisionis, sigillum iustitiae fidei*), entitled "De usu sacramentorum," Melanchthon wrote: "Non igitur merentur remissionem peccatorum, non iustificant, sed sunt notae, quae incurrunt in oculos ad commonefaciendos nos ad credendum, sicut verbum incurrit in aures, *ut moveat cor ad credendum.*" The fourth reference is the *Sententiae Veterae* (*CR*, 23:751): "Adest Deus et impellit *ac movet corda* per haec quae auribus atque oculis percipimus." Also, in the *Sententiae* (*CR*, 23:746), it is stated that the Sacrament was instituted "so that through it God may move and excite our minds to belief [*ut per ea Deus movet et exuscitet mentes ad credendum*]."

[25] Thomas M. Finn, "It Happened One Saturday Night: Ritual and Conversion in Augustine's North Africa," *Journal of the American Academy of Religion* 58, no. 4 (winter 1990): 589. Finn cites Monica Wilson, "Nyakyusa Ritual and Symbolism," *American Anthropologist* 56 (1954), 230, as the immediate source for this "anthropological axiom." Wilson's assertion that rituals disclose what most moves a people is also cited by Victor Turner, *The Ritual Process: Structure and Anti-structure* (Chicago: Adline, 1969; repr. Ithaca: Cornell Univ. Press, 1977), 6. "What moves them most," according to both Wilson and Turner, is the result of ritual's revealing the values of the group "at their deepest level" (Wilson, 241).

[26] Catherine Bell, "The Ritual Body and the Dynamics of Ritual Power," *Journal of Ritual Studies* 4, no. 2 (summer 1990): 299.

[27] See n. 16, above.

needs to begin with an examination of the intellectual and historical context from which it emerged (chapter 1). It is crucial to understand this context if we are to have any idea of the shape and character of his thought.[28]

At the same time, however, a more complete appreciation of what Melanchthon meant by "to move the heart" requires attention to late-medieval ritual practice and an emergent Reformed Protestantism (chapters 2 and 3) because of his effort to steer a middle course between the claims of both Rome and Zurich about what this way of acting and speaking does. The specific features of this formulation involve attention to *both* the force of the Word *and* the physical and visible action of the rite and are, therefore, the topic of chapter 4.

The task of the final chapter (chapter 5) is to show how such a rhetorical perspective on a heart being moved can be used to interrogate as well as to provide a window into some of the key concerns of current ritual practice and theory. Scholars have become especially interested in better understanding the mental and physical, affective and subjective, as well as cognitive dimensions of ritual experience.[29] We can hear in their discussions the same appreciation of self, emotion, and knowledge that animated Melanchthon's recasting of the role of ritual. In fact, some now argue that these dimensions are nothing less than "the crux of ritual."[30] Refusal or failure to deal with them "represents an enormous barrier to an understanding of the subject."[31]

Just as Melanchthon would employ the rhetorical concept of *movere,* with its accompanying views of knowledge, emotion, and selfhood, to achieve a better answer to the question of what ritual activity does, so in the late twentieth century, these matters are being seen as what is distinctive about its way of working. An exploration of Melanchthon's understanding of what is involved in "a movement of the heart," therefore, should be significant in its implications and compelling in its importance.

---

28 E.g., Michael Rogness, *Philip Melanchthon: Reformer Without Honor* (Minneapolis: Augsburg Publishing House, 1969), 2; and Wengert, *Melanchthon's Annotationes in Johannem,* 167ff.
29 Barbara G. Myerhoff, Linda A. Camino, and Edith Turner, "Rites of Passage," in *Encyclopedia of Religion,* ed. Mircea Eliade (New York: Macmillan, 1987), 12:383.
30 Ibid.
31 Ibid.

1. RENAISSANCE HUMANISM AND MELANCHTHON'S *THEOLOGIA RHETORICA*

A NEW OUTLOOK AND A NEW LEARNING

One of the favorite myths about Melanchthon is that his theology was pervasively and degeneratively "intellectualizing," a reduction of "Luther's direct and explosive addresses to academic form."[1] He is said to have understood Christian revelation as a certain kind of propositional knowledge that could be expressed in the form of ideas. While it is true that Melanchthon had "a passion for the proposition,"[2] for the cognitive meaning of doctrine, the knowledge he sought was "a very living knowledge of both the power and goodness of God."[3] The purpose or goal of this knowledge was "for motivation and Christian action, eventually that action which rendered us to God and God to us."[4] What Melanchthon sought to understand was

> always a matter of both knowledge and passion. Knowledge without passion was for him barren scholasticism; passion without knowledge, frightening fanaticism.[5]

Melanchthon's conception of knowledge as intellectually and affectively powerful belongs to a larger set of anthropological assumptions associated with that new outlook and new learning known as Renaissance Humanism. Suggesting as it does both a cultural revival and a secular philosophy, definitions of Renaissance Humanism have occupied historians since the appearance of Jacob Burckhardt's *The Civilization*

---

1 Eric W. Gritsch and Robert W. Jenson, *Lutheranism: The Theological Movement and Its Confessional Writings* (Philadelphia: Fortress Press, 1976), 64. For a different viewpoint, see Wengert, *Melanchthon's Annotationes in Johannem*, 121ff., 233; John R. Schneider, *Philip Melanchthon's Rhetorical Construal of Biblical Authority: Oratio Sacra*, Texts and Studies in Religion, vol. 51 (Lewiston, N.Y.: Edward Mellen, 1990), 234ff.; and Shuger, *Sacred Rhetoric*, 64–68.

2 Schneider, *Melanchthon's Rhetorical Construal of Biblical Authority*, 236.

3 Melanchthon, *LC*, 98. Translation altered, following Schneider: *cognitio* = knowledge.

4 Schneider, *Melanchthon's Rhetorical Construal of Biblical Authority*, 236.

5 Ibid., 238.

of the Renaissance in Italy more than a century ago[6] and have affected understandings of Melanchthon's theology as well.

If one adopted, for example, a formerly "traditional" view of Renaissance Humanism as a decisive break with the Middle Ages and as marked by consequent individualistic, anti-scholastic, and anti-Christian emphases that serve as the origins of what is characteristically modern, then Melanchthon's theology would be seen as gyrating between this pole and Luther's reformation.[7] If Renaissance Humanism's critical and rational habits of mind and affirmation of a new philosophy of life expressed in assumptions about the scope of the free were also characteristic of Melanchthon, then his views would stand in sharp opposition to Luther's understanding of justification, the bondage of the will, and the central note of faith as trust in the Gospel message. Or, if Renaissance Humanism lacked a sacramental piety and displayed a critical attitude toward ritual as the falsifying element that prevented "true" Christian worship, it would be seen as the source of Melanchthon's lack of interest in the sacraments, even of his reaching the point, "like all humanists,"[8] of being able to do without them.

Yet how one defines and understands Renaissance Humanism is crucial to an assessment of Melanchthon's intellectual development and theological orientation. Our task in this chapter, accordingly, is to provide a perspective on this movement of intellectual and cultural revival that can give us the necessary angle on his conception of theology's nature and task. First, we shall compare and contrast some older definitions of Renaissance Humanism with the more recent consensus of meaning regarding its meaning and character – especially the emphasis on humanism's valuing of a particular group of studies such as rhetoric for the design of graceful, persuasive, and effective communication. Secondly, we shall see how an understanding of rhetoric's effectiveness, summed up in the verb *movere*, produced a notion of theology as *theologia rhetorica*, best exemplified in Erasmus, but now recognized as certainly applicable to Melanchthon as well.[9] Lastly, we shall examine Melanchthon's concept of rhetoric and show how it helped him to define his position on important theological issues, to develop a particular manner of biblical interpretation, and to

---

6 Jacob Burckhardt, *The Civilization of the Renaissance in Italy*, trans. S. G. C. Middlemore (New York: New American Library, 1960).

7 E.g., Wengert, *Melanchthon's Annotationes in Johannem*, 58.

8 Herman Sasse, *This is my body: Luther's Contention for the Real Presence in the Sacrament of the Altar*, rev. ed. (Adelaide: Lutheran Publishing House, 1977), 255.

9 Charles Trinkaus, *The Scope of Renaissance Humanism* (Ann Arbor: Univ. of Michigan Press, 1979), 258.

present theological formulations that were very much concerned with affective, practical consequences in people's lives such as an understanding of religious ritual.

RENAISSANCE HUMANISM AND THE REVIVAL OF RHETORIC

In the early fifteenth century, a manuscript that had been lost for nearly six hundred years was rediscovered in a monastery dungeon. It was a copy of Quintilian's (A.D. 40–95) *Institutio oratorica*, or *Education of an Orator*, a work that had blended the theoretical and educational aspects of rhetoric and had influenced how it was taught over the centuries.[10] Along with a similar recovery of a complete text of Cicero's *De Oratore*, these finds were instrumental in the emergence of that intellectual and cultural movement known as Renaissance Humanism. Not so long ago, this movement was enthusiastically singled out by scholars for its so-called "modernity," individualism, anti-scholasticism, and affirmation of a new philosophy of life expressed in assumptions about the scope of free will. This involved, in turn, a strong reaction to what was perceived as the "pointless, arid intellectual speculation over trivia" associated, in the humanists' minds, with scholasticism.[11]

This "traditional" conception of the Renaissance, first articulated in the work of Jacob Burckhardt (published in 1860), saw it as a clear break from the Middle Ages, and, thus, the birth of modern consciousness.[12] Over against medieval Christian culture with its corporate structures and transcendental imperatives, Burkhardt argued that the Renaissance was marked by individualism, secularism, and moral autonomy. In fact, it was this distinct and peculiarly significant chapter in Western European history that gave "the highest development to individuality" and brought out "the full, whole nature of man" who now "recognized himself" as an individual.[13]

One consequence of such an emphasis on the Renaissance's "modernity" was to disregard the specificities and diversities of religious practices and writings. Also overlooked in an interpretation that emphasized the Renaissance as the birth of modern consciousness was the continuing preoccupation of scholastic and humanist alike with defining and defending traditional Christian doctrine. More recent scholarship

---

10 James Anderson Winn, *Unsuspected Eloquence: A History of the Relations between Poetry and Music* (New Haven & London: Yale Univ. Press, 1981), 122; Prentice A. Meador, "Quintilian and the *Institutio oratorica*," in *A Synoptic History of Classical Rhetoric*, ed. James J. Murphy (Davis, Calif.: Hermagoras Press, 1983), 151–176.
11 See the discussion of scholasticism by Alistair E. McGrath, *Reformation Thought: An Introduction* (London: Basil Blackwell, 1988), 50–66.
12 Burckhardt, *The Civilization of the Renaissance in Italy.*
13 Ibid., 65.

has deemphasized, reformulated, or subverted these "modernist" notions of the Renaissance by relating religious thought and movements, social conditions, etc., within the larger frame of Renaissance culture.[14] It has been observed that

> Religion remained a vital force in Renaissance society and the religious problem of the age was not the loss of faith but rather the inability of the bureaucratized, politicized institutional church to contain and creatively direct the spiritual energies of a society still deeply Christian.[15]

Also dispelled has been the commonly held view that the flowering of art, learning, and culture was solely or even primarily an Italian phenomenon. Instead, scholars are now demonstrating that the revival of letters and the generation of new modes of artistic expression had many sources outside of Italy. These often arose in response to numerous local needs, specific to the political, economic, social, and religious climates of principalities and regions all across Europe.[16]

"Humanism" and its attendant definitions, like the Renaissance, has also been understood in various ways. Some scholars emphasize that humanism was neither a clear break with the Middle Ages nor a forerunner of what is now called "secular humanism." Others point out that humanism's methods and concerns did not express a substantive philosophy but constituted an area of scholarly and literary activity that sought not to copy classical culture and its values, but to employ them in a creative way for shaping and interpreting contemporary experience.[17] These influential ideas had something to offer: "through them men came to think differently about themselves and the world."[18]

In spite of this diversity of viewpoints, it is possible to speak of "an emergent consensus" among scholars on the nature of humanism.[19] The meaning and significance

---

[14] See Charles Trinkaus, "Humanism, Religion, Society: Concepts and Motivations of Some Recent Studies," *Renaissance Quarterly* 29, no. 4 (winter 1976): 676–713.

[15] Charles G. Nauert, Jr., "Renaissance Humanism: An Emergent Consensus and Its Critics," *Indiana Social Sciences Quarterly* 33 (1980): 9.

[16] See the recent volume, *The Renaissance in national context*, ed. Roy Porter & Mikulas Teich (Cambridge: Cambridge Univ. Press, 1992).

[17] E.g., John Francis Tinkler, "Humanism as Discourse: Studies in the Rhetorical Culture of Renaissance Humanism, Petrarch to Bacon," (Ph.D. diss., Queens Univ., Kingston, Ontario, Canada, 1983), 7–22.

[18] John Stephens, *The Italian Renaissance: The Origins of Intellectual and Artistic Change Before the Reformation* (London and New York: Longman, 1990), xiii.

[19] The term is Charles G. Nauert's. See his "Renaissance Humanism: An Emergent Consensus and its Critics," 5–20. See also William J. Bouwsma, "Changing Assumptions in Later Renaissance Culture," *Viator* 7 (1976):74–96 (subsequently published in *A Usable Past* [Berkeley: Univ. of California Press, 1990]); Paul Oskar Kristeller, *Renaissance Thought: The Classic, Scholastic, and Humanist Strains* (New York: Harper & Row, 1961), 3–23; James J. Murphy, ed., *Renaissance*

of this intellectual and literary movement are equated with the revival of classical rhetoric, that art of eloquent and persuasive discourse which also enabled one to explain the process of human communication. This common bond that united the humanists no matter how separated in time or outlook, was, as Hanna Gray wrote in her now classic essay, "a conception of eloquence and its uses"[20] – in short, classical rhetoric.

According to Gray, a significant reason for humanism's assertion of the central role of rhetoric in education and culture had much to do with "a horror of abstract speculation carried on for its own sake."[21] At the same time, however, along with their condemnation of an attitude toward knowledge that stressed the abstract and the intellectual, humanists were very much interested in the persuasive communication of important truths that were truly useful and directly relevant for human life. Knowledge is to be lively, immediate, and persuasive enough not only to inform one's reason but also to stimulate one's will for practical ends.

Although Melanchthon's theology has been a focal point of study during the time a consensus on the meaning of humanism began to emerge, those historical theologians who have sought to understand better his turn of mind or habits of thought have not always taken advantage of the more useful concepts of humanism and rhetoric that are now available. Some of the discussions reflect older definitions of humanism as a new philosophy of life centering on the freedom of the will. Consider, for example, the following introduction to humanism in Michael Rogness' study of the place of Melanchthon in the development of Lutheran theology:

> The impetus behind Humanism was the Renaissance rediscovery of man. The Humanists sought to escape the harsh life and somber tones of the Dark Ages and recapture the grandeur of ancient Greece and Rome. They gloried in the beauty of nature and the capacity of man's spirit....Man's creativity was given free reign in painting, sculpture, architecture, music, and all culture.[22]

Others have restricted Melanchthon's interests to ancient languages or have operated with a notion of rhetoric that was so narrow that its entirety as an epistemology, a hermeneutic, and a framework for ethics was unknown.[23] Yet everything depends

---

Eloquence: Studies in the Theory and Practice of Renaissance Rhetoric, ed. (Berkeley: Univ. of California Press, 1983).

20 Hanna H. Gray, "Renaissance Humanism: The Pursuit of Eloquence," in *Renaissance Essays*, ed. Paul Oskar Kristeller and Philip P. Wiener (New York: Harper, 1968), 200.

21 Ibid., 203.

22 Rogness, *Reformer without Honor*, 2.

23 This criticism has been directed to Wilhelm Maurer's *Der junge Melanchthon zwischen Humanismus und Reformation*, 2 vols. (Gottingen: Vandenhoek and Ruprecht, 1967–1969), cited by

on a definition of humanism, as Timothy J. Wengert has forcefully reminded us, if we are to assess adequately the sense, let alone the innovative force of Melanchthon's way of doing theology.[24] Wengert's own definition of humanism "as interest in *bonae litterae*, rhetoric, and history, [and] *not* as a particular theological program,"[25] owes much to the recent and more tenuous consensus that now equates humanism with the revival of rhetoric.

Protagonists of rhetoric in early Lutheran thought, historical theologians, and cultural historians – when discussing its importance for evangelical theology and proclamation – cite regularly Luther's formula: "*Dialectica docet, rhetorica movet. Illa ad intellectum pertinet, haec ad voluntatem.*"[26] Melanchthon's statements from his first rhetorical handbook published in 1519, *De rhetorica libri tres*, and his later *Elementorum rhetorices* of 1531, make the same point:

> That you might know the nature of the studies about which I am speaking: the argument is the same for both the rhetorician and the dialectician: the one [dialectic] navigates between the limits of a proposed theme with sails somewhat more tightly drawn; the other [rhetoric] wanders more freely. The language of the one [dialectic] is accommodated to *teaching*, the other [rhetoric] to *moving*....[27]

> The distinction, to put it perhaps more properly, is that the end or purpose of dialectics is *to teach*, but the function of rhetoric is *to move* and stimulate minds and thus to affect a person.[28]

To understand more fully the nature not only of Renaissance Humanism's assimilation and synthesis of rhetoric but also of Melanchthon's own conceptualization of

---

Wengert in his *Melanchthon's Annotationes in Johannem*, 144. See Amy Seltzer, "Erasmus, for the Sake of Argument" (Ph.D. diss., Dept. of Rhetoric, Univ. of California, Berkeley, 1990), on the vital importance of counteracting the long tradition of separating rhetoric as expression from rhetoric as thought.

24 Wengert, *Melanchthon's Annotationes in Johannem*, 25.

25 Timothy J. Wengert, "Caspar Cruciger Sr.'s 1546 'Enarratio' on John's Gospel: An Experiment in Ecclesiological Exegesis," *Church History* 61, no. 1 (March 1992): 70, n. 36.

26 "Dialectic teaches, rhetoric moves. The one pertains to the intellect, the other to the will" (*D. Martin Luthers Werke: Tischreden*, 6 vols (Weimar, 1912–1921), 2:359, 18f. [2199A]); e.g., Klaus Dockhorn, "*Rhetorica movet*: Protestantischer Humanismus und karolingische Renaissance," in *Rhetorik: Beiträge zu ihrer Geschichte in Deutschland vom 16.–20. Jahrhundert*, ed. Helmut Schanze (Frankfurt: Athenaion, 1974), 21; Karl-Heinz zur Mühlen, "Rhetorik in Predigten und Schriften Luthers," *Luther Jahrbuch* 57 (1990): 257.

27 *De rhetorica libri tres* (Leipzig: Valentin Shumann, 1521). "Nam scias, quae sit ratio studiorum de quibus dico, commune argumentum est rhetori et dialectico, hic intra fines propositi negocii velis contractoribus navigat, ille evagatur liberius, *huis ad docendum, illius ad movendum est accommodata oratio*...."

28 Sister Mary J. LaFontaine, "A Critical Translation of Melanchthon's 'Elementorum Rhetorices Libri Duo,'" 85. "Iuxta hoc discrimen proprius dialecticae finis est docere, rhetoricae autem permovere atque impellere animos, et ad adfectum aliquem traducere...." The original Latin text is in *CR* 13:413–506.

this theory of discourse, it is important to be reminded, for a moment, of its basic categories.[29] These include the five stages of composition:

- *inventio*   – the discovery of material
- *dispositio*   – structure and arrangement of an oration or composition
- *elocutio*   – formulation in language
- *memoria*   – memorization
- *pronuntiatio*   – appropriate delivery

Rhetoricians also distinguished three kinds of oral discourse, and which, by extension, could include any work of literature:

- *epideictic*   – ceremonial discourse devoted to praise or blame
                     and intended to strengthen or deepen shared beliefs;
- *deliberative*   – legislative discourse involving persuasion and dissuasion,
                     as in political discourse;
- *forensic*   – judicial discourse concerned with proof or disproof,
                     as in a law court

Further, there were the main rhetorical styles, which were ranked according to levels or intensities of emotional involvement that a speaker or writer sought in a reader or listener:

- *plain style*   – "the most current idiom of standard speech"
- *middle style*   – "consists of words of a lower, yet not of the lowest
                     and most colloquial, class of words"
- *grand style*   – "a smooth and ornate arrangement of impressive words."[30]

Finally, a speaker or writer sought to accomplish three things: *docere* (to teach), *delectare* (to delight), and *movere* (to move). This concept of the "duties of an orator" involved a combined action of *teaching – delighting – moving* "in a complex knot that cannot be undone or cut."[31]

Because rhetoric's power is in affecting thoughts, judgments, feelings, and actions of others, scholars spent considerable time in elaborating how an oration was to be arranged and styled. If the goal was to affect the intellect, i.e., "to teach" (*docere*), the

---

29 Summaries of these categories are readily available in any rhetorical textbook and history of rhetoric. E.g., *The Rhetorical Tradition: Readings from Classical Times to the Present*, ed. Patricia Bizzell and Bruce Herzberg (Boston: Bedford Books of St. Martin's Press, 1990); Kennedy, *Classical Rhetoric.*

30 *Rhetorica ad Herennium*; cited in Brian Vickers, *In Defence of Rhetoric* (Oxford: Clarendon Press, 1988), 80.

31 Barilli, *Rhetoric*, 30.

style was more "plain." If the goal was "to delight" (*delectare*), the style was more in the "middle." If the goal was "to move" (*movere, emovere, permovere, flectere*), the rhetor employed the "grand style." Historian of rhetoric Brian Vickers provides a useful analogy:

> The Grand Style was allowed to use all the figures [of thought and sound], to achieve maximum effect; it was like a gale force 9; the Middle Style was force 5, the *genus humile* [i.e., "plain style"] force 3, with a correspondingly smaller power to affect the listener or reader.[32]

An ongoing difficulty for the ancient or classical rhetorical tradition, however, and one that Renaissance humanism sought to overcome, was the "faculty" psychology of the human person. Such a psychology viewed the person as composed of various and separate "faculties" or powers, "each directed towards a different object and responsible for a distinct operation."[33] While this faculty approach had the advantage of providing a model for the observation and explanation of human behavior, it could not account for the distinctive, emotive working of rhetoric. If *movere* was directed to the emotions of the hearer, it was necessary to understand and to utilize the emotional capacities of human beings for persuasive purposes if rhetoric was to be at all powerful and passionate discourse. But, over the long haul, such discourse continued to be seen as inherently deceptive because it played upon the desires and opinions of a basically ignorant if not imbecilic audience.[34]

A resolution, or at least a more helpful perspective on this ancient dichotomy of intellect and emotion was offered by Augustine's adaptation of classical rhetoric for Christian purposes. Among his important contributions was his revision, based on Christian epistemological and theological foundations, of the Ciceronian affective triad of teaching, delighting, and moving. Over against a pervasive and tenacious view of emotion as at best subrational, Augustine's ability to distinguish reason from volition and argument from pathos, resulted in a point of view that could closely interweave feeling, willing, knowing, and loving. This meant that emotion, instead of undermining the will, was key to how it worked, was, in fact, synonymous with the subjective experience of volition. The important point is that affectivity, "instead of

---

32 Vickers, *In Defence of Rhetoric*, 284.

33 Katharine Park, "The Organic Soul," *The Cambridge History of Renaissance Philosophy*, ed. Charles B. Schmitt et al. (Cambridge: Cambridge Univ. Press, 1988), 466.

34 Our discussion is based on Shuger, *Sacred Rhetoric*, 41–50.

being an irrational perturbation, thus moves into the center of spiritual experience."[35]

Although Augustine never connected this psychology of spiritual experience as fundamentally affective with rhetorical issues, subsequent discussions of Christian eloquence did, especially those of Renaissance humanism. These scholars saw how important, if not crucial, this understanding of affectivity was to a conception of sacred rhetoric that could best communicate the intentions and themes of Christian faith and life in a powerful and moving way. One historian has, in fact, concluded that rhetoric's effectiveness in moving the emotions, "summed up in the verbs *movere* and *flectere*," is possibly also its greatest contribution to the Renaissance, "being adopted *everywhere*, in rhetorical theory and practice, in poetics, music, and even painting,"[36] and, as we shall now see, in theology as well!

THEOLOGIA RHETORICA: AN AFFECTIVE, PRACTICAL THEOLOGY

This emphasis on *movere* helped to bring the realization that the nexus of relationships among God, human beings, nature, history, and society needed to be conceptualized more broadly and more experientially.[37] Such an emphasis contrasted sharply with traditional modes of thought, especially classical and theological anthropology, which had dominated the intellectual scene for centuries. The human person, as we have just seen, was understood as a hierarchy of faculties – intellect, will, and appetite – ruled by the intellect.

As this anthropology corresponded less and less with the realities and needs of late-medieval social life, scholastic theology came to be seen as increasingly abstract and irrelevant. It could not address the experience and feelings of living individuals. The stage was set, therefore, for the development of a style of thought that would be more experiential. Because of humanism's ongoing reclamation of the classical heritage of antiquity, a project itself motivated by the need to connect Christian beliefs with current cultural and intellectual problems, close at hand was a definite body of theory and practice that seemed immediately practical and useful – the rhetorical tradition.

This tradition unfolded in the Renaissance in a curious, controversial, and complex fashion. There were various Greek, Latin, and Christian rhetorical traditions

35 Ibid., 46.
36 Brian Vickers, "The recovery of rhetoric: Petrarch, Erasmus, Perelman," *History of the Human Sciences* 3, no. 3 (October 1990): 422. My emphasis.
37 Trinkaus, *The Scope of Renaissance Humanism*, 446.

that exercised considerable influence on how sacred rhetoric was conceptualized and practiced. Although these traditions differed significantly from one another in terms of style, range, and responses sought and produced, they did provide key resources for the important task of integrating theology, psychology, and language – for the mediation between Word and world.

This curious, if not controversial, mixture of Classical theory and practice and its Christian adaptations dating from the time of Augustine provided the foundation and engendered a new mood, a new way of doing theology – the *theologia rhetorica* of Renaissance humanism. Described once as an understanding of the elements of Christian theology as embedded in the feelings and experiences of living individuals, this *theologia rhetorica* involved a most salient definitional and psychological shift. In fact, it has been stated recently that this humanist rhetorical emphasis in time "wrought a profound intellectual change," and "a reorganization of consciousness."[38]

The intellectual and speculative concerns of faith seeking understanding gave way to more volitional and experiential emphases.[39] The view of the person that resulted was

both less and more than intellectual, less because it attributed so much power to other aspects of the personality, more in its recognition of the primacy in human experience of the inner life and the realm of subjectivity.[40]

As both theory and strategy of communication, rhetoric was rooted in a set of profound anthropological assumptions about the human personality, the positive value of the human passions and the human body, and the social-relational character and dynamic of human existence and experience. As such, rhetoric as a mode of thought and as a practice of discourse was understood as

the essential bond of human community, and therefore of supreme value for an increasingly complex society struggling to develop more effective patterns of communal life. Enthusiasm for rhetoric was most intense among townsmen responsible for welding the inchoate mass of individuals thrown together within the urban walls into a genuine community. Rhetoric thus provided a natural foundation for

---

[38] Ronald G. Witt, "Medieval Italian Culture and the Origins of Humanism as a Stylistic Ideal," in *RH*, 1:54.

[39] Marjorie O'Rourke Boyle, "Rhetorical Theology: Charity Seeking Charity," Response to William J. Bouwsma, "Calvinism as *Theologia Rhetorica*," *Center for Hermeneutical Studies in Hellenistic and Modern Culture Protocol of the Fifty-fourth Colloquy, 28 September 1986*, ed. Wilhelm Wuellner (Berkeley: Graduate Theological Union & Univ. of California-Berkeley, 1987), 24.

[40] William J. Bouwsma, "Review Article: 'Renaissance Humanism: Foundations, Forms, and Legacy,'" *Church History* 59, no. 1 (March 1990): 69.

the new urban culture of the Renaissance, and it operated at every level of human interaction, both private and public.[41]

This understanding of communication that sought full engagement with the total range of human experience was accompanied also by a changed conception of what comprises human knowledge.[42] Since rhetorical communication sought to persuade or "to move" a hearer by an appeal to the emotions rather than by trying to convince by an appeal to the mind, this meant that knowledge, too, was a total experience and not confined to the intellect alone.

Instead of localizing knowledge in the intellect, the humanists understood it as a total experience involving the feelings, penetrating the heart, shaping the will, and stimulating the whole person to some active response. Knowledge, in this conception, had to be subjectively appropriated in order to constitute, as we might say, "really" knowing.[43]

The human personality, therefore, was "an infinitely complex being, a dynamic and unpredictable bundle of energies, simultaneously sensual, passionate, intellectual, and spiritual…a mysterious unity."[44] The *theologia rhetorica* of Renaissance humanism regarded the essence of human being *not* from the viewpoint of what was highest but in terms of what was central – "its core (*cor, coeur*)."[45] This awareness or view of a human being as a mysterious unity helps us to understand better why early Reformation theologians emphasized "the heart."

The *theologia rhetorica* of Renaissance humanism, moreover, has been described as "an affective, practical theology" directed at the emotional, heart-felt conviction that an orator aspires to produce in [his] hearers.[46] Christian teaching and preaching were to be enunciated so clearly and powerfully that they could be existentially appropriated by the believer because he or she knew and felt the Gospel to be certain.

---

41 William J. Bouwsma, "Changing Assumptions in Later Renaissance Culture," *Viator* 7 (1976): 423.

42 William J. Bouwsma, "The Spirituality of Renaissance Humanism," in *Christian Spirituality II: High Middle Ages and Reformation*, edited by Jill Raitt in collaboration with Bernard McGinn and John Meyendorff, vol. 17 of *World Spirituality: An Encyclopedic History of the Religious Quest* (New York: Crossroad, 1987), 236.

43 Ibid., 238.

44 Ibid.

45 Bouwsma, "Review Article," 69.

46 Siegfried Wiedenhofer, "Humanismus und Reformation: Zur ökumenischen Bedeutung eines historischen Zusammenhangs," in *Werden und Wirkung der Reformation*, ed. L. Graf zu Dohna and R. Mokrosch (Darmstadt, 1986), 20–21; see his *Formalstrukturen humanistischer und reformatorischer Theologie bei Philipp Melanchthon*, 2 vols. (Bern: Herbert Lang and Frankfurt am Main und Munchen: Peter Lang, 1976).

This necessity for clarity and certainty had grown out of a larger crisis about the nature of knowledge that had begun several centuries earlier. The growing skepticism about the capacity of human beings to grasp the essences of things and to know God's ways and intentions, while embraced by some humanists, was regarded with horror by others. Among the responses to the intellectual and existential challenge posed by skepticism was the reassertion by Luther, Melanchthon, and other reformers, of God's goodness and the place of human beings in the divine creation.[47] Another way to deal with the skeptical threat was to experiment with different ways of knowing. Perhaps assisting such experimentation was the shift in religious consciousness that had first appeared in the twelfth century and was characterized by an increasingly interior, affective or emotional piety. One writer has stated recently that this shift was "marked by the desire for a felt rather than a reasoned faith."[48]

The major issue was: how could one establish the foundations of intellectual certainty, given the disjunction between words and things, *verba* and *res*? A consequence of rejecting the traditional sovereignty of human reason to know the world as it is was the awareness that knowledge is historically contingent and a changed conception of what it means to "know" something. Whether in the narrower sense of knowledge gained through the senses or in the wider sense of knowledge learned from experience, what was emerging was not so much the truth claims of what was to be known but, rather, its value – its utility for human life and action.

The intellectual and speculative concerns with faith seeking understanding had given way, therefore, to more volitional and experiential emphases.[49] This conception of knowledge that is to be a total experience – one that includes the feelings, enters the heart, molds the will, and incites the whole person to some lively response – helps us to understand better the sort of humanism that shaped and influenced Melanchthon. It was a practical and affective theology – a *theologia rhetorica*. The following summary of its major characteristics can serve as a bridge to our consideration of Melanchthon's own humanist methods and practices and their role in his approach to important theological issues, his particular manner of biblical interpretation, and his careful design of an evangelical message that could have powerful, affec-

47 Robert L. Rosin, "The Reformation Response to Skepticism: Ecclesiastes Commentaries of Luther, Brenz, and Melanchthon," (Ph.D. diss., Dept. of History, Stanford Univ., 1985).

48 Timothy Verdon, "Environments of Experience and Imagination," *Christianity and the Renaissance*, ed. Timothy Verdon and John Henderson (Syracuse, N.Y.: Syracuse Univ. Press, 1990), 11.

49 O'Rourke Boyle, "Rhetorical Theology: Charity Seeking Charity," 24.

tive, practical consequences in people's lives: "to bring about healing, comfort, or trust in those who heard it."[50]

The Major Characteristcs of Humanism's Affective, Practical Theology

- a reform theology, more rhetorical than logical-systematic
- a theology more focused on the substance and reality of Christian faith in its decisive, primary form
- a theology that is strictly Christocentric
- a critical theology over against "tradition"
- a scriptural theology that understands itself as true revelation
- a practical theology understood as a type of proclamation concerned with the Christian life and the question of salvation
- an affective theology that occurs in the dynamic of the spirit of Christ
- an existential theology that is communicated not only in the objective categories of doctrine but also in the form of personal witness [seen psychologically, the intellect is subordinate to affect and integrated into it]

Based on Wiedenhofer, "Humanismus und Reformation: Zur ökumenischen Bedeutung eines historischen Zusammenhangs," 20–21. There is a comparable summary in his *Formalstrukturen*, 1:158–160.

DIALECTICA DOCET, RHETORICA MOVET: MELANCHTHON'S AFFECTIVE, PRACTICAL THEOLOGY

Thus far, we have seen that rhetoric was not only a theory and art of discourse with clarity as a concern and action as its goal. It was also an approach to knowledge, a style of inquiry interested in the utility, intelligibility, and direct relevance of thought and knowledge for human life.[51] These concerns and approaches, as will be evident shortly, were also present in Melanchthon's own concept of rhetoric.

Several years before Melanchthon's appointment as a professor of Greek language and literature at the University of Wittenberg in 1518, a call for its reform along humanist lines was already underway. What this meant was a curricular emphasis on the study of biblical languages, the so-called "pure sources of Christian doctrine, i.e., the Bible and Church History," mathematics, and rhetoric.[52] Melanchthon's inaugural professorial lecture of August 29, 1518, entitled *De corrigendis adolescentiae studiis*, voiced similar concerns for curricular reform.[53] But our particular interest in

---

50 Wengert, *Melanchthon's Annotationes in Johannem*, 210.

51 Jerrold Seigel, *Rhetoric and Philosophy in Renaissance Humanism* (Princeton: Princeton Univ. Press, 1969), xi–xvii, 200–262.

52 Wengert, *Melanchthon's Annotationes in Johannem*, 25–28.

53 The original texts are in *CR*, 11:15–25, and *MW*, 3:29–42. There is an English translation by Ralph Keen, "On Correcting the Studies of Youth," in his *A Melanchthon Reader* (New York and Bern: Peter Lang, 1988), 47–57.

this lecture is the conception of rhetoric that Melanchthon presents, one that always emphasizes the importance of dialectic – a particular kind of critical inquiry that is necessary for discovering and knowing what can be said on a given subject for the purposes of persuasion.[54]

After recounting and condemning many long centuries of scholarly decay in the first part of this inaugural lecture, Melanchthon turned to a lengthy discussion of the role of the liberal arts and the fundamental role of dialectic. In doing so, he was rejecting, adopting, and developing in new directions an approach to the study of language and knowledge that had begun with Lorenzo Valla's *Repastinatio dialecticae et philosophiae* (1439) and Rudolph Agricola's watershed work of synthesizing dialectic and rhetoric, *De inventione dialectica* (1479), constructed around the *officia oratoris*: teaching, moving, and delighting.[55] Thus, Melanchthon can say, "Logic [i.e., dialectic] treats all the power and the distinctions of language...[and] indicates what you should pay attention to...."[56] Understood both as a system of philosophical argument and as a system of rules and methods for asking questions or for investigating subjects, dialectic could serve several functions: as a method of critical thinking, as a way of describing and handling complex things, as a method of sharpening one's discourse. Its goal, however, in the words of a modern commentator, was "to unleash all the power of language to persuade of truth."[57] With this description of the functions of dialectic, Melanchthon then concludes: "These are the parts of that which we call dialectic, others rhetoric: for authors vary in names, while the art is the same."[58]

Dialectic had once formed the basis for an understanding of rhetoric (e.g., as in Aristotle). In fact, rhetoric was regarded as a form of dialectic, in that it employed similar investigative processes or involved parallel movements, "virtually identical in content...."[59] Both were concerned with what constitutes knowledge, how such knowledge is to be discovered and employed in human communication.

Dialectic and rhetoric had become separated, however, and were often defined in terms of their differences rather than their similarities. In the Middle Ages, for exam-

---

54 See Lisa Jardine, "Humanist Logic," in *The Cambridge History of Renaissance Philosophy*, 173–198; also Peter Mack, *Renaissance Argument: Valla and Agricola in the Traditions of Rhetoric and Dialectic* (Leiden: E. J. Brill, 1993).

55 See Mack's summary, *Renaissance Argument*, 121–125.

56 "De corrigendis adolescentiae studiis 1518," in *MW*, 3:34: "Logicum vim omnem ac discrimina sermonis tractat...[et] indicat quid observes...."; see Schneider, *Melanchthon's Rhetorical Construal of Biblical Authority*, 54.

57 Schneider, *Melanchthon's Rhetorical Construal of Biblical Authority*, 54.

58 "De corrigendis adolescentiae studiis 1518," 34: "Hae partes illius sunt, quam nos dialecticam, alii rhetoricam vocant: Nominibus enim variant auctores, cum ars eadem sit."

59 Kennedy, *Classical Rhetoric*, 65.

ple, dialectic assumed a life of his own, becoming the intellectually dominant part of education.[60] Rhetoric, on the other hand, was to be that more practical task that involved official letter-writing.

A notable feature of Renaissance Humanism was its reassessment of the relationship between dialectic and rhetoric. The emphasis was placed on the finding part of both – a part known as *inventio*. An increasing dissatisfaction with abstract methods of discussion and logical structures produced a rethinking of the classical heritage of persuasion. Such a rethinking as one finds in Rudolph Agricola and subsequently in Melanchthon consisted of an interrelating of inquiry, argument, exposition, and emotional persuasion. That is, in considering what to say, one needs to know how to find convincing material, and to know how to organize it in such a way as to simultaneously teach, move, and please a listener or a reader.[61]

Agricola's insistence that teaching and moving, dialectic and rhetoric, belong together would be reflected in Melanchthon's conception of these uses of language. Although regarded as somewhat of a revolutionary by some historians of rhetoric, Agricola "stood on its head the classical dictum that orators must move, please, and teach."[62] Although assessments of Agricola's achievement differ,[63] his emphasis that *movere* and *docere* exist simultaneously influenced Melanchthon's subsequent rhetorical, theological, and homiletical writings.[64]

---

60 Mack, *Renaissance Argument*, 8–14.

61 Ibid., 120.

62 John Monfasani, "Humanism and Rhetoric," in *RH*, 196. Agricola has been sometimes called the "father of German humanism." We have noted already that his *De inventione dialectica* was an original, important, and highly influential pedagogical work. For recent discussions of the revolutionary impact of Agricola's work, see Marc Cogan, "Rodolphus Agricola and the Semantic Revolutions of the History of Invention," *Rhetorica* 2, no. 2 (summer 1984): 163–194, and Mack, *Renaissance Argument*, which has a chapter on Melanchthon's rhetorical and dialectical works (pp. 320–333).

63 E.g., did he collapse the traditional *officia oratoris* into one, "to teach," or did he regard teaching and moving as of a single piece because teaching seeks emotional, passionate involvement with the most important issues of human life? See Shuger, *Sacred Rhetoric*, 61–62.

64 Mack, *Renaissance Argument*, 321ff; See also Kees Meerhoff, "Logic and Eloquence: A Ramusian Revolution?" *Argumentation* 5, no. 4 (November 1991): 357–374; idem, "The Significance of Philip Melanchthon's Rhetoric in the Renaissance," in *Renaissance Rhetoric*, ed. Peter Mack (New York: St. Martin's, 1994), 46–62; Judith Rice Henderson, "Erasmian Ciceronians: Reformation Teachers of Letter Writing," *Rhetorica* 10, no. 3 (summer 1992): 273–302; and Mary Thomas Crane, *Framing Authority: Sayings, Self, and Society in Sixteenth-Century England* (Princeton: Princeton Univ. Press, 1993), 17–25. Meerhoff's essay on Melanchthon's rhetoric appeared as I was completing this study. My own emphasis on the simultaneity of teaching and moving in Melanchthon closely parallels Meerhoff's insight that the Melanchthonian rhetorical-theological "system" consists of "the two complementary goals" of "teaching and appealing to the emotions" (p. 53).

Historians of rhetoric as well as historical theologians identify Melanchthon's re-union of these two arts as a major theoretical innovation.[65] This joining of dialectic and rhetoric exemplified what has been termed recently as "Northern Methodical Humanism."[66] Both in his inaugural oration, which he delivered upon his arrival in Wittenberg in 1518, and in his *De rhetorica libri tres*, published a year later, Melanchthon presented his proposals for such a reunion. In the latter, he wrote that "rhetorical considerations have to do with practical matters" and dialectic "embraces demonstration or apodeixis – i.e., a readily, intelligible system of instruction."[67]

Such a heightened and self-conscious awareness of method signaled a change of emphasis in how one was to undertake the tasks of interpretation and theological formulation. Instead of pursuing abstract, metaphysical speculation as a way to knowledge, Melanchthon argued that the theologian needed to be concerned with the deepest existential questions and to understand the clearest cognitive claims of biblical doctrine so that receptive readers' and hearers' hearts could be transformed.[68] Thus, in the 1521 *Loci communes*, we can observe him thinking "existentially," as he proceeds from the cognitive to the affective. There is the "what" and "when" of sin, law, and grace, but also their power or effect: e.g., *quid peccatum – vis peccati et fruc-tus, de lege – de vi legis*, and *quid evangelium – de vi evangelium*. The progression is from "knowledge" to "efficacy," to a particular purpose or goal.

By closely allying (or reuniting) dialectic with rhetoric as Agricola had done, what emerges is an insistence on their fundamental similarity. The importance that Melanchthon attached to dialectical and rhetorical analysis of texts – that the two need to be taught together – helps to explain the sort of knowledge in which he was interested. It was to be a total experience involving both reason and emotion. The af-fective concerns of humanist theological thinking were oriented to a subjective ap-propriation of knowledge – "really" knowing, as we might say.[69] Knowledge of God's saving activity *pro homine*, for example, is to be knowledge of God's saving activity

[65] E.g., John McNally, "Melanchthon's Earliest Rhetoric," in *Rhetoric: A Tradition in Transition,* ed. Walter R. Fisher (East Lansing, Mich.: Michigan State Univ. Press, 1974), 33–40; Schneider, *Melanchthon's Rhetorical Construal of Biblical Authority,* 65–95; Wengert, *Melanchthon's Annotationes in Johannem,* 167–212.

[66] Anthony Grafton and Lisa Jardine, *From Humanism to the Humanities* (Cambridge: Harvard Univ. Press, 1986), 122–157.

[67] Cited in McNally, "Melanchthon's Earliest Rhetoric," 37.

[68] Schneider, *Melanchthon's Rhetorical Construal of Biblical Authority,* 218.

[69] Bouwsma, "The Spirituality of Renaissance Humanism," 238.

pro me.[70] The human personality, as we saw earlier, was understood as a complex, dynamic, unpredictable, and mysterious unity.[71] The anthropology of Renaissance Humanism's *theologia rhetorica* regarded the essence of human being, then, *not* from the viewpoint of what was highest but in terms of what was central – "its core (*cor, coeur*)."[72] Such an awareness helps us to understand better the emphasis that early Reformation theologians, including Melanchthon, placed upon "the heart."

This larger context of changing attitudes toward human knowing helps to explain Melanchthon's emphasis that knowledge be clear, certain, and useful. He also seemed to be insisting that the noetic and the affective, or interpretation and conviction, belong together. In his approach to biblical texts, for example, Melanchthon was preoccupied not only with their content but also with their purpose. This linkage (or, as some scholars have noted, "fusion") has been described in terms of *cognitio* and *affectus* – i.e., knowledge and passion.[73]

When we turn to Melanchthon's 1519 *De rhetorica libri tres*, in order to see more clearly this binding together of rhetoric and dialectic, we encounter, first of all, a discussion of the duties of the orator, the kinds of rhetoric, and the parts that an oration was to have. So, at least initially, we have the traditional list of invention, arrangement, style, memory, and delivery. Then, Melanchthon presents the *genera dicendi* – epideictic, deliberative, and forensic. And, finally, there is the classical and conventional framework for the arrangement of one's oration or composition into its connected parts – introduction, assertion of main point, defense of the main point, refutation of possible objections, and a concluding summary.

In addition to these characteristics, which identify Melanchthon's *De rhetorica libri tres* as rather typical of a work of northern European rhetoric, there is a major theoretical innovation of making demonstrative or epideictic rhetoric into the basic genre of discourse. Traditionally, this *genus dicendi* had been one of praise and blame addressed to mere spectators and concerned with the present. Melanchthon altered this central concern and proposed instead that epideictic "is concerned primarily with instruction, and only secondarily with praise and blame." More specifically, according to Melanchthon,

---

70 Klaus Haendler, *Wort und Glaube bei Melanchthon: Eine Untersuchung über die Voraussetzungen und Grundlagen des melanchthonischen Kirchensbegriffes*, Quellen und Forschungen zur Reformationsgeschichte, Band 37 (Gütersloh: Gütersloher Verlaghaus Gerd Mohn, 1968), 403.
71 Bouwsma, "Review Article," 69.
72 Ibid.
73 Wiedenhofer, *Formalstrukturen*, 1:196.

the epideictic genre, or theory of teaching is that which sets down by means of established places, and thereby discloses the nature and character of each subject in such a manner that, if the thing in its own right is at all capable of being understood, it cannot elude the inquirer. There are two functions to this genre: having immediately at hand by means of the proper places all that can be said about a given subject; and that of meting out those places in the order which will most effectively insinuate knowledge into the hearer's mind.[74]

John McNally has observed that Melanchthon's theoretical addition

was in essence an attempt to remake rhetoric into what it had been for Cicero and Quintilian: *the* art or theory of public communication concerned with and responsible for every aspect of its subject, from preliminary "situational" analysis, through research, strategic arrangement, and artistic expression to final presentation to and evaluation by an audience.[75]

In his subsequent *Institutiones rhetorices* of 1521 and *Elementorum rhetorices* of a decade later, Melanchthon continued to emphasize the teaching function of rhetoric but included it in separate *genus*, the so-called *genus didaskalikon* that he had added to the traditional three of epideictic, forensic, and deliberative. At the outset of this 1531 handbook, we encounter a discussion of why one should study rhetoric. It provides a useful way to read literary texts and "make proper judgments in long controversial matters."[76]

Then, after a discussion of the duties of the orator, we find a treatment of the distinction between dialectic and rhetoric and Melanchthon's assertion, "So great is [their] resemblance that scarcely any distinction can be observed between them."[77] While he noted how dialectic had been a matter of finding and preparing arguments for the use of rhetoricians and rhetoric adding "the vesture of words," Melanchthon reiterated that the two cannot be divorced. The purpose of dialectic is to teach (*docere*) "but the function of rhetoric is to move (*permovere*) and stimulate minds (*animos*) and thus to affect a person."[78]

To illustrate how dialectic and rhetoric work together [indeed they are so closely linked to each other that they "cannot be completely separated"], Melanchthon provided the examples of how to discuss virtue and penance:

---

[74] *De rhetorica libri tres*; cited in McNally, "Melanchthon's Earliest Rhetoric," 39.
[75] McNally, "Melanchthon's Earliest Rhetoric," 39.
[76] LaFontaine, "Melanchthon's 'Elementorum Rhetorices Libri Duo,'" 85.
[77] Ibid., 82.
[78] Ibid., 85.

dialectics must be used to show what virtue is, and what are its causes, its degrees, and its effects. But when he exhorts people to be virtuous, the principles of rhetoric must be followed. When we discourse about penance, the principles of dialectics must be used to teach men what penance is and what are its degrees. But the principles of rhetoric must be used to exhort men to do penance.[79]

The discussion then proceeds to the three kinds of rhetoric – declamatory or praise and blame, deliberative, and judicial. But now comes the new genus with teaching as its purpose:

> I myself recommend adding a fourth kind, and I borrow the name for it from the Greek and call it *didaskalikon*. This, indeed, is concerned with dialectic [and] it should not be ignored, especially in these days when it is a great use in Church matters where it is not so much a matter of platform speaking, but where wise men of dialectics can teach the dogmas of religion so that they are better understood (or, known).[80]

After providing some additional examples of epideictic rhetoric working as a form of teaching – such as how a statement of praise of Christ is actually a certain kind of definition "for it praises the person of Christ"[81] because it recalls who he is and what he has done, Melanchthon shows more specifically that teaching is a matter of forcefulness and usefulness:

> So the purpose of the didactic kind of instruction is to produce knowledge in individuals, as for instance when someone teaches what the Gospel is, how we can bring it about that God should think and pronounce us righteous, what faith is....[82]

The manner in which such knowledge was to be achieved employed a procedure built upon the "questions" of Aristotle's *Posterior Analytics* to search out and bring to light things belonging to a text. T. H. L. Parker has commented on Melanchthon's general concept of method:

> The programme is quite clear: The critic's way is one of search and discovery, his purpose is to find and coordinate the major concepts, his office to reduce confusion to order. He is an explorer, hacking his way through the undergrowth of dead languages and foreign customs and at the end of the journey assembling and relat-

---

79 Ibid., 85–86.
80 Ibid., 88.
81 Ibid., 89.
82 Ibid., 95.

ing the manifold specimens that he has collected. His journey is *inventio*, his specimens *loci*.[83]

In the 1519 *De rhetorica*, in the dialectics of 1520, in the 1521 *Institutiones rhetoricae*, and in the 1531 *Elementorum rhetorices*, Melanchthon presented a list of *inveniendi organa*, which would enable students to know "whatever can be known about any subject...."[84] These questions were:

• *An sit*	– Does it exist?
• *Quid sit*	– What is it?
• *Quibus causis partibusve constet*	– Of what causes or parts does it consist?
• *Unam an multa*	– Is it one or many?
• *Quae partes*	– What are its parts?
• *Quae comparatio partium*	– What is the comparison of parts?
• *Quae officia*	– What are its functions?
• *Quae affinia*	– What are its affinities?
• *Quae contraria*	– What are its contraries?

We know that in Melanchthon's exegetical work, the first question that he would ask of a verse was, "*Quid sit?*" But the second, and the most crucial question to be asked of a verse was, "*Quae officia?*" This is the text's purpose or goal. Moreover, as Melanchthon argued in his *Compendaria Dialectices Ratio* of 1520,

> nothing else is more diligently [to be] sought than what the use of a thing is.... A dialectician investigating the nature of a thing always establishes some proper office of the proposed theme.[85]

Just what this "proper office" is, however, is a matter of debate among some Melanchthon scholars. Some regard the *officium* or "efficacy" of a text and/or theological concept [e.g., the nature of religious ritual and its place in Christian life] as "*affektive Wirkung*" – its affective or emotional force.[86] Others regard this as a reductive misreading of how Melanchthon employed a dialectical method in union with rhetoric. Yet we need to remember that he used this method in order to make

---

83 T. H. L. Parker, *Calvin's New Testament Commentaries* (Grand Rapids, Mich.: William R. Eerdmans Publishing Company, 1971), 33.

84 Cited in Schneider, *Melanchthon's Rhetorical Construal of Biblical Authority*, 72; Wengert, *Melanchthon's Annotationes in Johannem*, 192–193.

85 Cited in Wengert, *Melanchthon's Annotationes in Johannem*, 208–209.

86 E.g., Haendler, *Wort und Glaube*, 500ff; Hans-Georg Geyer, *Vom Geburt des wahren Menschen: Probleme aus den Anfängen der Theologie Melanchthons* (Neukirchen: Neukirchener Verlag des Erziehungsvereins GmbH, 1965).

effect "as much a part of the *meaning* of the text as its definition."[87] Whether an *affektive Wirkung* of a text or a theological concept is "reductive" is an issue that requires additional examination of both Melanchthon's rhetoric and his anthropology. The important point at this juncture is that the *officium* of a text is often soteriological, even psychological, in nature because of its interest in how comfort, trust, or healing can be brought about. Clear and certain knowledge of what the text says reaches its goal in the hearer or reader, not simply by having performed a cognitive or intellective function, but by having involved the entire person.

Melanchthon's insistence on the importance of dialectic and its close connection with rhetoric helps us to understand his concern with the practical, affective effects of scriptural interpretation and theological formulation. Dialectic, as we have seen, is the method for content: determining an understanding that is appropriate to the nature of the subject matter. Rhetoric has to do with the affective relation of the subject matter to human beings. Thus we could say (perhaps simplistically) that dialectic has to do with intellect and rhetoric with affect. In fact, in his first edition of the dialectic, the *Compendaria Dialectices Ratio* of 1520, Melanchthon plays with such categories. But he also ties dialectic to another (affective!) category, namely certainty.

Dialectic and its analytical questions, especially *Quid sit?* and *Quae officia?* reveal the structure of things as a way of obtaining a certainty for the rhetorician. Without dialectic, the rhetorician would remain enmeshed in the uncertainty of language and speech.

Thus, dialectic has to do with certain knowledge. "I am certain, therefore I speak." In theology, the entire enterprise stands or falls on certainty. Dialectic, then, plays a crucial role. But we have noted how the affective is at the heart of Melanchthon's interest. Knowing a thing, for Melanchthon, is not ever merely a cognitive, intellective event. It involves the entire being and brings certainty, and in the case of the gospel, comfort. Thus, in the *Loci communes* of 1521, he can even describe the sacraments, i.e., Christian ritual, as offering reassurance and a feeling of certainty to the recipient:

> If God himself were to speak to you face to face or show you some peculiar pledge of his mercy as, for instance, a miracle, you would consider it nothing else than a sign of divine favor. As for these signs, then, you ought to believe with as much certainty that God is merciful to you when you receive baptism and participate in the Lord's Supper as you would if God himself were to speak with you or to show forth some other miracle that would pertain peculiarly to you.[88]

---

87 E.g., Wengert, *Melanchthon's Annotationes in Johannem*, 209.
88 Melanchthon, *LC*, 135.

RHETORIC AND RITUAL ONCE AGAIN

This union of dialectic and rhetoric and the application of their precepts to the interpretation of texts, and, as we have just seen, to the interpretation of Christian ritual, particularly the sacraments, suggests a bringing together of theory and practice.[89] We know, for example, that rhetorical theory was used by Protestant and Catholic reformer alike to reconceptualize the nature and task of preaching as passionate and powerful oratory.[90] Melanchthon himself viewed preaching as vivid and forceful, because its goal was to elicit "a firm trust (*fiducia*) in the mercy and promises of Christ, a movement not only of the intellect but also of the heart and will."[91] In doing so, he regarded preaching in particular as a medium with a distinctive way of working, that saw itself addressing the ear, the eye, and the heart simultaneously.

The understanding of preaching as working in such a distinctive manner sharpens the question of how useful are the categories and processes of rhetoric, especially *docere* and *movere*. Can they be employed for further exploration of the ritual framework in which preaching and sacrament are situated? Rhetoric and ritual, as we noted in the introduction to this study, possess great power. Melanchthon senses that they are somehow related. Both are able to explain a social world, to shape and define community, to generate a certain kind of knowing, and to stretch the daily experience of human beings into grander, nobler, and more delightful meanings.[92] It has also been argued that a particular type of rhetoric, epideictic discourse, actually performs the functions of ritual: it generates a kind of knowledge that is different from ordinary knowledge; it constitutes and promotes community; it offers participants guidance in conducting their lives.[93]

Turning specifically to Christian ritual, it has been observed how the mood of praise associated with epideictic is also that of the liturgy.[94]

The liturgy was a celebration and, more emphatically, a celebration which was thanksgiving – Eucharist. "Lift up your hearts," the celebrant sang as he began the most sacred part of the service. Why? In order to "give thanks to the Lord, our God." The traditional description of the Mass as a "sacrifice of praise," a description recited in the Canon of every Mass, was employed by some of the

---

89 Meerhoff, "Logic and Eloquence," 363.

90 See Shuger, *Sacred Rhetoric*, 55–117.

91 Ibid., 68; see also Melanchthon "*De modo et arte concionandi,*" in *SM,* vol. 5, part 2, 51.

92 E.g., Condit, "The Functions of Epideictic," 284–298.

93 Carter, "Ritual Functions of Epideictic Rhetoric," 212–217.

94 John W. O'Malley, *Praise and Blame in Renaissance Rome: Rhetoric, Doctrine, and Reform in the Sacred Orators of the Papal Court, c. 1450–1521* (Durham, N.C.: Duke Univ. Press, 1979), 75.

[Renaissance] preachers, and the appropriateness of an oration of praise in a cere-mony of praise would not be lost on them.[95]

Epideictic could also perform other functions within a ritual context: to better ex-press commitment, rally strength, form a vision, or to inspire others to accept the challenge of the times.[96] Or, epideictic rhetoric could serve, as it did later in the Catholic Reformation of the sixteenth century, to impart Catholic truth – the truth that the liturgy was regarded as teaching, enacting, and embodying. Knowledge of this truth, however, was to be no mere intellectual assent. The wills of the faithful needed to be "moved" to virtue, their souls bent, and their hearts melted.[97]

Melanchthon was apprehensive about the use of epideictic for Christian discourse, however, because its congratulatory propensities and uncommon appreciation of the so-called "dignity of man" overshadowed what he perceived as its original teaching function. In his view, epideictic rhetoric was finally unable to "effect little in oth-ers."[98] Did this mean, then, that he would view Christian ritual as effecting little in others as well? Or, by asserting that rhetoric aims principally at cognition, would he develop the notion that ritual performs a teaching function only?

We have seen, however, that Melanchthon did not restrict rhetoric to teaching alone but saw it as "mov[ing] and stimulat[ing] minds and thus... affect[ing] a per-son."[99] On the basis of his own statements about rite "moving hearts,"[100] *movere* is still connected with Christian ritual practice as a whole. From our consideration of Melanchthon's "affective, practical theology" within the larger framework of

95 Ibid.

96 Frederick John McGinness, "Rhetoric and Counter-Reformation Rome," 16, 262–263.

97 Ibid., 251–252. It needs to be pointed out, however, that these characteristics of the rhetorical model of preaching, known as the *genus didaskalikon*, were "Lutheran" in origin. John W. O'Malley has shown how the homiletic manual of the Spanish cleric, Alfonso Zorilla, that introduced this genre to Roman Catholic clergy was "constructed out of wholesale borrowings from Lutheran sources—Melanchthon, Dietrich, and Apinus" ("Content and Form in Sixteenth-Century Treatises on Preaching," in *Renaissance Eloquence: Studies in the Theory and Practice of Renaissance Rhetoric*, ed. James J. Murphy [Berkeley: Univ. of California Press, 1983], 245). Zorilla "made extensive use" of Melanchthon's *Elementorum Rhetorices*. Frederick John McGinness calls Zorilla's use of Melanchthon "wily piracy" and "plagiarism" (pp. 270–271). When Lutheran doctrine was "too blatantly obvious," Zorilla substituted traditional Catholic concerns. Saint Robert Bellarmine especially regarded the *genus didaskalikon* "as an exceptionally suitable means for imparting a clear knowledge of safe and sound doctrine and all the other *res necessariae ad salutem* (McGinness, 271)." As we have seen, Melanchthon had initially made epideictic the *basic* rhetorical genre in his *De Rhetorica* of 1519. His subsequent theoretical modifications can be described as making rhetoric "dialectical rhetoric." As we have also seen, Melanchthon viewed "teaching" as providing a knowledge that involves the whole being. The kind of knowing that "dialectic rhetoric" seeks is not ever merely cognitive or intellective.

98 Ibid., 42.

99 LaFontaine, "Melanchthon's 'Elementorum Rhetorices Libri Duo,'" 85.

100 See Introduction, notes 1 and 24.

Renaissance Humanism's *theologia rhetorica*, we have an initial historical and methodological context in which to understand better why he might seek to answer the question of the nature of ritual and its place in the Christian life in terms of a heart being moved. If rhetoric and dialectic affected and shaped his understanding of theological issues more broadly, one would think that such a method should equally affect his view of the nature and purpose of Christian ritual. But as we are about to see in the next two chapters, such a view also emerged as a response to the claims of late-medieval ritual practice (chapter 2) and the sharp distinctions between the spiritual and the material characterizing the Swiss-led Reformation's new theology and practice of worship (chapter 3).

2. RITUAL: LATE-MEDIEVAL ROMAN PRACTICE AND UNDERSTANDING

"NOW BREAD, NOW GOD"[1] :THE SACRED & SOCIAL POWER OF LATE-MEDIEVAL RITUAL PRACTICE

We have been so accustomed to viewing the later Middle Ages as simply a gloomy hiatus between two great periods of drama and high achievement – the economic, political, religious, and intellectual flowering of Europe in the twelfth and thirteenth centuries and the Renaissance and Reformation in the late fifteenth and early sixteenth centuries. Our picture of the context in which the Reformation occurred is one of "ecclesiastical decadence, theological bankruptcy, and religious decline so grievous" that traditional patterns of church life were adhered to only by "the most truly committed and most deeply devout."[2]

These older perspectives and interpretations have given way over the past twenty years or so to a broader and deeper assessment of the religious – cultural context in which the Reformation took place. Detailed investigations of ecclesiastical institutions and governance, currents of reform, theological developments, modes of spirituality both clerical and lay, and increased appreciation of the symbolic function of ritual in significantly defining group identity and social relations – all of these scholarly contributions, many of them assisted by the insights of sociologists, cultural anthropologists, feminist historians, and students of comparative religion, have given us a picture of the late-medieval context as one in which religious life was frequently a vital reality. No longer are the late Middle Ages viewed as simply a "pitiable story of decline."[3]

---

1 Miri Rubin, *Corpus Christi: The Eucharist in Late Medieval Culture* (Cambridge: Cambridge Univ. Press, 1991), 53.
2 Francis Oakley, "Religious and Ecclesiastical Life on the Eve of the Reformation," in *Reformation Europe: A Guide to Research*, ed. Steven Ozment (St. Louis: Center for Reformation Research, 1982), 6; see also his *The Western Church in the Later Middle Ages* (Ithaca: Cornell Univ. Press, 1979).
3 Oakley, "Religion and Ecclesiastical Life on the Eve of the Reformation," 10.

It was in this late-medieval context that Philip Melanchthon's expression, "to move the heart" began to take shape. And shortly after the Reformation was underway began the great sixteenth-century debate, "unparalleled in scale and intensity," about the meaning, function, and form of ritual.[4] At issue were the power dynamics that connected the divine and human realms as well as those that governed relations in the human realm. A useful way to think further about these dynamics is to plot them along two axes. There is a vertical axis of "sacred" or "spiritual" power and a horizontal axis of sociopolitical and economic power.[5] In this chapter, the task is to provide examples of how these axes were conceptualized in late-medieval Catholicism. In the next chapter, our focus will be on an emergent Reformed Protestantism's approach to these matters. Melanchthon's expression, "to move the heart," was an effort to steer a course between these two sensibilities.

HISTORICAL BACKGROUND OF LATE-MEDIEVAL LITURGICAL DEVELOPMENTS

The axis of sacred power includes phenomena such as the power of creating and maintaining the world and the power to be found in particular objects. It is an ontological power that belongs to and characterizes sacred or ultimate reality.[6] When one looks at medieval Christianity, for example, we find this sacred power located especially in the Mass, i.e., the eucharist or Lord's Supper. Located at the busy intersection of the two axes of sacred power and sociopolitical/economic power, the Mass, "turned bread into flesh – a fragile, small, wheaten disc into God...host, ritual, God among mortals."[7] As such, the Mass was regarded as

> the most powerful manifestation of the sacred in the profane world, the Real Presence of Christ....This doctrine was inseparable from the perception of Christ's sacrificial and saving death on the cross, completed in his resurrection. Far from being "unchristian" or semi-pagan, late-medieval religion was powerfully Christocentric, stressing as its main doctrine the Incarnation of Christ and his saving death. It was the humanity of Christ, especially his willingness to suffer for the sins of all, that formed the focal point of piety.[8]

---

4 Burke, "The repudiation of ritual," 226.
5 Barbara Holdredge, "Introduction: Towards a Phenomenology of Power," *Journal of Ritual Studies* 4, no. 2 (summer 1990): 5–6.
6 Ibid., 8.
7 Rubin, *Corpus Christi*, 1.
8 Scribner, "Reformation movements in Germany," 71–72.

Medieval liturgical developments, however, are often disparagingly evaluated by many contemporary scholars as being crude and objectionable. Especially singled out were the claims for the "material efficacy of ritual" – its power to effect changes in the physical world. "Divine power, embodied in the Church and its sacraments," Carlos Eire has written, "reached down through innumerable points of contact to make itself felt: to forgive or punish, to protect against the ravages of nature, to heal, to soothe, and to work all sorts of wonders."[9]

Yet such developments dare not be seen not simply as flights of fancy but as viable, consistent pieties and theologies suited to the mentality of the times. Each liturgical tradition, as Robert Taft has reminded us, seeks to express its particular view of what is perceived to be the Christian message and to make it alive for the genius of the age. It is at the intersection of tradition and culture that people worship and that the theological craft is exercised.[10]

When, for example, the markedly brief, simple, and sober Roman liturgy[11] "migrated" to what is now France and Germany in the seventh and eighth centuries, drama and elaborate ceremonial were added and more prolix prayer texts were composed. Of particular interest is the increased use of gestures, bells, candles, and the growing place of drama to make worship more available and accessible to the faithful. One reason for this development was that the language of worship was no longer the vernacular.

Another example is that since the brief, almost too succinct, and emotionally reserved Roman rite "spoke too little to the circumstances prevailing among other peoples,"[12] its texts were expanded and elaborated. There was also an increase in the dramatic, more demonstrative, ritual action of the priest that served to underscore the words he spoke. There was a corresponding decrease or, better, shift in the manner of lay participation as the role of the priest and his communion was heightened.[13]

---

9 Carlos Eire, *War Against the Idols: The Reformation of Worship from Erasmus to Calvin* (Cambridge: Cambridge Univ. Press, 1986), 1.

10 Robert F. Taft, "The Liturgy of the Great Church: An Initial Synthesis of Structure and Interpretation on the Eve of Iconoclasm," *Dumbarton Oaks Papers* 34–35 (1980–1981): 45–75.

11 Edmund Bishop, in his classic essay "The Genius of the Roman Rite," noted its simplicity. The "purely Roman elements," according to Bishop, were "marked by simplicity, practicality, a great sobriety and self-control, gravity, and dignity." These included the collect, the epistle, the blessing before the Gospel, the Gospel, the *Orate frates*, and the collect called the "secret," "and all that follows up to the Pax Domini (viz the Preface, Canon, Lord's Prayer, and the short prayer immediately following), the postcommunion collect, and the *Ite missa est*" (in *Liturgica Historica* [Oxford: Clarendon Press, 1962], 1–19; this essay was first printed in 1899).

12 Herman Wegman, *Christian Worship in East and West: A Study Guide to Liturgical History*, trans. Gordon W. Lathrop (New York: Pueblo Publishing Co., 1985), 152.

13 Ibid., 186.

The older communal actions of entrance, offertory, and communion were truncated into priestly actions. Other corporate elements were omitted or abbreviated. Homily and intercessions disappeared. The rite of peace, once shared by the entire assembly, became a brief versicle and response accompanied by a gesture ("*V.* The peace of the Lord be with you alway. *R.* And with your spirit.").[14]

Surrounding this Latin liturgy, beginning in the tenth century, were dramatic "sketches" based on biblical stories and subsequently translated into the vernacular.[15] Not to be confused with the medieval mystery plays, these dramas were sometimes performed within the liturgy, and "worked" much like tropes (e.g., textual elaborations of the Kyrie) or processions. The dramatizations of the Christmas story, Holy Week, and the life of Mary flourished in many European countries and, in later centuries, found their way to Latin America, the Philippines, and elsewhere including the United States.

Other examples of liturgical drama included the procession with palms, the dramatic chanting of the passion narrative, the veneration of the cross, the washing of the feet, etc. This heightening of the visual and the dramatic reflected a fundamental, more radical disjunction between symbol and reality that has characterized much of the Christian West until modern times.

This mentality or horizon of understanding could not perceive much less understand that words and images are systematically layered symbols. A major reason for this is that the Franks and other Germans could not think "symbolically" but only in terms of what was visible and tangible to them.[16] With respect to the eucharist, older patristic interpretations of "image" and "likeness" applied to the presence of Christ made no sense and gave way to a focus on things: "no longer did the celebration image the death of Christ but the food imaged Christ himself."[17] Subsequent eucharistic controversies, first in the ninth century and then in the eleventh century, led to significant transformations both in theology and piety.[18] In the preference for exactness, for some sort of one-to-one correspondence between word and object, between symbol and object, the eucharist could not be "symbolic." It had to be "real." With this focus on the holiness of the eucharist as a "thing," albeit powerful, the

---

14 John Harper, *The Forms and Orders of Western Liturgy from the Tenth to the Eighteenth Century* (Oxford: Clarendon Press, 1991), 113.

15 Wegman, *Christian Worship in East and West,* 177.

16 Alexander Gerken, O.F.M., "Historical background of the new direction in Eucharistic doctrine," *Theology Digest* 21(1973): 48.

17 Ibid.

18 See the summary in Rubin, *Corpus Christi,* 14–20.

result was a reifying or objectifying of Christian worship.[19] A logical conclusion of this mentality that was so focused on the "reality" of the eucharist was transsubstantiation, the claim that bread and wine were wholly changed into the body and blood of the historic Christ. One writer has labelled these developments in eucharistic piety and theology as "the crisis of the sacramental idea."[20] Metaphorical language had broken down and medieval people could not hold several levels of meaning simultaneously in dynamic tension. The overall result, then, was that the idea of eucharistic celebration changed:

> In the first place, the old communal service tended to become a cultic concern of the clerics who knew Latin and the rites, and it had only indirect contact with the faithful. Worship thereby became hieratic and separated from the people. Furthermore, the symbolic thought and feeling that had marked the liturgy up to that time had to make way for an analytic manner of thought. "Mystery" no longer meant "sign that points beyond itself" or symbol, but "incomprehensible" and "invisible." The view of God's salvation and God's grace became more material and thinglike. Sacraments tended to be thought of as "channels" of grace, with the result that the relationship between faith and sacrament became less obvious. As a further consequence, the internal dynamic of worship was bent toward a more static experience of the liturgy in which the faithful participated receptively rather than actively.[21]

Moreover, the preference for the immediacies of concrete experience can be seen as contributing to what has been called a "historicizing" tendency in Christian worship and life. Props, costumes, extended dialogue, and dramatic roles began to transform worship into realistic theater. Crucifixes showing the beaten, bloodied Christ began to appear. We see for the first time the appearance of the creche at Christmas. There was a hunger for the natural, the real, the literal, the historical – "to bring God down to earth and to see and touch him."[22]

This accent, however, was not new. Already in the New Testament and in early Christianity, "seeing" was a common way to express what Christian experience was all about. The Gospel of John and the stories of the Easter appearances of Jesus, the

---

19 John F. Baldovin, "Christian Worship to the Eve of the Reformation," in *The Making of Jewish and Christian Worship*, vol. 1 of *Two Liturgical Traditions*, ed. Paul F. Bradshaw and Lawrence A. Hoffman (Notre Dame, Ind.: Univ. of Notre Dame Press, 1991), 175.

20 Ferdinand Pratzner, *Messe und Kreuzeopfer: Die Krise der sakramentalen Idee bei Luther und in der mittelalterischen Scholastik* (Wien: Herder, 1970).

21 Wegman, *Christian Worship in East and West*, 185. As we shall see, however, the lay experience of the liturgy was not quite so "impoverished" as historians, including Wegman, have made it out to be.

22 Nathan Mitchell, *Cult and Controversy: The Worship of the Eucharist Outside Mass* (New York: Pueblo, 1982), 373ff. Our discussion at this juncture is dependent on Mitchell.

book of Revelation, Augustine's illumination, St. Benedict's perception of the whole world in a ray of light are just a few examples of identifying *seeing* with grace and the intuition of faith.

More recently, due to studies of psychological development, we have become very aware of the critical role that vision plays in our sense of reality. At the same time, however, we have been also made aware that our use of visual metaphors to connote "mind" and "knowing" can suggest that reality is static or that disengagement and objectification are central to the construction of knowledge. We can take up this issue later, but it is significant that the New Testament gives attention to both the use of visual metaphors and metaphors that suggest speaking, listening, connection and conversation:

> This flesh-taking Word reveals its power in water, light, and birth, and in a life-giving bread, in a body touched, held, sensed, and seen, in a community of love. The Apostle Paul, on the other hand, is fond of the vocal, the Word heard and responded to in faith. He understands the relationship between God and humankind as a conversation that reached its highest point of intensity in the life and death of Jesus.[23]

It is within this larger framework of understanding human life and human relationships as constituted by both vision and voice, seeing as well as saying, that we turn to late-medieval liturgical practice, especially the Mass, which was central to the religious vitality of the time.

THE LATE-MEDIEVAL MASS

The Mass was the central public ritual of the Christianity of pre-Reformation Europe. It not only reflected but also shaped faith and life as lived social and personal reality.[24] It was "a site for assertion and encounter, and thus of articulation of identities,"[25] clerical and men and women. For the clergy, the Mass symbolized the essence of their office. They possessed the power by virtue of ordination to make

---

[23] Ibid., 385

[24] Our discussion depends on John Bossy's now classic essay, "The Mass as a Social Institution 1200–1700," *Past and Present*, no. 100 (1983): 29–61, although Steven Ozment, in *Protestants*, warns us of Bossy's romanticizing of traditional Catholicism and caricaturing of Protestantism (pp. 35–40). Ozment also points out the gaps in Bossy's presentation of medieval Catholicism as "the perfect religion of family and society" (p. 36). Nonetheless, Bossy's portrayal of the Mass is instructive because his (over-)emphasis on community and institution helps us to better understand the Reformation's and especially Melanchthon's concern with ritual's impact upon an individual.

[25] Rubin, "The Eucharist and the Construction of Medieval Identities," in *Culture and History 1350–1600: Essays on English Communities, Identities, and Writing*, ed. David Aers (Detroit: Wayne State Univ. Press, 1992), 43.

Christ present, his very flesh and blood. For laymen and laywomen, the Mass was a source of power and experience, enabling them to express fears, hopes, and anxieties, as well as providing them health and salvation.

Thus, the writer of the *Lay Folks' Mass Book* could assert that the Mass was "the worthiest thing, most of the goodness in all this world...."[26] Social historians have underscored this assertion. But, first, it is necessary to look at what the mass comprised. The full, public, sung mass of the last two hundred years or so before the Reformation consisted of the following elements[27]:

Fore-Mass

- Preparatory Prayers
- Introductory Psalm (Introit) "exposing the predicament of unredeemed humanity and a confession of sin"
- Kyrie
- "Announcement of redemption" in the Gloria
- "A series of declarations of faith" including readings from the scriptures and the Nicene Creed
- Prone (or "bidding prayers")

Offertory

- Offertory and preparation of the bread and wine for sacrifice; "the congregation prepared itself by such means and contributing to the support of its pastor"
- Priest's washing of hands and secret prayer over the gifts

Eucharistic Service

- Preface and Sanctus
- Canon – "expressed in terms of sacrifice and including as its chief event the consecration of the bread and wine, by which they became the body and blood of Christ"
- Elevation of the host
- Lord's Prayer
- Agnus Dei
- Prayer for Peace
- Kiss of Peace

---

26 Bossy, "The Mass as a Social Institution," 30.

27 Our summary combines Bossy, "The Mass as a Social Institution," 32, and Virginia Reinburg, "Liturgy and the Laity in Late Medieval and Reformation France," *Sixteenth Century Journal* 23, no. 3 (1992): 547. The description of these items is Bossy's.

- Communion, or sequence of events connected with the reception of the eucharist
- Various concluding matters – e.g., postcommunion prayer, the blessing of the congregation by the priest before its departure, Last Gospel (John 1.1–14)

This was the central public ritual of the Western Church from the thirteenth century to the Reformation. The restructuring of the Mass by church administrators and intellectuals into a visual and vocal theophany helped to shape an experience of a powerful work capable of procuring salvation.[28] This was *salus* in the sense of deliverance for Christians from the whole concatenation of dooms, dangers, anxieties and tribulations that loomed over their corporal and spiritual existence. The overtones of such deliverance were more exactly conveyed by the German *Heil* than by any English equivalent. As sacrifice, the Mass renewed or recapitulated Christ's atonement. It re-enacted the payment to God that was necessary to appease God's anger.

But at the same time, the Mass embodied the existing socio-legal and political arrangements of the time. It was viewed as restoring diplomatic or social relations between God and humanity and return of the universe to a condition of peace. Medieval commentators on the Mass pointed out rather regularly, if not unanimously, the theme of the return of the universe to a condition of peace. According to these commentators, the opening words of the *Gloria in excelsis* said it all: "Glory be to God on high, and on earth peace to people of good will." What was announced by the angels to the shepherds was peace and friendship between God and humanity, angels and humanity, and among Christians in late-medieval Europe..

This declaration, moreover, was expressed by believers' participation in communion, common union, the wholeness of Christ and Christ's church. Even as communion of the faithful declined, the ceremonies of the kiss of peace and the distribution of the "blessed bread" [i.e., the leavened bread offered by the laity, blessed by the priest, and then distributed after Mass] became more central to lay experience, even replacing communion.[29] A primary benefit of the Mass, therefore, was as much social as it was strictly "religious." It represented a social universe and a social reality – the

---

[28] See these additional social-historical portrayals of medieval liturgical practice: Rubin, *Corpus Christi*; Charles Zika, "Hosts, Processions and Pilgrimages: Controlling the Sacred in Fifteenth-Century Germany," *Past and Present* no. 118 (February 1988): 25–64; Bossy, *Christianity in the West*, 57–75; Bossy, "The Mass as a Social Institution," 29–61; Robert W. Scribner, "Ritual and Popular Religion in Catholic Germany at the Time of the Reformation," *Journal of Ecclesiastical History* 35 (1984): 47–77.

[29] Reinburg, "Liturgy and the Laity in Late Medieval and Reformation France," 539, 541.

Christian community as an assembly of distinct parts and as a transcendent whole. What the faithful saw, heard, and did – "reading" the ritual gestures of the priest as well as their own – was an experience of participation rather different than that outlined in the various manuals for the clergy. While not as doctrinally informed, lay participation was significant nonetheless because it was an experience of "social and spiritual solidarity among God, the Church, and the lay community."[30]

These were the larger needs and perceptions to which the Mass provided an expression, promotion, and reproduction. John Bossy has observed how this ritual event presented the faithful with the opportunity "to combine sociability with the worship of God."[31] Although liturgists and reformers have complained that the Mass was hardly a communal act because it was offered by the priest alone, largely in silence, sometimes out of sight of the assembly, and in an unintelligible ritual language, this particular ritual practice embodied and created a sense of collective identity. Vernacular expositions of the Mass encouraged a kind of lay participation that was less concerned with whether congregants were aware of a ceremonial representation of eucharistic doctrine or Christ's original sacrifice.

More specifically, according to Bossy,

> We need not suppose that congregations were ignorant of what the priest was doing at the altar, if only because his performance was frequently criticized. The average parishioner, who would probably not be up to that, nevertheless *knew what he needed to know*. He knew that the priest was making sacrifice and satisfaction for the living and the dead; he knew that he would make God actually present in the Host before consuming it. If he was not a heretic or unbeliever he knew that this extraordinary event represented the best thing that could have happened in the universe, a deliverance from the power of evil, a reconciliation of God and man from which any amount of consequential good might follow, in this world and the next. If he could say his paternoster, and had been to confession and communion, he knew that these effects were something to do with the painful tasks of repenting your sins and loving your neighbor.[32]

Late-medieval piety and theology regarded the efficacy of the Mass as "the social miracle," and with it, the symbolization of a social universe and social reality hierarchically arranged. The locus of the sacred in such an arrangement – or at least, nearness to it – was to be found in the professionally religious, the monks and the clerics, while ordinary lay life was a zone of spiritual underdevelopment.[33]

---

30 Ibid., 542.
31 Bossy, *Christianity in the West*, 66.
32 Ibid., 57.
33 Charles Taylor, *Sources of the Self: The Making of the Modern Identity* (Cambridge: Harvard Univ. Press, 1989), 218.

Nevertheless, all was not as idyllic as some of these social-historical portrayals of late-medieval practice might suggest. Some studies have indicated increasing instances of conflicts concerning religious practice and power. In late fifteenth century Germany, for example, we hear of how the liturgical and popular religious practice of the elevation of the host, the bearing of it in communal procession, its veneration through pilgrimages, and its use as a potent, sacred object against diabolical interventions in the material and spiritual realms precipitated "irrational outbreaks of social disorder…," "psychological frenzy, the spurning of traditional authority and the total breakdown of social relationships…."[34]

Popular belief in transformed hosts and eucharistic miracles had grown and intensified. This gave rise to controversies over whether pilgrimages to bleeding-host shrines were proper expressions of belief, if they were indeed "sacred places." These pilgrimages had become the occasion for a religiosity that the clergy found difficult to control. Precipitating these pilgrimages were increasing political conflict, agrarian crisis, and economic depression. Thousands of young men and women, "barefoot, half-naked, without money, food and preparation, hit the road."[35]

Such instances of conflict raised larger and more fundamental questions of how sacred power was to be accessed, produced, and controlled. "If not properly controlled," as Charles Zika has written, "[then there is] clearly…an avenue which allows one to circumvent proper authorities and establish a direct relationship between the devotee and the object of worship."[36] At the same time, difficulties of maintaining "the social miracle" of late-medieval Christianity surfaced the question of how to bridge the gap between theological knowledge and religious behavior. Inability to do so would constitute a considerable danger to theological purity, ecclesiastical control, and social hierarchy.

A way was found, however, by emphasizing a belief-system "to which practices would have to conform and through which they would be thereby legitimated."[37] Theologically, the host was portrayed as embodying real sacramental presence. Practically, this meant that the Church could better control the religious action and expression of the faithful because of the need to conform to theological doctrine. "In

---

34 Zika, "Host, Processions, and Pilgrimages," 57ff.
35 Ibid., 58.
36 Ibid., 59.
37 Ibid.

this way," states Charles Zika, "theological discourse is given preeminence in the production of religious truth and in the creation of individual religious needs."[38]

A significant result of the attacks on pilgrimages and the efforts to purify what proper host devotion should involve was the attempt to establish a pastoral clergy. The priestly role was to be regarded as one of teaching and providing pastoral care in the community of faith.

> He is to communicate the knowledge of basic doctrine and ritual to the simple and care for their spiritual needs. Such teaching and care necessarily involve the communication and creation of religious beliefs and practices considered appropriate by the clergy. The emphasis upon the sinner as a leper to be healed by personal contrition and the priest-physician's counsel and absolution, the emphasis on the host as spiritual food administered by the priest rather than sacred object, the emphasis on scripture and carefully defined theological doctrine as the criteria according to which religious practices are authorized – these emphases suggest the creation of new strategies in the relation between ecclesiastical officers and the laity, and mediate a new perception of religiosity firmly circumscribed by the active intervention of clerical knowledge and clerical practice.[39]

Eventually, however, the late-medieval church would be unable to meet these individual religious needs. Religiously-minded laity who sought a theology and a spirituality that could satisfy and discipline them experienced increasing difficulty because of a lack of options and resources. The sacrament of penance did not always relieve religious and psychological anxiety. Moreover, a distinctive concept of lay religious life was acutely absent; lay piety was to be patterned on clerical and/or monastic piety with its traditionally contemplative and ascetic ideals. Those who desired to lead a more fully spiritual life were counselled to imitate as fully as possible such ideals.[40]

An increasingly literate, socially mobile urban laity who were coming to value simplicity, directness, and respectful treatment in all spheres of their lives found such monastic and clerical piety ill-suited to them.[41] Traditionally singled out at this juncture is Luther's religious experience and theological insight that would resolve this crisis in late-medieval piety and provide relief from the burdens of the church "by demanding that [people] live simple, sober lives, prey not to presumption, superstition, or indulgence, but merely as human beings."[42]

---

[38] Ibid.
[39] Ibid., 64.
[40] See Ozment, *The Age of Reform*, 204–222.
[41] Ibid., 220.
[42] Ibid., 438.

THE GREAT DEBATE ABOUT RITUAL BEGINS

It is difficult at first to understand, much less appreciate, why such an intense debate should arise over the meaning, function, and form of religious ritual, the "social miracle" that it was said to enact, and the opportunities it provided for assertion, encounter, and the articulation of a particular kind of person.[43] Recent studies have shown, as we have noted already, that this "social miracle" and other uses of the eucharist were not always as idyllic as some historians would have us believe. Steven Ozment has observed, for example, that medieval Christianity "was also a religion of hierarchy and law, seemingly obsessed with segregating the clergy from the laity and with regulating every aspect of the latter's life...."[44] Moreover, these various uses of the eucharist would prove to be very problematic when viewed from the perspective of the spirituality and theology of the Reformers. That access to the sacred could be controlled and manipulated was regarded as presumptuous at best and blasphemous at worst.

The "great debate over ritual," however, was not so much centered on symbolic representation but rather on the location of and access to the "reality" with which ritual itself and those who participate in it purport to deal.[45] Was such a "reality" to be viewed in the usual fashion? That is, was there a *material* kind of "reality" on the one hand and a *spiritual* kind of "reality" on the other?

In this two-level view of reality,

> [t]here is the material kind of reality, defined by characteristics that make it available to our senses: it is visible, tangible, audible, etc. And there is spiritual reality, defined by the absence of all such characteristics: it is invisible, intangible, inaudible, etc. Spiritual things are God, angels, human souls. Material things are bodies, even Christ's risen body.[46]

A humanist critique of late-medieval piety and worship, born of a desire to restore Christianity to some primitive purity, argued that a warm, living faith was possible only if the material and the spiritual were radically separated.[47] What was essential in this critique was the inner life of the spirit, one characterized by a more intimate rela-

---

[43] Bossy, *Christianity in the West*, 57–75.

[44] *Protestants: The Birth of a Revolution*, 40.

[45] The following discussion is based on Robert W. Jenson, "The Supper," in *Christian Dogmatics*, ed. Carl E. Braaten & Robert W. Jenson, (Philadelphia: Fortress Press, 1984), 2:358–361; Jenson, "Of Another Spirit," *Lutheran Theological Seminary Bulletin* 62, no. 1 (winter 1982): 3–13; and Robert J. Goeser, "Whither Lutheranism?" *Lutheran Quarterly*, n.s., 1, no. 1 (spring 1987): 40–53.

[46] Jenson, "Of Another Spirit," 9–10.

[47] Eire, *War Against the Idols*, 28ff.

tionship with God and, hence, free from externals, from objects, from a mode of worship that was dependent on ceremonies and on the senses.

Two spheres of existence, the material and the spiritual (visible and invisible), are juxtaposed, and it is clearly stated that true religion can only be experienced in the invisible realm. The material, visible world can never be the focus of true piety, since it is a distortion of reality, or, at best, incapable of bringing one to the truth.[48]

One can appreciate this critique and the emergent conception of the nature of worship when one recalls the excessive ceremonialism and the focus on externals that characterized the worship of late-medieval Christianity. It was commonly held that most ceremonies had been created by the apostles who evangelized the West. Such ceremonies, moreover, were perceived to be free from error since the Church that uses them is guided by the Spirit in matters of such grave importance.[49]

Both humanists and reformers regarded the emotional and sensuous experience of the Mass, with its focus *and* claim to bring together the spiritual and the material, as especially dangerous. It was a misplaced faith in external and outward forms and only distracted people from the true worship of God.[50]

This two-level system for reality – material and spiritual – thus became very problematic.[51] How is one to conceptualize and then to affirm Christ's bodily presence in the church's sacramental worship? Moreover, how is one to regard the soteriological dimension of this event? Is what is said and done containing, communicating, or simply pointing to God's grace and forgiveness?

If one is operating with the material-spiritual distinction, then the following options are available. The distinction can be overcome, as it was in the practice and theology of medieval Catholicism, by a miracle of God's sheer omnipotence.

But if the bodily presence of Christ is a miracle worked afresh each time, then if the Supper is to function in the life of the Church, this must be a predictable miracle. We must know how to make it happen; that is, there must be authorized secondary agents of the miracle. So Thomas [Aquinas]: the power of consecration resides in a formula of consecration, "This is my body," and in ordination's authorization by God to certain persons to speak this formula truly.[52]

---

48 Ibid., 34.
49 Reinhold Theisen, O.S.B., *Mass Liturgy and the Council of Trent* (Collegeville, Minn.: The Liturgical Press, 1965), 29–70, 87–107.
50 Eire, *War Against the Idols*, 37.
51 Our discussion follows Jenson, "Of Another Spirit," 10–11.
52 Ibid., 10.

Another option, one that would characterize the Swiss-led Reformation's under-standing of the church's worship, was to make the spiritual-material distinction even sharper. Christ's presence is a "spiritual" presence. Bread and cup can only serve as a means or as a reminder of that presence since the body of Christ remains in heaven. Because Christ is "there," he cannot also be in the bread and cup.

It is this two-level system for reality and its consequences for the practice and the-ology of the Church's worship that also needs to be kept in mind when considering why Melanchthon would speak of its power "to move the heart." His viewpoint would emerge, not only as a response to the "now bread, now God" affirmation of late-medieval Catholicism, but also to the spiritualism of the Swiss-led Reformation and its agenda for changing the worship of the entire *corpus Christianorum.*

The critique of traditional claims for religious ritual, together with efforts to sim-plify it, thus needs to be viewed from a different perspective, one that is both hermeneutical and practical. Among the targets of this critique were the less than in-tellectually engaged participation of the laity and any understanding of the Mass "as transaction – monetary, legal, or otherwise."[53] Just as significant is the sort of re-lationship with Christ that such a transaction notion involves – that it is comparable to the relationship that one has with a secular lord or judge. Melanchthon's statement about Word and rite "moving the heart" was also a part of this critique of what the Mass aspired to do and the sort of person it sought to make and to articulate. But his offering of a different approach to understand ritual experience, with a resulting dif-ferent perspective on the sort of person that such experience makes,was also very much shaped, as we shall now see, by his reaction to the practice and sensibility of the Swiss-led Reformation.

---

53 Reinburg, "Liturgy and the Laity in Late Medieval and Reformation France," 545.

3. RITUAL: REFORMED PROTESTANTISM'S PRACTICE AND UNDERSTANDING

IS CHRISTIAN RITUAL "REAL"?

When Melanchthon's *Answer to the Anabaptists*, with his initial use of "to move the heart" to interpret the purpose and power of Christian ritual, appeared in 1528, he had been teaching and publishing for a decade. He was the author of nine biblical commentaries, the first edition (1521) of the *Loci Communes*, Latin and Greek grammars, and a series of handbooks on rhetoric and dialectic. He had also become a controversialist and spokesperson for the Wittenberg Reformation and, by 1528, an active protagonist in the great debate about ritual, especially as it focused on the nature and purpose of the Lord's Supper.

This first and most enduring theological battle of the Reformation had begun eight years earlier with Luther's *Babylonian Captivity of the Church*, his attack on the medieval practice and interpretation of the sacraments. The Mass in particular was the focus of this attack with its powerful display as the climax of priestly power "to move God," as it were, to change his attitude toward humankind from an unfavorable to a favorable one.[1] Melanchthon's own response to Luther's position on these matters was positive, if not enthusiastic.[2] In fact, he had been developing his own understanding of "signs" as visible testimonies and expressions of God's graciousness that occur in the church's sacramental or ritual life.

But by the mid-1520s, a new dimension had been introduced into the great debate about ritual. An earlier humanist critique of false worship, with ritual being the falsifying element, was taken up by the Swiss-led Reformation and its chief architect,

---

[1] See Gritsch and Jenson, *Lutheranism*, 70ff.; also James F. White, *Protestant Worship: Traditions in Transition* (Louisville: Westminister/John Knox Press, 1989), 36ff. That the Mass was intended "to move God" is suggested in the text of the canon where the priest prays that God might "accept this, our oblation," and "dispose our days in your peace, save us from eternal damnation, and number us in the flock of your elect" (*Prex eucharistica*, ed. Anton Hängii and Irmgard Pahl [Freiburg: Editions Universitaires, 1968], 431).

[2] Rogness, *Reformer Without Honor*, 51.

Ulrich Zwingli. According to some scholars, it was Zwingli who brought this debate to its decisive moment – "the question of liturgy, i.e., the mode of presence of divinity in Christian ritual...."[3]

A similar perception of this debate has been voiced by Guy Swanson in his *Religion and Regime*. He argued that the Reformation's division of Western Christianity was rooted in a radical and fundamental difference of how God's presence was experienced in the human world.[4] Swanson wrote:

> The division of Christianity in the sixteenth century concerned this difference in experience: all Christians held the presence of God to be their ultimate concern. Catholic doctrines declared that, as Christ, God's own spiritual essence was always present in bread and wine consecrated in the Mass and always embodied in the organization and acts of the visible church existent in time. Reformation Protestants denied those doctrines and any other which suggested that God's essential qualities were even partially embodied in "created things."[5]

While Swanson has been castigated by some Reformation historians for his oversimplified definitions of Catholicism and Protestantism in terms of transcendence and immanence,[6] more recent scholarship has emphasized the strident transcendentalism and spiritualism that came to characterize the theology and practice of Reformed worship. In fact, any worship that focused attention on outward form rather than on inward substance was regarded as idolatrous. The war against ritual waged by the Swiss-led Reformation was "a war between *caro* and *spiritus*, between the things of this world and those of heaven."[7]

The net effect of this war between *caro* and *spiritus*, according to Jonathan Z. Smith, was "a major revolution" in Western thought:

> ritual is not "real"; rather, it is a matter of "signification" for Zwingli, or of "metonymy" for Theodore Beza. A wedge was decisively driven between symbol and reality; there was no necessary connection between them.[8]

For the early Lutheran movement, however, the great debate over ritual was not so much "a crisis of symbolic representation" as certain social historians and historical

---

3 J. P. S. Uberoi, *Science and Culture* (Delhi, 1978), 25; cited in Smith, *To Take Place: Toward Theory in Ritual*, 99.

4 *Religion and Regime: A Sociological Account of the Reformation* (Ann Arbor: Univ. of Michigan Press, 1967), 1ff.

5 Ibid., 1.

6 See Steven Ozment, *The Reformation in the Cities: The Appeal of Protestantism to Sixteenth-Century Germany and Switzerland* (New Haven: Yale Univ. Press, 1975), 9–11.

7 Eire, *War Against the Idols*, 31.

8 Smith, *To Take Place: Toward Theory in Ritual*, 100.

anthropologists would have it. Rather, the issue, as noted in the previous chapter, was the very location of and access to the "reality" with which ritual itself and those who participate in it claim to deal. By steering a middle course between transcendence and immanence, and remaining open to the use of material objects in worship, the ritual strategy and interpretation of the Wittenberg Reformers were very different than those of late-medieval Catholicism and Swiss-led Protestantism.

We see this difference in Melanchthon's attempt to steer a middle course between a Roman Catholic concept of efficacious signs and a Zwinglian view of worship as only psychologically or socially efficacious made possible by the presence of Christ's power.[9] As a humanist, Melanchthon's approach centered more on the practical and present aspects of evangelical faith. Such an approach, as we shall see, shaped his understanding of Word and rite as well.

His 1528 tract, *Answer to the Anabaptists*, is, as far as we know, the first time he uses the phrase "to move the heart" in reference to what Word *and* rite do. The immediate context is one of how to respond to a Zwinglian/Anabaptist understanding of sacrament, on the one hand, and to a late-medieval concept of the embodiment of divine power in church and sacrament:

> But in this age men take delight in a certain wisdom which is plainly absurd and wrangle about ceremonies and likewise about human traditions without any end. In the meantime, there is great silence about repentance, faith, the cross, love, and all good works.... Now, since there are so many dangerous dissensions about the Sacraments, it seems best in this place to touch upon these controversies....[10]

But in order to understand better how and why Melanchthon sought this middle position in the great debate about ritual, we must examine more closely the emergence of the dichotomy between "true" worship and "false" worship in early Reformed Protestantism. This involves, in particular, a consideration of its theological foundations.

---

9 E.g., Ralph W. Quere, "Melanchthonian Motifs in the Formula's Eucharistic Christology," in *Discord, Dialogue, and Concord: Studies in the Lutheran Reformation's Formula of Concord*, ed. Lewis W. Spitz and Wenzel Lohff (Philadelphia: Fortress, 1977), 58–73.
10 *MS*, 104.

SPIRIT AND WORD: FOUNDATIONS OF A NEW THEOLOGY
AND PRACTICE OF WORSHIP

The Swiss-led Reformation took its bearings from the powerful idea that "the pure Word of God" or "Scripture alone" calls the church to reconstruct its entire life. Ulrich Zwingli, inspired initially by an evangelical humanism, sought to make "the written biblical word of God the existentially appropriate word of God verbally proclaimed, attuned to time and audience."[11] Some have noted that Zwingli was the first of the Reformers to use the *sola scriptura* principle, although it is more accurate to say that he viewed Scripture as "from the Spirit" and it "can be understood only where the Spirit gives understanding."[12]

Both Spirit and Scripture played a central and vital role in Zwingli's theology. The Spirit teaches a person inwardly in order to create faith. The Word speaks directly to the human heart which is guided and illuminated by the Spirit. Zwingli's emphasis on the importance of the Spirit has led to an interpretation of his thought as "spiritualist" or "pneumatological." He characteristically stressed the interior character of religion and saw it as primarily concerned with internal attitudes rather than with external observances.[13]

Shortly after being named *Leutpriester* or "people's priest" of the Great Minster in Zurich, Zwingli embarked upon a practice of preaching directly from Holy Scripture instead of using the lessons appointed in the lectionary. His intent in these sermons was to allow the Scripture "to speak out in all its living coherence, by means of consecutive expository preaching."[14] More explicitly, such preaching, "with God's help" was to be "to the glory of God and of His only Son, our Lord Jesus Christ, as well as to the true salvation of souls and the edification of pious and honest people."[15]

Over the course of the next four years, Zwingli's preaching tended to focus on two major themes: "the centrality of Christ, and the worthlessness of 'invented external worship.'"[16] It was out of his exegetical work, especially on those passages related to commands concerning worship, that Zwingli's preaching led to concrete developments and results. He had understood these commands as providing a blueprint for

---

[11] Fritz Busser, "The Spirituality of Zwingli and Bullinger in the Reformation of Zurich," in *Christian Spirituality II: High Middle Ages and Reformation*, 303.

[12] W. P. Stephens, *The Theology of Huldrych Zwingli* (Oxford: Clarendon Press, 1986), 59.

[13] McGrath, *Reformation Thought*, 50.

[14] Gottfried W. Locher, *Zwingli's Theology: New Perspectives* (Leiden: E. J. Brill, 1981), 1–2.

[15] Ibid., 5–6; Locher cites *Heinrich Bullingers Reformationsgeschichte*, I, 12.

[16] Eire, *War Against the Idols*, 78.

behavior: "Any tradition that did not square with these commands was therefore to be disregarded."[17] For Zwingli, the goal was clear: the Bible must speak clearly again if the people of Zurich are to serve God. And for the Bible to speak with such clarity, worship must change; it must become a preaching service.[18]

By 1523, Zwingli's preaching had sufficiently mobilized public opinion, thus setting in motion a chain of events that would come to characterize the Reformation process in cities such as Zurich and elsewhere.[19] By his preaching, Zwingli had already provided the initial stimulus. Then came popular support to which the city government would respond by consolidating and moderating the called-for changes.

Zwingli's preparation for the public disputation, which would be the Zurich Reformation's turning point, included the publication of sixty-seven "Conclusions" as debate topics. Among them, conclusions XVII and XVIII stand out:

XVII. Christ is the only eternal high priest. Therefore those who have called themselves high priests have opposed the honour and power of Christ, yea, cast it out.

XVIII. Christ, having sacrificed himself once, is to all eternity a certain and valid sacrifice for the sins of all the faithful. Therefore the mass is not a sacrifice, but a remembrance of the sacrifice and assurance of the salvation Christ has given us.[20]

Although medieval interpretations of the Mass had held "remembrance" and "sacrifice" together, they came to be opposed categories in the Reformation debates and polemics over the nature of the Lord's Supper. Melanchthon and Luther emphasized Christ's promise and testament while Zwingli focused on the remembrance of and thanksgiving for a sacrifice that had already occurred.

One scholar has noted that Luther's emphasis was more "objective" while Zwingli's was more "subjective."[21] Zwingli's "subjectivism" has been noted especially in reference to his "spiritualism," or, as some scholars prefer, his pneumatology.[22] Note, for example, his summary of the Word of God's clarity and power:

---

17 Ibid.

18 Locher, *Zwingli's Theology*, 6

19 Our discussion here follows Ozment, *The Reformation in the Cities*, 131ff.

20 Cited in Alasdair I. C. Heron, *Table and Tradition: Toward an Ecumenical Understanding of the Eucharist* (Philadelphia: Westminster, 1983), 115.

21 Ibid. Melanchthon, as we shall subsequently see, tried to hold together, albeit in a dynamic tension as a doctrine of grace requires, the "objective" and "subjective" dimensions of Word and rite; see Ralph Walter Quere, *Melanchthon's Christum Cognoscere: Christ's Efficacious Presence in the Eucharistic Theology of Melanchthon* (Nieukoop: B. DeGraaf, 1977), 89–90, 109.

22 E.g., Busser, "Spirituality of Zwingli and Bullinger," 301–302; Locher, *Zwingli's Theology*, 178–180.

Do you feel that the Word is renewing you, that God begins to be dearer to you than before you harkened to human teachings? Then be sure that God has brought this about in you. Do you feel that it makes you certain of the grace of God and of eternal salvation? Then that comes from God. Do you feel that it makes you small and insignificant, whereas God is great in you? Then that is a work of God. Do you feel that the fear of God begins to make you more happy than sad? Then that is a certain work of the Word and Spirit of God. May God give you these feelings. Amen.[23]

In addition to emphasizing the work of the Word and of the Spirit, this passage also hints at what would have very significant consequences for the theology and practice of worship. Unlike the Lutheran movement, which sought to hold Word and Spirit together, as an external work of God upon the human heart, Zwingli distinguished between the two. A key New Testament text for him in this regard was the sixth chapter of John.

He interpreted this chapter and its references to eating the flesh of Christ and drinking Christ's blood as a "spiritual" reality, "a sacramental eating and drinking."

When you comfort yourself in Christ, then you eat his body *spiritually*, that is to say, trusting in Him who assumed humanity for your sake, you remain unafraid taking a stand in God against all the arrows of despair. When you, however, come with this spiritual food, to the Lord's Supper, and thank the Lord for this favour, for the redemption of the soul, whereby you are delivered from despair's destruction, and for the pledge, by which you are assured of eternal bliss; when you share with, with the bretheren, bread and wine which are the symbolic body of Christ, then, in a true sense you eat *sacramentally*, you are indeed doing inwardly what you undertake outwardly. Then the soul will be strengthened through the faith to which you bear witness with these symbols.[24]

Such an interpretation exhibits what is regarded as one of the chief characteristics of Zwingli's theology – his antithesis between the "spiritual" and the "material." Nothing is to usurp the place of God in worship. There can be no inner or outer object of faith, for true worship and piety "clings to the one and only God."[25] Zwingli's dictum – "Nothing, therefore, of ours, is to be added to the Word of God, and nothing taken from his Word by rashness of ours" – with its sharp distinction between creator and creature would provide "the foundation of the Reformed interpretation of worship."[26]

---

[23] Cited in Busser, "Spirituality of Zwingli and Bullinger," 303.

[24] Cited in Locher, "Zwingli's Theology," 319.

[25] "Commentary on True and False Religion," *Latin Works*, 2.92; cited in Eire, *War Against the Idols*, 85.

[26] Eire, *War Against the Idols*, 85.

One result is that sacrament is only a physical, visible sign of something "spiritual." If it is "spiritual," then it is not "really present." Yet what is "spiritual" does signify the atonement of Christ and God's good favor based on that atonement. But it is a signifying that points only to the past and not to a present realization of the Word's power.[27] Zwingli's overriding concern is to safeguard the Reformation principle of salvation by grace alone. And it is only through Christ alone, and not the sacraments, that such grace is received. The believer is to wholly trust God.

A decisive difference between the Zwinglian and Lutheran views was based on the interpretation of the "is" in the words of institution. Zwingli was convinced that "this is my body" was not to be understood as a literal identification of the bread with the body of Christ. Rather, according to biblical usage, "is" frequently meant "signifies." Also, for Zwingli, the familiar arguments of the pastness of the atonement, Christ's place at the right hand of God, the spiritual presence of Christ's divinity to faith could only lead to the conclusion that "the sacrament can only be a sign of a spiritual reality which is not present."[28]

The deeper issues at stake have to do with the incarnation and whether God is present in concrete historical forms like preached Word and the sacrament. Zwingli's separation of Word and Spirit left him with a different response to the question of the relationship between the divine and human realms – or, what one scholar has termed a different "*vision of reality.*"[29] Does "reality" consist of the material, visible, tangible, audible *and* the spiritual, invisible, intangible, inaudible?

If so, then affirmations about the complete, human, and bodily presence of Christ in the church's sacramental worship become very problematic conceptually. The solution of the medieval church to such a problem, as we saw in the previous chapter, was to say that presence can happen only by God's miraculous intervention. It is worked afresh each time the Lord's Supper is celebrated. But for such a presence to happen, one needs identifiable miracle workers, a priesthood, who can speak the formula of consecration. And such a notion of "institutionalized miracle-working" was denied by all the Reformers.

The two possible ways of dealing with this question of Christ's presence are either to maintain the spirit/matter distinction and so to make of such a presence a "spiritual" one. Bread and cup are reminders of that presence. Or, one can dissolve

---

27 Our discussion follows Robert James Goeser, "Word and Sacrament: A Study of Luther's Views as Developed in the Controversy with Zwingli and Karlstadt" (Ph.D. diss., Yale Univ., 1960), 204ff.
28 Ibid., 207.
29 See Jenson, "Of Another Spirit," 7ff. Our discussion follows Jenson.

the spirit/matter distinction altogether by making the Word comprehend and bring with it the reality of which it speaks. But, then that would involve a redefinition of embodied presence – not in terms of physicality or temporality – but in terms of "availability."

> It is in this way that Christ is "bodily" present where the bread and wine are. God addresses us, he calls to us. And he calls us to *himself,* i.e., he directs himself to places where we may locate him....When he addresses himself to this world, when he addresses himself to space, he always so speaks as to grant himself as our reciprocal addressee, as to make himself available, as to give us bodies that we can grasp as him.[30]

A major consequence of the Zwinglian spirit/matter distinction, however, was to make sacramental worship primarily a sign of faith and commitment:

> The sacraments are, then, signs or ceremonials by which a man proves to the Church that he either aims to be, or is, a soldier of Christ, and which inform the whole Church rather than yourself of your faith.[31]

Yet, interestingly, as a sign, a sacrament for Zwingli does not "signify." It does not really *do* anything. It does not even strengthen faith.[32] What a sacrament does is to "point to" Christ who alone brings salvation. Any "body of Christ" that is to be found is not in the elements of the Lord's Supper, but in the Church,

> they who here eat and drink are one body, one bread; that is, all those who come together to proclaim Christ's death and eat the symbolical bread, declare themselves to be Christ's body, that is, members of his church; and as this church holds one faith and eats one symbolical bread, so it is one bread and one body.[33]

For Zwingli, the Lord's Supper provides the occasion for the worshiping community to give thanks for Christ's redemptive death, to testify to their identity as Christians, thus binding themselves "to the Christian life and to [their] fellow Christians."[34] As such, the Lord's Supper is a communal act and testifies to the conviction that believers are not saved alone but as members of the body of Christ.

Another consequence of Zwingli's separation of the physical and the spiritual was "a war against ritual." He was profoundly suspicious of anything external or outward

---

30 Ibid., 13.

31 Cited in Locher, *Zwingli's Theology,* 317; see also Heron, *Table and Tradition,* 117.

32 W. P. Stephens, *The Theology of Huldrych Zwingli,* 235.

33 *Huldreich Zwinglis Sämtliche Werke,* ed. Emil Egli et al., 3:802, lines 30–35; cited in William R. Crockett, *Eucharist: Symbol of Transformation* (New York: Pueblo Publishing Company, 1989), 139.

34 W. P. Stephens, *The Theology of Huldrych Zwingli,* 235; see also 185.

in religion and this included forms of worship. In all fairness to Zwingli, one needs to recall the late-medieval context of practice and piety and the attachment (which some call "superstitious") to people, places, things, and sacraments. Also, the church did not hesitate to exploit this attachment financially.[35] For Zwingli, such preoccupation with externals or "outward religion" usurped God's place and placed human works in his stead.

With the stress on "interior religion," the complexities of the relationships among words, images, and rituals and the "reality" they are supposed to contain, communicate, or point to become very problematic. A frequent charge levelled by the Swiss-led Reformation was that traditional practice was "empty," if not idolatrous. Simplicity was the goal.

The practical consequences of Reformed Protestantism's interpretation of the church's worship involved a more radical move away from existing rites in order to shape a pattern of worship that approximated early Christian practice.[36] Such practice was understood to thus be more in line with "the apparently simple rites" instituted by Christ himself – water-baptism and the sharing of his meal of bread and wine. "Ceremonially more drastic" than either Catholicism or Lutheranism, this involved not only a change in the furnishings and decorations of the place of worship; it meant a change in the "meaning" of worship – what some scholars have termed either its "domestication" or the "repudiation of ritual" altogether.[37]

One can say, instead, that the "meaning" of worship was changed. For Zwingli reversed the function of a sacrament. It is related more to what the believer does rather than what the believer is given. The value of worship, moreover, is not at all soteriological, but consists of its psychological and teaching power since Christ is already present in the souls of the believers by faith.

Beginning in 1525, the manner in which worship occurred in the austere whiteness of the churches in Zurich bore witness to Zwingli's sundering of the spiritual realm from the material. Sermon and Lord's Supper stood in irreconcilable opposition to a religious experience that involved sight and sound, smell and movement.

---

35 See Ozment's discussion of the numerous fees which parish clergy collected from laity (*Age of Reform*, 212ff; *Protestants*, 11ff).

36 Susan J. White, "Christian Worship Since the Reformation," in *The Making of Jewish and Christian Worship*, ed. Paul F. Bradshaw and Lawrence A. Hoffman (Notre Dame, Ind.: Univ. of Notre Dame Press, 1991), 187.

37 Geoffrey Wainwright, *Doxology: The Praise of God in Worship, Doctrine, and Life* (New York: Oxford, 1980), 267; Wegman, *Christian Worship in East and West*, 327; Burke, "The repudiation of ritual in early modern Europe"; Thomas A. Brady, Jr., "In Search of the Godly City," in *The German People and the Reformation*, ed. R. Po-chia Hsia (Ithaca: Cornell Univ. Press, 1988), 21.

Externals such as music, vestments, incense, ritual gestures, and images were of no avail to the worshiper. Faith was the only reality, that invisible action of the Holy Spirit in the human heart:

> "Faith" is from the invisible God and it tends toward the invisible God, and is something completely apart from all that is sensible. Anything that is body, anything that is of the senses, cannot be an object of faith.[38]

Before we turn to an initial examination of the understanding of the Christian ritual/worship that Melanchthon sought to present, Zwingli's diametrically opposed understandings of true and false belief – one based on the Word, invisible and heard, the other on the visible and the seen – must be borne in mind. At the same time, as we saw in the previous chapter, the practice and theology of late-medieval Catholicism, needs to be recalled as well.

WORD *AND* RITE

At the outset of his tract, *Answer to the Anabaptists*, Melanchthon discussed two matters – what a sacrament is and what are the uses of the sacraments. To define a sacrament, he used the classic saying of Augustine: "Let the Word be added to the element and it becomes a Sacrament." There is the element or the sign that signifies the promised grace *and* the Word by which the sign has been instituted by God in order to promise grace.

As he inaugurated his discussion of the "use" of the sacrament, he had in mind the Zwinglian notion that a sacrament is primarily a badge or token of Christian identity:

> In the first place, therefore, we should know this, that the sacraments have not been instituted merely for the purpose of being marks to distinguish Christians from Gentiles, as the toga distinguished Romans from Greeks or as the vesture distinguishes monks. Some do write that Sacraments have been instituted that we may show the Gentiles through them that we believe in Christ and that we may profess our faith before men and by our example invite others to take up the doctrine of Christ.[39]

---

38 Zwingli, "Answer to Valentin Compar," in *Huldreich Zwinglis Sämtliche Werke*, ed. Emil Egli, et al., 3:798, lines 14–17; cited in Charles Garside, Jr., *Zwingli and the Arts* (New Haven: Yale Univ. Press, 1966), 178.

39 "Answer to the Anabaptists," in *MS*, 105.

Instead, Melanchthon wrote,

> But we should feel that Sacraments are signs of the divine will toward us and not merely signs of our profession toward men. For the fleece was to Gideon, not merely a mark by which his army would be distinguished from the enemy, as if by some signal of the camp, but rather it was a sign of the will of God and and a pledge of promised victory.[40]

Melanchthon continued by affirming how the sacraments are, like Gideon's fleece, signs of God's will and a remembrance of Christ and Christ's benefits. Then, he wrote,

> As the will of God is shown in the Word or in the promise, so also is it shown in a sign as in a picture. As the Word is perceived in our ears to arouse [*excitet*] faith in our hearts, so a sign occurs to our eyes that it may also arouse faith in our hearts. Therefore Augustine wrote that a Sacrament is the visible Word, because it signifies the same thing as the promise does, and is, as it were, a picture of the divine will, just as the Word is the voice of the divine will.[41]

For Melanchthon, signification was both outward and inward – objective *and* subjective. For Zwingli, any signification or "efficacy," if you will, was inward only. And what was produced "inwardly" was produced by the "freedom of the divine Spirit," and *not* by any outward sign. According to Melanchthon, however, one could not separate the outward and the inward without jeopardizing just how it is that God's will and work reach the human heart.

In the very next paragraph of this tract, however, we find a more explicit equivalent to Melanchthon's statement in the Apology of the Augsburg Confession about Word and rite "moving the heart." Here the position he was addressing is the Roman position that sacraments justify or are effective *ex opere operato*:

> For they are in error who think that they merit the remission of sins by this work, when they eat the Lord's Supper. Paul teaches that we are justified not by works but by faith. And just as hearing the Word without faith does not justify, so using a Sacrament without faith does not justify. For even the Sacrament itself is, as I have said before, some sort of visible Word.[42]

---

40 Ibid., 105–106.
41 Ibid., 106.
42 Ibid.

Then comes the text with the "movement of the heart" language:

> Just as the voice is perceived by our ears, so the Sacrament confronts our eyes *to move our hearts* to believe. And since the Sacraments contain promises, so we finally use them correctly when we believe that we attain those things which are promised, for promises require faith, as Paul teaches in Romans 4.[43]

What Melanchthon was doing in this tract, then, was articulating a position that was neither Zwinglian (the grace of the sacrament is effective *ex opere operantis* – the bread and wine understood as Roman toga!) nor Roman (grace is effective *ex opere operato*). Instead the sacraments are effective signs of God's will, the visible word of God, that work faith in the person. Simply stated, then, Melanchthon's position was that sacraments are "signs of God's will" against Zurich and effective, i.e., "heart moving" to faith against Rome.[44]

It is interesting to note how these insights of Melanchthon into Word and rite "moving the heart" parallel Luther's Large Catechism. While different in method and use of language, the point is curiously the same. Luther noted,

> This is the reason why these two things are done in Baptism: the body has water poured over it, though it cannot receive anything but the water, and meanwhile the Word is spoken so that the soul may grasp it.

> Since the water and the Word together constitute one Baptism, body and soul shall be saved and live forever: the soul through the Word in which it believes, the body because it is united with the soul and apprehends Baptism in the only way it can. No greater jewel, therefore, can adorn our body and soul than Baptism....[45]

One key difference between Melanchthon and Luther at this juncture was that for Luther, the eyes are of no help. For Melanchthon, however, they are another way to the heart. Yet earlier in his discussion, Luther did insist on the externality of Word and sacrament:

> Yes, [the object of faith] must be external so that it can be perceived and grasped by the senses and thus brought into the heart, just as the entire Gospel is an external, oral proclamation.[46]

Luther mentioned the result of bringing word/sign into the heart just a bit later in the discussion: "God's works, however, are salutary and necessary for salvation, and

---

43 Ibid. My emphasis.

44 My thanks to Professor Timothy J. Wengert of the Lutheran Theological Seminary at Philadelphia for these insights.

45 Martin Luther, Large Catechism 4.45–46; in *BC*, 442.

46 Ibid., 4.30, 440

they do not exclude but rather demand faith. For without faith they could not be grasped."[47] God's work requires faith. And God's work is of just such an external nature so that it can be brought into the human heart. Underneath the differences between Luther and Melanchthon, the point is the same. For Luther, God's external work of water and word demanded, required, faith! For Melanchthon, God's word and work "move the heart" through eye and ear.

A MIDDLE COURSE

Melanchthon's desire to steer a middle course between medieval Catholicism's *ex opere operato* and Zwingli's spiritualistic view that drove a wedge between symbol and reality has not always been understood. This was true in his own time as well as in the case of subsequent interpreters.[48] One consequence of his interest in the entirety of ritual action – its use, purpose, and goal – was a description of Christ's presence and the effect of that presence in ways that would not get bogged-down in either "materialist" or "spiritualist" categories.

Scholars have noted Melanchthon's preference for expressions such as *in sacramento, in ritu,* or *in actu* when describing Christ's presence.This has been labelled as "efficacious" or "ritual" presence.[49] Over against theological attempts to answer the "how question" of Christ's presence in the Lord's Supper (attempts that made him very uneasy), Melanchthon's emphasis on the rite as a whole is often viewed as a "deviation" from Luther's view of an embodied presence in the elements of bread and wine that gave forgiveness, life, and salvation. Yet within Melanchthon's perspective as a whole, there is his language that Christ is present in the ritual action *with* the bread and wine to forgive, to strengthen and confirm faith – even "to move the heart to believe and take hold of faith."

Is the emphasis and perspective of Melanchthon so different from that of Luther's? Because he has synthesized "presence" and "efficacy" in order to connect a so-called "sacramental" presence of Christ with human participation and use, does he need to be vilified as a "proto-Calvinist" or "crypto-Calvinist"? Is this a defection from "Lutheran" doctrine?[50]

An older scholarship, operating with certain conceptions of humanism (i.e., humanism as too preoccupied with free will or individualism and as basically anti-reli-

---

47 Ibid., 4.36, 441.
48 See the discussion in Quere, *Melanchthon's Christum Cognoscere*, 8–10, 383–390.
49 Ibid. See also his "Melanchthonian Motifs in the Formula's Eucharistic Christology," 58–73.
50 E.g., Sasse, *This is my Body*, 252ff.

gious or too confident in human capacities), has read Melanchthon's sacramental theology as continuing to exhibit "humanist" tendencies.[51] Presumably, this meant that he was not all that interested in sacrament, liturgy, and ritual or that his materialistic fears led him to emphasize presence in celebration, i.e., in the ritual action, instead of in the elements. Also, Melanchthon is often regarded as understanding faith in a too intellectual or a too propositional fashion – as *constanter assentiri omni verbo Dei*,[52] even though one would look in vain in any of his writings for an equation of faith with doctrinal knowledge. For Melanchthon,

> the central note of faith was always trust – reliance upon Jesus Christ as Savior. The knowledge to which faith clings is the simple Gospel message of the cross and resurrection, not a complex theological system.[53]

More recent scholarship has corrected, even overturned these formerly conventional interpretations by treating them in fresh ways, principally by situating Melanchthon amidst more adequate understandings of humanism and the developing theology of Luther. We can thus be delivered from the notion "that Melanchthon's career at Wittenberg must be seen as a series of crises and breaks...," or that he was continually torn between humanist and evangelical emphases.[54] For, as E. Gordon Rupp has noted,

> When all has been said about Melanchthon's humanism, about his ability to synthesize – about his "Melanchthon – and" (as against "Luther – or"), he did fatefully and deeply understand what Luther meant by the gospel, and that he received at this point, or rather what with Luther he rediscovered in the Bible, was not a set of notions of doctrines, but an initiation into the experience of salvation, of a forgiven and regenerated soul, set at peace and liberty by grace, and turned from disobedience to a new life, within the redeemed community, within a forgiven and edifying solidarity, through the action of the Word.[55]

Within such a broader framework, we can better appreciate Melanchthon's idea of a manifold presence of Christ – a presence working efficaciously, ecclesially, ritually, elementally, and personally. This process engages participants, who are enabled to assent to and trust in that presence and authority. These ideas are all of a piece and have soteriological consequences. For since the Lord's Supper is a rite, a sign of the

---

51 Ibid.

52 *LC*, 92: "It [faith] is constantly to assent to every word of God...."

53 Rogness, *Reformer Without Honor*, 61.

54 Wengert, *Philip Melanchthon's Annotationes in Johannem*, 233.

55 E. Gordon Rupp, "Philip Melanchthon and Martin Bucer," *A History of Christian Doctrine: In Succession to the Earlier Work of G. P. Fisher*, ed. Hubert Cunliffe-Jones (Philadelphia:Fortress Press, 1980), 375.

promise to be used in faith, a ceremony added to the promise, "the body and blood of Christ are presented [*exhibentur*]...so that we may know that we are loved, cared for, and preserved by him."[56] It is in this particular way of acting and speaking, then, that the gospel is embodied in order "to strike" and "to move the heart." With such matters in mind, we turn now to a more explicit consideration of what Melanchthon understood as comprising this "movement of the heart."

---

[56] Melanchthon, *Loci* of 1535, in *CR* 21:479; cited in Quere, "Melanchthonian Motifs...", 72.

4. "AGAIN AND AGAIN THE HEART": MELANCHTHON'S RHETORICAL UNDERSTANDING OF CHRISTIAN RITUAL

INTRODUCTION

"Again and again the heart," wrote Heinrich Bornkamm over thirty years ago to underscore the centrality of the heart for Melanchthon's understanding both what it meant to be a particular kind of person and how he or she experienced the gospel.[1] Unlike the compartmentalized anthropology of Scholasticism that visualized human being as a hierarchy of faculties governed by the intellect, Melanchthon preferred to think of the *totus homo*. As a humanist, he was inclined to emphasize not what was highest but what was central – the core (*cor, coeur*) – "the heart."[2]

This perspective had profound implications for understanding what the Gospel was and how it worked in the event of audible and visible communication called the worship of the church. The emphasis on "the heart" involved a recognition of the primacy in human experience of the realms of feeling and subjectivity. As Word and rite of the Gospel, this event did not so much aim to convince one who participated by an appeal to the mind. Rather, like rhetoric, it sought to *move* the whole human being – "the heart" – the source and center of all that one is – to believe and take hold of faith. If we recall, for a moment, how Melanchthon paired dialectic with *docere* and rhetoric with *movere*, then a rhetorical understanding of the distinctive working of Christian ritual has to do with the effective relation of "subject matter" – in this instance Word *and* rite – to human beings.[3]

---

[1] "Melanchthons Menschenbild," *Philip Melanchthon: Forschungsbeiträge zur vierhundertensten Wiederkehr seines Todestages dargeboten in Wittenberg 1960*, ed. Walter Elliger (Göttingen: Vandenhoeck & Ruprecht 1961), 88.

[2] Bouwsma, "Review Article," 69.

[3] See Klaus Haendler, *Wort und Glaube bei Melanchthon: Eine Untersuchung über die Voraussetzungen und Grundlagen des melanchthonischen Kirchensbegriffes*, Quellen und Forschungen zur Reformationsgeschichte Band 37 (Gütersloh: Gütersloher Verlagshaus Gerd Mohn, 1968), 35–36.

This rhetorical understanding of the workings of the Gospel meant a reconceptualization or recovery of preaching as passionate and expressive discourse. The singular power of words and the Word sought a transformation of both self and the world – what Melanchthon described in one of his homiletical writings as "renovation and spiritual life" where the "better emotions" – fear of God or faith, patience or love – manifest a selfhood created by a firm trust in the mercy and promises of Christ.[4]

But Melanchthon also used *movere* – the *officium* of the grand style – to describe how the Gospel works in the total action of what happens in Christian ritual, especially in the Lord's Supper: "the rite itself enters through the eyes to move the heart."[5] In the previous chapter, we noted his desire to steer a course between the Roman concept of sacramental worship as efficacious signs that justify and the Zwinglian reduction of Christ's presence to a spiritual efficacy. By doing so, Melanchthon placed the action of Word and rite in the God who makes believers. This was the "objective" basis of the divine-human relationship.

At the same time, however, the so-called "objectivity" of the church's worship should and/or needed to correspond to "the subjective feelings and experiences of believers...."[6] Melanchthon was keenly interested in unfolding this "subjective" dimension by analyzing how faith and love spring from worship's saving gift, the effect of God's grace upon human beings.[7] In his rhetorical understanding of Scripture, for example, he emphasized its power to move not merely the mind but to be also an instrument of God's spiritual work in changing the heart. There is a sense that this movement of the heart is both the work of the Spirit and "*also* a quite human psychological process."[8] One would think, therefore, that we could explore Melanchthon's understanding of the purpose and power of the church's worship in a similar fashion. For a theological claim for what this event is and does strongly suggests, if not requires, that it happens somewhere and looks and sounds like something. That is, there is an accent on discovering experientially what theology claims and seeks to understand.

---

4 Melanchthon, *SM*, vol. 5, pt. 2, 51.
5 Melanchthon, Apology of the Augsburg Confession 13.5, in *BC*, 212. The Latin text [*BS*, 292] reads as follows: "ita ritus ipse incurrit in oculus, ut moveat corda."
6 Jaroslav Pelikan, "Luther and the Liturgy," in *More About Luther*, Martin Luther Lectures, vol. 2 (Decorah, Iowa: Luther College Press, 1958), 37.
7 Quere, *Melanchthon's Christum Cognoscere*, 109, 172ff.
8 Schneider, *Melanchthon's Rhetorical Construal of Biblical Authority*, 141.

With these introductory considerations, we have a framework for this chapter. Our task is to explore Melanchthon's use of the rhetorical concept *movere* to name and understand how God's saving action is enacted and experienced in Christian ritual.

THEOLOGICAL INSIGHT AND RITUAL CONSEQUENCE

The religious experience and theological insight of the sixteenth century Lutheran Reformation have been variously described as "justification by faith," "the rediscovery of the gospel," and as "an encounter with and discovery of the Word of God."9 While there is general agreement that this theological insight grew out of particular concern for biblical interpretation and the sort of language that could be the gospel's "living voice," the matter of how to approach and to understand the ensuing ritual/liturgical expressions of such an insight are much more controverted.

Discussions of what the early Lutheran movement sought to achieve liturgically emphasize either its intent to remain within the mainstream of historic catholic tradition or its desire to reshape the understanding and practice of the worship of the church. Both of these emphases, however, have tended toward one-sidedness either by being too textually-based or too theologically-preoccupied. Also, they have been insufficiently attentive to recent Reformation studies that remind us of the necessity of calling attention to "all the forces that shape historical experience."10 What this means for our purposes is to become more aware of the various forces and factors shaping and influencing what the liturgical expressions of the early Lutheran movement aspired to accomplish for worshiping communities and why.

In the sixteenth century, Western Christianity witnessed a significant redesign, if not reconceptualization, of its symbolic order. The Mass, which had been central and vital to the experience and understanding of the sacred, "now bread, now God,"11 became "evangelical" so that the clear, unambiguous word of promise could be communicated powerfully and meaningfully to those present.12 A significant consequence of this symbolic redesign and reconceptualization for a lay experience of re-

9 See Goeser, "Whither Lutheranism?" 41; Michael B. Aune, "Issues in Contemporary Lutheran Worship Theory and Practice," *Worship Textbook*, ed. Patrick J. Keifert (St. Paul, Minn.: Luther Northwestern Theological Seminary, 1985), 1.

10 Steven Ozment, introduction to *Religion and Culture in the Renaissance and Reformation*, ed. Steven Ozment, Sixteenth Century Essays and Studies, vol. XI (Kirksville, Mo.: Sixteenth Century Journal Publishers, Inc., 1989), 4.

11 Rubin, *Corpus Christi*, 53.

12 See James S. Preus, "Neglected Problems in the Eucharistic Dialogue," *Currents in Theology and Mission* 3 (1976), 279–287.

ligious ritual was an insistence that it be doctrinally informed, intellectually engaged.[13]

Among those who have rued such a development are social historians of the Reformation and numerous students of Christian liturgy.[14] They argue that it was both a "domestication" of worship and a repudiation of ritual, since the new operative notion was to be *lex docendi, lex orandi* rather than the *lex orandi, lex credendi* of traditional Catholicism.[15] Lurking behind these evangelical liturgies that were designed to teach about the faith rather than to celebrate it, moreover, was a different model of communication and relationship between God and mortals, and between mortals – the model of "classically inspired eloquence"[16] or rhetoric. Then, as well as now, as we saw in the introduction to this study, rhetoric and ritual are often perceived as being mutually exclusive, if not altogether contradictory. Yet both are suspected of possessing great power.

We saw in chapter 2 how the ritual practices of late-medieval Catholicism claimed that

> Heaven was never too far from earth. The sacred was diffused in the profane, the spiritual in the material. Divine power, embodied in the Church and its sacraments, reached down through innumerable points of contact to make itself felt: to forgive or punish, to protect against the ravages of nature, to heal, to soothe, and to work all sorts of wonders.[17]

It was over against such humbling and such audacious claims for the embodiment of divine power in the Church's sacramental system that the early Lutheran movement's critical and fundamental hermeneutic of the Word engendered an utterly different conception of what was supposed to be happening in religious ritual.[18] This activity was still regarded as possessing great power, but what makes it so is the Word, the *viva vox evangelii* in Scripture and in church and beyond them, not the sacerdotal office.

---

13 Reinburg, "Liturgy and the Laity in Late Medieval and Reformation France," 545–546.

14 E.g., Robert W. Scribner, *Popular Culture and Popular Movements in Reformation Germany* (London & Ronceverte: The Hambledon Press, 1987); Brady, "In Search of the Godly City," 14–29; Bossy, *Christianity in the West*; Bossy, "The Mass as a Social Institution 1200–1700," *Past and Present* no. 100 (1983): 29–61; Louis Weil, "Facilitating Growth in Faith Through Liturgical Worship," in *Handbook of Faith*, ed. James Michael Lee (Birmingham, Ala.: Religious Education Press, 1990), 208–209.

15 Rene Bornert, *La réforme protestante du culte à Strasbourg au XVIe siècle (1523–1598)* (Leiden: E. J. Brill, 1981), 596.

16 Bossy, *Christianity in the West*, 98.

17 Eire, *War Against the Idols*, 1.

18 See Preus, "Neglected Problems in the Eucharistic Dialogue," 279–287.

Much of the early sixteenth century discussion of the practice and theology of the church's worship, however, was caught up in the technical debates about the sacramental elements and the modes of Christ's presence. Melanchthon's point of view, grounded in his articulation of Reformation theology using the categories of Renaissance rhetoric, was one that can be described as a joyful affirmation of the effectiveness of the spoken, written, and pictured Word. His language of the Word striking the ear and the rite moving or exciting to faith in the heart exemplified a preference to emphasize the use and purpose of sacramental worship within the church and in the new life of the justified believer. The result, as Peter Fraenkel has noted, was a "functional" interest rather than a strictly systematic-theological one.[19]

In the framework of this "functional" interest, Melanchthon spoke of *processes* and their effects – *ritus, usus* – instead of things such as bread, wine, body, blood and what they are.[20] He wanted to unfold an understanding of the giving of Christ in the performance of the sacramental rite, which he regarded as some sort of "event." While Melanchthon has been vilified for having such a "vague" sacramental/eucharistic theology, what is often overlooked is his affirmation of the substantial presence of Christ. But his overall interest was one that has been described as centered more on "the real communication,"[21] – its objective and subjective dimensions – than on trying to explain the particular manner of Christ's presence, which, like the Trinity, he considered a mystery.[22]

"THE REAL COMMUNICATION"

It is difficult to understand Melanchthon's more process-oriented, event approach to the effects of sacramental worship. Such difficulty stems from a lack of awareness of his humanist dialectical-rhetorical method, with its twin emphases on *certitudo* and *utilitas*. We saw in our earlier discussion in chapter 1 and in the introduction to this chapter that the humanist model of human being, its anthropology and psychology, envisaged something more unpredictable and mysterious than Scholasticism's faculty psychology of a well-ordered personality ruled by the intellect. Rather than flatten the essence of human being to a single, dominant dimension of intellect or reason, humanists and rhetoricians recognized that a human being is a composite of reason and

---

19 "Ten Questions Concerning Melanchthon, the Fathers, and the Eucharist," *Luther and Melanchthon*, ed. Vilmos Vajta (Philadelphia: Muhlenberg Press, 1961), 147ff.

20 Ibid.

21 Quere, *Melanchthon's Christum Cognoscere*, 268 n. 564.

22 *LC*, 21: "We do better to adore the mysteries of Deity than to investigate them."

emotion. We find not so much a reform of traditional faculty psychology as a diversification, an encouragement to value formerly disparaged faculties. Thus, a human being has a body and is imaginative; in the imagination, reason and emotion meet to move the heart and will.

The consequences of such an anthropology for an understanding of communication, particularly "Christian communication," was a view of the Gospel, not as "a set of statements giving information" but, rather possessing a "more than rational, active character" that is able to convey "grace and power of conversion, the self-revelation and saving presence of God."[23] From a rhetorical vantage point, the goal of communication was to make something happen in another human being or in a group of human beings. In order to make something happen, there needed to be an appeal to the deepest possible level of the human personality – "the heart."[24]

We noted earlier that for a humanist, rhetorical understanding of the human personality was accompanied by a changing conception both of what it meant "to know something" and of what knowledge should be. We might also say that there was a changing conception of what communication should be – a broader, more experiential sort of event in which one is not only informed but also touched, confounded, inflamed, and moved.

Melanchthon, for example, emphasized that knowing needed to be practical and useful, relevant to the experience of living individuals in specific historical moments. His emphasis that the human personality is molded and controlled by something deep within gives us additional insight into the workings of the mind. What occurs there is more profound than either reason or will. The mind or intellect is not simply a cold, objective instrument that receives and processes information. Rather, it perceives the communication of knowledge as saturated with affect, which, for a humanist like Melanchthon, was an asset because it narrowed the gap between theory and practice, belief and action. Also, these changing notions of the human personality, of knowledge, of communication helped to enlarge the importance of divine revelation while simultaneously intensifying the relationship between God and human beings *and* giving a greater role to human subjectivity.

In the sixteenth century, however, there were no vocabularies for describing "subjectivity" and its corollaries such as "the real self" or "the inner life." To be sure,

---

23 Peter Fraenkel, "Revelation and Tradition: Notes on Some Aspects of Doctrinal Continuity in the Theology of Philip Melanchthon," *Studia Theologica* 13 (1959): 100.

24 See Lewis W. Spitz, "Humanism and the Protestant Reformation," in *RH*, 3:194: "The Gospel ... moves the heart, and for the reformers as for humanist rhetoricians, speaking with synecdoche, the heart stands for the whole man including his emotions."

there were assumptions about inward experience as well as ways to talk about and analyze feelings and the inmost sensations of the human heart. "Experience" tended to be associated with "feeling" and "sensation." Those terms which were closest to our understandings of "feelings" and "emotions" were "affections," and, often in poetry as well as in theology, "passions." Although the "passions" were usually contrasted with or opposed to "reason," they were also viewed as playing a vital role in how the person responded to God's presence.[25] Instead of being deceptive and subrational, they become the experiential component of faith, love, and knowledge. They are part of the noetic *and* affective response to God's action on the mind and heart. Melanchthon wrote, for example, of the mind being "moved," "excited," "inflamed," and "stimulated" to embrace the benefits of Christ. But he would also emphasize that faith was an emotion, a firm trust (*fiducia*) in the mercy and promises of Christ – a movement of the intellect *and* of the heart and will.

Whatever sort of self that was constituted and/or reconstituted by what we have been calling "the real communication" was one in which intellectual precision and passionate force had been joined. This sense of the proximity, even the interweaving of the noetic and the affective, was characteristic of Melanchthon's understanding, as we have also noted earlier, as well. The significance or import of this distinguishing and joining of knowing and feeling was what was at stake in his emphasis upon *certitudo* and *utilitas*.

It is interesting, moreover, that one of the terms contained in the Latin title of the 1521 *Loci*, namely *hypotyposis*, is a particularly key rhetorical strategy, in which the orator or writer so narrates an event that it seems to be going on before our very eyes. The strategy is employed to bring things forcefully, vividly to the sight or mind that there is no doubt whatsoever that their import and significance are clear.

Such clarity and power are what Melanchthon meant by the "perspicuity" and "certitudo" of his subject matter – in this instance, the Scripture's message of the offer of salvation in Christ. In fact, the message was so clear that it can be totally assented to *and* confidently trusted. Melanchthon was keen to make sure that faith has a certain object and that such certainty is coordinated with the human need to be convinced, persuaded, and moved – so that one "takes hold of faith," i.e., *concipiant*. The word *concipiant* means "to take completely in, absorb, grasp by senses or intellect, to begin to feel" that what is said, heard, and done is indeed the Gospel promise. This was the same rhetorical strategy which Melanchthon employed in the Apology

---

25 See the discussion in Anne Ferry, *The 'Inward' Language: Sonnets of Wyatt, Sidney, Shakespeare, Donne* (Chicago: Univ. of Chicago Press, 1983), 46.

of the Augsburg Confession when he described how the rite "enters through the eyes to move the heart." Such a concern with vividness and *hypotyposis* grew out of the need to emphasize God's presence in such a way that its felt significance can be articulated as well as experienced. This was the human side of the encounter – the certitude of faith that trusts the Word and the Promise.

This conception of theology which was at once "practical and affective" and anti-speculative has been nicely visualized by Siegfried Wiedenhofer in his study of Melanchthon's theology and theological method.[26] This method was based on an interpretation of 1 Timothy 4.13: "Until I arrive devote your attention to the public reading of the scriptures, to exhortation, and to teaching." Melanchthon had altered the sequence of the terms "reading," "exhortation," "teaching," bringing them into the more logical and psychological order, *lectio, doctrina, consolatio*.[27]

Melanchthon's Theological Method

	LECTIO	DOCTRINA	CONSOLATIO
Revelation	"Fact"	Content	Effect
Text	Scripture	Articles of Faith	Law & Promise
Psychology	Intellect /Mind	Intellect	Affect /Will
Rhetoric	Utterance	Teach	Move
Wissenschaft		Grammar/Dialectic	Rhetoric
Theology		Exegesis/Dogmatics Interpretation/ Methodological/ Systematic Explanation & Presentation of Articles of Faith	Homiletics/ Sermon
Proclamation	Read/Lecture	Knowledge	Experience/ Action of Exciting the Affections
Sermon		Teaching/ Catechesis	Affective sermon

Based on Wiedenhofer, *Formalstrukturen*, 1:335.

---

26 Wiedenhofer, *Formalstrukturen*, 1:335.

27 Meerhoff notes that Melanchthon used 1 Tim. 4.13 on at least ten different occasions, and that this passage was the basis for a Melanchthonian homiletic theory ("The Significance of Philip Melanchthon's Rhetoric," 53).

Wiedenhofer notes how *doctrina* for Melanchthon had an "active" and "passive" sense. As "active," it was teaching, process, occurrence. As "passive," it was content and subject. He also observes that *doctrina* had a wide frame of meaning for Melanchthon that included revelation, tradition, proclamation, preaching, faith, theology. According to Peter Fraenkel, these terms are "verbal nouns" that express activities, functions, processes of God's self-revelation and gift of grace, of Gospel preaching and teaching – a subject matter "at work."[28]

Consolatio was Melanchthon's way of speaking of the effect of revelation, both as knowledge and as existential accomplishment of faith. It happens in the application of the promise, in its practical employment in the new life of the believer. Wiedenhofer notes how *consolatio* is both a matter of *praxis*, "the energetic practice of faith in the Christian life," and a psychological process that involves the intellect and the affections, i.e., the "heart" and the "will." The affections are specified further as "fear," "trust," "hope," "love," and "joy" and are to characterize the Christian life marked by growth in faith and in intellectual understanding.[29]

Melanchthon's understanding of the *certitudo* and *utilitas* of the subject matter of theology and proclamation "at work" as a trustworthy foundation for faith and life involved a definable intellectual *and* psychological process. It began with "historical faith" – "an acknowledgement of the historical story of Christ," the acknowledgement of the history of divine revelation – that led to existential appropriation. It was a "fiducial faith" which is established in the center of life of human beings – the *cor*, the heart.

"MOVING THE HEART"

The "heart," as we noted at the beginning of this chapter, was central to Melanchthon's understanding both of the person and how he or she experienced the gospel. In the 1521 *Loci communes*, he had articulated this understanding over against the tripartite psychology and anthropology of classical and scholastic thought – where the person is composed of sensual appetite, intellect, and will.

At the outset of the *Loci*, Melanchthon divided the human being into two parts – cognition, i.e., our capacity to know, perceive, understand, and reason; and the will, or the affections – i.e., the source of our feelings, drives, desires, and passions. But unlike classical and scholastic thinkers who regarded the intellect as supreme,

---

28 Ibid.; also Fraenkel, "Revelation and Tradition," 113–117.
29 Wiedenhofer, *Formalstrukturen*, 1:333–334.

Melanchthon argued that "cognition serves the will" because he was "convinced by experience and practice that the will cannot bring forth love, hate, and similar affections by its own power."[30]

A year earlier, in his 1520 oration entitled *Small Declamation concerning the study of Paul,* Melanchthon had argued in a very similar fashion:

> Some of the ancients thought that reason in man functions like a charioteer and called the passions the horses. But reason is conquered by passion. Holding the reins in vain, the charioteer is borne on by the horses. Nor does the team heed curb. Rather the passions shake off reason in the same way that the horses of the sun's chariot did Phaeton. This power of sin is conquered by the grace of Christ alone.[31]

It did not take long for Melanchthon to conclude, finally, that the categories of intellect and will were altogether unrealistic. In the *Loci,* he wrote:

> I do not think it greatly matters at this point to separate the feelings from what is called the intellect, and the appetite of the feelings from the higher appetite [i.e., the "will"].... For what is will if it is not the fount of the affections? *And why do we not use the word "heart" instead of will? For the Scriptures call the most powerful part of man the "heart," especially that part in which the affections arise...*and since God judges hearts, *the heart must be the highest and most powerful part of man.*[32]

Affectus is one of those key terms, like fiducia, that was of great importance for Melanchthon's entire thinking. In classical rhetoric, *affectus* was the Latin word for emotion, a translation of the Greek *pathos.* It is regarded as key to the entire persuasive process: "[There is persuasion] through the hearers when they are led to feel emotion by the speech; for we do not give the same judgment when grieved and rejoicing or when being friendly and hostile."[33] *Affectus* and *pathos* were distinguished from *ethos,* the character of the speaker. For Aristotle, ethos was "the controlling factor in persuasion."[34] *Pathos* was in the audience, however, and referred to "the more

---

30 *LC,* 27.

31 *MW* 1:39. Both Geyer and Meerhoff note the significance of this oration for Melanchthon's developing theology. *Doctrina* is not something abstractly intellectual but is to be applied to life: "Therefore, if your salvation is a matter of your heart, if to know Christ and Christ's grace is your real concern, take into your hands finally the divine books of Paul" (*MS,* 40). Meerhoff characterizes Melanchthon's system as twofold. It is both rational and affective: "Gospel ... implies knowledge about God's will, about Christ, and his gifts (*beneficia*) to mankind, about justice, and so on; it is also a promise, a vivifying force, as it dispenses hope and consolation" ("The Significance of Philip Melanchthon's Rhetoric," 53).

32 *LC,* 23, 27. My emphasis.

33 Aristotle *Rhetorica* 1. 2. 5., trans. George A. Kennedy, in *On Rhetoric: A Theory of Civic Discourse* (New York: Oxford Univ. Press, 1991), 38.

34 Ibid., 1. 2. 4 (Kennedy, 38). In an accompanying note (p. 37 n. 40), Kennedy remarks that *ethos* for Aristotle "is regarded as an attribute of a person, not of a speech."

violent emotions [which] command and disturb."[35] They are "almost entirely concerned with anger, dislike, fear, hatred, and pity."[36]

Classical rhetorical theory could not escape the old dichotomy of reason and emotion. In Cicero, for example, the latter was a substitute for reasoned conviction. It played upon the desires and opinions of ignorant people. In Quintilian, there is a very revealing discussion that at first tries to hold thought and emotion together. But then he concluded that the purpose of passionate discourse is fundamentally to deceive.

> But the peculiar task of the orator arises when the minds of the judges require force to move them, and their thoughts have actually to be led away from the contemplation of the truth…. For as soon as they begin to be angry, to feel favourably disposed, to hate or pity, they begin to take a personal interest in the case, and just as lovers are incapable of forming a reasoned judgment on the beauty of the object of their affections, because passion forestalls the sense of sight, so the judge, when overcome by his emotions, abandons all attempt to enquire into the truth of the arguments, is swept along by the tide of passion, and yields himself unquestioning to the torrent.[37]

In Augustine's Christian adaptation of classical rhetoric, we encounter a more incisive analysis of the emotions in which they were interwoven with feeling, loving, knowing, and willing. Affectivity, or better, emotion, moved into the center of religious experience. It was no longer regarded solely as irrational perturbation. Nor did Augustine regard emotion as undermining or subverting rational judgment. Rather, affectivity was intimately involved in the mind's quest to know God.

The implications of this view of the emotions would come to underlie numerous subsequent discussions of Christian rhetoric, Melanchthon's included. In turn, while Melanchthon and other humanist rhetoricians accepted and argued in terms of the older faculty psychology, the faculties which they emphasized implied a very different understanding of human being. The will or the heart came to occupy center stage. The essential point, as Melanchthon would exemplify in his own work, is that the will is both separate from and elevated above reason. He wrote, "knowledge serves the will … and is borne along by its own affection."[38]

Where it was once thought that the heart and will could be carried to God by discursive reasoning, Melanchthon's rhetorical standpoint indicates that no amount of

---

[35] Quintilian *Institutio oratoria* 4. 2. 10, trans. H. E. Butler (Loeb, 1960).
[36] Ibid., 6. 2. 20.
[37] Ibid., 6. 2. 5–6.
[38] *LC*, 23–24.

rational argument can make the invisible and remote objects of faith available, intelligible, vivid, concrete, and/or sensible. What moves the will and the emotions – the heart, the *affectus humanus*, is not rational probability because "the heart is ultimately beyond the power of both the intellect as well as the will...."[39]

Melanchthon's claim that rhetoric "moves"[40] – and, by extension, the church's ritual – rested upon a very basic and careful distinction in his thought as a whole. It is his distinction between *humana iustitia* and *iustitia Christiana*. Or, as he formulated the distinction elsewhere, there is the *affectus humanus* and *novus affectus*, or "law and gospel." "Human righteousness" and "human affection," though God-given, are "that endlessly repeated human striving for what is one's own, and thus is directed against God's will."[41]

In his commentary on Colossians, Melanchthon compared human and Christian righteousness, emphasizing the necessity of understanding the difference between them so that reason and philosophy (i.e., *all* the disciplines except theology) could serve their God-ordained purpose in the world.[42] Although human righteousness, or "philosophy," was a gift of God, it could only instruct "in earthly matters and not religious doctrine."[43] It provided useful knowledge for morality and was relevant for social dealings and political affairs. *But*, when it came to teaching about the will of God, "it goes entirely wrong."[44] Human righteousness was incapable of accepting "that reality is governed by God." It asserted that social righteousness was enough and did not see any need for the Holy Spirit "to move" or transform the heart."[45]

Melanchthon's constant emphasis, however, was that such a "movement of the heart" is the spiritual work of God. It is a divine gift that can "alter, change, and direct the affections" for the good, for an altogether new life.[46] The Spirit of God changes the heart and empowers to action. Melanchthon seemed to accept the paradox, present in other sacred rhetorics of the period, that the affective power of reli-

---

[39] Haendler, *Wort und Glaube*, 500; see also Wiedenhofer, *Formalstrukturen*, 1:155.

[40] Recall this claim in his *De rhetorica libri tres* of 1519 and again in the *Elementorum rhetorices libri duo* of 1531. In *De Rhetorica*, Melanchthon asserted that the language of rhetoric "is accomodated...to moving." In the *Elementorum rhetorices*, he stated, "...the function of rhetoric is *to move* and stimulate minds [or, 'souls'] and thus to affect a person."

[41] Wiedenhofer, *Formalstrukturen*, 1:155.

[42] Melanchthon, *Paul's Letter to the Colossians*, trans. D. C. Parker (Sheffield, England: The Almond Press, 1989), 46ff. For the original text, see "Scholia in Epistulam Pauli ad Colossenses" in *MW*, 4:230ff.

[43] Ibid. (Parker translation), 47.

[44] Ibid., 52.

[45] Ibid., 53–54.

[46] "Annotationes in Evangelium Matthaei" [Annotations to the Gospel of Matthew], in *MW*, 4:150.

gious discourse, as well as the ability to feel and to experience its power, is a divine gift.

Yet, as we noted at the outset of this chapter, he sensed that on some level such a "movement" is very much a psychological process as well. There is "a believing subject" who is "the object of God's spiritual action in the world."[47] He or she "is the one upon which this action impinges, and upon whom and in whom the action is carried out."[48] The knotty question that surfaces at this juncture is "the relation between human effort and divine initiative, and the connection between language and self and God."[49] This question is also at the center of what the church's ritual is and does. If activities that are normally attributed to the self are "the result of God's activity; the self seems to have little of its own left to do."[50]

This question of selfhood and subjectivity has become crucial in much contemporary thought and research. Over against individualistic ideologies that presuppose a given, fully-formed human being existing prior to his or her entry into a symbolic order of language or discourse, theoretical and critical stances in a number of disciplines have "de-centered" the subject. "The autonomous, transcendent self," writes theologian Timothy Sedgwick, "is an illusion."[51] Such "de-centering" of the human subject is "old news" from both Classical and Christian perspectives. The experience of God, as Melanchthon emphasized, is produced by the activity of God and so forms a different understanding and relationship with the world and with God. The selfhood or "moved heart" formed in the interaction between the Spirit and the human being is an activity, not an autonomous, unique entity. It is a loving response, experienced as *fiducia* (trust) and as *notitia* (an existential knowledge of Christ and of Christ's benefits).[52]

This affect of the heart towards God cannot occur, as Melanchthon relentlessly repeated and emphasized, without the Spirit's gracious gift. And, such affects were "not merely the disorderly impulses of the treacherous body but expressions of the energy and quality of the heart, that mysterious organ which was the center of the personality, the source of its unity and its ultimate worth."[53] The affections, therefore, were

---

47 Haendler, *Wort und Glaube*, 495
48 Ibid.
49 Shuger, *Sacred Rhetoric*, 230.
50 Ibid., 232.
51 "The Import of Foucault for Understanding Christian Faith," *St. Luke's Journal of Theology* 34, no. 2 (March 1991): 76.
52 Haendler, *Wort und Glaube*, 501–513.
53 William J. Bouwsma, "The Two Faces of Humanism: Stoicism and Augustinianism in Renaissance Thought," in Heiko Oberman with Thomas A Brady, Jr., eds., *Itinerarium Italicum: The*

the essential resources of the human personality and seen as somehow constitutive of religious experience as well. In fact, we have seen already how Melanchthon underlined both their irrepressible power[54] and their positive value. Over against the scholastic view of the affections as a "weakness of nature," he argued that, on the contrary, "the heart and the affections must be the highest and most powerful part of man."[55]

Melanchthon also argued that the consequence of control over the affections (if such control were truly possible) would *not* be rationality but insincerity. An attendant consequence is the presentation of an inauthentic self. Such a psychological insight has been regarded recently as "a shrewd contribution to Renaissance concern...with the problem of friendship and hypocrisy."[56] It may be also a remarkable foreshadowing of modern psychology's discovery of the subconscious, that human being is shaped and controlled by something deep within, more profound than either intellect or will.[57]

Melanchthon's theological and psychological insights into the nature and role of the affections help to explain how he viewed both sin and grace. "Sin is a depraved affectus, a depraved activity of the heart against the law of God...the dominant affection of man's nature is love of self."[58] But faith, too, sprang from the affections. "This trust in the goodwill or mercy of God first calms our hearts and then inflames us to give thanks to God for his mercy...."[59] For Melanchthon, therefore, passion could be overcome but only through a stronger passion. *Affectus vincitur affectus* ["it is possible for affection to overcome affection"[60]] – which is "God's consuming fire for human beings,"[61] the Spirit's gift of new and good affects.

With the concept of *affectus*, Melanchthon tried to understand both the state of mind or disposition of a person as well as his or her conduct or behavior. In short, *affectus* had a double aspect – impulses and behavior *and* a frame of mind in which one felt, perceived, and sensed as a whole, a sort of "experiential and practical knowl-

---

Profile of the Italian Renaissance in the Mirror of Its European Transformations (Leiden: E. J. Brill, 1975), 47; subsequently published in *A Usable Past: Essays in European Cultural History* (Berkeley: Univ. of California Press, 1990); here, as below, I cite the original edition.
     54 *LC*, 30: "When an affection has begun to rage and seethe, it cannot be kept from breaking forth."
     55 Ibid., 29.
     56 Bouwsma, "The Two Faces of Humanism," 47.
     57 Rogness, *Reformer Without Honor*, 143.
     58 *LC*, 31.
     59 Ibid., 92.
     60 Ibid., 27.
     61 Ibid., 32.

edge."[62] A primary theological issue in all of this, as we have noted, is the relationship of divine and human agency in this affective understanding of faith, that is, of the relation between grace and the heart. The whole person needed to be changed, to be *moved* through a conversion. The whole person, therefore, requires a new heart.[63]

It has been noted recently that Melanchthon's replacement of the "will" with "heart" indicated a commitment "with theological as well as rhetorical implications...."[64] If "willing" is an emotion, it is hardly a matter of free choice. We do not choose our feelings and our hearts cannot be moved by reason alone "but only by grace – and eloquence."[65] But what is involved in being "moved"? What is this "faith" which one is "to believe and take hold of"?

"TO BELIEVE AND TAKE HOLD OF FAITH": MOMENTS IN A MOVEMENT

Early Lutheran rhetoric and ritual sought to provide an expression of the Gospel that would be vividly immediate, dramatically forceful, and emotionally intense. The goal of such expression – audible in Word and visible in rite – was to change minds and empower lives capable of dealing with and interpreting the world in constructive, even redemptive ways.

For Melanchthon, the faith to which one is moved is composed of cognitive and affective elements, distinguishable yet joined. These elements are *notitia*, (knowledge), and *fiducia* (trust). His programmatic statement on faith as "knowledge" appears in the 1521 *Loci*:

> For from these things [the "fundamentals" of "sin," "law," and "grace"] Christ is known, since to know Christ means to know his benefits, and not as *they* teach, to reflect upon his natures and the modes of his incarnation.[66]

This emphasis on "knowing Christ" is sometimes regarded as the origin of Melanchthon's penchant for intellectualizing or rationalizing Christian faith. More recent scholarship, along with a re-reading of some of his important texts such as the rhetorical handbooks, enables us to see instead that the knowing in which Melanchthon was interested was no mere scratching of the intellect. His linking of

---

62 Hans-Georg Geyer, *Vom der Geburt des wahren Menschen: Probleme aus den Anfängen der Theologie Melanchthons* (Neukirchen-Vluyn: Neukirchener Verlag, 1965), 74ff.

63 Bornkamm, "Melanchthons Menschenbild," 88.

64 Shuger, *Sacred Rhetoric*, 134.

65 Ibid., 134–135.

66 *LC*, 21–22. According to Meerhoff, these Pauline concepts of law and gospel "possess a two-way impact, on reason and on the emotions" ("Significance of Philip Melanchthon's Rhetoric," 53).

notitia and *cognitio Christi* with other concepts such as *fiducia, promise,* and *benefit* indicate that a particular kind of knowing is at stake.[67] "Unless you know why Christ put on flesh and was nailed to the cross," Melanchthon wrote in the 1521 *Loci,* "what good will it do you to know merely the history about him?"[68] Moreover,

> Of what use is it to know that God is merciful if one's own heart is not touched by the realization "that he is merciful to *you?*" To have this experience is "to know God truly."[69]

Melanchthon's emphasis on a particular kind of knowing can also be seen in his *Elementorum Rhetorices Libri Duo:*

> It is faith therefore by which we give assent to the promise of God that Christ would be a sacrifice (propitiation) for us. This faith embraces two things: the acknowledgement of history (*noticiam historiae*) and trustingly assenting (*fiduciam assientientem*) to a promise to which that history refers.[70]

"To know Christ" is not simply to be equated with an understanding of doctrine about Christ. Rather, it is a knowledge that is connected to *promise,* i.e., Melanchthon's overarching rubric for understanding God's relationship to humanity, the saving God *pro nobis. Promise* becomes specific in *benefit* – which for Melanchthon included Christ's saving work, atonement, justification, sanctification, grace. Such matters are the "objective" basis of God's gracious will and God's attitude toward humanity. But there is also the "subjective" effect of the *promise* and *benefit,* knowledge of Christ as *assured* knowledge that mitigates the distrust of the heart. Such knowledge is soteriologically and experientially significant, involving the knower as person. It is existential and participatory knowledge. In this way of knowing Christ, the affective was central to Melanchthon's interest.

Simple acknowledgement of "the story about Christ," then, does not constitute essential, real, or true faith, for it is a detached, even inhuman knowing. Rather, for real faith even to exist, it must be "taken to heart." Melanchthon portrays this most significant side of faith with a term which has distinctly emotional connotations – *fiducia* (trust). He wrote in the Apology of the Augsburg Confession, for example,

---

[67] This is Quere's insight. See his *Melanchthon's Christum Cognoscere,* 115ff.

[68] *LC,* 22.

[69] Robert Stupperich, *Melanchthon,* trans. Robert H. Fischer (Philadelphia: Westminster Press, 1965), 46.

[70] LaFontaine, "Melanchthon's 'Elementorum Rhetorices Libri Duo,'" 106.

that faith "is not merely knowledge in the intellect but also trust in the will."[71] Or, "true faith is a knowing in the heart and a moving of the will."[72]

Yet this affective orientation and understanding allowed Melanchthon to clarify further the intellectual component of faith as well. In the 1521 *Loci*, he asked:

> What, therefore, is faith? It is constantly to assent to every word of God; this cannot take place unless the Spirit of God renews and illuminates our hearts. Further, the Word of God is both law and gospel. To the law threats are joined. Scripture calls that by which man believes those threats "fear," and calls that by which he trusts the gospel or divine promises "faith."[73]

Melanchthon's connection of his theology of law and gospel with rhetorical affect thus produced a concept of faith as "the affect-charged trust in the divine mercy."[74] Yet to regard faith as an emotion was perhaps "too radical for the sixteenth and seventeenth centuries" since it vanishes from Lutheran rhetorics after Melanchthon's death (1560).[75]

One should not conclude, however, that by emphasizing the affective component of faith, Melanchthon is interested in some kind of "warm-heartedness." Rather, his keen awareness of the gracious working of the Spirit made him particularly sensitive to the issue of the relationship between divine and human agency in both the affective force of rhetoric and faith. The cause of such faith does not lie within human power. In fact, one is spiritually powerless. Melanchthon thus notes in the 1521 *Loci*,

> internal affections are not in our power, for by experience and habit we find that the will cannot in itself control love, hate, or similar affections, but affection is overcome by affection.[76]

Only when God's Holy Spirit, sometimes called by Melanchthon "the gift of new affections,"[77] renews and enlightens the heart is one moved to understand and to experience faith as knowledge and as trust.

---

71 Melanchthon, Apology of the Augsburg Confession 4.304, in *BC*, 154.

72 Cited in Schnell, *Die homiletische Theorie Philipp Melanchthons*, 89.

73 *LC*, 92.

74 Rolf Schäfer, *Christologie und Sittlichkeit im Melanchthons frühen Loci*, Beiträge zur historischen Theologie 29 (Tübingen, 1961), 8; cited in Schnell, *Die homiletische Theorie Philipp Melanchthons*, 89. See also Schäfer, "Melanchthons Hermeneutik im Römerbrief Kommentar von 1532," *Zeitschrift für Theologie und Kirche* 60 (1963): 216–235; and Shuger, *Sacred Rhetoric*, 65–68.

75 Shuger, *Sacred Rhetoric*, 72.

76 *LC*, 27.

77 Wiedenhofer, *Formalstrukturen*, 1:126–27. Melanchthon develops the conception of the "new affections" as the most prominent gift of the Spirit in his 1519–1520 lectures on Matthew. For the text of these lectures, see "Annotationes in Evangelium Matthei," in *MW*, 4:133–208.

While he widened the cognitive element of faith in the later editions of the *Loci* to include assent to all the articles of faith, to Christ's forgiveness of sins, to the expression of the Word of God as law and gospel, yet the affective side of faith remained its most important moment.[78] For the believer can not really know in the abstract but needs to know experientially the effect of this history about Christ – his death and resurrection and his promise of the forgiveness of sins and new life. This *divina historia* becomes significant for the believer when he or she is seized, comprehended, and grasped in a personal relationship to its effect. He did not totally lose sight of or disregard faith's affective character and dynamic.[79] Following his discussion of dogmatic sermons in the homiletical tract entitled *De modo et arte concionandi*, for example, Melanchthon then emphasizes that *all* preaching is to move the emotions, for its goal is "renovation and spiritual life" attained by "inserting the better emotions into the soul," such as faith, patience, and love.[80]

Such a firm trust in the mercy and promises of Christ, is the result of an action, a *motus* or "*movement*" of the will which, for Melanchthon, was the same as "a movement of the heart."[81]

> Just as the movement of the eyes cannot be divided into parts, so also neither the movement of the mind or the will can be divided, and yet faith brings together the acknowledgement [of Christ] in both the intellect and the will and leads it to accept the proffered blessing, namely, assent to the promise.[82]

A further elaboration of this emphasis is provided in Melanchthon's *Liber de Anima*. Here he persistently refused to separate emotion from either the will [which for Melanchthon is the same thing as "the heart"] or the intellect as Scholastic theology had done with its notion of the will and the intellect as comprising the rational soul, which alone is able to know or desire God.[83] Melanchthon, however, wove tightly together human desire, the senses, and the ability to know, "so that man loves God, takes pleasure in him and obeys him."[84]

---

[78] Schnell, *Die homiletische Theorie Philipp Melanchthons*, 89–95.

[79] Ibid., 91–92.

[80] *SM*, vol. 5, pt. 2, 51.

[81] Haendler, *Wort und Glaube*, 501; see Dockhorn, "*Rhetorica movet*," 30; and Shuger, "The Christian Grand Style in Renaissance Rhetoric," *Viator* 16 (1985): 351–352.

[82] *Elementorum rhetorices*, 107. My emphases.

[83] Debora Shuger, "Morris Croll, Flacius Illyricus, and the Origin of Anti-Ciceronianism," *Rhetorica* 3, no. 3 (summer 1985): 282.

[84] "On the Soul," in *A Melanchthon Reader*, trans. Ralph Keen (New York & Bern: Peter Lang, 1988), 241.

His psychology and anthropology also emphasized the "affects." They "follow thought and have their rightful place in the heart."[85] Melanchthon notes that these affects are

> movements of the heart following something, pursuing or avoiding objects, which since they either aid or destroy nature often accompany movements either of sadness or destruction when the nature is wounded, or pleasant motions of pleasure or joy when the heart acquiesces in the object.... Affect is the movement of the heart or the will following cognition....[86]

The understanding of emotion which informed these discussions is not at all like our regnant contemporary notions which equate it solely with feeling or physiological perturbation. Rather, it is a knowing or a coming to know and, as such, results in a fundamental way of apprehending the world. Thus, when Melanchthon speaks of certain emotions which are to characterize the response of faith – tranquillity, joy, prayer, delight, love, freedom, hope – he is speaking of an active sensibility that orients a person to others, to the world, and to God. It is a sensibility at once psychological and social. This seems to be similar to recent insights into emotion as "a kind of language of the self"; "a statement about a person's relationship to the world;"or "as about the ways in which the social world is one in which *we* are involved."[87] In his "Summary of Ethics," for instance, Melanchthon spoke of emotion "as a certain kind of spur" for inciting to things that must be done – e.g., virtue, justice, equality, friendship, mutual faith, and benevolence.

Being "moved," then, is to believe and take of hold of faith as knowledge and trust. *Movere* is not just "deceptive and subrational obfuscation or dangerous enchantment."[88] It is an interweaving of the *notitiae historiae* of Christian faith with the person or "*subiectum, in quo haec geruntur*": "the subject in which these things occur."[89] This believing subject, however, is not the Cartesian "I" but the object of God's spiritual action.[90] And such action produces *notitia* and then *fiducia*, "a

85 Ibid., 243.

86 Ibid., 243, 280.

87 Catherine Lutz and Geoffrey M. White, "The Anthropology of Emotions," *Annual Review of Anthropology* 15 (1986): 417, 421; see Michael J. Hyde, "Emotion and Human Communication: A Rhetorical, Scientific, and Philosophical Picture," *Communication Quarterly* 32, no. 2 (spring 1984): 120–132; Hyde, "Existentialism as a Basis for the Theory and Practice of Rhetoric," in *Rhetoric and Philosophy*, ed. Richard A. Cherwitz (Hillsdale, N.J.: Lawrence Erlbaum Associates, Publishers, 1990), 213–251.

88 Shuger, *Sacred Rhetoric*, 138.

89 LaFontaine, "Melanchthon's 'Elementorum Rhetorices Libri Duo,'" 109.

90 Haendler, *Wort und Glaube*, 495.

movement of the heart."[91] This "heart," "is not Plato's unruly horse but the '*domicilium Dei.*'"[92]

It is clear from this consideration of the moments in the movement of the heart that knowledge and emotion constitute the response of faith. It is an affective knowledge which has grasped the word of salvation and the content of that word.[93] The postcommunion prayer in Luther's *German Mass* seems to summarize well what constitutes a "movement of the heart":

> We give thanks to thee, Almighty God, that thou hast refreshed us with this thy salutary gift; and we beseech thy mercy to strengthen us through the same in faith toward thee, and in fervent love among us all; for the sake of Jesus Christ our Lord. Amen.[94]

The focus is not upon abstract doctrine but upon God's *beneficia* – God's deeds and actions. As such, the appeal was to the emotions which are not merely the disorderly, unstable impulses of an unreliable body, but are the center of the human personality – its "core" (*cor, coeur*).[95] The "movement of the heart" that was sought, therefore, was both a matter of feeling as well as knowing. *Notitia* and *fiducia* are intellectual passion and passionate understanding engendered by the Spirit of God who works faith and trust.

Rhetoric and ritual in Melanchthon's perspective strategically address the problem of the relationship between God and humankind, especially the problem of whether God was truthful in his judgment of human nature and destiny and whether life was meaningful, despite all evidence to the contrary. Yet this rhetorical speech and ritual action – Word and rite – do not rectify or solve this problem, so that it is a problem no longer. Things most definitely do not work that way. Instead, rhetoric and ritual seek to create a transformation of a believer's orientation to this problematic human situation. This change in orientation is "moving the heart" from a state of uncertainty and doubt to a state of belief and trust in God's words and promises.

Understandings of being "moved" or "persuaded" were thus situated in a wider framework of understandings of self, emotion, and knowledge. The "heart," for example, was an approximation for what we today call the self. "Emotion" was not something subrational or subethical and the antithesis of reason, but was viewed

---

91 Ibid., 502.

92 Debora Shuger, "Morris Croll, Flacius Illyricus, and the Origin of Anti-Ciceronianism," 282.

93 Haendler, *Wort und Glaube*, 509.

94 Luther, "The German Mass," in *LW*, 53:84.

95 Bouwsma, "Review Article," 69.

more favorably as the center of the human personality. This more unified picture of being human meant that the process of communication sought to be a total experience and not confined to the intellect alone.[96]

Such a wider framework thus involved a complex of theological, epistemological, and psychological assumptions.[97] The making of a word, a promise, a message – what Melanchthon and other Reformers called "Gospel" – accessible to ear and eye, to thought and feeling, occurred in the context of *movere*. This accessibility meant that Word and rite were to participate in all the characteristics of human language and expression – dialogical, interactive, attentiveness, vividness, dramatic force, and emotional intensity. Such accessibility also bore the stamp of subjectivity. If Word and rite disclose the "Gospel" as spoken and visible, they seek to evoke a perception of God as gracious and a corresponding trust or confidence that is to characterize a particular kind of person. Here is a notion of subjectivity or selfhood as an activity, as a loving, trusting response. As Debora Shuger has noted, "The Christian self emerges in its loving response to God's drawing, a response created by God's presence within the heart."[98]

WORD AND RITE: CREATING AN IDENTITY

The great sixteenth-century debate about Christian ritual and Melanchthon's concern for its distinctive way of working belong to what may be described as a larger, early modern discourse over the nature of the person.[99] Playing a key role in a developing understanding of how the self was constituted was religious ritual, especially Holy Communion with its capacity to define the social and moral community that, in turn, provided the reference for self-understanding.

In a similar fashion, the most powerful symbol of late-medieval culture – namely, the eucharist – had been known and experienced in the making of personal and collective identities at all social levels.[100] Although for some social historians, the eucharist was the "social miracle,"[101] or the passive reflection of the social body, more

---

96 Bouwsma, "The Spirituality of Renaissance Humanism," 238; see Barilli, *Rhetoric*, 30.
97 Shuger, *Sacred Rhetoric*, 193ff.
98 Ibid., 235.
99 David Warren Sabean, *Power in the Blood: Popular Culture and Village Discourse in Early Modern Germany* (Cambridge: Cambridge Univ. Press, 1984), 1–36, 199–213.
100 Miri Rubin, "The Eucharist and the Construction of Medieval Identities," in *Culture and History 1350–1600: Essays on English Communities, Identities and Writing*, ed. David Aers (Detroit: Wayne State Univ. Press, 1992), 43–63.
101 Bossy, *Christianity in the West*, 57–75.

recent studies have demonstrated that participants in this rite used it in different ways and for different reasons.

Miri Rubin, for example, has explored how this central ritual served as a site for the articulation of the identity of the priest, especially the essence and power of his office, and of a community that was to be whole and orthodox.[102] As such, the eucharist belonged to a larger, over-arching pastoral project: "to provide a system of ideas and practices for the life of a *societas christiana*."[103] This intent, Rubin has noted, was "to provide a viable, resilient, predictable, and all-encompassing cultural system for the application in all areas of life, and for the use of men and women everywhere."[104] In terms of practice and ritual effect, what became central was the consecration. This dramatic moment, surrounded by incense and the ringing of bells, marked the transformation of bread into God. This was where salvation indeed resided.

Actual participation in communion, however, was a rare and awesome practice. Nonetheless, a certain kind of participation was invited and claims were increasingly made that witnessing the elevation of the white, thin, round disc – "now bread, now God" – could be a source of power and experience for those present. Offered and promised were "release and ecstasy, a space for the expression of fears, hopes, and anxieties."[105]

Yet people did not always regard and use the eucharist as the church intended. Historical evidence indicates that this very body of Christ was used for mystical flights, healing and magic, and to reinforce a sacramental worldview – "a hegemonic symbolic system," as it has been termed.[106] The eucharist, thus, had no single meaning, either as source of salvation and health or as primary identity of Christian orthodoxy. Rather, it offered multiple meanings and constructed what was not and ought not to be as well such as Jews and heretics. As the heart of the late-medieval church's symbolic system, the eucharist "was being constituted and reconstituted, defining and being defined by experience and expediency, need and repressed desire."[107]

The eucharist's communication of such disparate and changing collective and personal messages were interpreted in conflicting and competing ways. The aspects of

---

102 Rubin, "The Eucharist and the Construction of Medieval Identities," 44.
103 Ibid., 48.
104 Ibid.
105 Ibid.
106 Ibid.
107 Ibid., 58.

power and persuasion that marked its design and dynamic were, by the early six-teenth century, exhausted or fragmented. While "creative tension in signification is the life-blood of any culture," the time does come "for change of the system of sym-bols and realignment of the language which must service difference and experi-ence."[108]

The backdrop sketched here – one concerned with how Christian ritual structures notions of self and identity – stands in sharp contrast to Melanchthon's assertion that such activity is "to move the heart to believe and take hold of faith." This contrast, however, is a good example of that change in a symbolic system and realignment of language just mentioned.

It has been observed that Melanchthon's changes and realignment of language re-garding Christian ritual, especially the Lord's Supper, were different from that of Luther or the other protagonists in the controversies over its nature and efficacy.[109] A major reason for this difference might be that Melanchthon was not a priest. Hence, his life and piety would not be as immersed in and shaped by this rite or by its ac-companying notions of exclusive power and status to make it happen. Moreover, it may be worth noting that Melanchthon abandoned the doctrine of transsubstantia-tion much earlier than Luther and his discussion of the eucharist in the 1521 *Loci Communes* was entitled, "Participation in the Lord's Table."[110] At any rate, both of these matters are suggestive as additional examples of what contributed to Melanchthon's "realignment of language" in order to service a particular kind of ex-perience and to articulate a certain kind of identity.

Moreover, his focus on a heart being addressed with the goal of being "moved" indicates that one exists in a certain kind of rhetorical situation or what are called to-day "webs of interlocution."[111] For Melanchthon, these "webs of interlocution" and the defining community in which they occur are shaped by the form and content of God's promises. "Promise" was a broad and complex term, often synonymous with "Word," "Gospel," "doctrine," "revelation."[112] The goal of its audible proclamation and visible depiction was participation in the world that this promise depicts where "God alone is the gracious initiator, actor, and fulfiller of his own promises."[113]

108 Ibid., 59.
109 Rogness, *Reformer Without Honor*, 51.
110 *LC*, 145ff.
111 Taylor, *Sources of the Self*, 36.
112 See Wiedenhofer, *Formalstrukturen*, 1:195, and the sources that he cites. See also Ronald F. Thiemann, *Revelation and Theology: The Gospel as Narrated Promise* (Notre Dame, Ind.: Univ. of Notre Dame Press, 1985), 97ff.
113 Thiemann, 110.

The sort of person that promise makes is one who believes and takes hold of faith – a person recently described as "the whole responsible self."[114] This equation of a heart moved with the whole responsible self, however, raises some interesting questions. What exactly is that? How does this jibe with more negative ideas about the heart as the soft, weak part of a person, something "worn on the sleeve" only with shame, etc., and with the view that "responsibility" comes out of rational, unpassionate consideration of one's obligations, etc.? Yet, in early Lutheran Reformation discourse, the self was not regarded in bi-partite or bi-polar terms. Rather, it was viewed as a whole, to be related to God and to the neighbor. Such a "responsible self" was, in short, responsive and relational.[115]

This view of the person as fundamentally "responsive" is basic not only to the development of a relationally based capacity to belong and to connect but also to participate in religious ritual – "a responsorial of familiar action and response."[116] In more theological language, since the person is not simply some receptacle of information, facts, teachings, and ideas, she or he can be *moved* in some fashion from all objectivity and detachment to radical levels of involvement, responsibility, and selfhood.[117]

Such a *movement*, it might be said, is a consequence of a certain way of doing theology and of interpreting biblical texts. The goal of both for Melanchthon was crucial, where he sought to bind together or to fuse content and effect. Wiedenhofer has observed that Melanchthon's overall concept of "revelation" with its two-fold structure of *Word* and *testimony* or *witness* exhibits an interest in what such revelation ultimately does or the goal it seeks. He has visualized this in the following manner[118]:

114 Robert J. Goeser, "The Doctrine of Word and Scripture in Luther and Lutheranism," *The Report of the Lutheran-Episcopal Dialogue Second Series 1976–1980* (Cincinnati: Forward Movement, 1981), 119.

115 See H. Richard Niebuhr, *The Responsible Self* (New York: Harper & Row), 1963.

116 Mary Frohlich, "The Responsorial Self," *Liturgy* 7, no. 2 (winter 1987): 41.

117 Goeser, "The Doctrine of Word and Scripture," 119.

118 Wiedenhofer, *Formalstruckturen*, 1:196.

Melanchthon's Understanding of the Nature and Purpose of Revelation

Wrath and Mercy

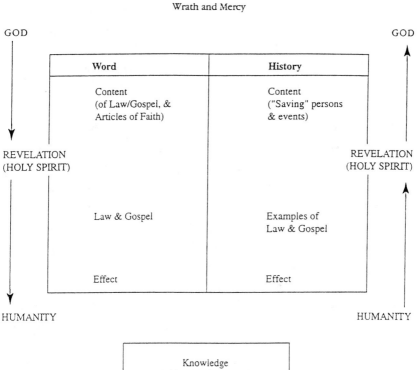

GOD

Word	History
Content (of Law/Gospel, & Articles of Faith)	Content ("Saving" persons & events)

REVELATION (HOLY SPIRIT)

Law & Gospel	Examples of Law & Gospel
Effect	Effect

HUMANITY

GOD

REVELATION (HOLY SPIRIT)

HUMANITY

Knowledge
(of Law & Gospel and
Articles of Faith)

Affect
Fear & Trust
(Experience of Fear & Consolation)

The achievement of such a *movement* is also one of the major goals and/or effects of rhetorical discourse. These include insight and knowledge as well as particular feeling or affect. One does not merely "get the point," but also becomes involved in the issue.[119] Early Lutheran theology's term for this feeling, insight, knowledge, and involvement, as we have seen, was "faith."

More theologically, *"cor ex motu Spiritus sancti intelligit"*: "the heart understands via the motion of the Holy Spirit."[120] "The heart" – i.e., the whole responsible self, is rooted in trusting and knowing God as sheer goodness.[121] One becomes human as one lives out of this trust and, in so doing, is moved into the possibilities of relationship and mutuality with God, neighbor, and creation. "This is the natural human condition," according to historical theologian Robert J. Goeser.[122]

A movement between content and effect/affect in both Melanchthon's theological program and in his scriptural interpretation thus seems to be matched in his view of the distinctive working of ritual practice as well.[123] No longer was its task to somehow "perform the dramatic coup of eliciting the supernatural out of the mundane."[124] One might say, rather, that it was to express and affirm "the mundane" – to provide a realistic assessment of the human condition in which "the self can now live again in relationship, in mutuality," where "it can now encounter God, creation, neighbor, and history instead of being insulated against them."[125] Most significantly, this meant that one could get on with day-to-day living, "confident about the ultimate matters."[126]

What is intriguing, even striking about this way of viewing Word *and* rite, theological discourse *and* ritual practice, are how these insights about the creating of a certain kind of identity, a particular kind of person, are echoed in some of the concerns of contemporary ritual theory. With the eschewing of definitional debates over what this activity *really* is and *does*, there has been more of a focus on those who par-

---

119 Jan Lindhardt, *Martin Luther: Knowledge and Mediation in the Renaissance* (Lewiston, N.Y.: The Edwin Mellen Press, 1986), 59, 63.

120 Ibid., 107.

121 Our discussion at this point is based on Goeser, "Whither Lutheranism?" 42–45.

122 Ibid., 44.

123 Wengert, in his *Philip Melanchthon's Annotationes in Johannem*, notes this "match" in Melanchthon's dialectical method with his scriptural interpretation and theological program. One would think, therefore, that this "match" would continue in Melanchthon's way of viewing the distinctive working of Christian ritual.

124 Bossy, *Christianity in the West*, 67.

125 Goeser, "Whither Lutheranism?", 44.

126 Stephen Ozment, "Luther and the Late Middle Ages: The Formation of Reformation Thought," in *Transition and Revolution: Problems and Issues of European Renaissance and Reformation History*, ed. Robert M. Kingdon (Minneapolis: Burgess Publishing Co., 1974), 128.

ticipate – and who in doing so have their worlds made mangageable and meaningful in such a way that they can live in it, deal with it, reinterpret it in a modestly constructive, even redemptive fashion. The task that awaits us in our final chapter, then, is to make more explicit these connections between Melanchthon's ideas and current ritual theory.

5. "A HEART MOVED": RETHINKING WHAT RELIGIOUS RITUAL DOES

INTRODUCTION: ECHOES OF MELANCHTHON'S CONCERNS IN CONTEMPORARY RITUAL THEORY

The great sixteenth-century debate about the meanings, forms, and functions of religious ritual seems uncannily modern. Melanchthon's concerns with the goal or use of a rite, his interest in its capacity to generate a certain kind of knowing and "to move" the person who is a concatenation of emotion, will, and intellect – i.e., "the heart" – are echoed in the work of some contemporary ritual theorists. They ask similar questions about how and why this activity is what it is and does what it does.[1] They also ask,

- How is this activity called ritual a way of knowing?[2]
- How does it offer reassurance and a feeling of certainty in the face of "existential uncertainties"?[3]
- How and why is it an expression of what most moves a people?[4]
- How does it articulate what it means to be a particular kind of person?[5]

These questions have emerged as a consequence of a significant shift in the study of ritual that has been underway over the past three decades. As a category of both scholarly analysis and human experience, ritual was once regarded with great suspicion. Depending on one's discipline, it could be thought of as wedded to the status quo, inherently if not rigidly conservative, or as a type of pathological behavior.

---

1 E.g., Grimes, *Ritual Criticism*; Bell, *Ritual Theory, Ritual Practice*; Smith, *To Take Place: Toward Theory in Ritual*; Tom Driver, *The Magic of Ritual* (San Francisco: Harper San Francisco, 1991)

2 Theodore W. Jennings, "On Ritual Knowledge," *Journal of Religion* 62 (1982): 113.

3 Peter G. Stromberg, *Language and self-transformation: A study of the Christian conversion narrative* (Cambridge: Cambridge Univ. Press, 1993), 120.

4 See above, p. 6 n. 25.

5 Howard Eilberg-Schwartz (paper presented to the Ritual Studies Group, American Academy of Religion Annual Meeting, San Francisco, 22 November 1992).

Moreover, there were bitter arguments over how to be more precise about ritual's nature and meaning, although such arguments have yet to produce a generally accepted
definition. Those scholars who have offered definitions in recent years have high-
lighted its special, expressive features, its formality and purposiveness, and its spatial
and/or temporal marking off from the routine of everyday life.[6] Yet these definitions,
according to one critic, "really tell us almost nothing, apart from some vague sort of
instruction, perhaps akin to: PAY ATTENTION – SOMETHING SPECIAL GOING ON
HERE AND NOW."[7]

This definitional quest (and warfare) has been giving way slowly, however, to more
open and dynamic approaches. One which has emerged as especially significant and
which is reminiscent of Melanchthon's understanding of the relationship between
form (in his instance *Word* and *rite*) and participants' achievement of a certain state
of thought and feeling are those which are more "practical" or "practice-oriented."
That is, there is a particular focus on human action and interaction with the goal of
explaining more forcefully and coherently what people are doing, why they are doing
it, and what their doing *does*. Called *practice theory*, this approach brings together a
variety of concerns and issues – the historical particularity of people and events, the
workings of cultures and institutions, and "the productive and creative potential of
human activity and human interactions."[8] Such a synthesis, writes Sherry B. Ortner,
"begin[s] to approach an adequate understanding of human phenomena."[9]

The use of *practice theory* for the study of ritual involves the realization that
"people *do* it,"[10] and who, in such doing, "seek to make their worlds manageable and
meaningful...."[11] Or, there is an interest in how *practice* embodies a particular
ordering of redeeming or saving power that provides participants with a way to deal
with, to construe their world in ways that envision and empower.[12]

In eschewing definitional warfare over whether ritual is some kind of indepen-
dently existing object that possesses a basic mechanism which operates more or less

6 Don Handelman, *Models and Mirrors: Towards an Anthropology of Public Events* (Cambridge:
Cambridge Univ. Press, 1990), 10–11. Handelman notes that these "definitions" have come from
three separate disciplines—sociology, social history, and anthropology.
7 Ibid., 11.
8 Sherry B. Ortner, "Cultural Politics: Religious Activism and Ideological Transformation Among
20th Century Sherpas," *Dialectical Anthropology* 14 (1989): 199.
9 Ibid.
10 Ortner, "Theory in Anthropology since the Sixties," 154.
11 Jean Comaroff and John Comaroff, introduction to *Modernity and Its Malcontents: Ritual and
Power in Postcolonial Africa*, ed. Jean Comaroff and John Comaroff (Chicago: Univ. of Chicago Press,
1993), xxix.
12 E.g., Bell, *Ritual Theory, Ritual Practice*, 83ff.

the same everywhere, it is more the case, as we noted earlier, that specific cultures identify and engage in certain kinds of activities that may be unique or congruent with other activities. In place of "ritual," there is "ritualization" – a particular "how" or "quality" of doing and saying that has a form of a distinctive sort and is undertaken for different reasons and effects.[13] This recognition of specificity involves a corresponding awareness that ritual or "ritualization" must be understood in its appropriate context. That is, this activity needs to be "historicized," taken down from the pedestal where certain historians, comparativists, and liturgical scholars have placed it, and "put to work" as a signifying or critical practice that can vitally function in the making or remaking of both personhood and collective identity.[14]

With these introductory considerations in mind, we can proceed to unfold more fully the connections between Melanchthon's perspective on the distinctive workings of religious ritual and those of contemporary ritual theory. Using *practice* as a point of departure, we hope to hear more clearly the same appreciation of knowledge, emotion, and self that animated Melanchthon's recasting of the role of ritual and which can, in turn, redirect our own thinking about what this activity is and does. To guide the discussion which follows, the chart below is offered.

Echoes of Melanchthon's Rhetorical Outlook in Contemporary Ritual Theory

1. RITUS, USUS	1. CULTURAL PRACTICE
2. SOTERIOLOGICAL EFFECT	2. REDEMPTIVE HEGEMONY
• Christ's presence	• ordering of redemptive power
• saving knowledge	• practical construal of the world that envisions and empowers
• reassurance & a feeling of certainty	• reassurance & a feeling of certainty
3. BEING "MOVED"	3. WHAT "MOVES" SOCIETY THE MOST
4. A CERTAIN KIND OF PERSON	4. GOAL OF A NEW PERSON

---

13 E.g., Grimes, *Ritual Criticism*; also Bell, *Ritual Theory, Ritual Practice*.

14 See Kelly and Kaplan, "History, Structure, and Ritual," 119, and Comaroff and Comaroff, introduction to *Modernity and Its Malcontents: Ritual and Power in Postcolonial Africa*, vii–xxxvii.

RITUS, USUS, AND RITUAL AS A CULTURAL PRACTICE

Earlier in chapter 1, we saw that the special Renaissance affinity for the classical art of rhetoric and its appropriation for theological purposes involved a certain kind of attentiveness to human experience. This *theologica rhetorica* did not begin with a list of doctrines or truths to be unfolded, but was oriented to the nexus of relationships among God, humanity, nature, history, and society. Christian theology needed to be conceptualized more experientially and anthropologically because it dealt with the feelings, attitudes, and behaviors of living individuals. We saw Melanchthon's own recognition of the need to take theory/theology out of academic obscurity in order to make it practically useful.

The title of cultural historian Nancy Struever's recent book, *Theory as Practice*, is an apt description of how Renaissance Humanists understood the inquiry in which they were engaged.[15] This involved a great deal more than reading and interpreting texts. It was a matter of presenting such inquiry as available practice. For the understanding of what was being read, interpreted, and written about had to do with the stuff of reality that demanded human engagement and toward which no human being could remain indifferent.

For example, the relocation of theological inquiry from the realm of abstract speculation to concern with existential or soteriological questions meant that the knowledge which was sought was to be a total experience. Earlier in our study, we noted that "to know" in this fashion involved the feelings, the heart, and the will – the whole human being – in some active response. The result for Melanchthon and other Northern European humanists such as Erasmus and Pirckheimer was to make of theology "an affective and practical science." "It does not remain at the level of the history of deeds done, but directs its view to the *scope* and *use* of history and thus to the real salvific presence of Christ."[16] This emphasis was, in short, *functional* because of its interest in the effects of an action upon an actor.

One way of conceptualizing and approaching this experiential matrix of historically, culturally, and socially constituted persons who employ a variety of interpretive strategies to make sense of the world, of others, and of themselves is to view it as an activity or "cultural practice." Such a concept and approach promises to offer a way

---

15 Nancy Struever, *Theory as Practice: Ethical Inquiry in the Renaissance* (Chicago: Univ. of Chicago Press, 1992).

16 Wiedenhofer, *Formalstrukturen*, 1:156.

to transcend the irksome dichotomies with which we love to "wrongly divide" human experience: subjective-objective, thought-action, emotion-cognition, tradition-change, individual-group, nature-culture, real-ideal.[17] This focus on "practice" in social and cultural studies brings with it a bundle of interrelated terms such as "practice, praxis, action, interaction, activity, experience, performance."[18] Accompanying such a focus is another bundle of terms which center on the doers of all this doing: "agent, actor, person, self, individual, subject."[19]

A "cultural practice" approach to contemporary ritual questions stems from an uneasiness and dissatisfaction with breaking up thought about worship into artificial chunks like symbol, metaphor, image, text, and structure, or pitting emotion against cognition, thought against action. For when one listens to what people say about what they actually *do* in religious ritual, it is quite clear that they have not been *not* ferreting out deep cultural meanings ensconced in highly complex verbal strategies or metaphorical arrangements. Nor have they been discovering that the greatest import resides in "the densest forests of symbols."[20] Rather, what seems to be going on with them is more a matter of "glimpsing," or perhaps better, "knowing" something of themselves, of God, of others, and of the world in which they live.[21]

An approach to religious ritual as a social and cultural practice and those whose practice it is grows from an understanding that cultures and cultural practices ("worship" and "ritual" or "worshiping" and "ritualizing") need to be studied not as reified wholes but as strategic ways of acting. Moreover, such ways of acting provide a means for people to know and understand their lives and to live in a world which makes some sense to them.[22] This means that those who study these ways of acting need to come to terms with the dynamic nature of social and cultural reality – with history, spontaneity, and human emotions.

The artificial chunk approach noted just a moment ago is a fragmented, unreal, detached sort of analysis which bears little resemblance to what people and their do-

---

17 Bell, *Ritual Theory, Ritual Practice*, 74–81.
18 Ortner, "Theory in Anthropology since the Sixties," 144.
19 Ibid.
20 The expression is Renato Rosaldo's; *Culture and Truth: Explorations in Social Analysis* (Boston: Beacon Press, 1989), 2.
21 See Barbara Myerhoff, "The transformation of consciousness," in *By means of performance: Intercultural studies of theatre and ritual*, ed. Richard Schechner and Willa Appel (Cambridge: Cambridge Univ. Press, 1990), 246.
22 See the following examples: Renato Rosaldo, *Culture and Truth: The Remaking of Social Analysis*; George E. Marcus and Michael M. J. Fischer, *Anthropology as Cultural Critique: An Experimental Moment in the Human Sciences* (Chicago: Univ. of Chicago Press, 1986); Grimes, *Ritual Criticism*; Bell, *Ritual Theory, Ritual Practice*; and Sabean, *Power in the Blood*.

ings might be all about. An approach in terms of "cultural practice," however, challenges us to take another look at traditional theological or doctrinal claims about the power or efficacy of religious ritual. How is this activity an eventful and powerful practice that can shape participants' sense of identity as involved, responsible selves *coram deo* and situated in a social reality clothed in the created and the historical, i.e., *coram hominibus?*[23]

In the sixteenth century, these questions were addressed from a rhetorical perspective. In a sense, rhetoric constituted the practice theory of the time. It, too, sought to transcend the dichotomies with which we "wrongly divide" human experience. We saw how the anthropological and psychological assumptions that undergirded this *theologia rhetorica* posited an understanding of the human personality as a mysterious unity of intellect, emotion, and will and whose essence was "the heart." Such an understanding, as we also saw, had profound implications for what it meant to know something. Because the mind was subject to the influence of the will and the passions, it could not be regarded as a cold, objective receiver and processor of knowledge. Rather, knowledge became a function of the whole person and was saturated with affect. A singular advantage of this view of knowledge and knower was to narrow the gap between theory and practice, belief and action.

SOTERIOLOGICAL EFFECTS AND REDEMPTIVE HEGEMONY

Melanchthon's own preferred way of speaking of Christian ritual activity as *ritus* or *usus* can be seen as an extension of his larger interests in the soteriological effects of scriptural interpretation, doctrinal formulation, and proclamation. With respect to ritual activity, his orientation was to how a participant uses this rite as a whole – how the so-called "objective" expression of Christ's sacramental presence produces a "subjective" effect of recognizing and "embracing [Christ's] benefit with a thankful mind."[24] Or, as emphasized repeatedly throughout this study, his focus was on a heart that has been "moved to believe and take hold of faith."

Ritual practice in almost all Christian traditions has a soteriological dimension, "whether containing, communicating, or simply pointing to God's grace and for-

---

23 Goeser, "The Doctrine of Word and Scripture," 119ff.

24 Melanchthon, "Declamatiuncula in Divi Pauli doctrinam" (1520), in *MW* 1:31, lines 11–13: "Siquidem Christum novisse non modo est res eius gestas tenere, sed grato animo beneficium complecti, quod per ipsum coelestis pater in universum terrarum orbem effudit, quo solo inter impias gentes et vere Christianos animos internoscitur." Cited in Quere, *Melanchthon's Christum Cognoscere*, 109.

giveness."[25] Soteriology is a rather idiosyncratic term, referring to such matters as life after death, the acquiring of a new outlook on life in the present, a possibility of self-transcendence, passage into a new mode of being.[26] Yet there seem to be some common threads or emphases including those of "power" and "change." The underlying assumption in soteriology is that there are two states of human existence: one a state of deprivation (sin, corruption) and the other "a state of release from that deprivation (salvation, liberation), and an event that transforms the first state to the second."[27]

In a Christian context, for example, the sort of "change" that is soteriological or "saving" in some sense has to do either with "a change in the very nature of reality" or with a change in the *perception* of reality that occurs because of what occurred in the life, death, and resurrection of Jesus of Nazareth.[28] The former understanding can be summarized as follows:

> It is clear that for the earliest believers in Jesus, change and history were the vehicles of salvation. Assuming the Jewish view of history, some of Jesus' disciples understood him to the Messiah who would usher in the Kingdom of God. This was to be a radical change in nature itself such that justice, harmony, and peace would be established in the place of the injustice, suffering, and death which characterized existence since Adam's fall before.[29]

Examples of soteriology or "salvation" understood as a change in the perception of reality would be those of Paul or John. It is or can be both a present and future phenomenon. The present state can be qualitatively different from the rest of human existence and is described by Paul in relational terms such as justification and reconciliation. Yet such a change is not simply a different understanding of reality *per se*, but is a belief that there will be a future change in reality, to which those who believe are already somehow conformed.[30]

A "sneak preview" of how this reshaping of experience is said to happen is sometimes regarded as a characteristic dynamic of how ritual "works" or is efficacious. "In genuine worship," claims Fred Clothey,

---

25 Quere, *Melanchthon's Christum Cognoscere*, 13.

26 See Peter Stromberg, *Symbols of Community: The Cultural System of a Swedish Church* (Tucson: Univ. of Arizona Press, 1986), 89–103.

27 Michael Root, "The Narrative Structure of Soteriology," *Modern Theology* 2, no. 2 (January 1986): 145–146.

28 Charles D. Hackett, "Psychoanalysis and Theology: Two Dialectics," *Journal of Religion and Health*, 25, no. 1 (spring 1986): 29–31.

29 Ibid., 30.

30 Ibid., 31; See Robin Scroggs, "The Heuristic Value of a Psychoanalytic Model in the Interpretation of Pauline Theology," *Zygon* 13, no. 2 (June 1978): 136–155.

not only does one experience new community – a participation in a larger, often heterogeneous body,with other persons – a community which often transcends the social boundaries brought into the ritual; one is also ushered into the presence of a transcending "other," experiences a timelessness that is beyond history and becomes aware of a general cosmic reality that gives meaning, context, and perspective to all the mundane realities of which one has been a part.[31]

While Clothey's claim exhibits the tendency to see ritual as possessing one basic mechanism operating more or less the same everywhere, (e.g., this is "genuine worship," as he says), nonetheless he has surfaced the key issue of the soteriological aspect or goal of this activity. For Melanchthon, this aspect was discussed in terms of presence and benefit. These days, ritual theorists speak of "redemptive processes" or "redemptive hegemonies." Drawn from recent understandings of power, social process, and how personhood is shaped, such a notion synthesizes what Kenelm Burridge has termed "redemptive process" and Antonio Gramsci's concept of "hegemony."[32]

A "redemptive process" has to do with what is taken to be the truth about power that can "save" and or "redeem." Such power is empowering, so to speak. It enables perception of "the truth of things" and provides certainty that what is perceived is indeed "true."[33] When this notion of "redemptive process" is combined with Gramsci's concept of "hegemony," his explanation of how various social practices, including religion, can produce meaning and value, we gain an entree into a lived system of meanings that serve to construct how one senses "reality" and understands his or her identity.[34] Such a vision of how power is ordered in the world can be regarded as empowerment to significant action, which – Melanchthon's case as we saw in the last chapter – included empowerment to justice, equality, friendship, mutual benevolence.

What is especially striking is that a human being, that concatenation of emotion, will, and intellect as Melanchthon was fond of reminding us, could not inspire such movement or empowerment on his or her own. Rather, Word *and* rite, used efficaciously by the Spirit, move the heart: they set a person within the purview of God's work and action – that power which "saves" and "redeems" – so that such work and action can be experienced as one's own.

---

[31] Fred Clothey, *Rhythm and Intent: Ritual Studies from South India* (Bombay: Blackie and Son, 1983), 4–5.

[32] Bell, *Ritual Theory, Ritual Practice*, 83.

[33] Kenelm Burridge, *New Heaven New Earth: A Study of Millenarian Activities* (New York: Schocken Books, 1969), 6–7.

[34] Bell, *Ritual Theory, Ritual Practice*, 83.

RITUAL AS A WAY OF KNOWING

This approach to experience was understood as a certain kind of knowing. Recall that for Melanchthon, as a rhetorical theologian, knowledge was no mere scratching of the intellect but rather "a total experience involving the feelings, penetrating the heart, shaping the will, and stimulating the whole person to some active response."[35] In this conception, knowledge "had to be subjectively appropriated in order to constitute, as we might say, 'really' knowing."[36] Knowledge of God's saving activity *pro homine*, for example, is to be knowledge of God's saving activity *pro me*.[37]

Melanchthon's *cognitio Christi*, therefore, was not a detached, inhuman kind of knowing. It was a knowing of

> his benefits [i.e., atonement, justification, sanctification, and grace], by which he has opened the way of salvation to the whole of earth; to perceive correctly why he came to earth, what may be obtained from him, of which things the flesh he assumed is a pledge, or the cross on which he met death doubtlessly for our sake.[38]

Contemporary epistemologists call this kind of knowledge "personal" or "participatory." It is a "coming to know" something as our own. Avery Dulles has observed,

> We know from our own body not by looking at it...but rather by dwelling in it, by using it, by relying on it. We know it...not by attending *to* it but by attending *from* it. Because we know the body in this subjective manner, it is cognitively identified with the knowing self. Analagously, we know by indwelling when we apprehend anything at all as specifically ours – for example, our home, our country, our family, our church, our culture, our traditions. None of these realities can be properly understood from without, through sheer spectator knowledge, but only from within, insofar as we appropriate and rely upon them – that is to say, by participatory knowledge.[39]

Such "participatory" knowledge involves the "knower" as a person and has the potential of transforming, of making an impact upon his or her commitments and behavior. In a Christian perspective, such knowing initiates a person into a particular relationship with God and, as such, aspires to shift his or her horizons, perspectives, and point of view. Melanchthon's own approach to knowledge exhibited a similar

---

35 Bouwsma, "The Spirituality of Renaissance Humanism," 238.
36 Ibid.
37 Haendler, *Wort und Glaube*, 403.
38 *LC*, 22.
39 Avery Dulles, "The Symbolic Structure of Revelation," *Theological Studies* 41, no. 1 (March 1980): 60–61.

emphasis on its participatory character as well. This is clear in his *cognitio Christum* dictum, as we have noted above. Moreover, he asserted that it is useless to know merely the history *about* Christ. Rather, one needs to know "why Christ put on flesh and was nailed to the cross."[40] His prefatory comments to Luther's 1519 *Operationes in Psalmos* summarize well his conception of what it means to know something:

> For what does it profit to know that the world was created by God, as Genesis indicates, unless you adore the mercy and wisdom of the creator? Furthermore, what will it profit you to have known that God is merciful and wise, unless you take it into your own soul that to *you* He is merciful, to *you* He is just, to *you* He is wise? And that is to truly know God. Nor has philosophy followed this utmost method of knowing God. It is peculiar to Christians.[41]

Contemporary ritual scholarship, also, is very interested in better understanding this activity's noetic or epistemic purpose, value, and function. The focus is not so much on the myth or founding narrative that ritual then purportedly illustrates but on the gaining of a kind of knowing by which participants can "construe and construct their world."[42] Such knowing can be further specified as "a mode of inquiry and discovery," as a particular focusing as well as forming of "a way of being and acting in the world," and a knowing of the said, seen, and done of ritual activity itself.[43]

What one seeks to discover in ritual activity is who one is and "how it is" with the world. It is "a search for an understanding of the world" as "a meaningful and intelligible order" – in short, an understanding of human culture as a specific way of life. This is "a standing under" in the literal sense where the self is oriented and related to some fundamental view of reality where one has a basis for human living.[44]

Another way to speak of "ritual as coming to know" is to see what is known as involving schemes of perception and interpretation. They are embodied schemes – schemes of a meaningful conception of the world within which one has his or her place as a person and as a member/participant in a community. But to know that such schemes are indeed the case, they need to be embodied. Participants "mind" themselves or attend through themselves in ritual. When engaged in the Lord's Supper, for example, they do not first think through what it is about and then per-

---

40 *LC*, 22.

41 *WA*, 5:25.

42 Jennings, "On Ritual Knowledge," 112.

43 Ibid., 112–113.

44 Edward C. Hobbs, "Recognition of Conceptuality as a Hermeneutical Tool," in *Texte und Untersuchungen zur Geschichte der altchristlichen Literatur*, Band 88, ed. F. L. Cross (Berlin: Akademie-Verlag, 1964), 472.

form it. Rather, they bodily do or act or are bodily done to or acted upon – hence, Melanchthon's statement about the Word "striking" and "entering" the eyes and ears. Or, recall that he discussed the Lord's Supper in the 1521 *Loci communes*, not in terms of the elements of bread and wine, but as "participation in the table of the Lord." What participants come to know, as a result, is the will of God toward them, a certain and assured knowledge that "excites and arouses faith."[45]

But while ritual "transmits" or communicates a particular knowledge, it also seeks to form a way of being and acting in the world.[46] One might say that there is a connection between "knowing that" and "knowing how." Theodore W. Jennings has argued in this regard that ritual governs or patterns a field of action:

> As early as the third century Cyprian remarked, "If we call God Father we should behave as his children." What Cyprian is proposing is that this ritual act may be understood as the epitome of all specifically Christian action – that is, as the precis of Christian ethics. This proposal is taken up by Karl Barth in a programmatic fashion through his announced intention to develop a specifically Christian ethic on the pattern of a commentary on baptism, the Lord's Prayer, and the eucharist. This proposal may be reformulated by the thesis that Christian ritual patterns all doing which is a doing *coram Deo*.[47]

Jennings' argument that ritual patterns human doing *coram Deo* is reminiscent of Melanchthon's interest in how the *communicatio* of the Lord's Supper serves to shape the new life of the justified believer.[48] His great concern with ritual's *purpose* and *use* meant, as we have seen in the previous chapter, that the communication or sharing of Christ's benefits believers was integral to their lives because it was "the concrete assurance and climax of Christ's working presence...."[49]

This sort of knowedge, notes Jennings, is very much a knowledge "gained in bodily action"[50] – which, in Melanchthon's instance, was the bodily action of believers eating the bread and drinking the cup of the Supper – participating in the table of the Lord as he was fond of pointing out. Such bodily action, moreover, was to ensue in the sort of knowledge that has an impact on one's being and acting in the world.

Recently, Catherine Bell has written that such embodiment is a matter of a participant taking in an interpretive scheme for the purpose of practically construing the

---

45 Quere, *Melanchthon's Christum Cognoscere*, 90.
46 Jennings, "On Ritual Knowledge," 112.
47 Ibid., 118.
48 See the discussion in Rogness, *Reformer Without Honor*, 35ff.
49 Ibid., 118.
50 Jennings, "On Ritual Knowledge," 119.

world in which one lives.[51] The interpretive scheme envisioned and articulated by Melanchthon – was one where a source of power and authority is extended to include those participating in the Lord's Table, thereby modestly empowering them to experience their world in constructive or redemptive ways.

But the experiencing of such knowledge as "personal" and "participatory" requires a catalyst. As rhetoricians clearly recognized in the sixteenth century and as scholars in a growing number of disciplines now realize, that catalyst is emotion. It provides an important "missing link" for bridging mind and body, individual and society, because it transforms knowledge into human understanding.[52] And it is also through knowing that "the self is made."[53]

EMOTION AS CATALYST: A FUNDAMENTAL WAY OF KNOWING

To be "moved," as we have seen in our discussion thus far, indicates that emotion has an active function. It has "the capacity to inspire in human beings the wonder and creativity for actively interpreting and organizing the apparent mysteries of life."[54] Our propensity, however, shaped by a cultural discourse consisting of certain assumptions about human nature as well as well-established dualisms [e.g., mind/body, thought/action, emotion/knowledge, etc.], is to view emotion as passive rather than as active. It has been extremely difficult for us to think of emotion otherwise.

Older rhetorical traditions, current interpretive theories of culture, and contemporary philosophical reflection challenge many of our stale preconceptions of emotion, and regard it as involving much more than a reference to some internal, physiological state. An emotion is not a thing, but a process that is best understood as a way of interacting and interpreting. It is how we connect and communicate with a socially constituted, relationally meaningful world of people, places, times, events, and concepts. Emotion, therefore, is fundamental to the constitution of our psychological,

---

[51] Catherine Bell, "The Authority of Ritual Experts," *Studia Liturgica* 23 (1993): 117.

[52] E.g., Nancy Scheper-Hughes and Margaret Lock, "The Mindful Body: A Prolegomenon to Future Work in Medical Anthropology," *Medical Anthropology Quarterly* 1 (1987): 28ff.

[53] See Rebecca J. Slough, "These Songs Are the Life We Live: A Discussion of Ritual, Knowledge, and Knowing" (paper presented to the Graduate Theological Union Interdisciplinary Workshop on Ritual Theory, spring 1990), 14.

[54] Hyde, "Emotion and Human Communication," 120.

rhetorical, poetic, political, and ethical life.[55] It is how we render our world meaningful "and with it our lives and our Selves."[56]

The hinge, the channel through which meaningful communication was accomplished was the *affectus*, the source of passion or emotion, the power to feel and to know.[57] As Brian Vickers reminds us, "We must be aware of using the clear-cut modern distinction between 'feelings and thoughts.'"[58] Thus, when rhetorical communication sought "to move" someone, this involved judgments and emotions: feeling intensely, willing, acting, understanding, believing, changing one's mind.[59] The sacred rhetoric of the Renaissance and Reformation, based as it was on both classical and Christian sources, sought to connect emotion and knowing, thereby providing an interpretation of how psyche, world, and language were interrelated.[60]

Contemporary scholarship distinguishes among the terms "emotion," "affect," and "feeling." All three connote interpretive, interactive, and cognitive processes of being related to or involved in a world of meaning. "Emotion" is a personal and participatory form of knowing by which one is aware of and engaged with the world and with others. Awareness and engagement can be transformative, especially when thoughts, opinions, and behaviors are influenced or changed.[61] We could also include the word "passion" here, as we did earlier. Robert Solomon uses "passion" "as the generic term to cover the entire range of those phenomena that may be said to "move" us."[62]

"Affect" is used more inclusively and embraces "moods," "dispositions," "characters," "personalities," et al. Some speak of "affect" as a larger "semantic domain" within which a full range of communicative means (linguistic, non-verbal, dis-

---

55 Ibid., 121ff; see also Lila Abu-Lughod and Catherine Lutz, "Introduction: emotion, discourse, and the politics of everyday life," in *Language and the politics of emotion*, ed. Catherine A. Lutz & Lila Abu-Lughod (Cambridge: Cambridge Univ. Press, 1990), 1–23; Michelle Z. Rosaldo, "Toward An Anthropology of Self and Feeling," in *Culture Theory: Essays on Mind, Self, and Emotion*, ed. Richard A. Shweder and Robert A. LeVine (Cambridge: Cambridge Univ. Press, 1984), 137–157.

56 Robert C. Solomon, *The Passions: The Myth and Nature of Human Emotion* (Notre Dame, Ind.: Univ. of Notre Dame Press, 1983), 169 (originally published by Anchor Press/Doubleday, 1976).

57 See Vickers, *In Defence of Rhetoric*, 276–286; Shuger, *Sacred Rhetoric*, 118–153; William J. Bouwsma, "The Two Faces of Humanism," in *Itinerarium Italicum*, 38ff.

58 Vickers, *In Defence of Rhetoric*, 277.

59 Rosemund Tuve, *Elizabethan and Metaphysical Imagery. Renaissance Poetic and Twentieth-Century Critics* (Chicago, 1947), 183; cited in Vickers, *In Defence of Rhetoric*, 277.

60 See Shuger, *Sacred Rhetoric*, 10–13.

61 Hyde, "Emotion and Communication," 216–218; Hyde, "Emotion as Communication," 128–129; also Robert Levy, "Introduction: Self and Emotion," *Ethos* 11, no. 3 (1983): 128–134.

62 Solomon, *The Passions*, 130.

course, interaction) are employed "against a backdrop of social contexts, social identities, and culturally constituted expectations."[63]

"Feeling" seems to be more immediate and experiential.[64] It "tell(s) us how the
world is in a vivid way, holding information in an active form so that it doesn't go
away."[65] Some philosophers and rhetoricians, however, are much less sanguine about
"feeling." In fact, they are quick to point out that "feeling" has nothing to do with
"emotion" as such or, at least, should not be confused with it.[66] Anthropologists are
not quite so adamant about sharply distinguishing "emotion" and "feeling," though
they are aware of the nuances *and* the commonalities. In the sacred rhetorics of the
Reformation, as we noted earlier, *movere* was directed to *affectio*, *affectus*, and/or
passio – the core of the human personality, i.e., "the heart."

These particular ways of thinking about and interpreting how it is that rituals express what moves people the most, however, rest upon an assumption that bears careful and critical re-examination. The assumption is that the fundamental task of ritual
is to "resolve" basic conflicts or contradictions that have emerged in personal/social
life, such as those that exist between religious belief and the real world.[67]

If rituals actually "worked" in this fashion, i.e., as solving or resolving contradictions and conflicts between religious belief and the real world, those who participated
in them would handle their problems with great aplomb or be healed of whatever it is
that ails and afflicts them.[68] It is more useful to proceed with a radically different assumption about what the central dynamic of ritual is.[69] What if we assumed, instead,
that rituals do not address nor resolve "fundamental contradictions" or "conflicts" at
all? Rather, let us say that they are strategic activities in which people participate in
order to deal practically with their specific circumstances.

While "resolution" of these circumstances may be implied in a ritual, it may be
more accurate to say that the way of acting and speaking in ritual provides a way to
know the world and to act in it. The manner in which one comes to know this is

---

63 Judith Irvine, "Language and affect: some cross-cultural issues,"in *Contemporary Perceptions of
Language: Interdisciplinary Dimensions, Georgetown Univ. Round Table on Languages and Linguistics
1982*, ed. Heidi Byrnes (Washington: Georgetown Univ. Press, 1982), 32.

64 See Helen Fay Nissenbaum, *Emotion and Focus* (Stanford, Calif.: Center for the Study of
Language and Information, 1985), 127ff; also Roy D'Andrade, "Cultural meaning systems," in
Culture Theory, 124.

65 Roy D'Andrade, "The cultural part of cognition," *Cognitive Science* 5 (1981): 191; cited in
Robert Levy, "Emotion, knowing, and culture," in *Culture Theory*, 218.

66 Solomon, *The Passions*, 57ff.; Hyde, "Emotion and Communication," 128–129.

67 See Bell, *Ritual Theory, Ritual Practice*, 35–37.

68 See F. Allan Hanson, "The semiotics of ritual," *Semiotica* 33–1/2 (1981), 169–178.

69 Bell, *Ritual Theory, Ritual Practice*, 35–37, 69–117.

through an emotional experience of insight and connectedness to others. Such an experience is one of "modest empowerment" where the person is afforded a certain sense of identity and enabled to have some sense of reality by virtue of which they can live in communication and relationship.[70] What can be said to occur is a certain embodied appropriation by a ritual participant of a set of schemes, values, perceptions, and interpretations of an order of power that is "redemptive." This is "is a strategic and practical orientation for acting" in which a person's sense of reality and identity is nuanced and confirmed.[71]

That these matters are among the communicative, social/psychological effects of Christian worship in a Lutheran tradition are indicated by the responses of worshipers themselves when asked what it is they have experienced. They do not report marvelous transformations either of head or of heart, but will speak of having been "moved," of having experienced what was said, seen, and done as "intensely meaningful." Or, they will indicate that they think and/or feel differently about themselves, others, God, and the world in which they live. They will mention receiving or achieving important insights about the self, experiencing a greater sense of belonging, feeling supported and enabled to function sensibly in the everyday world. Anthropological studies indicate that what persons are doing with such talk is employing "a kind of language of the self – a code for statements about intentions, actions, and social relations" or making "a statement about [their] relationship with the world."[72] In this perspective, "[e]motions are about the ways in which the social world is one in which *we* are involved."[73]

The ability or capacity to engage in such talk and to experience such emotion as entailing both feelings and cognitive orientation is strikingly similar to an older rhetorical psychology that viewed it as active and purposive. Traditions of existential philosophy also remind us that emotions

> function as vehicles for the active sensibility of human beings....they emerge in the interaction between a person and the world as the world is perceived by the person through an act of consciousness. An emotion operates as an act of consciousness; it serves to orient a person toward the world in a certain way.[74]

---

70 Ibid.
71 Ibid., 85.
72 Lutz and White, "The Anthropology of Emotions," 417, 421.
73 Michelle Z. Rosaldo, "Toward an Anthropology of Self and Feeling," 143.
74 Hyde, "Existentialism as a Basis for the Theory and Practice of Rhetoric," 216.

The earlier Lutheran Reformation's use and understanding of *movere*, grounded in the rhetorical and theological features of emotion as an interweaving of the affective and the cognitive, is similar in its emphasis. What is articulated is not an introspective self-consciousness but an expression of the dynamic of seeking and being sought, a yoking of "the complexly intertwined activities of self and spirit."[75] Selfhood is formed in such an interaction.

The affective power of religious ritual, rhetorically construed, is not the result of pathos or deception but is a divine gift. Yet the recognition that such power is a gift is interwoven with human psychological and social processes – the noetic and the affective. Or, as Melanchthon would emphasize, the *quid* and the *quid pro nobis*: "to know Christ is to know Christ's benefits."[76] A contemporary assessment of these processes as "meaning-making" is suggestively similar:

> Meaning-making is the activity of composing and being composed by the connections among things. To have meaning in one's life is to recognize pattern in the disparate elements of existence, to seek order, significance, and wholeness. Meaning is anchored in trust and is the ground of hope. Without it, human beings cannot survive. In its most comprehensive dimensions, this meaning-making activity is the activity of faith, carried out in a dialectic between fear and trust, hope and hopelessness, alienation and belonging....

> We are personally engaged in this meaning-making, symbolizing, faith activity, *yet ultimately we cannot do it alone; it is a profoundly relational activity.* And thus it is that a participant in the central ritual of Christian faith – the eucharist – is identified as a "communicant," a participant in a web of communication by which the fabric of human life is composed and re-composed.[77]

WHAT DOES IT MEAN TO BE A PARTICULAR KIND OF PERSON?

What emerges from these considerations of what is involved in "a heart's being moved" is that the sort of "movement" which occurs is a matter of empowerment, knowledge, and understanding. What is made, expressed, and articulated is a particular kind of person,[78] one who seeks to live a simple, undeluded life, "prey not to presumption, superstition, or indulgence, but merely as [a] human being."[79] Such a

---

[75] Shuger, *Sacred Rhetoric*, 240.

[76] *LC*, 21.

[77] Sharon Daloz Parks, "Communication, Ritual as," *The New Dictionary of Sacramental Worship*, ed. Peter E. Fink, S.J. (Collegeville: The Liturgical Press, 1991) 236. My emphasis.

[78] Eilberg-Schwartz, (paper presented to the Ritual Studies Group, American Academy of Religion Annual Meeting, San Francisco, 22 November 1992).

[79] Ozment, *The Age of Reform*, 438.

person, moreover, cannot be a self on his or her own but only in relation to a defining community, a web of communication, an "other" of some kind, as the following homiletical snippet makes particularly clear:

> The first truth to come tumbling out of that blustering, dizzying era called the Reformation is that I am nothing, you're nothing, not a human, not a person *without the other*; that selfhood is neither something inherent nor something you become through exercise...but that you are because there is another; that you not merely need the other, you cannot think, you have no identity, cannot say "I," "me," or "mine" without the other. The other side of this coin reads "grace alone." To be a person is to have another, another you did not make, fancy, or construct, but who was there before you ever were, who is or will be while you're still here and after you've gone – a given, a gift.[80]

Beliefs, values, and being a particular kind of person involve "a changed ethic" because the significant human activity of "moving the Good into the world" is no longer restricted to a special spiritual or sacred area.[81] What the redesigned ritual practice of the Lutheran Reformation sought to provide was a different interpretive scheme for how participants not only view the world but also act in it. This means that

> [s]piritual isolation is at an end. One is moved into responsibility for one's neighbor just in the freedom and uncertainty of history and the givenness of creation. This is so wonderfully evident in the recognition of the neighbor: the absolute command that I recognize the neighbor as a "thou." If I do not love my neighbor, I hate my own humanity...so intimate is the oneness of the race [where we are] to be on tip-toe anticipating the needs of the neighbor [who is] equally creature of God....[82]

Earlier in this book, we noted that rhetoric and ritual "have not a little in common." Both modes of expression are ways of knowing, ways of shaping and structuring reality, and ways of being a particular kind of person. Both aim at engaging the whole self. This means, in a specific sense, the activity of what we call the *will* or the *heart*. "Willing" sums up the whole person, and includes thinking and feeling, but transcends both as well.[83]

Being "moved," then, is not simply an elemental feeling or an "oh, wow" matter. It does not happen or emerge *ex nihilo*. Rather, it is an interpretive process that en-

---

80 Roy A. Harrisville, "Texts in Context: God's Yes (2 Corinthians 1:20)," *Word and World* 11, no. 3 (summer 1991): 322.

81 Goeser, "Whither Lutheranism?" 44.

82 Ibid., 48.

83 Douglas John Hall, *Thinking the Faith* (Minneapolis: Augsburg Publishing House, 1989), 382–383.

gages the heart, "the whole, responsible self"[84] in interaction with the indwelling Spirit. Here is an example of a differently understood, if not differently constituted, self. And, here is a perspective on not just *what* is experienced, but a change in *how* experience occurs. It is not simply a mere registering of sensory data nor an individualistic, idiosyncratic "warm feeling." Rather, we see a *process* that entails both feelings and cognitive orientations. It provides, as we noted earlier, the catalyst that transforms knowledge into human understanding, thereby bringing intensity and commitment to human action.[85]

Douglas John Hall's recent discussion of this way of knowing, which he labels "trust," is very helpful here because of its connection to our earlier consideration of *fiducia*. Hall has written:

> ...when a person moves over into this kind of personal knowledge of someone else, it is something which involves not only *rational* activity but the activity of the whole self. This means in a specific sense the activity of what we call the *will*....Willing...is a summing up of the whole person, inclusive of thinking and inclusive of feeling, but transcending both....It is the knowing of an encounter between persons who indeed know they they will *never* know each other fully in the fact-knowledge sense, and will *never* acknowledge in one another fully everything that really *is* significant, but who nevertheless determine to commit themselves to one another.[86]

When applied to an experience of ritual, these features and dynamics thus expose and express the implicit cognitive and emotional model or idea that a culture has of and for itself.[87] For the tradition of the Lutheran Reformation, such a model or idea has usually been described theologically using the categories of "promise" and "faith." But this model or idea also points to or issues in a particular kind of social experience. Melanchthon noted in his 1521 *Loci communes* that "we are born into a life that is social," that we are bound to others.[88]

The early Lutheran Reformation's radical reassessment of both God and the human project gave both a distinctively down-to-earth meaning. This was singularly different from how the order of salvation and the relationship of human beings to God in this life had been conceptualized. There was no ontological continuum between God and humankind. The burden of salvation was placed squarely upon God

---

[84] Goeser, "The Doctrine of Word and Scripture," 118.
[85] Scheper-Hughes and Lock, "The Mindful Body," 28–29.
[86] Hall, *Thinking the Faith*, 382–383.
[87] See Volney Gay, "Ritual and Self-Esteem in Victor Turner and Heinz Kohut," *Zygon* 18 (1983): 273.
[88] *LC*, 51.

so that the religious problem was *not* one of individual moral transformation into the likeness of God. The problem was one of trust and belief that God was indeed truthful and trustworthy.

> Or, put another way, the "transformation" now at issue was from a state of doubt and uncertainty to a state of trust and belief in words and promises which lacked immediate verification. The basic question became not whether one was inwardly and outwardly righteous, but whether God was truthful in his judgment of human nature and destiny, whether, despite all evidence to the contrary, life was meaningful.[89]

Such truthfulness and trustworthiness were seen as central to both theological discourse and in ritual practice. For the latter, this meant that its task was no longer to somehow "perform the dramatic coup of eliciting the supernatural out of the mundane."[90] Rather, it sought to express and affirm "the mundane" – to provide a realistic assessment of the human condition in which "the self can now live again in relationship, in mutuality," where "it can now encounter God, creation, neighbor, and history instead of being insulated against them."[91] Most significantly, this meant that one could get on with day-to-day living, "confident about the ultimate matters."[92]

A comparable emphasis exists in some current culture writing and theorizing as well as in some contemporary philosophical discussions of identity and selfhood. Stephen A. Tyler has written recently, for example, that a post-modern ethnography

> does not move toward abstraction, away from life, but back to experience. It aims not to foster the growth of knowledge but to restructure experience, not to understand objective reality, for that is already established by common sense, nor to explain how we understand, for that is impossible, but to reassimilate, to reintegrate the self in society and to restructure the conduct of everyday life.[93]

It is significant that in contemporary philosophical discussions of the sources of modern selfhood, especially those that challenge, if not reject, the turn to subjectivity as *mere* subjectivity at the mildest and sheer nihilism at the worst, the Reformation

---

89 Steven Ozment, "Luther and the Late Middle Ages: The Formation of Reformation Thought," *Transition and Revolution: Problems and Issues of European Renaissance and Reformation History*, ed. Robert M. Kingdon (Minneapolis: Burgess Publishing Company, 1974), 127.

90 Bossy, *Christianity in the West*, 67.

91 Goeser, "Whither Lutheranism?" 44.

92 Ozment, "Luther and the Late Middle Ages,"128.

93 Stephen Tyler, *The Unspeakable: Discourse, Dialogue, and Rhetoric in the Postmodern World*, The Rhetoric of the Human Sciences (Madison: Univ. of Wisconsin Press, 1987), 211–212.

has been singled out for its "new radical revaluation of ordinary life...."[94] Its anti-subjectivistic emphasis has been pointed out as well.[95] The sort of subjectivity envisaged by the Lutheran Reformation is correlative with the message, word, or promise of the Gospel. Such a communication attains its goal, as we saw in chapter 4, only as it engenders knowledge of God, of Christ, and of his benefits, and, at the same time, trust and commitment. Moreover, "The entire modern development of the affirmation of ordinary life was foreshadowed and initiated, in all its facets, in the spirituality of the Reformers."[96]

Some recent reflection on ritual, with its analysis of the construction and the deployment of "the ritual body," is also similar to the Lutheran Reformation's emphasis upon "the distinctively down-to-earth."[97] The modest empowerment that is said to occur in ritual and is sometimes reported as having occurred, as we noted earlier, is not for the purpose of resolving contradictions between the conditions of ordinary life and the key assumptions of a religious-cultural order. Rather, what is proposed is a rather practical way of dealing with one's circumstances.

The Lutheran Reformation's rhetorical and ritual practices sought to empower people to live merely as simple, undeluded human beings – who know and trust in the God who makes them believers *and* Christs for their neighbor.[98] These practices sought "to move the heart" from a state of doubt and unbelief to one of trust and belief that it is *this* world *coram Deo* and *coram hominibus* that is envisaged and proclaimed, and not some other.

The purpose and power of religious ritual lie in its capacity to provide a particular interpretation or re-interpretation of the world. This is not always the romanticized and mystified efficacy of this activity as a central, transformative cultural process. Yet it is a purpose and power "adequate to the task of experiencing [the] world in constructive or redemptive ways."[99] For it is in such a world that one comes to know and feel that the Word and the Promise can be trusted after all.

---

94 Taylor, *Sources of the Self,* 218.
95 Sacvan Bercovitch, *The Puritan Origins of the American Self* (New Haven: Yale Univ. Press, 1975), 25.
96 Taylor, *Sources of the Self,* 218.
97 Bell, *Ritual Theory, Ritual Practice,* 94–117.
98 Ozment, *The Age of Reform,* 438.
99 Bell, "The Authority of Ritual Experts," 117.

CONCLUSION

We have just seen that Philip Melanchthon's use of "to move the heart" to interpret the distinctive working of religious ritual can still speak to our own theoretical context in which similar questions are being asked about the nature and purpose of this way of acting. In interrogating and interpreting his work with regard to the concerns of current ritual practice and theory, it was necessary to issue three challenges. The first was directed to those who see the great sixteenth-century debate about religious ritual as eventually resulting in the repudiation of this sort of activity. Their view of ritual as possessing one basic mechanism operating more or less the same everywhere avoided or overlooked the fact that it assumes different forms, is undertaken for different reasons and effects, and is very historically determined. Hence, I argued that a term such as "ritual" needed both pliability and nuance in order not to deny history and subjectivity but to take such dynamics seriously and to view them in a different way.

The second challenge was to an interpretation of the sixteenth-century's reconceptualization Western Christianity's symbolic order that saw rhetoric and ritual as distinct from one another rather than uniquely related. In exploring this relationship, we were able to see that both kinds of cultural practice seek to explain a social world, to shape and define a community, to generate a certain kind of knowing, and to construct a particular sort of person.

The third challenge was to a conventional Melanchthon scholarship's image of him as the great intellectualizer of the Lutheran Reformation who had little or no interest in the practical, affective dimensions of faith and life. Recent studies of his methods of interpreting scripture, his application of rhetorical theory to preaching, and his formulating of theological positions with an eye to their effects in the lives of believers, however, enabled us to proceed with the agenda and argument of this book.

REVIEWING THE AGENDA AND ARGUMENT OF THIS BOOK

The striking analogies between Melanchthon's approach to religious ritual and our own theoretical interests derived from similarities in the historical and cultural fabric then as well as now. A brief review of his cultural-experiential background that largely contributed to the emergence of "to move the heart" and to the shape of our own agenda in this book will clarify this point.

Melanchthon's intellectual milieu was one marked by serious inquiry that sought to relocate theological reflection and discourse from an abstract, theoretical realm to the realm of a practice responsive to human experience. Understanding this milieu known as Renaissance Humanism was crucial, as Melanchthon scholars assert, if we are to adequately and fully appreciate his thought.

Since the first instance of Melanchthon's use of "to move the heart" occured in a 1528 tract (three years prior to its appearance in the Apology of the Augsburg Confession) in which he was out to find a position on the church's ritual practice that was neither Roman (grace is effective *ex opere operato*) nor Zwinglian (the bread and wine as Roman toga, a marker of identity), it was necessary to explore both of these positions. For Melanchthon, the sacraments were effective signs of God's will, the visible word of God, that worked faith in believers. His emphasis on "signs of God's will" against Zurich and effective, i.e., "heart moving" to faith against Rome was one of steering a middle course.

Much of the early sixteenth century discussion of the practice and theology of the church's worship was caught up in the technical debates about the sacramental elements and the modes of Christ's presence. Melanchthon's point of view, grounded in his articulation of Reformation theology using the categories of Renaissance rhetoric, was one that has been described as a joyful affirmation of the effectiveness of the spoken and written Word. His language of the Word striking the ear and the rite moving or exciting to faith in the heart exemplified a preference to emphasize the use and purpose of Christian ritual within the church and in the new life of the justified believer. The result, as Peter Fraenkel has noted, is a "functional" interest rather than a strictly systematic-theological one.[1]

Melanchthon's "functional" interest meant a view and practice of sacred discourse (preaching to be sure but also "rite") as passionate and affective. Such discourse

---

[1] "Ten Questions Concerning Melanchthon, the Fathers, and the Eucharist," 147ff.

sought the response of faith. It was in this response that the self emerged and became oriented toward God and toward the world. "A heart moved" was both a matter of feeling as well as knowing. It was an apprehension as intellectual passion and passionate understanding engendered by the Spirit of God who worked faith and trust. Discussions of being "moved" during the time of the Reformation and in Melanchthon's thought, therefore, were situated in a wider framework of understandings of self, emotion, and knowledge.

The shape which Melanchthon's emphasis and approach took, therefore, involved strategies of description, interpretation, and explanation. Descriptively, he singled out human sensory faculties, namely the eyes and ears. Interpretively, he sought to show how ritual has a real, practical effect on a person. As an explanation, he emphasized how ritual can function as a vehicle for a particular emotional expression (and a transformation of emotion) which Melancthon conceived of as *fiducia* – the perception or knowledge of God as gracious *and* a corresponding trust or confidence in God.

Our final task was to show how Melanchthon's understanding of what is involved in "a heart moved" can still speak to us. Contemporary scholarship, for example, has been rethinking the special efficacy or power of ritual. This efficacy may not always be the power once claimed – i.e., the delivery of sacramental grace to the faithful or the accumulation of a wide range of spiritual and mundane benefits. Nevertheless, ritual is regarded and experienced as having "a particularly persuasive effect" on the sense of identity and social reality of those who participate.[2] To speak of "a persuasive effect" clearly points to what rhetoricians label as one of the *officia* or ends of oratory – that of moving the emotions (*movere*), and thereby the wills of living individuals. This "persuasive effect" has to do with their reinterpretation of the world in ways that envision and empower.

SOME FINAL OBSERVATIONS

An important result of my study has been to demonstrate two important aspects of ritual practice that are often misunderstood – its embeddedness in particular historical and cultural frames of reference on the one hand, and on the other, its continuity across time as a medium that in general has a distinctive way of working. Such a way

---

2 E.g., *Journal of Ritual Studies* 4, no. 2 (summer 1990), special issue based on the Proceedings of the University of California, Santa Barbara Conference on Ritual and Power. See especially Barbara A. Holdredge, "Introduction: Towards a Phenomenology of Power," 5-37, and Catherine Bell, "The Ritual Body and the Dynamics of Ritual Power," 299-313.

of working for Melanchthon involved an addressing the ear, the eye, and the heart simultaneously.

Another result has been to show that once ritual is not viewed as possessing some intrinsic, universal mechanism, those who seek to understand it in some way draw heavily on the ideas and attitudes of their times. While much is being written about ritual today and some approaches contradict other approaches,[3] we can hear in some of these, as the foregoing chapter sought to demonstrate, the same appreciation of self, emotion, and knowledge that animated Melanchthon's recasting of the role of ritual. Also, when ritual strays too far away from a focus on the heart, then correctives emerge. So, in the sixteenth century as well as our own, when there is an overintellectualization, an overemphasis on the community (and, hence, on the institution), we look for other ideas to help us explain the nature and purpose of ritual. For Melanchthon, these were ideas drawn from the understanding of the person found in Renaissance (and Reformation) Humanism's *theologia rhetorica*. For contemporary ritual theory, these ideas emerge from alternative conceptualizations of "self" and "experience" that are available in both the humanities and the social sciences.

Melanchthon's time was marked by a heightened awareness of different modes of social, theological, and psychological organization. This, in turn, brought a corresponding interest in how an identity is shaped, how a self is formed. Yet such awareness and interest did not always occur at the expense of the specificities and diversities of religious practices and writings as some modern scholars have claimed.[4] In fact, with their marked lack of interest in Christian traditions or Christian practices, the early modern notions of self and experience that are advanced by these scholars occur without taking Christianity seriously. But in considering Melanchthon's approach to ritual practice and interpretation, we encounter "the heart" as subjectivity, as interiority, as an individual. But this self was neither independent nor able to be a source of movement toward God. Melanchthon univocally rejected this notion. Yet such a movement is experienced by a truly human being who is a concatenation of emotion, will, and intellect. God, Christ, redemption, and being moved are not simply cre-

---

3 See Bell, *Ritual Theory, Ritual Practice* (esp. pp. 13–66), for a summary of some of these contradictory approaches. For example, does ritual express or communicate a mental orientation? Does it endow "meaning upon experience" (p. 15)? Does it effect social and/or individual change? Can ritual be "read" like a text? Is it a certain kind of cultural experience? Is it benignly transformative? In short, what does ritual do and how does it "do what we say it does" (p. 169)?

4 See David Aers' criticism of the tendency in recent literary study to all but ignore such specificities and practices: "A Whisper in the Ear of Early Modernists: or, Reflections on Literary Critics Writing the 'History of the Subject,'" in *Culture and History 1350-1600: Essays on English Communities, Identities and Writing*, ed. David Aers (Detroit: Wayne State University Press, 1992), 177-202.

ations of ritual actors themselves, for Melanchthon never says "the heart moves toward," but rather the heart is moved by Word and rite.

The emphasis on being moved that was characteristic of Melanchthon's understanding of sacred discourse, and, as we have shown in this study, of his understanding of religious ritual thus raises questions about the relationship between divine initiative and human effort. The linking of rhetoric, ritual, and soteriology suggests, as
Debora Shuger has observed, a "self that seems to have little of its own left to do."[5]
But we need to recall that our notions of the self are rather peculiar. Clifford Geertz
has pointed out, for example, that we tend to think of the self as

> a bounded, unique, more or less integrated motivational and cognitive universe, a
> dynamic center of awareness, emotion, judgment, and action organized into a dis-
> tinctive whole and set contrastively both against other such wholes and against its
> social and natural background....[6]

We saw that the self constituted or formed by sixteenth century rhetoric and ritual,
however, was more interactive and relational. One's response to God resulted in a
certain kind of self; one's response to the things of this world constituted a different
self.[7] The rhetoric, ritual, and soteriology connection – with its understanding of the
Gospel as a particular kind of communication and the form of human response as
one of "faith," involved a subjectivity characterized by a joyful trust or confidence in
God "that makes us all children of the promise...."[8]

The dilemma for modern theorists, however, is that while they reject the notion of
an autonomous, unified subject, they still want to posit ritual's capacity to engage a
person in relatively active forms of assent to and experience of divine (or redemptive)
presence and authority. Despite the "untroubled atheism" of contemporary theory
and discourse on the self,[9] there is an interest in looking at how experience can be re-
demptively powerful or personally defining in some way. A helpful reminder might
be to think of such redemptive empowerment as "faith" or "trust." One scholar has
written recently that to believe or to trust is much like falling in love.[10] A person is

---

5 Debora K. Shuger, *Sacred Rhetoric: The Christian Grand Style in the English Renaissance*.
(Princeton: Princeton University Press, 1988), 232.

6 Clifford Geertz, "'From the Native's Point of View': On the Nature of Anthropological
Understanding," in *Local Knowledge: Further Essays in Interpretive Anthropology* (New York: Basic
Books, 1983), 59.

7 Shuger, *Sacred Rhetoric*, 233.

8 Richard Waswo, *Language and Meaning in the Renaissance* (Princeton: Princeton University Press,
1987), 240.

9 Michael Edwards, "Not I," *Comparative Criticism: An Annual Journal. Representations of the Self*
12 (1990), 26.

10 Gerhard O. Forde, *Theology is for Proclamation* (Minneapolis: Fortress Press, 1990), 137–141.

truly and really involved. It is a certain kind of human experience. And then there is Philip Melanchthon's emphasis *contra omnes rationes humanae* concerning the movement of the heart by the grace of God. Of course, the whole human being is involved, but in a way to preclude all boasting.

Whether this is the "subjection" that characterises so-called postmodern identity is not really the point. For if one is looking for a radical deconstruction of self, glance at the New Testament or at the Lutheran Reformation with their insights into the labyrinthine depths of human self-deception and their particular understanding of the de-centered subject, a "not I," as one writer has stated recently.[11] At the same time, however, a salutary dialectic is at work:

> The more the "I" is asserted, the more the "not I" intervenes to replace it. The more the "not I" increases, the more the "I" becomes capable, capacious to receive it.[12]

We can say, then, that when a heart is moved by the grace of God *and* by the distinctive working of Word and rite, there is a corresponding subjectivity. One is allowed to become a particular kind of person who now can construe the world in ways that envision and empower – just as Philip Melanchthon claimed some four-and-a-half centuries ago, when he wrote: "As the Word enters the ears to strike the heart [*ut feriat corda*], so the rite itself enters through the eyes to move the heart [*ut moveat corda*] to believe and take hold of faith."[13]

---

[11] Edwards, "Not I," 25-38.
[12] Ibid., 38.
[13] Apology of the Augsburg Confession 13.5, in *BC*, 212.

BIBLIOGRAPHY

A. PRIMARY SOURCES

Melanchthon, Philip. "Adversus anabaptistas iudicium" [Answer to the Anabaptists, 1528]. Translated by Charles L. Hill. In *Melanchthon: Selected Writings*. Edited by Elmer E. Flack and Lowell J. Satre. Minneapolis: Augsburg Publishing House, 1962. Latin text in *Melanchthons Werke*, edited by Robert Stupperich et al. Vol. 1, *Reformatorische Schriften*, edited by Robert Stupperich. Gütersloh: C. Bertelsmann Verlag, 1951.

————. "Annotationes in Evangelium Matthaei" [Annotations to the Gospel of Matthew]. In *Melanchthons Werke*, edited by Robert Stupperich et al. Vol. 4, *Frühe exegetische Schriften*, edited by Peter F. Barton. Gütersloh: Gütersloher Verlagshaus Gerd Mohn, 1963.

————. "Apology of the Augsburg Confession." Translated by Jaroslav Pelikan. In *The Book of Concord: The Confessions of the Evangelical Lutheran Church*. Edited by Theodore G. Tappert. Philadelphia: Fortress Press, 1959. Latin text in *Die Bekenntnisschriften der evangelisch-lutherischen Kirche*. 6th ed. Göttingen: Vandenhoeck & Ruprecht, 1967.

————. "De modo et arte concionandi." In *Supplementa Melanchthoniana: Werke Philipp Melanchthons, die im Corpus reformatorum vermisst werde*. Vol. 5, bk. 2, *Philipp Melanchthons Schriften zur Praktischen Theologie: Homiletische Schriften*, edited by Paul Drews and Ferdinand Cohrs. Leipzig: R. Haupt, 1929. Reprint, Frankfurt: Unveränderte Nachdruck, 1968.

————. "De officiis concionatoris." In *Supplementa Melanchthoniana: Werke Philipp Melanchthons, die im Corpus reformatorum vermisst werde*. Vol. 5, pt. 2, *Philipp Melanchthons Schriften zur Praktischen Theologie: Homiletische Schriften*, edited by Paul Drews and Ferdinand Cohrs. Leipzig: R. Haupt, 1929. Reprint, Frankfurt: Unveränderte Nachdruck, 1968.

————. "Scholia in Epistulam Pauli ad Colossenses." In *Melanchthons Werke*, edited by Robert Stupperich et al.. Vol. 4, *Frühe exegetische Schriften*, edited by Peter F. Barton. Gütersloh: Gütersloher Verlagshaus Gerd Mohn, 1963.

————. "Sententiae Veterum." In *Philippi Melanthonis Opera quae supersunt omnia*. Edited by C. K. Bretschneider and H. E. Bindseil. Vol. 23. Halle: apud C. A. Schwetschke et filium, 1847. The *Opera* constitute volumes 1–28 of the *Corpus Reformatorum* (99 vols., Halle, Berlin, and Leipzig, 1834–).

————. *De rhetorica libri tres.* Leipzig: Valentin Schumann, 1521. Originally published 1519.

————. *Institutiones rhetoricae.* Strasbourg: J. Herwagen, 1523. Originally published 1521.

————. *Loci communes theologici* of 1521. Translated by Lowell J. Satre. In *Melanchthon and Bucer,* edited by Wilhelm Pauck. Vol. 19 of *The Library of Christian Classics.* Philadelphia: Westminster Press, 1969.

————. *Paul's Letter to the Colossians.* Translated by David C. Parker. Historic Texts and Interpreters in Biblical Scholarship. Sheffield, England: The Almond Press, 1989.

————. *Philippi Melancthonis de rhetorica libri tres.* Wittenberg, 1519.

————. *Römerbrief-Kommentar* of 1532. In *Melanchthons Werke in Auswahl,* ed. Robert Stupperich et al. Vol. 5. Gütersloh: C. Bertelsmannn Verlag and Verlagshaus Gerd Mohn, 1951-1963.

B. TRANSLATIONS

LaFontaine, Sister Mary J. "A Critical Translation of Philip Melanchthon's 'Elementorum Rhetorices Libri Duo.'" Ph.D. dissertation, University of Michigan, 1968.

McNally, John. "Melanchthon's Earliest Rhetoric." In *Rhetoric: A Tradition in Transition,* Edited by Walter R. Fisher. East Lansing, Mich.: Michigan State University Press, 1974.

C. SECONDARY SOURCES: MIDDLE AGES, RENAISSANCE, AND REFORMATION

1. General Studies

Aers, David. "A Whisper in the Ear of Early Modernists: or, Reflections on Literary Critics Writing the 'History of the Subject.'" In *Culture and History 1350-1600: Essays on English Communities, Identities and Writing.* Edited by David Aers. Detroit: Wayne State University Press, 1992.

Barnes, Andrew E. "Review Essay: Religious Reform and the War Against Ritual." *Journal of Ritual Studies* 4, no. 2 (winter 1990): 127–133.

Beckwith, Sarah. "Ritual, Church and Theatre: Medieval Dramas of the Sacramental Body." In *Culture and History 1350–1600: Essays on English Communities, Identities and Writing.* Edited by David Aers. Detroit: Wayne State University Press, 1992.

Bornert, Rene. *La réforme protestante du culte à Strasbourg au XVIe siècle (1523-1598).* Leiden: E. J. Brill, 1981.

Bossy, John. *Christianity in the West 1400–1700.* Oxford: Oxford Univ. Press, 1985.

———. "The Mass as a Social Institution 1200-1700." *Past and Present*, no. 100 (1983): 29-61.

Bouwsma, William J. "Changing Assumptions in Later Renaissance Culture." *Viator* 7 (1976). Subsequently published in *A Usable Past: Essays in European Cultural History*. Berkeley: University of California Press, 1990.

———. "Review Article: 'Renaissance Humanism: Foundations, Forms, and Legacy.'" *Church History* 59, no. 1 (March 1990): 65-70.

———. "The Spirituality of Renaissance Humanism." In *Christian Spirituality II: High Middle Ages and Reformation*, edited by Jill Raitt in collaboration with Bernard McGinn and John Meyendorff. Vol. 17 of *World Spirituality: An Encyclopedic History of the Religious Quest*. New York: Crossroad, 1987.

———. "The Two Faces of Humanism: Stoicism and Augustinianism in Renaissance Thought." In *Itinerarium Italicum: The Profile of the Italian Renaissance in the Mirror of Its European Transformations*. Edited by Heiko A. Oberman with Thomas A. Brady, Jr. Leiden: E.J. Brill, 1975. Subsequently published in *A Usable Past: Essays in European Cultural History*. Berkeley: University of California Press, 1990. Page citations are to the original edition.

Boyle, Marjorie O'Rourke. "Rhetorical Theology: Charity Seeking Charity." Response to William J. Bouwsma, "Calvinism as *Theologia Rhetorica*." Center for Hermeneutical Studies in Hellenistic and Modern Culture Protocol of the Fifty-fourth Colloquy, 28 September 1986. Edited by Wilhelm Wuellner. Berkeley: Graduate Theological Union & University of California-Berkeley, 1987.

Brady, Thomas A. Jr. "In Search of the Godly City." In *The German People and the Reformation*. Edited by R. Po-chia Hsia. Ithaca & London, Cornell University Press, 1988.

Brann, Noel. "Humanism in Germany." In *Humanism Beyond Italy*. Vol. 2 of *Renaissance Humanism: Foundations, Forms, and Legacy*, edited by Albert Rabil, Jr. Philadelphia: University of Pennsylvania Press, 1988.

Burckhardt, Jacob. *The Civilization of the Renaissance in Italy*. Translated by S. G. C. Middlemore. New York: New American Library, 1960.

Burke, Peter. "The repudiation of ritual in early modern modern Europe." In *The Historical Anthropology of Early Modern Italy: Essays on Perception and Communication*. Cambridge: Cambridge University Press, 1987.

Busser, Fritz. "The Spirituality of Zwingli and Bullinger in the Reformation of Zurich." In *Christian Spirituality II: High Middle Ages and Reformation*, edited by Jill Raitt in collaboration with Bernard McGinn and John Meyendorff. Vol. 17 of *World Spirituality: An Encyclopedic History of the Religious Quest*. New York: Crossroad, 1987.

Cogan, Marc. "Rodolphus Agricola and the Semantic Revolutions of the History of Invention." *Rhetorica* 2, no. 2 (summer 1984): 163-194.

Crane, Mary Thomas. *Framing Authority: Sayings, Self, and Society in Sixteenth-Century England*. Princeton: Princeton Univ. Press, 1993.

Eire, Carlos. *War Against the Idols: The Reformation of Worship from Erasmus to Calvin.* Cambridge: Cambridge Univ. Press, 1986.

Garside, Charles Jr. *Zwingli and the Arts.* New Haven: Yale University Press, 1966.

Gilbert, Neal. *Renaissance Concepts and Method.* New York and London: Columbia Univ. Press, 1960.

Goeser, Robert J. "The Doctrine of Word and Scripture in Luther and Lutheranism." In *The Report of the Lutheran-Episcopal Dialogue, Second Series 1976-1980.* Cincinnati: Forward Movement, 1981.

———. "Word and Sacrament: A Study of Luther's Views as Developed in the Controversy with Zwingli and Karlstadt." Ph.D. dissertation, Yale University, 1960.

Grafton, Anthony and Jardine, Lisa. *From Humanism to the Humanities.* Cambridge: Harvard University Press, 1986.

Gray, Hanna H. "Renaissance Humanism: The Pursuit of Eloquence." In *Renaissance Essays.* Edited by Paul Oskar Kristeller and Philip P. Wiener. New York: Harper, 1968.

Jenson, Robert W. "Of Another Spirit." *Lutheran Theological Seminary Bulletin* 62, no. 1 (winter 1982): 3-13.

———. "The Supper." In *Christian Dogmatics.* Edited by Carl E. Braaten & Robert W. Jenson. Vol. 2. Philadelphia: Fortress Press, 1984.

Kristeller, Paul Oskar. *Renaissance Thought: The Classic, Scholastic, and Humanist Strains.* New York: Harper & Row, 1961.

Lindhardt, Jan. *Martin Luther: Knowledge and Mediation in the Renaissance.* Texts and Studies in Religion 29. Lewiston, N.Y.: The Edward Mellen Press, 1986.

Locher, Gottfried W. *Zwingli's Theology: New Perspectives.* Leiden: E. J. Brill, 1981.

Mack, Peter. *Renaissance Argument: Valla and Agricola in the Traditions of Rhetoric and Dialectic.* Leiden: E. J. Brill, 1993.

McCue, James F. "Liturgy and Eucharist: West." In *Christian Spirituality II: High Middle Ages and Reformation*, edited by Jill Raitt in collaboration with Bernard McGinn and John Meyendorff. Vol. 17 of *World Spirituality: An Encyclopedic History of the Religious Quest.* New York: Crossroad, 1987.

McGrath, Alistair E. *Reformation Thought: An Introduction.* London: Basil Blackwell, 1988.

Meerhoff, Kees. "Logic and Eloquence: A Ramusian Revolution?" *Argumentation* 5 (1991): 357–374.

Monfasani, John. "Humanism and Rhetoric." In *Humanism and the Disciplines.* Vol. 3 of *Renaissance Humanism: Foundations, Forms, and Legacy*, edited by Albert Rabil, Jr. Philadelphia: University of Pennsylvania Press, 1988.

Nauert, Charles G. Jr., "Renaissance Humanism: An Emergent Consensus and Its Critics." *Indiana Social Sciences Quarterly* 33 (1980): 5-20.

Oakley, Francis. "Religious and Ecclesiastical Life on the Eve of the Reformation." In *Reformation Europe: A Guide to Research.* Edited by Steven Ozment. St. Louis: Center for Reformation Research, 1982.

———. *The Western Church in the Later Middle Ages.* Ithaca: Cornell University Press, 1979.

Oftestad, Bernt Torvild. "'Historia' und 'Utilitas': Methodologische Aspekte der Abendsmahltheologie bei Martin Chemnitz." *Archiv für Reformationsgeschichte* 77 (1986): 186-225.

Ozment, Steven. "Luther and the Late Middle Ages: The Formation of Reformation Thought." In *Transition and Revolution: Problems and Issues of European Renaissance and Reformation History.* Edited by Robert M. Kingdon. Minneapolis: Burgess Publishing Company, 1974.

———. Introduction to *Religion and Culture in the Renaissance and Reformation.* Edited by Steven Ozment. Sixteenth Century Essays and Studies, vol. XI. Kirksville, Mo.: Sixteenth Century Journal Publishers, Inc., 1989.

———. *Protestants: The Birth of a Revolution.* New York: Doubleday, 1992.

———. *The Age of Reform 1250-1550: An Intellectual and Religious History of Late Medieval and Reformation Europe.* New Haven: Yale University Press, 1980.

———. *The Reformation in the Cities: The Appeal of Protestantism to Sixteenth-Century Germany and Switzerland.* New Haven: Yale University Press, 1975.

Porter, Roy, & Mikulas Teich, eds. *The Renaissance in national context.* Cambridge: Cambridge University Press, 1992.

Park, Katharine. "The Organic Soul." In *The Cambridge History of Renaissance Philosophy.* Edited by Charles B. Schmitt, general editor; Quentin Skinner and Eckhard Kessler, editors; and Jill Kraye, associate editor. Cambridge: Cambridge Univ. Press, 1988.

Parker, T. H. L. *Calvin's New Testament Commentaries.* Grand Rapids, Mich.: William R. Eerdmans Publishing Co., 1971.

Pelikan, Jaroslav. "Luther and the Liturgy." In *More About Luther.* Martin Luther Lectures, vol. 2. Decorah, Iowa: Luther College Press, 1958.

Reinburg, Virginia. "Liturgy and the Laity in Late Medieval and Reformation France." *Sixteenth Century Journal* 23, no. 3 (1992): 526–547.

Rosin, Robert L. "The Reformation Response to Skepticism: Ecclesiastes Commentaries of Luther, Brenz, and Melanchthon." Ph.D. dissertation, Dept. of History, Stanford Univ., 1985.

Rosin, Wilbert H. "In Response to Bengt Hägglund: The Importance of Epistemology for Luther's and Melanchthon's Theology." *Concordia Theological Quarterly* 44, nos. 2-3 (July 1980): 134-140.

Rubin, Miri. "The Eucharist and the Construction of Medieval Identities." In *Culture and History 1350–1600: Essays on English Communities, Identities and Writing.* Edited by David Aers. Detroit: Wayne State Univ. Press, 1992.

————. *Corpus Christi: The Eucharist in Late Medieval Culture.* Cambridge: Cambridge University Press, 1991.

Sabean, David Warren. *Power in the Blood: Popular Culture and Village Discourse in Early Modern Germany.* Cambridge: Cambridge University Press, 1984.

Sasse, Herman. *This is my body: Luther's Contention for the Real Presence in the Sacrament of the Altar.* Revised edition. Adelaide: Lutheran Publishing House, 1977,

Scribner, Robert W. "Ritual and Popular Religion in Catholic Germany at the Time of the Reformation." *Journal of Ecclesiastical History* 35 (1984): 47-77.

————. *The German Reformation.* Atlantic Highlands, N.J.: Humanities Press International, Inc., 1986.

————. "The Reformation movements in Germany." In *The New Cambridge Modern History.* 2d ed. Vol. 2, edited by G. R. Elton. Cambridge: Cambridge University Press, 1990.

————. *Popular Culture and Popular Movements in Reformation Germany.* London & Ronceverte: The Hambledon Press, 1987.

Seigel, Jerrold. *Rhetoric and Philosophy in Renaissance Humanism.* Princeton: Princeton University Press, 1968.

Seltzer, Amy. "Erasmus, for the Sake of Argument." Ph.D. dissertation, Department of Rhetoric, University of California at Berkeley, 1990.

Spitz, Lewis W. "Humanism and the Protestant Reformation." In *Humanism and the Disciplines.* Vol. 3. of *Renaissance Humanism: Foundations, Forms, and Legacy.* Edited by Albert Rabil, Jr. Philadelphia: University of Pennsylvania Press, 1988.

Stephens, John. *The Italian Renaissance: The Origins of Intellectual and Artistic Change Before the Reformation.* London and New York: Longman, 1990.

Stephens, W. P. *The Theology of Huldrych Zwingli.* Oxford: Clarendon Press, 1986.

Struever, Nancy S. *Theory as Practice: Ethical Inquiry in the Renaissance.* Chicago & London: The University of Chicago Press, 1992.

Swanson, Guy. *Religion and Regime: A Sociological Account of the Reformation.* Ann Arbor: University of Michigan Press, 1967.

Tinkler, John Francis. "Humanism as Discourse: Studies in the Rhetorical Culture of Renaissance Humanism, Petrarch to Bacon." Ph.D. dissertation, Queens University, Kingston, Ontario, Canada, 1983.

Trinkaus, Charles. "Humanism, Religion, Society: Concepts and Motivations of Some Recent Studies." *Renaissance Quarterly* 29, no. 4 (winter 1976): 676-713.

————. *In Our Image and Likeness.* 2 vols. London: Constable & Co., 1970.

————. *The Scope of Renaissance Humanism.* Ann Arbor: University of Michigan Press, 1979.

Verdon, Timothy. "Environments of Experience and Imagination." In *Christianity and the Renaissance*. Edited by Timothy Verdon and John Henderson. Syracuse, N.Y.: Syracuse University Press, 1990.

Wengert, Timothy J. "Caspar Cruciger Sr.'s 1546 'Enarratio' on John's Gospel: An Experiment in Ecclesiological Exegesis." *Church History* 61, no. 1 (March 1992): 60–74.

Wiedenhofer, Siegfried. "Humanismus und Reformation: Zur ökumenischen Bedeutung eines historischen Zusammenhangs." In *Werden und Wirkung der Reformation*. Edited by L. Graf zu Dohna and R. Mokrosch. Darmstadt, 1986.

Witt, Ronald G. "Medieval Italian Culture and the Origins of Humanism as a Stylistic Ideal." In *Humanism in Italy*. Vol. 1 of *Renaissance Humanism: Foundations, Forms, and Legacy*, edited by Albert Rabil, Jr. Philadelphia: University of Pennsylvania Press, 1988.

Zika, Charles. "Hosts, Processions and Pilgrimages: Controlling the Sacred in Fifteenth-Century Germany." *Past and Present* no. 118 (February 1988): 25-64.

2. Philip Melanchthon

Bizer, Ernst. *Theologie der Verheissung: Studien zur Theologie des jungen Melanchthon*. Neukirchen: Verlag der Erziehungsverein, 1964.

Bornkamm, Heinrich. "Melanchthons Menschenbild." In *Philip Melanchthon: Forschungsbeiträge zur vierhundertensten Wiederkehr seines Todestages dargeboten in Wittenberg 1960*. Edited by Walter Elliger. Göttingen: Vandenhoeck & Ruprecht 1961.

Fraenkel, Peter. "Revelation and Tradition: Notes on Some Aspects of Doctrinal Continuity in the Theology of Philip Melanchthon." *Studia Theologica* 13 (1959): 97-113.

————. "Ten Questions Concerning Melanchthon, the Fathers, and the Eucharist." In *Luther and Melanchthon*. Edited by Vilmos Vajta. Philadelphia: Muhlenberg Press, 1961.

Geyer, Hans Georg. *Vom Geburt des wahren Menschen: Probleme aus den Anfängen der Theologie Melanchthons*. Neukirchen: Neukirchener Verlag des Erziehungsvereins GmbH, 1965.

Haendler, Klaus. *Wort und Glaube bei Melanchthon: Eine Untersuchung über die Voraussetzungen und Grundlagen des melanchthonischen Kirchensbegriffes*. Quellen und Forschungen zur Reformationsgeschichte Band 37. Gütersloh: Gütersloher Verlagshaus Gerd Mohn, 1968.

Maurer, Wilhelm. *Der junge Melanchthon zwischen Humanismus und Reformation*. 2 vols. Göttingen: Vandenhoeck and Ruprecht, 1967–1969.

Meerhoff, Kees. "The Significance of Philip Melanchthon's Rhetoric in the Renaissance." In *Renaissance Rhetoric*. Edited by Peter Mack. New York: St. Martin's Press, 1994.

Muhlenberg, Ekkehard. "Humanistisches Bildungsprogramm und reformatorisches Lehre beim jungen Melanchthon." *Zeitschrift für Theologie und Kirche* 65 (1968): 431-444.

Neuser, Wilhelm. *Der Ansatz der Theologie der Philipp Melanchthons*. Neukirchen: Kr. Moers, 1957.

Quere, Ralph W. "Melanchthonian Motifs in the Formula's Eucharistic Christology." In *Discord, Dialogue, and Concord: Studies in the Lutheran Reformation's Formula of Concord*. Edited by Lewis W. Spitz and Wenzel Lohff. Philadelphia: Fortress Press, 1977.

————. *Melanchthon's Christum Cognoscere: Christ's Efficacious Presence in the Eucharistic Theology of Melanchthon*. Nieuwkoop: B. DeGraaf, 1977.

Rogness, Michael. *Philip Melanchthon: Reformer Without Honor*. Minneapolis: Augsburg Publishing House, 1969.

Rupp, E. Gordon. "Philip Melanchthon and Martin Bucer." In *A History of Christian Doctrine: In Succession to the Earlier Work of G. P. Fisher*. Edited by Hubert Cunliffe-Jones. Philadelphia: Fortress Press, 1980.

Schäfer, Rolf. "Melanchthons Hermeneutik im Römerbrief Kommentar von 1532." *Zeitschrift für Theologie und Kirche* 60 (1963): 216-235.

————. *Christologie und Sittlichkeit im Melanchthons frühen Loci*. Beiträge zur historischen Theologie 29. Tübingen, 1961.

Schneider, John R. *Philip Melanchthon's Rhetorical Construal of Biblical Authority: Oratio Sacra*. Texts and Studies in Religion, vol. 51 Lewiston, N.Y.: The Edwin Mellen Press,1990.

Schnell, Uwe. *Die homiletische Theorie Philipp Melanchthons*. Arbeiten zur Geschichte und Theologie des Luthertums 20. Berlin: Lutherisches Verlaghaus, 1968.

Shuger, Debora K. "Morris Croll, Flacius Illyricus, and the Origin of Anti-Ciceronianism." *Rhetorica* 3, no. 3 (summer 1985): 269-284.

Sick, Hansjörg. *Melanchthon als Ausleger des Alten Testament*. Tübingen: J. C. B. Mohr, 1959.

Stupperich, Robert. *Melanchthon*. Translated by Robert H. Fischer. Philadelphia: The Westminster Press, 1965.

Wengert, Timothy J. *Philip Melanchthon's Annotationes in Johannem in Relation to its Predecessors and Contemporaries*. Geneve: Librairie Droz, S.A., 1987.

Wiedenhofer, Siegfried. *Formalstrukturen humanistischer und reformatorischer Theologie bei Philipp Melanchthon*. 2 vols. Bern: Herbert Lang and Frankfurt am Main und München: Peter Lang, 1976.

D. RHETORIC

Aristotle. *On Rhetoric: A Theory of Civic Discourse.* Translated by George A. Kennedy. New York: Oxford University Press, 1991.

Barilli, Renato. *Rhetoric.* Translated by Giulana Menozzi. Minneapolis: Univ. of Minnesota Press, 1989.

Bizzell, Patricia and Bruce Harzberg, eds. *The Rhetorical Tradition: Readings from Classical Times to the Present.* Boston: Bedford Books of St. Martin's Press, 1990.

Carter, Michael F. "The Ritual Functions of Epideictic Rhetoric: The Case of Socrates' Funeral Oration." *Rhetorica* 9, no. 3 (summer 1991): 209-232.

Condit, Celeste Michelle. "The Functions of Epideictic: The Boston Massacre Orations as Exemplar." *Communication Quarterly* 33 (1985): 284-298.

Dockhorn, Klaus. "*Rhetorica movet:* Protestantischer Humanismus und karolingische Renaissance." In *Rhetorik: Beiträge zu ihrer Geschichte in Deutschland vom 16.-20. Jahrhundert.* Edited by Helmut Schanze. Frankfurt: Athenaion, 1974.

Henderson, Judith Rice. "Erasmian Ciceronians: Reformation Teachers of Letter Writing." *Rhetorica* 10, no. 3 (summer 1992): 273–302.

Hyde, Michael J. "Emotion and Communication: A Rhetorical, Scientific, and Philosophical Picture." *Communication Quarterly* 32, no. 2 (spring 1984): 120-132.

————. "Existentialism as a Basis for the Theory and Practice of Rhetoric." In *Rhetoric and Philosophy.* Edited by Richard A. Cherwitz. Hillsdale, N.J.: Lawrence Erlbaum Associates, Publishers, 1990.

Kennedy, George A. *Classical Rhetoric and Its Christian and Secular Tradition from Ancient to Modern Times.* Chapel Hill, N.C.: University of North Carolina Press, 1980.

————. *The Art of Persuasion in Greece.* Princeton: Princeton University Press, 1963.

McGinness, Frederick John. "Rhetoric and Counter-Reformation Rome: Sacred Oratory and the Construction of the Catholic World View, 1563-1621." Ph.D. dissertation, Department of History, University of California, Berkeley, 1982.

Meador, Prentice A.. "Quintilian and the *Institutio oratorica.*" In *A Synoptic History of Classical Rhetoric,* 151–176. Edited by James J. Murphy. Davis, Calif.: Hermagoras Press, 1983.

Mühlen, Karl-Heinz zur, "Rhetorik in Predigten und Schriften Luthers." *Luther Jahrbuch* 57 (1990): 257-259.

Murphy, James J. "One Thousand Neglected Authors: The Scope and Importance of Renaissance Rhetoric." In *Renaissance Eloquence: Studies in the Theory and Practice of Renaissance Rhetoric.* Edited by James J. Murphy. Berkeley: University of California Press, 1983.

Murphy, James J., compiler. *Renaissance Rhetoric: A Short-Title Catalog of Works on Rhetorical Theory from the Beginning of Printing to A.D. 1700.* New York & London: Garland Publishing Company, 1981.

Murphy, James J., ed. *Renaissance Eloquence: Studies in the Theory and Practice of Renaissance Rhetoric.* Berkeley: University of Calfornina Press, 1983.

O'Malley, John W. "Content and Form in Sixteenth-Century Treatises on Preaching." In *Renaissance Eloquence: Studies in the Theory and Practice of Renaissance Rhetoric.* Edited by James J. Murphy. Berkeley: University of California Press, 1983.

―――. *Praise and Blame in Renaissance Rome: Rhetoric, Doctrine, and Reform in the Sacred Orators of the Papal Court, c. 1450-1521.* Durham, N.C.: Duke University Press, 1979.

Plett, Heinrich. *Rhetorik der Affekte.* Tubingen: Max Niemeyer Verlag, 1975.

Quintilian. *Institutio oratorica.* Translated by H. E. Butler. Loeb Classical Library. Cambridge: Harvard University Press, 1960.

Schrag, Calvin O. *Communicative Praxis and the Space of Subjectivity.* Bloomington, Ind.: Indiana University Press, 1986.

Shuger, Debora K. "The Christian Grand Style in Renaissance Rhetoric." *Viator* 16 (1985): 351–352.

―――. *Sacred Rhetoric: The Christian Grand Style in the English Renaissance.* Princeton: Princeton University Press, 1988.

Sloane, Thomas O. *Donne, Milton and the End of Humanist Rhetoric.* Berkeley: University of California Press, 1985.

Vickers, Brian. *In Defence of Rhetoric.* Oxford: Clarendon Press, 1988.

―――. "The recovery of rhetoric: Petrarch, Erasmus, Perelman." *History of the Human Sciences* 3, no. 3 (October 1990): 415-441.

Waswo, Richard. *Language and Meaning in the Renaissance.* Princeton: Princeton Univ. Press, 1987.

E. RITUAL

Bell, Catherine. "The Authority of Ritual Experts." *Studia Liturgica* 23, no. 1 (1993): 98-120.

―――. "The Ritual Body and the Dynamics of Ritual Power." *Journal of Ritual Studies* 4, no. 2 (summer 1990): 299-313.

―――. *Ritual Theory, Ritual Practice.* Oxford: Oxford University Press, 1992.

Clothey, Fred. *Rhythm and Intent: Ritual Studies from South India.* Bombay: Blackie and Son, 1983.

Eilberg-Schwartz, Howard. Paper presented to the Ritual Studies Group, American Academy of Religion Annual Meeting, San Francisco, 22 November 1992.

Finn, Thomas M. "It Happened One Saturday Night: Ritual and Conversion in Augustine's North Africa." *Journal of the American Academy of Religion* 58, no. 4 (winter 1990): 589-616.

Gay, Volney. "Ritual and Self-Esteem in Victor Turner and Heinz Kohut." *Zygon* 18 (1983): 271-282.

Grimes, Ronald L. *Ritual Criticism: Case Studies in Its Practice, Essays on Its Theory.* Columbia, S.C.: University of South Carolina Press, 1990.

Hanson, F. Allan. "The semiotics of ritual." *Semiotica* 33-1/2 (1981), 169-178.

Holdredge, Barbara. "Introduction: Towards a Phenomenology of Power." *Journal of Ritual Studies* 4, no. 2 (summer 1990): 5-37.

Jennings, Theodore W. "On Ritual Knowledge." *Journal of Religion* 62 (1982): 111-127.

Kelly, John D., and Martha Kaplan. "History, Structure, and Ritual." *Annual Review of Anthropology* 19 (1990): 119-150.

Myerhoff, Barbara G., Camino, Linda A. and Turner, Edith. "Rites of Passage." In *Encyclopedia of Religion*, edited by Mircea Eliade. Vol. 12. New York: Macmillan, 1987.

————. "The transformation of consciousness in ritual performances: some thoughts and questions." In *By means of performance: Intercultural studies of theatre and ritual.* Edited by Richard Schechner and Willa Appel. Cambridge: Cambridge University Press, 1990.

Parks, Sharon Daloz. "Communication, Ritual as." In *The New Dictionary of Sacramental Worship.* Edited by Peter E. Fink, S.J. Collegeville, Minn.: The Liturgical Press, 1991.

Slough, Rebecca J. "These Songs Are the Life We Live: A Discussion of Ritual, Knowledge, and Knowing." Paper presented to the Graduate Theological Union Interdisciplinary Workshop on Ritual Theory. Berkeley, Calif., spring 1990.

Smith, Jonathan Z. *To Take Place: Toward Theory in Ritual.* Chicago: University of Chicago Press, 1987.

Turner, Victor. *The Ritual Process: Structure and Anti-structure.* Aldine: Chicago, 1969. Reprint, Ithaca, N.Y.: Cornell University Press, 1977.

Wilson, Monica. "Nyakyusa Ritual and Symbolism." *American Anthropologist* 56 (1954): 228-241.

Zuesse, Evan. "Ritual." In *Encyclopedia of Religion*, edited by Mircea Eliade. Vol. 12. New York: Macmillan, 1987.

F. LITURGICAL STUDIES

Aune, Michael B. "Issues in Contemporary Lutheran Worship Theory and Practice." In *WorshipTextbook.* Edited by Patrick J. Keifert. St. Paul: Luther Northwestern Theological Seminary, 1985.

Baldovin, John F. "Christian Worship to the Eve of the Reformation." In *The Making of Jewish and Christian Worship*. Vol 1, *Two Liturgical Traditions*, ed. Paul F. Bradshaw and Lawrence A. Hoffman. Notre Dame, Ind.: Univ. of Notre Dame Press, 1991.

Bishop, Edmund. "The Genius of the Roman Rite." In *Liturgica Historia*. Oxford: Clarendon Press, 1962.

Crockett, William R. *Eucharist: Symbol of Transformation*. New York: Pueblo Publishing Company, 1989.

Harper, John. *The Forms and Orders of Western Liturgy from the Tenth to the Eighteenth Century*. Oxford: Clarendon Press, 1991.

Heron, Alasdair I. C. *Table and Tradition: Toward an Ecumenical Understanding of the Eucharist*. Philadelphia: The Westminster Press, 1983.

Mitchell, Nathan. *Cult and Controversy: The Worship of the Eucharist Outside of Mass*. New York: Pueblo, 1982.

Pratzner, Ferdinand. *Messe und Kreuzeopfer: Die Krise der sakramentalen Idee bei Luther und in der mittelalterischen Scholastik*. Wien: Herder, 1970.

Taft, Robert F. "The Liturgy of the Great Church: An Initial Synthesis of Structure and Interpretation on the Eve of Iconoclasm." *Dumbarton Oaks Papers 34–35* (1980-1981): 45-75.

Theisen, Reinhold, O.S.B. *Mass Liturgy and the Council of Trent*. Collegeville, Minn.: The Liturgical Press, 1965.

Underhill, Evelyn. *Worship*. New York: Harper, 1936.

Wainwright, Geoffrey. *Doxology: The Praise of God in Worship, Doctrine, and Life*. New York: Oxford University Press, 1980.

Wegman, Herman. *Christian Worship in East and West: A Study Guide to Liturgical History*. Translated by Gordon W. Lathrop. New York: Pueblo Publishing Co., 1985.

Weil, Louis. "Facilitating Growth in Faith Through Liturgical Worship." In *Handbook of Faith*. Edited by James Michael Lee. Birmingham, Ala.: Religious Education Press, 1990.

White, James F. *Protestant Worship: Traditions in Transition*. Louisville: Westminister/John Knox Press, 1989.

White, Susan J. "Christian Worship Since the Reformation." In *The Making of Jewish and Christian Worship*. Vol. 1, *Two Liturgical Traditions*, ed. Paul F. Bradshaw and Lawrence A. Hoffman. Notre Dame, Ind.: University of Notre Dame Press, 1991.

G. CULTURAL AND ANTHROPOLOGICAL STUDIES

Abu-Lughod, Lila and Catherine Lutz. "Introduction: emotion, discourse, and the politics of everyday life." In *Language and the politics of emotion*. Edited by

Catherine A. Lutz & Lila Abu-Lughod. Cambridge: Cambridge University Press, 1990.

Bercovitch, Sacvan. *The Puritan Origins of the American Self.* New Haven: Yale University Press, 1975.

Burke, Peter. "Historians, Anthropologists, and Symbols." *Culture Through Time: Anthropological Approaches.* Edited by Emiko Ohnuki-Tierney. Stanford: Stanford University Press, 1990.

Comaroff, Jean, and John Comaroff. Introduction to *Modernity and Its Malcontents: Ritual and Power in Postcolonial Africa.* Edited by Jean Comaroff and John Comaroff. Chicago: University of Chicago Press, 1993.

D'Andrade, Roy G. "Cultural meaning systems." In *Culture Theory: Essays on Mind, Self, and Emotion.* Edited by Richard A. Shweder and Robert A. LeVine. Cambridge: Cambridge University Press, 1984.

———. "The cultural part of cognition." *Cognitive Science* 5 (1981): 179-195.

Edwards, Michael. "Not I." *Comparative Criticism: An Annual Journal. Representations of the Self* 12 (1990): 25–38.

Ferry, Anne. *The "Inward" Language: Sonnets of Wyatt, Sidney, Shakespeare, Donne.* Chicago: University of Chicago Press, 1983.

Geertz, Clifford. "'From the Native's Point of View': On the Nature of Anthropological Understanding." In *Local Knowledge: Further Essays in Interpretive Anthropology.* New York: Basic Books, 1983.

Handelman, Don. *Models and Mirrors: Towards an anthropology of public events.* Cambridge: Cambridge University Press, 1990.

Irvine, Judith. "Language and affect: some cross-cultural issues." In *Contemporary Perceptions of Language: Interdisciplinary Dimensions, Georgetown University Round Table on Languages and Linguistics 1982.* Edited by Heidi Byrnes. Washington: Georgetown University Press, 1982.

Levy, Robert. "Emotion, knowing, and culture." In *Culture Theory: Essays on Mind, Self, and Emotion.* Edited by Richard A. Shweder and Robert A. LeVine. Cambridge: Cambridge University Press, 1984.

———. "Introduction: Self and Emotion." *Ethos* 11, no. 3 (1983): 128-134.

Lutz, Catherine, and Geoffrey M. White."The Anthropology of Emotions." *Annual Review of Anthropology* 15 (1986): 405-436.

Marcus, George E. and Fischer, Michael M. J. *Anthropology as Cultural Critique: An Experimental Moment in the Human Sciences.* Chicago: University of Chicago Press, 1986.

Nissenbaum, Helen Fay. *Emotion and Focus.* Stanford, Calif.: Center for the Study of Language and Information, 1985.

Ortner, Sherry B. "Cultural Politics: Religious Activism and Ideological Transformation Among 20th-Century Sherpas." *Dialectical Anthropology* 14 (1989): 197–211.

————. "Theory in Anthropology since the Sixties." *Comparative Studies in Society and History* 26 (1984): 126-165.

Rosaldo, Michelle Z. "Toward An Anthropology of Self and Feeling." In *Culture Theory: Essays on Mind, Self, and Emotion*. Edited by Richard A. Shweder and Robert A. LeVine. Cambridge: Cambridge University Press, 1984.

————. *Knowledge and Passion: Ilongot Notions of Self and Social Life*. Cambridge Studies in Cultural Systems. Cambridge: Cambridge University Press, 1980.

Rosaldo, Renato. *Culture and Truth: Explorations in Social Analysis*. Boston: Beacon Press, 1989.

Scheper-Hughes, Nancy and Lock, Margaret. "The Mindful Body: A Prolegomenon to Future Work in Medical Anthropology." *Medical Anthropology Quarterly* 1 (1987): 6-41.

Solomon, Robert C. *The Passions: The Myth and Nature of Human Emotion*. Anchor Press/Doubleday, 1976. Reprint, Notre Dame, Ind.: University of Notre Dame Press, 1983.

Stromberg, Peter. *Symbols of Community: The Cultural System of a Swedish Church*. Tucson: University of Arizona Press, 1986.

————. *Language and self-transformation: A study of the Christian conversion narrative*. Cambridge: Cambridge Univ. Press, 1993.

Taylor, Charles. *Sources of the Self: The Making of the Modern Identity*. Cambridge: Harvard University Press, 1989.

Tyler, Stephen. *The Unspeakable: Discourse, Dialogue, and Rhetoric in the Postmodern World*. The Rhetoric of the Human Sciences. Madison: University of Wisconsin Press, 1987.

Uberoi, J. P. S. *Science and Culture*. Delhi, 1978.

Winn, James Anderson. *Unsuspected Eloquence: A History of the Relations between Poetry and Music*. New Haven & London: Yale Univ. Press, 1981.

H. THEOLOGICAL STUDIES

Dulles, Avery. "The Symbolic Structure of Revelation." *Theological Studies* 41, no. 1 (March 1980): 51-73.

Forde, Gerhard. *Theology is for Proclamation*. Minneapolis: Fortress Press, 1990.

Goeser, Robert J. "Whither Lutheranism?" *Lutheran Quarterly*, new series, 1, no. 1 (spring 1987): 40-53.

Gritsch, Eric W. and Jenson, Robert W. *Lutheranism: The Theological Movement and Its Confessional Writings*. Philadelphia: Fortress Press, 1976.

Hackett, Charles D. "Psychoanalysis and Theology: Two Dialectics." *Journal of Religion and Health*, 25, no. 1 (spring 1986): 29-31.

Hall, Douglas John. *Thinking the Faith*. Minneapolis: Augsburg Publishing House, 1989.

Harrisville, Roy A. "Texts in Context: God's Yes (2 Corinthians 1.20)." *Word and World* 11, no. 3 (summer 1991): 321–324.

Hobbs, Edward C. "Recognition of Conceptuality as a Hermeneutical Tool." In *Texte und Untersuchungen zur Geschichte der altchristlichen Literatur*, Band 88. Edited by F. L. Cross. Berlin: Akademie-Verlag, 1964.

Preus, James S. "Neglected Problems in the Eucharistic Dialogue." *Currents in Theology and Mission* 3 (1976): 279-287.

Root, Michael. "The Narrative Structure of Soteriology." *Modern Theology* 2, no. 2 (January 1986): 145-146.

Scroggs, Robin. "The Heuristic Value of a Psychoanalytic Model in the Interpretation of Pauline Theology." *Zygon* 13, no. 2 (June 1978): 136-155.

Sedgwick, Timothy. "The Import of Foucault for Understanding Christian Faith." *St. Luke's Journal of Theology* 34, no. 2 (March 1991): 75–89.

INDEX

Jane Gardam is the only writer to have been twice awarded the Whitbread/Costa Prize for Best Novel of the Year, for *The Queen of the Tambourine* and *The Hollow Land*. She also holds a Heywood Hill Literary Prize for a lifetime's contribution to the enjoyment of literature. She is the author of five volumes of acclaimed stories: *Black Faces, White Faces* (David Higham Prize and the Royal Society for Literature's Winifred Holtby Prize); *The Pangs of Love* (Katherine Mansfield Prize); *Going into a Dark House* (Silver Pen Award from PEN); *Missing the Midnight*; and *The People on Privilege Hill*. Her novels include *God on the Rocks*, which was shortlisted for the Booker Prize; *Faith Fox*; *The Flight of the Maidens*; the bestselling *Old Filth*, which was shortlisted for the Orange Prize in 2005; *The Man in the Wooden Hat*; and *Last Friends*. Jane Gardam was born in Yorkshire. She now lives in east Kent.

'What a lot Jane Gardam knows about love and its accommodations; the rich contradictory play of desire and loyalty, the sudden storms of feeling that assail the edifice of a marriage. And how elegantly and intelligently and kindly she writes about the instinctive, tendril-like gropings of one human heart towards another' Jane Shilling, *Telegraph*

Praise for *Old Filth*

'Told with compassion and great style. Gardam seems to get better as she gets older' John Humphrys, *New Statesman*, Books of the Year

'Superb ... quiet beauty, sly wit and heartbreaking humanity ... the author has poignantly distilled a life less ordinary into 259 unforgettable pages' *Sunday Times*

'Gardam pulls off the near-impossible trick of great emotional depth delivered with wingtip lightness. Her characters are drawn with rich humour, and Old Filth himself is a marvellous, moving creation whose company you find yourself sad to leave'
Telegraph

'The really outstanding work of fiction I've read this year, predictably neglected by the Booker judges, is Jane Gardam's *Old Filth*. A Rembrandt portrait of a lawyer from birth to death, it shuttles between east and west, love and heartbreak, murder and pity, repaying patience with luminous wisdom'
Amanda Craig, *New Statesman*, Books of the Year

'This life story of Sir Edward Feathers QC sparkles with Gardam's wit, sensibility and poignancy and it deservedly earned an Orange Prize nomination ... a fictional life of absorbing, emotional sophistication about memory, loss and the vestiges of empire. It is a beautiful, melancholy novel which captivates, saddens and delights'
Observer

'Gardam, always the supreme novelist of young girls, also does old age brilliantly and proves that she can penetrate the male psyche convincingly too. She is on top form here: words come at you from startling angles; time shifts and shunts. It's the view from the crow's nest of old age: the distant past is more real than yesterday and insights intrude violently on the old routines'
Guardian

'Excellently observed and quietly moving ... Gardam invents an apparently composed character, and then disassembles him into pieces which – on closer inspection – look jagged and in poor repair'
Independent on Sunday

OLD FILTH

JANE GARDAM

ABACUS

To Raj Orphans and their parents

ABACUS

First published in Great Britain in 2004 by Chatto & Windus
First published in paperback by Abacus in 2005
Reissued in 2014 by Abacus

9 10 8

Copyright © Jane Gardam 2004
Introduction copyright © Jane Gardam 2013

The moral right of the author has been asserted.

A CIP catalogue record for this book
is available from the British Library.

ISBN 978-0-349-13949-4

Printed and bound in Great Britain by
Clays Ltd, St Ives plc

Papers used by Abacus are from well-managed forests
and other responsible sources.

MIX
Paper from
responsible sources
FSC® C104740

Abacus
An imprint of
Little, Brown Book Group
Carmelite House
50 Victoria Embankment
London EC4Y 0DZ

An Hachette UK Company
www.hachette.co.uk

www.littlebrown.co.uk

Contents

Lawyers, I suppose, were
children once

(Inscription upon the statue of a child
in the inner Temple Garden in London)

Introduction

I was on the first list of Abacus authors forty years ago, in 1973, and like the other five, I have never strayed. Sadly, the others are now dead and indeed I might well have stopped writing by now too. This, however, didn't happen because in 2002 I was telephoned by Richard Ingrams, Editor of *The Oldie*, and asked to write a short story for the Christmas edition of the paper.

I said I hadn't any ideas. He said, 'Oh, come on, you can write one on your head.' This so flattered me that I sat down and wrote a story about two old gentlemen lawyers, life-long enemies who became reconciled in a snow-storm in Dorset one Christmas Eve. The reconciliation is the more unlikely and delicate because the dead wife of one of the old gentleman (Sir Edward Feathers) had for years been in love with the other (Sir Terence Veneering) – or so it had always been said.

The novel that emerged from the story was *Old Filth*. It was a title my hardback publisher deplored but I hung on to it and my editor at Abacus, Richard Beswick, liked it – Filth is an acronym, well known in the Orient where the two lawyers were celebrated advocates and became judges, and stands for Failed In London Try Hong Kong. It is a joke some two hundred years old and is inaccurate, for it is hard for anyone who is a failure to survive in Hong Kong. The notion upset a certain number of members of The Inns of Court in London, but enchanted others, who took *Old Filth* to their hearts and so two years later I wrote a sequel, *The Man in the Wooden Hat*, telling the same story of Old Filth but from his wife's point of view. Now I am finishing the third in this trilogy, *Last Friends*, about the same set of characters, retired now to Dorset and grown old in what looks to the world like peace and harmony. But age does not often bring these things, even to the rich and admired and supremely self-confident. To the end they – we – have hidden lives. Particularly, there are always hidden childhoods. 'Keep the child in view', wrote Dickens in a note on the manuscript of *The Old Curiosity Shop* when he thought he was losing sight of Little Nell.

There have been many enquiries about the identity of Old Filth. All I can tell you is that he once passed me in the street. It was rather like the extraordinary vision the Baroness Orczy had over a century ago when she encountered The Scarlet Pimpernel. She was standing on the platform of a London tube station, looking into the tunnel where the next train would in a minute arrive, and as she stood waiting, an urbane figure emerged, walking elegantly along the track. He was not of the present day, perfectly dressed, proceeding with panache, good-looks and pride. 'The damned, illusive pimpernel.' The books followed in a spate.

I had not heard this story when I first encountered Old Filth. I was walking along Piccadilly on the south side, thinking of nothing much, when a tall old man stepped in front of me from the glass doors of The Ritz Hotel. He passed through the arches, looked carefully left and right and stepped intrepidly out across the road, disappearing up Dover Street past Elizabeth Frink's bronze horse. He was wearing a frock coat, pale yellow silk socks, black polished shoes and kid gloves. He carried a black furled umbrella and his fine old face was thoughtful; even rather beautiful. He seemed oblivious of the mob of many colours and conditions around him. He had what is called 'a military moustache' but he was not a soldier for he carried an expensive though weathered briefcase, heavy with papers, the baggage of a lawyer. I knew this because I was married to a lawyer though he was not like this one, being tempestuously untidy and taken up with the Arts. This one must have been a senior judge, though the senior judges I had met were not really like this one either. They were paler and tireder. This one was like an illustration from an Edwardian novel. Or one's granny's photograph album. I looked around for the film crew.

'I saw a ghost today,' I told my husband as he peeled potatoes for supper, and described him.

'Was he wearing black shoes?'

'Yes.'

'Was he wearing a hat?'

'No.'

'Then he wasn't a ghost. He's still about. Some dotty eccentric. You'll see him again. Probably has tea at the Ritz every day. Probably American.' I have never seen him again but I continue to write about him: his childhood as an orphan of the Raj, his near-breakdown in an evil, fostered childhood, his salvation through a marvellous school master and first friend: his adventures at sea during the war, his struggle – made harder by a stammer – to become an advocate and, in particular, his love for his wife. And perhaps for another woman, too.

At a party given in London over twenty years ago I met the poet Stevie Smith who asked me who I was.

'A Wimbledon housewife,' I said 'who writes novels.'

'But,' said Stevie Smith 'Who are you *really*?' and she peered up at me, bent double under a shawl through wisps of grey hair. Who was – is – Sir Edward Feathers 'really'? *Last Friends* begins with his memorial service in the Temple Church where everyone is praising a transparently splendid man. Yet somehow not always the same one. Even in death Old Filth is a master of disguise.

Jane Gardam
Kent, April, 2013

PART ONE

Scene: Inner Temple

The Benchers' luncheon-room of the Inner Temple. Light pours through the long windows upon polished table, silver, glass. A number of Judges and Benchers finishing lunch. One chair has recently been vacated and the Benchers are looking at it.

The Queen's Remembrancer: I suppose we all know who that was?

Junior Judge: I've no idea.

Senior Judge: It seemed to be a famous face.

The Common Sergeant: It was Old Filth.

JJ: *What*! But he must have died years ago. Contemporary of F.E. Smith.

CS: No. It was Old Filth. Great advocate, Judge and – bit of a wit. Said to have invented FILTH – Failed In London Try Hong Kong. He tried Hong Kong. Modest, nice chap.

SJ: Hard worker. Well – the Pollution Law. Feathers on Pollution.

CS: Filth on Filth.

SJ: An old joke. He must be a hundred.

CS: Nowhere near. He's not been retired all that long. Looks a great age, though.

QR: Transparent. You could see the light through him.

CS: Magnificent looks, though. And still sharp.

QR: He's up here doing things to his Will. He's got Betty with him. She's still alive too. They've had a soft life.

Far Eastern Bar. And made a packet. Looked after themselves.

CS: Never put a foot wrong, Old Filth. Very popular.

QR: Except with Veneering.

SJ: Yes, that was odd. Out of character.

QR: For such a benevolent old bugger. D'you think there are mysteries?

SJ: Old Filth mysterious?

QR: It's a wonder he's not just a bore.

CS: Yes. But he's not. Child of the Raj, public school, Oxford, the Bar – but he's not a bore. Women went mad for him.

QR: Coffee? You going through?

CS: Yes. Ten minutes. My Clerk's packing in the next case. He'll be ranting at me. Tapping his watch.

QR: Yes. This isn't Hong Kong. Coffee? But it was good to see the old coelacanth.

CS: Yes. Yes, indeed it was. Tell our grandchildren.

The Donheads

He was spectacularly clean. You might say ostentatiously clean. His ancient fingernails were rimmed with purest white. The few still-gold hairs below his knuckles looked always freshly shampooed, as did his curly still-bronze hair. His shoes shone like conkers. His clothes were always freshly pressed. He had the elegance of the 1920s, for his garments, whatever they looked like off, always became him. Always a Victorian silk handkerchief in the breast pocket. Always yellow cotton or silk socks from Harrods; and some still-perfect from his old days in the East. His skin was clear and, in a poor light, young.

His colleagues at the Bar called him Filth, but not out of irony. It was because he was considered to be the source of the old joke, Failed In London Try Hong Kong. It was said that he had fled the London Bar, very young, very poor, on a sudden whim just after the War, and had done magnificently well in Hong Kong from the start. Being a modest man, they said, he had called himself a parvenu, a fraud, a carefree spirit.

Filth in fact was no great maker of jokes, was not at all modest about his work and seldom, except in great extremity, went in for whims. He was loved, however, admired, laughed at kindly and still much discussed many years after retirement.

Now, nearing eighty, he lived alone in Dorset. His wife Betty was dead but he often prattled on to her around the house. Astonishingly in one so old, his curly hair was not yet grey. His eyes and mind alert, he was a delightful man. He had always been thought so. A man whose distinguished life had run steadily and happily. There was no smell of old age about his house. He was rich and took for granted that it (and he) would be kept clean, fed and laundered by servants as it had always been. He knew how to treat servants and they stayed for years.

Betty had been successful with servants, too. Both she and Old Filth had been born in what Americans called the Orient and the British Raj had called the Far East. They knew who they were, but they were unselfconscious and popular.

After Betty's death the self-mockery dwindled in Old Filth. His life exploded. He became more ponderous. He began, at first slowly, to flick open shutters on the past that he had, as a sensible man with sensible and learned friends (he was a QC and had been a Judge), kept clamped down.

His success as an advocate in Hong Kong had been phenomenal for he had had ease, grasp, diligence and flair. His career had taken off the minute he had begun to be briefed by the Straits-Chinese. It was not just that scraps of eastern languages began to re-emerge from his childhood in Malaya, but a feeling of nearness to the Oriental mind. When Old Filth spoke Malay or (less ably) Mandarin, you heard an unsuspected voice. Chinese, Malay and Bengali lawyers – though often trained at Oxford and the Inns of Court – were thought to be not straightforward but Filth, now Old Filth and after his retirement often Dear Old Filth, had found them perfectly straightforward, and to his taste.

All his life he kept a regard for Chinese values: the courtesy, the sudden thrust, the holiness of hospitality, the pleasure in money, the decorum, the importance of food, the discretion, the cleverness. He had married a Scotswoman but she had been born in Peking. She was dumpy and tweedy with broad Lanarkshire shoulders and square hands, but she spoke Mandarin perfectly and was much more at home with Chinese ways and idiom than she ever felt on her very rare visits to Scotland. Her passion for jewellery was Chinese and her strong Scottish fingers rattled the trays of jade in the street markets of Kowloon, stirring the stones like pebbles on a beach. 'When you do that,' Old Filth would say – when they

6

were young and he was still aware of her all the time – 'your eyes are almond-shaped.' 'Poor Old Betty,' he would say to her ghost across in another armchair in the house in Dorset to which they had retired and in which she had died.

And why ever Dorset? Nobody knew. Some family tradition somewhere perhaps. Filth said it was because he disliked everywhere else in England, Betty because she felt the cold in Scotland. They both had a dismissive attitude towards Wales.

But if any old pair had been born to become retired ex-pats in Hong Kong, members of the Cricket Club, the Jockey Club, stalwarts of the English Lending Library, props of St Andrew's Church and St John's Cathedral, they were Filth and Betty. People who would always be able to keep servants (Filth was very rich), who would live in a house on The Peak, be forever welcoming hosts to every friend of a friend's friend visiting the Colony. When you thought of Betty, you saw her at her round rosewood dining table, looking quickly about her to see if plates were empty, tinkling her little bell to summon the snakey smiling girls in their household livery of identical cheongsams. Old Filth and Betty were perfectly international people, beloved ornaments at every one of the Memorial Services to old friends, English or Chinese, in the Cathedral. In the last years these deaths had been falling thick and fast upon them.

Was it perhaps 'The Pound' that drew them to Dorset? The thought of having to survive one day in Hong Kong on a pension? But the part of Dorset they had chosen was far from cheap. Betty was known to 'have her own money' and Filth had always said merrily that he had put off making Judge for as long as possible so that he hadn't to live on a salary.

And they had no children. No responsibilities. No one to come back to England for.

Or was it – the most likely thing – the end of Empire? The drawing-near of 1997? Was it the unbearableness of the thought of the arrival of the barbarians? The now unknown, but certainly changed, Mainland-Chinese whose grandparents had fed the baby Miss Betty on soft, cloudy jellies and told her frightening fairy tales?

Neither Filth nor Betty cared for the unknown and already, five years before they left, English was not being heard so much in Hong Kong shops and hotels and, when it was heard, it was being spoken less well. Many familiar English and Chinese had disappeared to London or Seattle or Toronto, and many children had vanished to foreign boarding schools. The finest of the big houses on The Peak were in darkness behind steel grilles, and at Betty's favourite jeweller the little girls behind the counter, who sat all day threading beads and who still seemed to look under sixteen although she had known them twenty years, glanced up more slowly now when she rang the bell on the armour-plated door. They kept their fixed smiles but somehow found fewer good stones for her. Chinese women she knew had not the same difficulty.

So suddenly Filth and Betty were gone, gone for ever from the sky-high curtains of glittering lights, unflickering gold, soft-green and rose, from the busy waters of the finest harbour in the world and the perpetual drama of every sort of boat: the junks and oil tankers and the private yachts like swans, and the comforting, bottle-green bulk of the little Star Ferries that chugged back and forth to Kowloon all day and most of the night. *This deck accommodates 319 passengers.* Filth had loved the certainty of the *19*.

So they were gone, far from friends and over seventy, to a house deep in the Donheads on the Dorset-Wiltshire border, an old low stone house that could not be seen from its gate. A rough, narrow drive climbed up to it, curving towards it and out of sight. The house sat on a small plateau looking down over forests of every sort and colour of English tree, and far across the horizon was a long scalpel line of milky, chalky downland, dappled with shadows drawn across it by the clouds. No place in the world is less like Hong Kong or the Far East.

Yet it was not so remote that a doctor might start suggesting in a few years' time that it might be kinder to the Social Services if they were to move nearer to civilisation. There was a village half a mile up the hilly road that passed their gate, and half a mile in the other direction, also up a hill for their drive ran down into a dip, were a church and a shop. There were other houses among the trees. There was even a house next door, its gateway alongside theirs, its drive curving upwards as did their own, though branching away. It disappeared, as did their own. So they were secluded but not cut off.

And it worked. They made it work. Betty was the sort of woman who had plotted that the end of her life would work, and Filth, having Betty, had no fears of failure. They changed of course. They discarded much. They went out and about very little. Betty wrote a great many letters. They put their hearts into becoming content, safe in their successful lives. Filth had always said – of his Cases – 'I am trained to forget.' 'Otherwise,' he said, 'how could I function?' Facts, memories, the pain of life – of lives in chaos – have to be forgotten. Filth had condemned men to death. Had seen innocent men convicted. As a Silk he reckoned that fifty per cent of his Cases had gone wrong. In Hong Kong the Judges lived in an enclave of palaces but behind steel gates guarded night and day.

In The Donheads they felt safe behind the lock of their old-fashioned farmhouse door that could never accidentally be left on the latch. Betty gardened, Filth read thrillers and biographies, worked now and then in his tool shed. He kept his Judge's wig in its oval black-and-gold tin box on the hearth, like a grey cat in a basket. Then in time, as there was nobody but Betty to be amused, he moved it to his wardrobe to lie with his black silk stockings and buckled shoes. He had not brought the Black Cap home.

Betty sat sewing. She often stared for hours at the trees. They went to the supermarket in Shaftesbury once a week in their modest car. A gardener came to do the heavy digging and a woman from a nearby village came in four times a week to clean, cook and do the laundry. Betty said that Hong Kong's legacy was to make foreigners unable to do their own washing. After Betty died, the gardener and the woman continued to work for Filth. Filth's lifetime of disciplined charm survived well.

Or so it seemed. Looking back, Filth knew that beneath his apparent serenity the years after Betty's departure had been a time of mental breakdown and that mental breakdown in someone conditioned to an actor's life (which is the Bar) can be invisible both to the sufferer and everyone else.

And this – the event he came to see as the beginning of enlightenment – occurred one Christmas, two years on. The cleaning lady started it.

Letting herself in with her door-key, talking as usual before she was over the threshold, '*Well*,' she said. 'What about this then, Sir Edward? You never hear a thing down this way till it's happened. Next door must have moved. Your next door. There's removal vans all up and down the drive and loads of new stuff being carried in. They say it's another lawyer from Singapore like you.'

'Hong Kong,' corrected Filth, as he always did.

'Hong Kong then. They'll be wanting a domestic I dare say, but they're out of luck. I'm well-suited here, you're not to worry. I'll find them someone if they ask. I've enough to do.'

A few days later Filth was told, courtesy of the village shop, the new neighbour's name. It was, as the cleaning lady had said, indeed that of another Hong Kong lawyer and it was the name of the only man in his professional life, or come to that his private life, that Old Filth had ever detested. The extraordinary effect this man had had upon him over many years, and it had been much remarked upon and the usually buttoned-up Filth had not cared, was like venom sprayed from the mouths of Chinese dragons.

And the same had gone for Terry Veneering's opinion of Old Filth.

Betty had never spoken of it. Kept herself apart. Became silent, remote. Filth's Clerk, other lawyers, found the enmity almost a chemical, physical thing. In Hong Kong, the Bar watched. Old Filth, delightful wise Old Filth and swash-buckling Veneering, did not 'have words' in Court, they spat poisons. They did not cross swords, they set about each other with scimitars. Old Filth believed that Terry Veneering was all that was wrong with the British masters of this divine Colony – jumped-up, arrogant, blustering, loud, cynical and common. And far too good at games. Without such as Veneering – who knows? Veneering treated the Chinese as if they were invisible, flung himself into pompous rites of Empire, strutted at ceremonies in his black and gold, cringed with sycophancy before the Governor, drank too much. In Court he treated his opponent to personal abuse. Once, when they were both still Counsel in an interminable case about a housing estate built over a Chinese graveyard (the housing estate mysteriously refused to prosper), Veneering spent days sneering at primitive beliefs. Or so Old Filth said in, and out of, Court. What Veneering said about Old Filth he never enquired but there was a mutual, seething dislike. Betty became haggard with the subject.

For Veneering got away with everything, snarled Filth. He bestrode the Colony on his thick legs like a colossus, booming on at parties about his own excellence. During a state visit by royalty he boasted about his boy at Eton. Later it was all 'my boy at Cambridge', then 'my boy in the Guards'. 'Insufferable,' cried Filth. Betty said, 'Oh, hush, hush.'

Filth's first thought – now – was: Well, thank God Betty's gone. His second thought was that he would have to move.

However, the next-door house was as invisible as Filth's, its garden secret behind the long band of firs that curved between their joint drives. These trees grew broader, taller, all the time, and even when the leaves of other trees fell and it became winter, there was neither sight nor sound of the new neighbour.

'He's a widower, living alone,' said the cleaning lady. 'His wife used to be a Chinese.'

Old Filth remembered then that Veneering had married a Chinese woman. Strange to have forgotten. Why did it stir up in him such a mixture of hatred and smugness – almost of relief? He remembered the wife now, her downward-looking eyes, the curious chandelier earrings she wore. He remembered her at the racecourse in a bright yellow silk dress, Veneering alongside – great coarse golden fellow, six foot two; his strangled voice trying to sound English public school.

Old Filth dozed off then with this picture before him, wondering at the clarity of an image thirty years old when what happened yesterday had receded into darkness. He was nearly eighty now. Veneering was a bit younger. Well, they could each keep their own corner. They need never meet.

Nor did they. The year went by and the next one. A friend from Hong Kong – young chap of sixty – called and said, 'I believe old Terry Veneering lives somewhere down here, too. Do you ever come across him?'

'He's next door. No. Never.'

'Next *door*? My dear fellow –!'

'I'd have been wise to move away.'

'But you mean you've never –?'

'No.'

'And he's made no . . . gesture?'

'Christopher, your memory is short.'

'Well, I knew of course you were . . . You were both irrational in that direction, but . . .'

Old Filth walked his friend down to the gate. Beside it stood Veneering's gate, overhung by ragged yews. A short length of drainpipe, to take a morning newspaper, was attached to Veneering's gate. It was identical to the one that had lain by Old Filth's gate for many years. 'He copied my drainpipe,' said Old Filth. 'He never had an original notion.'

'I've half a mind to call,' said Christopher.

'Well, you needn't come and see me again if you do,' said courteous Old Filth.

Seated in his car in the road the friend considered the mystery of what convictions survive into dotage and how wise he had been to stay on in Hong Kong.

'You don't feel like a visit, Eddie?' he asked out of the car window. 'Why not come out for Christmas? It's not so much changed that there'll ever be anywhere in the world like it.'

But Filth said he never stirred at Christmas. Just a taxi to the White Hart at Salisbury, for luncheon. Good place. No paper hats. No streamers.

'I remember Betty with streamers tangled up in her hair and her pearls and gold chains. In Hong Kong.'

But Filth thanked him and declined and waved him off.

On Christmas morning, Filth thought again of Christopher, as he was waiting for the taxi to the White Hart, watching from a window whose panes were almost blocked with snow, snow that had been falling when he'd opened his bedroom curtains five hours ago at seven o'clock. Big, fast, determined flakes. They fell and fell. They danced. They mesmerised. After a few moments you couldn't tell if they were going up or down. Thinking of the road at the end of his drive, the deep hollow there, he wondered if the taxi would make it. At twelve-fifteen he thought he might ring and ask, but waited until twelve-thirty as it seemed tetchy to fuss. He discovered the telephone was dead.

'Ah,' he said. 'Ha.'

There were mince pies and a ham shank. A good bottle somewhere. He'd be all right. A pity though. Break with tradition.

He stood staring at the Christmas cards. Fewer again this year. As for presents, nothing except one from his cousin Claire. Always the same. Two handkerchiefs. More than he ever sent her, but she had had the pearls. He must send her some flowers. He picked up one large glossy card and read *A Merry Christmas from The Ideal Tailor, Century Arcade, Star Building, Hong Kong to an old and esteemed client*. Every year. Never failed. Still had his suits. Twenty years old. He wore them sometimes in summer. Snowflakes danced around a Chinese house on stilts. Red Chinese characters. A rosy Father Christmas waving from a corner. Stilts. Houses on stilts.

Suddenly he missed Betty. Longed for her. Felt that if he turned round now, quickly, there she would be.

13

But she was not.

Outside there was a strange sound, a long, sliding noise and a thump. A heavy thump. It might well be the taxi skidding on the drive and hitting the side of the house. Filth opened the front door but saw nothing but snow. He stepped quickly out upon his doorstep to look down the drive, and behind him the front door swung to, fastening with a solid, pre-War click.

He was in his bedroom slippers. Otherwise he was dressed in trousers, a singlet – which he always wore, being a gentleman, thank God – shirt and tie and the thin cashmere cardigan Betty had bought him years ago. Already it was sopped through.

Filth walked delicately along the side of the house in his slippers, bent forward, screwing his old eyes against the snow, to see if by any chance . . . but he knew that the back door was locked, and the French windows. He turned off towards the tool shed over the invisible slippery grass. Locked. He thought of the car in the garage. He hadn't driven now for some time, not since the days of terror. Mrs Thing did the shopping now. It was scarcely used. But perhaps the garage –?

The garage was locked.

Nothing for it but to get down the drive somehow and wait for the taxi under Veneering's yews.

In his tiptoe way he passed the heap of snow that had fallen off the roof and had sounded like a slithering car. 'I'm a bloody old fool,' he said.

From the gate he looked out upon the road. It was a gleaming sheet of snow in both directions. Nothing had disturbed it for many hours. All was silent, as death. Filth turned and looked up Veneering's drive.

That too was pristine silk, unmarked by birds, unpocked by fallen berries. Snow and snow. Falling and falling. Thick, wet, ice cold. His thinning hair ice cold. Snow had gathered inside his collar, his cardigan, his slippers. All ice cold. His knobbly hands were freezing as he grasped first one yew branch and then the next. Hand over hand he made his way up Veneering's drive.

He'll be with the son, thought Old Filth. That or there'll be some ghastly house party going on. Golfers. Old cobwebs from the Temple. Smart solicitors. Gin.

But the house when it came in view was dark and seemed empty. Abandoned for years.

Old Filth rang the bell and stood on the porch. The bell tinkled somewhere far away inside, like Betty's at the rosewood dining-table in the Mid Levels.

And what the hell do I do now? He's probably gone to that oaf Christopher and they are carousing in the Peninsular Hotel. It'll be – what? Late night now. They'll have reached the brandy and cigars – the cigars presented in a huge shallow box, the maître d' bowing like a priest before the sacrament. The vulgarity. Probably kill the pair of them. Hullo?

A light had been switched on inside the house and a face peered from behind a curtain in a side window. Then the front door was opened slightly by a bent old man with a strand or two of blond hair.

'Filth? Come in.'

'Thank you.'

'No coat?'

'I just stepped across. I was looking out for my taxi. For the White Hart. Christmas luncheon. Just hanging about. I thought I'd call and . . .'

'Merry Christmas. Good of you.'

They stood in the drear, unhollied hall.

'I'll get you a towel. Better take off your cardigan. I'll find you another. Whiskey?'

In the brown and freezing sitting-room a jigsaw puzzle only one eighth completed was laid out over a huge table. Table and jigsaw were both white with dust. The venture looked hopeless.

'Too much damned sky,' said Veneering as they stood contemplating it. 'I'll put another bar on. I don't often sit in here. You must be cold. Maybe we'll hear your car from here, but I doubt it. I'd guess it won't get through.'

'I wonder if I might use your phone? Mine seemed to be defunct.'

15

'Mine too, I'd guess, if yours is,' said Veneering. 'By all means try.'

The phone was dead.

They sat before two small, red wire-worms stretched across the front of an electric fire. Some sort of antique, thought Filth. Haven't seen one like that in sixty years. Chambers in the years of the Great Fog.

In a display case on the chimney-piece he saw a pair of exotic chandelier earrings. The fire, the earrings, the whiskey, the jigsaw, the silence, the eerily-falling snow made him all at once want to weep.

'I was sorry to hear about Betty,' said Veneering.

'I was sorry about Elsie,' said Filth, remembering her name and her still and beautiful – and unhappy – Chinese face. 'Your son –?'

'Dead,' said Veneering. 'Killed. Army.'

'I am most terribly sorry. So dreadfully sorry. I hadn't heard.'

'We don't hear much these days,' said Veneering. 'Maybe we don't want to. We had too many Hearings.'

Filth watched the arthritic stooped old figure shamble across the room to the decanter.

'Not good for the bones, this climate,' said Veneering, shambling back.

'Did you think of staying on?'

'Good God, no.'

'It suited you so well.' Then Filth said something very odd. 'Better than us, I always thought. Better than me, anyway. And Betty never talked about it. She was very Scotch, you know.'

'Plenty of Scots in Hong Kong,' said Veneering. 'You two seemed absolutely welded, melded, into the place. Betty and her Chinese jewellery.'

'Oh, she tried,' said Filth sadly. 'She was very faithful.'

'Another?'

'I should be getting home.'

It dawned on Old Filth that he would have to ask a favour of Veneering. He had already lost a good point to him by calling round wet to the skin. Veneering was still no fool. He'd spotted the telephone business. It would be difficult to regain his position. Maybe make something out of being the first to break the silence? Maturity. Magnanimity. Water under the bridge. Christmas Day. Hint at a larger spirit?

He wouldn't mention locking himself out.

But how was he to get home? Mrs Thing's key was three miles off and she wasn't coming in again until New Year's Day. He could hardly stay here – Good God! With Veneering!

'I've thought of coming to see you,' said Veneering. 'Several times as a matter of fact, this past year. Getting on, both of us.'

Old Filth was silent. He himself had not thought of doing anything of the sort, and could not pretend.

'Couldn't think of a good excuse,' said Veneering. 'Bit afraid of the reception. Bloody hot-tempered type, I used to be. We weren't exactly similar.'

'I've forgotten what type I was,' said Filth, again surprising himself. 'Not much of anything, I expect.'

'Bloody good advocate,' said Veneering.

'You made a damn good Judge,' said Filth, remembering that this was true. 'Better than I was.'

'Only excuse I could think of was a feeble one,' said Veneering. 'There's a key of yours here hanging in my pantry. Front door. Chubb. Your address is on the label. Must have been here for years. Neighbours being neighbourly long ago, I expect. Maybe you have one of mine?'

'No,' said Filth. 'No, I've not seen one.'

'Could have let myself in, any time,' said Veneering. 'Murdered you in your bed.' There was a flash of the old black mischief. 'Must you go? I don't think there's going to be a taxi. It would never make the hill. I'll get that key – unless you want me to hold on to it. For an emergency?' (Another hard look.)

'No,' said Filth with Court decorum. 'No, I'll take it and see if it works.'

On Veneering's porch, wearing Veneering's (ghastly) over-coat, Filth paused. The snow was easing. He heard himself say,

'Boxing Day tomorrow. If you're on your own, I've a ham shank and some decent claret.'

'Pleasure,' said Veneering.

On his own doorstep Filth thought: Will it turn?

It did.

The house was beautifully warm but he made up the fire. The water would be hot, thank God. Get out of these clothes. Hello? What?

He thought he heard something in the kitchen. Hello? Yes?

He went through and found it empty. The snow had stopped at last and the windows were squares of black light. He thought, peering forward into the gloaming: Someone is looking in. But he could see no signs of footprints anywhere, and drew the curtains. He peeped into cupboards to make sure of things for tomorrow. Didn't want to look a fool. There was a can of shark's fin soup. Tin of crab-meat. Good rice. Package of parmesan. Avocado. Fine. Fine.

Behind him in the hall he heard something like a chuckle.

'Who the hell is that? Hello?' (Had the fellow had two keys? *Murdered you in your bed.*)

'Edward, Edward, stop these fantasies! You are too old. You are no longer seven.' A man's voice. Good God, I'm going senile. 'Yes, Sir,' he said. 'Kettle. Hot water bottle. Bath. I'm old.'

The phone rang.

'You back safely?' asked Veneering's voice. 'I thought I'd try the phone. We're in touch again.'

'Oh. Thanks, Veneering. One o'clock tomorrow?'

'Yes. Would you like me to bring my chessmen?'

'Got some. Maybe next time.'

'Next time.'

So it wasn't Veneering, he ruminated in the bath, idly watching his old greying pubic hair floating like fern on the delicious hot water. Steam filled the bathroom. He almost slept.

Better get out. Somehow. Or it'll be all over.

He turned his lanky frame so that he was on all fours, facing the porcelain floor of the bath, balanced on his spread hands and his sharp knees (one of them none too excellent), and slithered his feet about to get some sort of purchase near the taps. Slowly the long length of him arose, feet squeaking a little. He pulled the plug out and watched the soapy water begin to drain, bubbling round his now rosy feet. He thought of another river. Black and brown babies splashing. A girl all warmth and laughter, his head against her thighs. The water gurgled away.

Getting more difficult. Must get a shower. Won't have one of those bloody mats with suction pads, though. Won't have what they call the Social Services. Veneering doesn't, you can see. Mind, Veneering doesn't look as if he has baths at all. Poor old bugger.

Wrapped in a white bath towel he padded about. Slippers, bath robe. Perfectly well. Take a little something to bed? No – eat it over the telly? Anchovy toast. Tea – enough whiskey. Ha! – blaze up, fire. Mustn't drop off.

'Don't drop off,' said a woman's voice. 'Don't drop off the perch! Not yet.'

'Hey, hello, what? Betty?'

But again, nobody there.

Hope I'm not feverish.

'And I'm not being a fool,' he shouted to the door of Betty's old bedroom and shut his own bedroom door behind him.

Perfectly in charge.

The bed was warm, and his own. Extraordinary really, the idea of sharing a bed. Bourgeois. Something Betty and I never talked about.

'This is not the time of frenzy,' he heard himself say out loud as the images of the day merged into dreams. He was clinging to someone on a boat-deck and the sea a silver skin. There was screaming but it was somewhere else and hardly woke him. 'We dealt with all that,' he said, 'in what they call my long, untroubled and uneventful life.'

'Sleep, Filth,' said a voice. 'Nobody knew you like I did.'

Which of them said that? he wondered.

Kotakinakulu

'Yes, yes, yes,' said Auntie May of the Baptist Mission, striding up the gangplank. 'Now then, here we are. Excellent.'

The motor launch, now and then trying its engine to see whether it would be safe to let it die, stirred the black water around it, rocked and snorted. All across the wide river, small waves slapped and tipped. Heat seemed to drip from the trees like oil. It was summer, the monsoon coming, and when it did the river traffic would die. This was why they were getting the baby home at only one week old. Otherwise he would have been stranded in the Port where he had gone to be born. Here they were, safely home, but it had been a near thing. A two-day journey and Auntie May, after she had seen him safely to his father's house, would have to make it back again herself, alone and at once.

On the journey out to the Port not much more than a week ago the baby not yet born had travelled the river in a native boat with his mother and the Malay woman who was now climbing the grass ladder to the landing stage, sorrowful and frightened, behind Auntie May. She had carried her own baby for she was the wet-nurse who had been taken to Mrs Feathers's confinement in case of an emergency should Mrs Feathers have been unable to feed the child herself.

Nobody had expected Mrs Feathers to die. The Clinic at the Port was good, the Baptist Mission efficient and known to her already for she had been a nurse before marriage to Feathers, the District Officer of Kotakinakulu province. She was a tough, lean Scot, like her husband, solid as a rock. She had nursed him through his war wounds of 1914, quieted his shell-shock, coped with his damaged ankle, born his mad rages, loved him. She had been born in the East herself, loved the climate, the river, the people, and had never ailed for a day of this her first and straightforward pregnancy. She had brought to the Clinic only the wet-nurse and her prayer book, knowing that she would be back within the month. As she left she had been helped a little into the open boat but had not looked back. The landing stage stood on its high crooked stilts with only one person watching the boat disappear round the bend of the river – a girl of twelve called Ada, the wet-nurse's eldest child. As stick-thin as the landing stage itself, the girl wound her arms about the rough branches and stayed long after the boat had disappeared.

Comfortable in the long low boat, Mrs Feathers in her loose cotton dress – never a sarong – she was the District Officer's wife – had scarcely looked pregnant. The baby had dropped low in the womb and become very quiet, which its mother knew meant the birth was imminent. In the Long House where they had rested that night, she had not worried that the child might be born early. With the peaceful happiness that often predicts labour, she had smiled and knitted a tiny lace jacket, fondly taking a strand of wool at a time and loosening it, holding it high. She had knitted most of the night, listening to the baboon on the roof clacking like a typewriter in short, unaccountable snatches of baboon monologue.

The wet-nurse, her own baby beside her, lay on the floor, terrified at being a day's journey down river from home. She whimpered.

'Now, now,' said Mrs Feathers, patting her. 'Hush, don't be afraid. Tomorrow we'll be at the Port and the next day the new baby will be here. I know. Then soon we shall all go home.' And she held up the jacket and looked at the pattern by the light of the kerosene lamp on the floor. She knew that the baby would be a girl and was finishing off the little garment with pink lacy scallops.

She finished the last scallop the following night in the Clinic but gave birth to a long, rangy, red-headed, eight-pound boy. She was delighted with him (Edward) and passed the jacket to the wet-nurse's silky brown baby, who never wore it, and the next day puerperal fever began its cruel course and three days later Mrs Feathers died.

Ten days after that, the Welsh missionary Auntie May was plodding firmly on board the river steamer which might be the last to run before the onset of the monsoon, one big hand on the rail of the gangplank, the other arm tight round the swaddled child. Behind came the weeping and now indispensable wet-nurse with her baby. She had wept for two days. Auntie May never wept.

She had, however, felt a great plunge of spirits as the river boat rounded the bend of the river before the District Officer's landing, for there was nobody there except for the same young girl sitting at the ladder's top with her arms tight round her knees. The boat lay in the water, silent, waiting for people to appear. Nobody. Auntie May knew that though there was neither telephone nor mail direct to the District Officer's quarters, and their attempt to send a cable had failed, the news of his wife's death would certainly have seeped through to Alistair Feathers. She had half-expected him to turn up at the Port to bring his son home himself. News flies fast through the jungle. Attendance at his wife's funeral would of course have been impossible, for the body had to be buried immediately, then, in Kotakinakulu province.

'Not here,' Auntie May allowed herself to say.

The wet-nurse was not surprised, however. Mr Feathers had not come down to the landing stage to see his wife leave. Their goodbye – for them, a very affectionate goodbye – a kiss on the cheek (however had this child been conceived?) – had taken place inside the verandah of the house. A quick embrace, then out and down the verandah steps, Captain Feathers calling to the others to be ready. The wet-nurse was being well-paid and had been groomed for her possible job of nursing the baby with quantities of good food, and watched over against the betel nut and alcohol. Her elder daughter had come down to the landing stage, helped Mrs Feathers to the gangplank – Mrs Feathers had suddenly turned and given the girl a kiss – and watched the boat sidle towards the current and then pass from sight.

Here the girl was now, against Captain Feathers's orders, and she had watched for two days, her legs pressed against the banana leaf barrier, desperately watching. At the Port these choppy waves had been nowhere to be seen and the river had run oily and thick, seemed hardly to move. Here though, up river, there were no glow-worm lights on the great invisible nets, no sounds of fishermen calling from boat to boat. No ghostly cartwheels of weed, flying like skaters on the surface of the running river, almost outstripping it. No crocodile snout at the Port. No plop or scream of waterbird dropping on prey. Here on the landing stage, up river, fat metallic lizards moved about, long jaws angled for grubs in the leaves. They moved silently around her feet. She kicked them away. They were harmless things.

And here was the river boat. Would Mrs Feathers be there? If she was indeed dead her strong, young body, her bright happy face would be already decaying in the wet earth of the Port's Christian cemetery.

The boat's engine reawakened with a roar and the boat approached the landing stage. Ada, the brown girl, twisted her arms tighter among the banana leaves. Here came lights. Men – not the District Officer – appeared to catch ropes.

The boat anchored, the engine stopped, the boat rocked and shuddered and Ada's mother and her baby sister and big Auntie May from the Mission began to disembark. Auntie May carried a light bundle.

When she had both feet on the rickety platform, Auntie May looked at the girl and asked if she were the wet-nurse's big daughter. Ada said yes, and looked at the bundle, and Auntie

May put it in her arms. Ada's mother went by, head-down over her own baby, afraid of seeing the District Officer somewhere in the shadows.

But there was no District Officer. Alistair Feathers was at his desk working, tonight not even drinking.

When Auntie May was admitted, he shook hands with her and sent for a servant to see her to her room, show her the bath-house, make sure that food was taken to her.

'I can stay for several days,' she said. 'I'll risk the monsoon. To see that all is as well as can be for him.'

'F-F-For him?'

'For your son. He is Edward. He's a fine boy.'

'Good. Good.'

He did not ask to see the baby who, by the time Auntie May left a week later, was the amazement of the village. A child with bright-blue eyes and white, white skin and curly chestnut hair. After Auntie May had left with a donation of ten pounds to the Mission, he gave orders for Ada to take charge of the child. Auntie May had already given orders (and the ten pounds) that Ada should sit each evening with the baby on the steps of his father's verandah. This she did for many months, but Alistair Feathers never came near.

During the monsoon Ada and the baby moved up the steps and on to the verandah and sat there listening to the deluge, the crashing steaming torrent of the rain, and at last the girl was told by the District Officer's servant to go away and take the child to live with her and his wet-nurse in their family hut.

And so the baby's first years were in the Long House among brown skins, brown eyes, scraps of coloured clothes, the Malay language; often sleeping, sometimes making musical singing, dreamily passing the time against the roar of the river and the rain. At night the lamps swung from the rafters and the baby watched the flames with their haloes of moths, heard the baboons with pleasure, saw the silver lizards without fear – their questing, swinging heads – and the geckos hooked into the mesh of the walls puffing out their lurid throats. He listened to the racket of the rats in the thatch, once watched with rapture as a fat snake came sliding up from a post-hole. Observed it being killed. He was satisfied by the nourishment of the wet-nurse but passionate in his love for the girl.

Soon he stretched to pat her face, suck her chin, her ear. One day, at two months, gazing at her he gave a crow of laughter like a boy of two. Because of the memory of the child's kind mother, the Long House respected him and accepted him, an ivory child in their warm dun dust, and he was passed about, rocked to sleep, talked to and sung to and understood only Malay. By the time he was one he rolled and tottered and waddled in the village compound with the other children. There were a number of pale-skinned half-caste children from the Raj's peccadilloes. Sometimes this child's father crossed the compound but seemed not to see him, not to notice his wife's chestnut curls.

The village observed the District Officer. Captain Feathers was a strong just governor, but nobody liked him. His child was given extra attention and, from Ada, intense, unswerving, obsessive adoration.

When the child was four and a half, Auntie May came back. Big and strong, off the boat and over the landing stage to the compound, she looked about her, at once spotting Edward with his orange hair, naked and sucking a mango, his feet and hands as pale with the mud of the compound as the other children's. She made no move towards him – the women were watching from the dark openings of the huts – but nodded and smiled in his direction, to his surprise, for his mouth fell open – and went on to climb the steps of the verandah.

She was expected: there had been correspondence for some time. But Captain Feathers had not been at the landing stage. She had not seen him for four and a half years but rumour had it that he was unchanged in his attitude to his son, that his shattered ankle was worse and that he was drinking heavily. It was said he had become eccentrically pedantically absorbed in his work and the management of his District. He was celibate. No girls were brought to him by their mothers as 'extra servants', though he was handsome still, his eyes bright with malaria. He turned away from the women's beauty to the beauty of the whiskey in the glass. It did not seem to harm him. He had the Scottish immunity. He drank alone, for he had no friends.

'Oh, Miss Neal. Auntie May. G-g-good evening.'

He looks tired, she thought.

She had come to take the child down to the Port, to be taught English for six months before the journey Home, where he would live with a Welsh family until he was eight. After that, he would go to his father's old Prep school and then his father's old Public school. Auntie May knew of the Welsh family with whom he was to be fostered. They were used to Raj Orphans. There would be home-cooked food, and it would be cheap (Alistair Feathers was a Scot). And there were two aunts about, his sisters, in Lancashire which was not really far away from North Wales.

'And of course,' said Auntie May at dinner, watching the lowering of the whiskey in the glass at the other end of the lamp-lit table, 'you will have to take him to Wales. In six months' time. And you will by then have paid for him in advance.'

Alistair Feathers's eyes stared. Outside, the madhouse noises of the jungle. Inside, the servant padding about, taking plates, setting down others, offering fruit.

'He seems well and happy,' he said. 'I have never seen the need for him to go Home. It's not the law.'

'You know perfectly well that it *is* the custom. Because of the risk of childhood illnesses out here. You went Home yourself.'

'I did,' said Alistair. 'So help me God.'

Auntie May on the whole agreed with him. She'd seen great damage. Some children forgot their parents, clung to their adoptive families who later often forgot them. There were bad tales. Others grew to say they'd had a much better time in England away from their parents, whom they did not care for. There were children who worked hard at growing stolid and boring, and made marriages only in order to have roots of their own at last. They never told anything. And Auntie May had never been sure about the ferocity of Eastern childhood diseases. But in this case there was no mother.

'You've had no leave in ten years, Alistair. It isn't safe. Nobody knows better than you what happens out here to District Officers who work too hard. They drink and go native.'

Alistair fastidiously poured another whiskey and said, 'At least I still change for dinner.'

He was in dinner jacket and black tie that would have been acceptable at the Ritz. Not a bead of sweat. Auntie May in sarong and sandals, her chin a little more whiskery, her arms resting almost to her elbows on the table a little more muscular, had put on weight and felt hot. She looked at Alistair and had to admire. She wanted to take his hand. Her hardest task now as she grew older in the Ministry was to deal with her longing to be touched – hugged, stroked by anyone, any human being – a friend, a lover, a child or even (and here she scented danger) a servant. Of either sex. She prayed about it, asking that God's encircling arms would bring comfort. They did not.

'Alistair, you have no choice. You have a son who has no mother. At Home there will be your sisters, both unmarried. They will love a little nephew. They don't answer any of my letters but you say you've been making arrangements, telling them? You have to take leave and accompany the boy home. It's what his mother would have done.'

Alistair rose and limped about, his crooked shadow everywhere. Outside in the steaming night there was an upsurge of voices across the compound and the crowing of a cock. A drum began to beat.

'It's the festival. They're sacrificing a cockerel.'

'You don't need to tell me, Auntie May.'

'Your son is watching. Do you think this is the right way of life for a Christian child?'

'He isn't a Christian child.'

'Yes, he is. I saw to that. He was baptised at birth. His mother held him. It's not the Baptist way but she asked for it. In case he didn't survive the river boat. He is baptised in the name of the Father, Son and Holy Spirit who have nothing to do with the slitting of a cock's gullet at the full moon.'

'They are calling on their god,' said Alistair. 'There is no God but God. I'm nearer to their gods than yours ever was to me in 1914. Can the child not go on as he is?'

'No,' she said and left it at that.

The next day she went looking for Edward and found him in the river shallows where Ada on the bank was rubbing at coloured cloths, the pair of them calling and laughing. Other children stood in the water sending showers of it over each other and Edward and Ada, with their round dark hands. Edward began to do the same and kicked more of it about with his long white feet. Ada, pretending to be furious, dropped her cloths and ran in amongst them, splashing back. All the heads bobbed away into the rocks like black floats. Edward splashed forward and took Ada round the waist and buried his face against her thighs. 'You are my leopard,' cried Edward Feathers in the Malay of the compound. 'My beautiful leopard and I want to *eat* you alive.'

This, thought Auntie May, will not do.

That night at dinner she said so.

'He goes Home, Alistair. If you won't take him, I will. I'm due some leave, too. There will be other English children on board. There always are. I'm told there may be two of his cousins joining a ship Home from Ceylon. We may pick them up. We shall be able to go the short way through Suez next year. Your sisters must organise warm clothes for Liverpool.'

'They wouldn't know how,' said Alistair. 'They're independent spinsters. Play a lot of golf.'

'Very well. I'll contact the Baptists. In Lancashire and in Wales. And I shall also –' she looked hard at him '– inform the Foreign Office. How well do you know your son, I wonder?'

'I see him.'

'I've sent for him to come here now. Tonight.' She clapped her hands and shouted for the servant in the Raj voice of thunder.

The servant looked at his master, but the master continued

to open and shut a little silver box that had been his wife's pin-box and now held his tooth-picks. Then he took up his glass and looked into its golden depths.

'Yes. Very well.'

Edward was brought in from just outside the door where he had been watching and holding Ada's hand. He blinked in the glare of light, stared at the tall man's queer clothes – the starched shirt, the gold watch chain – and the gleam of the table-silver and glass he had never seen before.

'Now then, Edward,' said Auntie May. 'Greet your father, please.'

The child looked mystified.

'Your father. Go on.'

She gave him a push. 'Bow, child. Hold out your hand.'

The child bowed but scarcely took his eyes from Alistair's pinched yellow face and sandy square moustache.

Alistair suddenly threw himself back in his chair, dropped the silver box on the table and looked straight at Edward for the first time. His wife's genial blue eyes looked back at him.

'Hullo,' he said, 'Hullo – Edward. And so you are going away?' Like Auntie May, he spoke in Edward's own Malay.

Edward wriggled and turned his attention to the silver box.

'Did you know that you will be going away?'

'They say so,' said Edward.

'You are going first with Auntie May to the Port. For half a year. To learn to speak English, like all British boys have to do.'

Edward fiddled with the box.

'You hear English spoken sometimes, don't you? You understand what it is?'

'Sometimes. Why do I have to? I can talk here.'

'Because you will one day have to go to England. It is called Home. They don't speak Malay there.'

'Why can't I stay here?'

'Because white children often die here.'

'I shall like to die here.'

'We want you not to die but to grow up big and strong.'

'Will Ada come?'

'We'll see.'

'Can I go back to Ada now?'

'Here,' the father called as the child made off to the verandah where Ada stood in the shadows. 'Here. Come back. Take this. It was your mother's,' and he held out the silver box.

'Does Ada say I can?'

'I say you can. I am your father.'

'You can't be,' said Edward.

Silence fell and Auntie May's hands began to shake.

The servants were listening.

'And why not?'

'Because you've been here all the time without me.'

Auntie May left with Edward next morning. She felt sick and low.

I'm lugubrious, unattractive, bossy and a failure, she told God. I shan't come here ever again. That man can rot.

Alistair, however, had been on the landing stage, leaning only a little on his stick, spick and span in his khaki shorts and sola topi. He had shaken hands with Auntie May, acknowledged Ada. Had shaken hands with the little boy, and asked if he had the box safe. Then he had given the order for the boat to be cast off, and had limped away.

'Wave,' said Auntie May, but Edward did not.

Nor did Alistair turn to look at his son's second – and last – journey down the black river.

As the trees on either winding bank blotted out the landing stage, Edward, who had been struck dumb by the sight of Ada left alone on the tottering platform, began to scream 'Ada, Ada, Ada!' and to point back up river. Auntie May held him tight, but he screamed louder, and writhed in her arms. She spoke sharply in Malay and he bit her shoulder, wriggled free and seemed about to jump overboard. A sailor caught him by the belt of the shorts that Auntie May had brought and that had astonished him. The sailor lifted him high. Water poured down the sailor's silky arms. 'Hai, hai, hai,' he laughed and Edward lashed out at him, sobbing. He was a tall, strong boy for four and a half but the boatman lifted him into the air like a swathe of flowers. Something of the boatman's smell and his happy eyes reminded the child of Ada, and the sobbing lessened and he went limp.

'Why does she stay? Why is she not here?'

'If she came with you, you would never learn English. You and she would talk Malay, as we are doing now.'

'I will talk Malay with you always.'

'Not after we get to the Port. You will learn something new. Ada will follow.'

'Follow?'

'She will follow to the Port when you have to go Home.'

Edward gave a shuddering, hopeless sob. He had just left Home. What would Ada do without him at Home? He was placed in Auntie May's lap and looked at her with eyes nearly mad and shouted 'Ada! Ada!' He tried to hit Auntie May, and swim for it, but she grabbed him in her muscular arms and tried to rock him. He became limp again. The sobs that shook his body began to become farther apart. He hiccupped and tried to speak, but it came out jerky and odd: 'Ek, ek, ek –' like the baboon on the roof. A cupfull of drink appeared from a bottle in Auntie May's bag. (Auntie May had negotiated these hateful kidnappings before.) The drink was dark and sweet and he gulped it in the middle of a last shuddering sob. She passed the empty cup to the boatman and rocked the child, allowing herself the pleasure of a child in her arms, knowing that this stringy, red-headed boy would never tempt her into lullabies or spoiling comforts. But he was warm against her broad chest, and now he slept. She seethed against the father, the system, the Empire which she had begun to think was not God's ordinance after all, and how had she ever thought it could be? Duty to these people was what mattered now. Well, to all people. Love and duty.

Six months later the two of them took ship to England alone. There was no sign of the District Officer, no sign of Ada, and they travelled steerage – Alistair had been vague to Auntie May about how much more money he had to spare, and she was nervous lest the child became over-excited by uniforms and orchestras. There was also the question of table manners for someone who had not sat at tables until six months ago at the Port. At first Edward had tried to eat beneath the table. The Mission had done better with his English than with his social graces. All that Auntie May had heard from Captain Feathers since they parted was a letter saying that all financial arrangements had been made for the boy and that he would come into his own money in time. His father's sisters had been written to and had the address of the Public school where he would go when he was fourteen. Money had been sent to the foster parents in Wales.

Auntie May wrote back, making sure the father had the boy's Welsh address correctly, and told him that a letter would be written by Edward every week as soon as he could write. She made clear that Edward was not himself at present. That, at the Port, while he had absorbed English easily – he would be a linguist she was sure – he had become passive and listless and glum and when he talked now it seemed to be with some difficulty, as if he had a constriction in the throat like an old clock trying to gear itself up to strike. 'A-a-a-a-a-ack.' You longed to say the word for him. You sometimes almost wanted to shake him for he seemed to be doing it on purpose. When the words were eventually freed from the clockwork in the gullet, or the mind, out they poured far too fast, and when he paused for breath it was 'ack-ack-ack, ek-ek-ek' again. At the Mission, other children had called him 'the monkey' and he had in fact become rather like one of the bony, pale-orange baboons with their hot red eyes.

He never asked for Ada again.

At Colombo the ship took on more passengers and Auntie May suspected that two of the many white children with their ayahs and mothers might be Edward's cousins travelling (of course) first-class. There had been rumours of this but she had made no enquiries. The two cousins were girls, one a little older than Edward the other even younger. They would be spending the next four years together, all three, in Wales, with the Didds family. Edward might be taunted for his father's apparent poverty if these cousins knew he was on the lower deck. There might be jealousy.

In this Auntie May was wrong. Whatever web the children were to make between themselves, it would always be too tight-knit for jealousy or taunts. But Auntie May kept her counsel, did her best with the stammering Edward as they crossed the molten-silver disc of the Indian Ocean beneath a beating sky. It was very hot in steerage but both were used to heat. From the upper deck in the first-class, dance-music floated down to them.

Inner Temple

Stately Old Filth – Eddie Feathers – was nodding after lunch for a moment in the smoking-room of the Inner Temple before taking a taxi to his family solicitor to make his Will.

It was autumn but very hot. The flowers in the Inner Temple garden blazed. The River Thames glittered, and, coming out of his post-prandial nap he was a gawky boy, crossing the equator again, watching mad capers by the grown-ups. Neptune in a green wig. Auntie May had been lying down and so he had wandered towards the upper deck and seen faces and elegance he'd never known. He stood and gawped. People were drinking coloured liquid out of vases on stalks, puffing smoke from their lips. Ladies with hard, sad eyes wore long tight glitter and laughed a lot. A man in black and white held a woman in gold, their bodies fused as they moved languidly about to the wailing, meaningless music. A wave of great desolation had swept across Eddie. He was never, ever after, to understand it. He knew that before long he'd be back on this ocean, maybe for eternity. He had no words for all this then, and not even now in the armchair in the Inner Temple, coffee cup alongside.

As he came round from the day-dream he heard two of his peers – old Judges he'd known for years – coming along the passage to the smoking-room talking about him. He had been sitting next to them at luncheon.

'Remarkably well preserved.'

34

'Well, he's from Commercial Chambers. Rich as Croesus. But he's a great man.'

'Pretty easy life. Nothing ever seems to have happened to him.'

Nothing.

Wales

The white-washed stone farmhouse stood high, with fields all around it and a view of rick-rack stone walls laid out towards cliffs above the sea. In front of the house was a farmyard of beaten earth and a midden with a headless chicken lying on it and a cockerel crowing near. The door of the farmhouse stood open. On the yard in front of it, spaced out well away from each other, were three children, Eddie the only boy and the tallest.

He was eight now, looked ten, and startlingly white, though this may have been the pallor of a red-head. He was standing almost to attention, as if awaiting execution or about to declaim a speech. The other two figures were also looking theatrical, set in their positions on stage. Waiting for something. Babs and Claire. Claire sat on the corner of the wall. Babs leaned darkly against an outhouse. Chickens ran about. The children were not speaking to each other.

Inside the house was Auntie May again, packing up. She was softer now, less bristly, about to marry another missionary and off to the Belgian Congo very soon. But first she was finishing her job with Edward Feathers. 'I never desert,' said Auntie May. 'Especially after such a tragedy as this.'

The tragedy was apparent, she thought, as soon as she'd seen Edward's closed face, his frightening dignity. He had stood there in shorts long-grown-out-of – could they have been those she'd found for him three-and-a-half years ago? – his hair cropped to near-baldness, his white face empty. 'Auntie May,' she'd said, 'You remember Auntie May?' He seemed not to know her. She looked at the two girls, whom she was to take away and look after until their parents – or some relatives somewhere – would come to claim them.

The children had been excused the funeral. People in the village had taken them in.

Babs, dark and unsmiling, stood picking at her fingernails, stage left. Pink little Claire sat on the wall, wagging her feet, down stage right. When Auntie May had arrived and said, 'I am Auntie May,' Claire had smiled and raised her arms to her for an embrace.

Babs had jerked away from Auntie May, as if expecting a blow.

Edward, whom Auntie May had cared for, did not go near her. He had looked at her once, then walked away through the gate in the stone wall, off-stage right, and now stood alone, gazing at the sea.

You would expect them to draw together, Auntie May thought.

'I'll see if all's ready,' she had said. 'I'll lock up the house.'

After Auntie May had gone into the house the children did not stir but began to observe a small motor car working its way towards them from the cliff road. It turned into the maze of stone walls. A car was rare. This car was fat and business-like with a cloth roof and rounded, tinny back and a high, rubber running-board down each side. Mudguards flowed like breaking waves over the solid wheels and the windows were made of orange celluloid, rather cracked. A short man jumped out and came jollily to the foot of the garden steps. He was talking.

'– I dare say,' he said. 'Eddie Feathers, I dare say? Excellent to meet you. I am your new Headmaster and my name is *Sir*. Always *Sir*. Understood? The school is small. There are only twenty boys. They call each other by their surnames. I have one assistant, Mr Smith. He is always called Mr Smith, my assistant, whatever his real name. Different ones come and go. This Mr Smith is something of a trial but very good at cricket, which

I am not. And so, good morning, Eddie, and these are your sisters, I dare say?'

'C-cou-cousins,' came out of Edward's mouth. He liked this man.

'I know nothing of girls,' said Sir. 'I know everything about boys. I am a very good teacher, Feathers, as your father may remember. By the time you leave my Outfit there is not a bird, butterfly or flower, not a fish or insect of the British Isles you will not recognise. You will also read Latin like a Roman and understand Euclid like a Greek.'

'Will he still have to do Welsh?' asked blonde Claire.

'Welsh! I should hope not.'

'What if you get a *stupid* boy?' asked Babs from the shadows (and thought: I do not like this man; he'll change Eddie).

'Eddie isn't stupid,' said Claire and, suddenly aware – for here came Auntie May with luggage – that Eddie was going away, she jumped from her plinth and hugged him as she had never done in all the terrible years since they met at Liverpool Docks. She began to cry.

'Sh-shut up, Claire.' Eddie turned to the man accusingly and said, 'Claire never cries.' He looked down at Claire's top-knot, felt her arms round him, did not know what to do about it and carefully removed himself.

'Auntie May,' said Auntie May to Sir. 'I am Auntie May.'

'Ah, the redoubtable Auntie May. You are seeing to the girls, I hear? This would be quite outside my territory. I teach only boys. My establishment is very expensive and very well-known. I am unmarried, as is Mr Smith, but let me say, for all things good should be noised abroad, that there is absolutely nothing unpleasant going on in my school. We are perfectly clean. There is nothing like that.'

'Well, that will be a change for him,' said Auntie May. 'There's been nothing pleasant here.'

'So I understand. Or rather I do not understand for such events are beyond comprehension in a well-run Outfit. There is no corporal punishment in my school. And there is no emotional hysteria. One can only suppose that these things are

38

the result of the mixture of the sexes. I *never* teach girls.'

'What happened here was not to do with a school. These children went to the village school.'

'Which accounts for the pink child's regional accent. Come, boy, say your goodbyes. At my school nobody leaves with an accent.'

'Goodbye,' said Eddie, looking only at Sir's face. He remembered to shake hands with Auntie May and say, 'Th-th-tha-thank you.' Ignoring the girls, for the three of them would all their lives be beyond formalities, he picked up some of his belongings, Auntie May some more and Sir none at all and they processed to the car, where Sir unfastened broad leather straps and the back was lifted, like the lid of a bread-bin.

'It's marvellous. Your car.'

'Marvellous, *Sir*.'

'Marvellous, Sir.'

Sir stood back and watched the luggage being put inside the bread-bin. Then he nodded at Auntie May, pointed to the dickie seat and watched Eddie climb in, Babs and Claire looking on nonchalantly from above.

'You have the address?' said Sir to Auntie May. 'And Feathers has yours? Not too many letters, please; we have work to do. He should write regularly to his father only. No letters from the girls or from this village. I think that was the understanding? Why does the boy stammer?'

'It began years ago.'

'Nothing in the least to worry about now,' said Sir, cranking an iron handle in front of the bonnet, then flinging it over the car into the dickie, just missing Eddie's head, and leaping behind the wheel to keep the engine alive. Without a toot or a wave or a word of farewell he reversed on the springy grass and flung the car back into the stony lane and went bounding between the low walls and out of sight; leaving a considerable silence.

It was Babs who burst into tears.

'Now then, this stammer,' said Sir, an hour or so later, 'I suppose it's never mentioned. That's the current policy.'

'It – it – it was. At the sch-school.'

'Ah, well they were Welsh. The Welsh have an easy flow and cadence. They can't understand those of us who haven't. I, for example, am not musical. Are you?'

'I d-don't know.'

'Chapel? Chapel?'

'I d-didn't sing. If I did they all turned and l-l-looked. Babs sang. B-b-b *can* sing.'

'The dark one?'

'She sang clear and sh-sh-sharp. Not at all sweet. Not Welsh singing. They d-didn't like it. So she went on.'

'A prima donna. Girls are very difficult. Hush. Stop a minute. I see swifts.'

He stopped the car in the middle of a leafy lane with trees. Swooping about in high pleasure were some dart-shaped birds cutting the air high and low and gathering invisible flies. 'Listen!' said Sir. 'Hear that?'

'It's rather like b-bells.'

'Good, good. You will never forget swifts now. There are birds, you know, who actually do sound like bells. They're bell birds and they call to each other across the rainforests of Eastern Australia. Don't let them tell you there are no rainforests in Australia. I have been there. Is that understood? I dare say?'

'Y-yes, Sir.'

'Good. And it is writhing with dragons.'

'D-d–, Sir?'

'They are a form of armadillo, enlarged wood-lice. (The common prawn is related to the wood-louse.) Fat low beasts and over-confident. Rather disgustingly beautiful.'

'Like the lizards in Kotakinakulu?' said Eddie, amazing himself by the memory of the platinum lizards with crocodiles' merciless eyes, steel slit of a long mouth, not seen since. . . .

'Seen some, have you? Interested Darwin. You'll have to tell the others, stammer or no stammer. Claudius had a stammer. Have you come across Claudius?'

'Claudius who?'

'Who, *Sir*. Claudius the Emperor of Rome. Splendid fellow. The Duke of York has a stammer. He's having lessons for it.'

'Did he get it in Wales?'

'I shouldn't wonder. Pity they didn't send him to me.'

On sped the car. When they reached main roads conversation ceased. Sir's long scarf kept flapping behind him into Eddie's face. A precarious mirror hooked to the car at the height of Sir's ear but in front of him showed Sir with concentrated gravity clenching his teeth on a curly pipe, unlit. Now and then he squeezed a grey rubber bulb attached to a small trumpet and a high bleat sounded off.

The rubber thing reminded Eddie of something vile. Old Mr Didds's constipation. Eddie's face disappeared from Sir's mirror, and Sir drew to the side of the road and stopped.

'Just letting her cool down somewhat. Where are you? On the floor, I dare say?'

Eddie was squashed down on the floor of the dickie, knees to chin and pale green.

'Feeling sick? Not unnatural. Breathe slowly. It may be the car. Others have felt the same.'

After a while Eddie scrambled up.

'You could come and sit beside me but I never allow it. You are in my care. Do you know much about cars?'

'It's the f-f-first –'

'First time in a car? Excellent. You can write the experience down. Did they teach you to write?'

'Yes. In a w-ay.'

'You mean they struck you with rulers? Beat you about the head?'

'Y-yes.'

'This does not happen in my Outfit. If you do not work – do not *try* – then Mr Smith takes you for a run. All weathers. Along the shores of the lake.'

'D-do we wear labels?'

'Labels?'

'We carried labels on our backs.'

'Did this happen to you?'

'To all of us, it d-did. Babs had UGLY. I had MONKEY.'

'And the pink girl?'

'Oh, she never got c-caught. Well, they l-liked her.'

'Nothing can be further from my Outfit,' said Sir, closing his eyes for a moment. 'What do you think of my mirror?'

'M-m-m?'

'On the car. It is very much the fashionable touch, invented I am surprised to say by a lady. The first driving mirrors were adapted from the powder-case in a lady's handbag. They were hand-held. So that you could see if anything was coming along behind. One day, they'll be compulsory for both sexes I dare say. I see you are unaware of powder-cases? Perhaps you know no ladies? Have you a mother?'

'She died when I was b-b-b –'

'Several boys in my Outfit have suffered similarly. We are almost all of the Raj. I try not to see any of the mothers.'

The car was re-cranked and off they went again. In the dickie it grew very cold about the ears. Eddie crouched down a bit but was afraid to take himself out of range of the mysterious powder-case mirror. Sir stopped in a wooded valley and passed Eddie a bottle of lemonade, taking a swig himself from a flask with a silver top and wrapped in basket work. Eddie smelled something powerful and sweet. It reminded him of the silver box which his father had given him and which he had given to Ada.

'Not long, now,' said Sir. 'We are on the borders of what is known as the English Lake District. It is the Old Kingdom of Cumbria and where I chose to set up my Outfit. I dare say you have not heard of our purple mountains and silver rivers?'

'I c-can't remember. Sir.'

'Never fell to the Romans. Home of the poet Wordsworth who had a happy education.'

'Y-yes, Sir.'

'You know all this, I dare say?'

'I did – didn't –'

'Can you read, Feathers?' Sir asked casually.

'N-n-not yet m-much.'

'Never mind. Won't take two ticks. Great times ahead. Now, here we are.'

A high and very ugly brown stone castle towered out of a mountain forest beside a black lake, and as they turned and began to climb up a drive edged with blue hydrangeas a bell rang ahead of them and various boys began to emerge from the undergrowth looking eager and wild. Sir gave a salvo on the bulb and the boys began to jog up the drive, beside the car, some of them cheering.

'Supper time,' said Sir. 'Sausages, with any luck. We've a good cook. You like sausages, I dare say?'

An elfin child burst out of the front door and flung himself in front of the car, arms spread.

'One day I'll turn you into a single dimension. A pancake. A pulp for a pie,' said Sir.

'Can I put the car in the garage for you, Sir?' said the alert-looking boy.

'Of course, of course. Rub it down, will you, and give it a drink?'

The boy took the driver's seat and, though his head was not far above the instruments panel, steered slowly and carefully into the garage where it fitted like a toy in a box.

'Very accurate boy,' said Sir. 'Name of Ingoldby. He's in charge of you for your first half-term. Very well done, Ingoldby. A garage to contend with.'

'It's not so much a garage,' said Ingoldby, 'as a kennel for a medium-sized dog. Hullo.'

'Ingoldby – Feathers,' introduced Sir, shaping the future.

The Donheads

Seventy years on in Dorset, an extraordinarily warm November, Teddy Feathers, Sir Edward, Old Filth was fussing about which tie to wear for a trip to London. He and Betty were going to the solicitors to make their Wills.

Downstairs in the hall Betty, perfectly ready, sat waiting on a sort of throne of gilded wood and faded, shredding silk which had been scarlet when they bought it in Bangladesh. She had found it in a cavernous incense-smelling shop in the back-streets of Dacca's Old Town. Stroking the pale rose satin now with her fingertips, she tried to remember what it was that had made her buy this chair. A bit of showing off, she thought. Well, some people brought back stuffed animals. She had asked if she might try sitting in it. It had been right at the back of the shop and she had looked out from it down the blackness to the dazzle of the doorway and the passing show of the street, the tangle of the rickshaws, the dignified old gentlemen in turbans, the women like briskly floating butterflies, the clusters of black heads in all the high windows. A procession of princelings had gone by, each carrying a silver dish piled with steaming plum pudding. Well of course she knew that it was only tin-foil and cow dung. But they were jolly and grave at the same time, like the Magi.

'Yes, I'll take it. I'll take the chair.'

And here it was now, standing on the Dorset parquet beside the teak chest, and her fingernails, rosy as the silk, were stroking it.

On the teak chest were net bags full of tulip bulbs waiting to be planted. Today would have been the perfect day for it. Tomorrow might be cold or wet and she would be feeling a bit done-in after this jaunt today. Why Filth still had to have a London solicitor she did not know. Twice the price and half the efficiency, in her experience. The very thought of London made her dizzy. No point in telling Filth. No arguing with Filth.

And the bulbs should have been in two weeks ago for she wasn't the walking talking calendar she used to be. She didn't like dropping to her knees very much, at any time. She'd even stopped in church, though it felt louche, just squatting. The Queen Mother still knelt in church. Well, probably. Filth said that Queen Mary had knelt until the very end.

Filth still kept to a timetable. He'd booked this appointment weeks ago. 3.30 p.m. Bantry Street, W.C.1. The Wills would now be ready for signing. He'd been urgent about it lately and she wondered if he'd been having the dizzies again. His slight heart attack was several years ago. She stroked the satin.

Then her fingers strayed to the bulbs in their bags and she touched them – like a priestess giving a blessing. The fat globes inside the nets made her think of the crops of shot game-birds laid out on a slab – somewhere in her childhood's China, maybe? And, as a matter of fact, thought Betty, stroking, these fat potential globes under their skins were very like a man's balls, when you came to think about it.

Not that I have, for years.

She heard Filth above stairs drop a shoe and swear.

But if I *seriously* think about it, as an artist might, or a doctor, or a lover dreaming. . . .

She closed her eyes and under the pile of bulb-bags the telephone began to ring. She felt about until she reached the receiver, pulled it free and said, 'Yes? Betty.' She said again, 'Yes? Hello? Betty,' knowing that it would be someone from her reading group, which was meeting in the village that afternoon, and which she had notified yesterday that she would be away. The writer they were studying (studying!) was driving all the way from Islington to interpret her novel for them. Betty thought that she ought to have better things to do. It must be like discussing your marriage with strangers. 'Hello? Is that you, Chloe?'

'Betty?' (A man.)

'Yes?'

'I'm in Orange Tree Road. Where are you?'

'Well, here.'

'Exactly where?'

'Sitting in the hall. By the phone. On the satin throne.'

'What are you wearing?'

'Wearing?'

'I need to see you.'

'But you're in Hong Kong.'

'I need to see you. To see your face. I've lost it. I have to be able to see you in the chair.'

'Well, I'm – we're about to go up to London. Filth's putting his shoes on upstairs. He'll be down in a minute. I'm dressed for London.'

'Are you wearing the amethysts?'

'Don't be ridiculous. It's nine o'clock in the morning.'

'Pearls.'

'Oh, well, yes.'

'Touch them. Are they warm? Are they mine? Or his? Would he know?'

'Yours. No, he wouldn't notice. Are you drunk? It must be after dinner.'

'No. Well, yes. Maybe.'

'Is – are you alone?'

'Elsie's lying down. Betty, Harry's dead. My boy.'

The line died as Filth came bounding down the stairs in a London suit and black shoes. He swirled himself into his overcoat and looked about for the bowler hat which he had resurrected. It lay among the tulips. He reflected upon it and then let it lie. Mustn't be antique. The taxi was here.

'Phone-call?'

'Nothing – cut off.'

*

They travelled first-class, though unintentionally as they both thought first-class was vulgar and only for expense-account people.

The ticket-collector, weighing up their age and clothes, had thought differently, seeing Teddy's rolled umbrella and Betty's glorious pearls and the rubbish on the floor around their polished shoes.

'You can upgrade, sir, if you like.' (The wife looks very pale.) 'Just the next compartment and four pounds extra if you're seniors.'

'Perfectly well here, thank you,' said Filth, but Betty smiled at the man's black Tamil face, gathered up her bag and gloves and set off on her jaunty heels down the coach, tottering through the swaying connecting doors towards the firsts, away from what she still called 'the thirds'.

They paddled through the water spilling out from under the doors of the W.C.s and settled in a blue velvet six-seater compartment. Four of the seats were slashed down the back with the stuffing coming out. Graffiti covered the ceiling but the floor was cleaner. Filth thought of the train to Kuala Lumpur, the mahogany and the hot food handed in, and sat facing his wife in the two unslashed seats on the window side. The fields, woods, hedges, uplands of Wiltshire, white chalk shining through the grass, flickered by.

Betty suddenly saw a hoopoe in a hedge. She looked at Filth to see if he had noticed it, but he was abstracted. The lines between his nose and mouth were sharp today, cruel as the slashes down the seats. Whatever had he to be bitter about?

His boy is dead. His boy, Harry.

The Tamil drew the door open.

'Better, sir?'

'Very nice,' said Betty.

'Four pounds? Is that *each*?' asked Filth.

'Don't bother with it, sir. When you look at the seats. . . . But it's cleaner. Take my advice and get straight into first-class on the way home. You'll be Day Returns?'

'Oh, yes. We don't stay in London longer than we can help.'

The man wondered why the lady's eyes were so bright. Like it was tears. Real old. Could be his grandma. And yet – she was smiling at him.

'We're going to London to sign our Wills.'

'Ma'am, I'm sure there's plenty of time.'

Filth blew his nose on a starched handkerchief and drew down his eyebrows as if in Court. 'In your profession, I wouldn't count on that.'

'Too right,' said the man. 'Takes our lives in our hands, we do on the railways. Safer flying. But that's how I like it. When you gotta go, you gotta go? Right?'

'Right,' said Betty.

'Quite right,' said Filth. He was noticing Betty, her face tired through the make-up. He looked at her again as the train swayed insolently through Clapham Junction. She must get her eyes seen to. They looked moist and strange. Old, he thought. She's never looked old before.

'Lunch?' he asked.

'What?'

'Where are you having lunch? Shall we go somewhere together? Simpson's?'

'But you're going to the Inner Temple.'

'I can change it. Nobody's expecting me. Don't know a soul there now.'

She was silent.

'Then we could get a taxi to the place – the solicitor – together. Not arrive separately. Hanging about on pavements.'

'No,' she said. 'I've made arrangements at the Club.'

'You don't have to go. There's never anybody else there.'

'That's why I go. To keep it going. I'm meeting somebody this time.'

'You didn't tell me.'

She thought: You didn't ask.

At Waterloo she stood with him for his taxi, the driver coming round to help him in. The door was slammed and he tapped his window and called 'Betty – where did you say you were going?'

but she was gone. He saw her as he was taken down the slope, fast as a girl on her still not uninteresting legs, nipping through the traffic towards the National Theatre side. Must be walking all the way to the Club, he thought with pride. Crossing the bridge, down the Strand, Trafalgar Square, the Mall, St James's, Dover Street. Remarkable woman for over seventy. She loved walking. Strange the hold that University Women's Club had over her. Never been there himself. Betty, of course, had never been to a university. She'd vanished now.

He had not seen her take a right down the steps towards the Film Theatre and the Queen Elizabeth Hall. In the National Theatre she took a tray and shoved it along in the queue of the audience for the matinee for *Elektra*.

She had no idea what she ate. She took the lift to the high level of the theatre and sat outside alone in the cold air. She was meeting nobody. There were buskers everywhere: acrobats, musicians, living statues, contortionists and a sudden deluge of sound from a Pavarotti in a loin cloth. The waves of the canned music made the pigeons fly. Two people sat down on the seat beside her, the girl with her hair in two wings of crinkled gold. Heavy, sullen, resentful, the boy slumped beside her, his mouth slack. The music and the voice blazed away.

His boy Harry is dead.

The girl lit a cigarette, her fingers and thumbs chunky with rings.

Rings on her fingers and bells on her toes – and goodness knows where else, thought Betty. She shall have music wherever she goes. Oh, I do hope so.

The girl was staring at her.

'I like your hair,' said Betty.

The girl turned away, haughtily. 'Nothing lasts long,' said Betty, and the boy said, 'We could go for a Chinese.'

They thought about it.

Then the two of them turned to each other on the seat and in one fluid movement entwined themselves in each other's arms.

His boy is dead, thought Betty and got up.

She wandered away down steep, spiral stairs and at the river-bank watched the water streaming by, the crowds, the silver wheel high in the air dotted with silver bullets. Beautiful. It jerked awake. Jerk, stop, fly. Round and round.

Terry's boy is dead.

And I'm not, she thought. Filth and I are going to live for ever. Pointlessly. Keeping the old flag flying for a country I no longer recognise or love.

When she saw the state of the traffic down the Strand she wondered if Filth would make it to the solicitor's in time. He liked ten minutes zizz after lunch in the smoking-room of the Inn. Hopeless without it. She thought of him, tense and angry, traffic-blocked in his taxi. A few years ago he'd have sprung out and walked. He had been a familiar sight, gown and papers flapping, prancing to the Law Courts. 'Look, isn't it Old Filth?'

When he'd been very young and not a penny, not a Brief, before she knew him, he'd always, he said, had a bowler hat for going home. 'Why?' she had asked.

'To have something to raise to a Judge.'

You never knew when Filth was being sardonic or serious.

He was not being sardonic today. With the help of the rolled umbrella he was signalling to taxis outside his Inn on the Embankment. He moved his feet rather cautiously and looked ancient, but still handsome, beautifully dressed, alert after his ten-minute nap, someone you'd notice. But the traffic streamed by him. Nothing stopped. He'd never get there. Too old for this now. He'd be late for Court. He began to be frightened as he used to be. His throat felt tight.

I'll walk to Bantry Street, thought Betty; his taxi might overtake me. And she struck out into the crowd. In her Agatha-Christie country clothes and pearls and polished shoes, she strode among an elbowing, slovenly riff-raff who looked at her as if she was someone out of a play. Pain and dislike, bewilderment and fear, she thought, in every face. Nobody at peace except the corpses in the doorways, the bundles with rags and bottles;

50

and you can't call that peace. She dropped money into hats and boxes as she would never have done in Dacca or Shanghai, and would have been prosecuted for doing in Singapore. Beggars again in the streets of London, she thought. My world's over. Like Terry's.

Her heart was beating much too fast and she slowed down at Bantry Street and felt in her handbag for a pill. But all was well. Here was Filth, grave and tall, being helped out of a taxi.

'Well, good timing,' he called. 'Excellent. Nice lunch? Anybody there?'

'No one I knew.'

'Same here. Only old has-beens.'

The Outfit

'Ingoldby – Feathers,' Sir had said outside the Prep school in the Lake District mountains.

Ingoldby that day became not only Eddie Feathers's first friend but a part of him. They sat down that evening side by side for the sausage supper. From the next morning they shared one of the ten double desks, with tip-up seats and a single inkwell. Listening to Pat Ingoldby's endless talk, Eddie, at first painfully and hesitantly, began to talk, too. Ingoldby waited patiently when the clock had trouble ticking, never breaking in. Over four years the stammer healed.

Despite Sir's strictness about no best friends and daily cold showers, nothing could be done about the oneness of Ingoldby and Feathers. They read the same tattered books from the library – Henty, Ballantyne and Kipling; picked each other for teams. They discussed the same heroes. Ingoldby was dark and slight, Eddie Feathers four inches taller and chestnut-haired, but they began to walk with the same gait. A funny pair. And they made a funny pair in the school skiff on the lake but almost always won. Ingoldby's wit and logic expunged the nightmares of Eddie's past. They were balm and blessing to Eddie who had met none previously. He never once mentioned the years before he arrived at Sir's Outfit and Pat never enquired about them or volunteered information about himself. The past, unless very pleasant, is not much discussed among children.

On Sports Day, Colonel Ingoldby arrived and Feathers was

introduced to him and soon Feathers was visiting the Ingoldbys in the school holidays. Sir wrote to Malaya describing the excellence of the Ingoldbys and saying that they would like to have Eddie with them for every holiday. A handsome cheque came from Kotakinakulu to Mrs Ingoldby and was graciously received (though there had been no accompanying letter).

At fourteen both boys were to move on to the same Public school in the Midlands and Mrs Ingoldby asked Eddie how he felt about continuing the arrangements. Would his aunts – whom he had only once seen – be jealous? Insulted? 'We've become so used to you, Eddie. Jack is so much older than Pat. They're too far apart to be close as brothers. I think Pat is lonely, to tell you the truth. Would you be *very* bored to become part of the family? Now, do say so if you would.'

'Of course I'd love to be.'

'I'll write to your father.'

From Malaya, there was silence, except for another cheque. Nor was anything heard from the aunts. Mrs Ingoldby said nothing about the money except, 'How very kind and how quite unnecessary,' and Eddie was absorbed into the Ingoldbys' life in their large house on a Lancashire hilltop where the Colonel kept bees and Mrs Ingoldby wandered vaguely and happily about, smiling at people. When Pat won an award to their next school, Colonel Ingoldby opened a bottle of Valpolicella which he remembered having drunk ('Did we dear?') on their honeymoon in Italy before the Great War. The following year Eddie won one, too, and there was the same ritual.

Mrs Ingoldby was Eddie's first English love. He had not known such an uncomplicated woman could exist. Calm and dreamy, often carrying somebody a cup of tea for no reason but love; entirely at the whim of a choleric husband, of whom she made no complaints. She was unfailingly delighted by the surprise of each new day.

The house was High House and stood at the end of a straight steep drive with an avenue of trees. Old and spare metal fences separated the avenue from the fields which in the Easter holidays of the wet Lancashire spring were the same dizzy green as the rice-paddies of South-East Asia. Far below the avenue to the West you could look down the chimneys of the family business which was a factory set in a dell. It was famous for making a particular kind of carpet, and was called The Goit, and through it, among the buildings of the purring carpet factory, ran a wide stream full of washed stones and little transparent fishes. 'I am told our water is particularly pure,' said Mrs Ingoldby to Eddie Feathers ('Such an interesting name').

'I suppose it has to be, for washing the carpets,' said Eddie. 'But what about all the dyes?'

'Oh, I've simply no idea.'

'Teddy' they called him, or 'My dear chap' (the Colonel). Pat called him 'Fevvers', as at school, but otherwise often ignored him. He was different at home and went off on his own. He sometimes sulked.

'He has these wretched black moods,' said Mrs Ingoldby, shelling peas under a beech tree. 'Does it happen at school?'

'Yes. Sometimes. It does, actually.'

'D'you know what causes them? He was such a *sunny* little boy. Of course he is so clever, it's such a pity. The rest of us are nothing much. I keep thinking it's my fault. One's mother becomes disappointing in puberty, don't you think? I suppose he'll just have to bear it.'

Eddie wondered what puberty was.

'I suppose it's just this tiresome sex business coming on. Not, thank goodness, *homo*-sex for either of you.'

'No,' said Eddie. 'We get too much about it from Sir.'

'Ah, Sir. And poor Mr Smith.'

'Yes,' said Eddie. 'and the Mr Smiths are always changing and Sir broken-hearted and we have to take him up Striding Edge and get his spirits re-started.' Eddie had come some distance since the motor-ride from North Wales.

'Your mother must feel so far from you, across the world.'

'Oh no, she's dead. She died having me. I never knew her.'

'And your poor father, all alone still?'

'I suppose so.'

'I'm sure he loves you.'

Eddie said nothing. The idea was novel. Bumble bees drowsed in the lavender bushes.

'*My* parents didn't love me at all,' said Mrs Ingoldby. 'They were Indian Army. My mother couldn't wait to get rid of me to England. She'd lost several of us. Such pitiful rows of little graves in the Punjab and rows of mothers, too. But she really wanted just to ship me off. I'm very grateful. I went to a marvellous woman and there was a group of us. We completely forgot our parents. My mother ran off with someone – they did, you know. Or took to drink. Not enough to do. They used to give orders to the Indian servants like soldiers – very unbecoming. Utterly loyal to England of course. Then my father lost all his money. He was rather pathetic, I suppose.'

'D-d-did he come to see you? In England?'

'Oh, I suppose so. Yes. I went to live with his sister, my Aunt Rose, when I grew up. It was very dull but I had nice clothes and she was very rich. I was never allowed to be ill. She was what is known as a Christian Scientist. Influenza in 1919 was tiresome. Everyone was dying. When my father turned up one day, a *footman* answered the morning-room door if you please (Aunt Rose had never opened a door in her life), and she just said, "Oh, there you are, Gaspard. You must be tired. Here is your little girl." D'you know, he burst into tears and fled. I can't think why. Oh, how lucky I was to meet the Colonel.'

Walking across the fields with Pat, Eddie made about the only comment on anyone's life he had ever made.

'Your mother seems to feel the same about everybody. Why is she always happy?'

'God – I don't know.'

'She's not bitter at all. Nobody liked her. Her parents sound awful if you don't mind my saying so.'

'You've had Aunt Rose and the footman? They were all barmy, if you ask me. Raj loonies.'

'She seems to feel – well, to like everybody, though.'

'Oh, no, she doesn't. They were brought up like that. Most of them learned never to like anyone, ever, their whole lives. But they didn't moan because they had this safety net. The Empire. Wherever you went you wore the Crown, and wherever you went you could find your own kind. A club. There are still thousands round the world thinking they own it. It's vaguely mixed up with Christian duty. Even now. Even here, at Home. Every house of our sort you go into, Liverpool to the Isle of Wight – there's big game on the wall and tiger skins on the floor and tables made of Benares brass trays and a photograph of the Great Durbar. Nowadays you can even fake it, with plenty of servants. It wasn't like that in my grandfather's generation. They were better people. Better educated, Bible-readers, not showy. Got on with the job. There was a job for everyone and they did it and often died in it.'

'I think my father will die in his. He thinks of nothing else. Sweats and slogs. Sick with malaria. And lost his family.'

Pat, who was unconcerned about individuals, slashed at the flower-heads. 'I'll be an historian. That's what I'm going to do. It's the only hope – learning how we got to be what we are. Primates, I mean. Surges of aggression. Today'll be history tomorrow. The empire is on the wane. Draining away. There will be chaos when it's gone and we'll be none the better people. When empires end, there's often a dazzling finale – then –? Germany's looming again, Goths versus Vizigoths.'

'But you'd fight for the Empire, wouldn't you? I mean – you'd fight for all this?' Eddie nodded over the green land.

'For the carpet factory? Yes, I would. I will.'

'You *will*. Fight then?'

'Yes.'

'So will I,' said Eddie.

Wandering about that last peacetime summer with the Ingoldbys, Pat now seventeen, Eddie sixteen, the days were like weeks, endless as summers in childhood. They walked for miles – and at the end of each day of sun and smouldering cloud and shining Lancashire rain – stopped at the avenue. In the soft

valley, more certain than sunset, the factory workers set off for
home after the five o'clock hooter, moving in strings up The
Goit and through the woods on paved paths worn into saucers
and polished by generations of clogs. Sometimes on the high
avenue, with the wind right, you could hear the horse-shoe
metal of the clogs on the sandstone clinking like castanets.

Wandering on, the two of them would watch the Colonel in
a black veil puffing smoke from a funnel stuffed with hay, and
swearing at his bees. 'If he'd only be quieter with them,' said
Pat. 'Want any help, Pa?'

'No. Get away, you'll be killed. They're on the rampage.'

'Oh – tea,' said Mrs Ingoldby. 'You're just in time. I'll get them
to make you some more of the little tongue sandwiches. Did
you have a good walk?'

'Wonderful, thanks. Any news?'

'Yes. Hitler's invaded Poland. Don't tell your father yet, Pat.
He can do nothing about it and there's his favourite supper.
Oxtail stew.'

'It's not all an act, you know,' said Pat, the thought-reader, Mrs
Ingoldby having gone up to change for dinner. 'It's a *modus
vivendi*. Old-fashioned manners.'

'I like it.'

'Not upsetting the guests, yes. But she keeps anything horrid
inside, for her own safety. My mother's not the fool she makes
herself out to be. She's frightened. Any minute now, and
farewell the carpet factory and security. It's going to be turned
over to munitions. Plough-shares into swords. It's been our safe
and respected source of income for two generations. This
house'll go. Jack's going into the Air Force, and I intend to.'

'You?'

'Yes. I suppose so. After I've got in to Cambridge. If they'll
have me. Get my foot in for later.'

He didn't ask about Eddie's plans.

'As I've been through the OTC,' said Eddie. 'I suppose I'll
go for a soldier. My father was in something called the Royal

Gloucesters – I don't know why. He might get me in there.'

'By the way,' said Pat, like his mother avoiding rocks in the river. 'All that about footmen and Ma – it's balls, you know. Too many Georgette Heyers.'

'But your mother's so –' (he was going to say innocent but it didn't seem polite) '– truthful.'

'She's self-protective,' said Pat. 'Can you wonder? She was through the Great War, too.'

That evening after dinner they listened to the wireless with the long windows open on to the lawn. A larch swung down black arms to touch the grass. A cat came out from under the arms and limped across the garden and out of sight. It was shaking its paws crossly.

The news was dire. After the Colonel had switched it off, you could hear the clipped BBC tones continuing through the open windows of the servants' sitting-room. Shadows had suddenly swallowed the drawing-room, and it was cold.

Mrs Ingoldby draped a rug about her knees and said, 'Pat, we need the light on.' The heart-breaking smell of the stocks in the nearest flower bed engulfed the room like a sweet gas.

Pat lit up a cigarette and the cat walked back over the grass, a shadow now. Two green lamps of eyes blinked briefly. Pat put the light on.

'Whatever's the matter with the cat?'

'Don't talk to me about the cat,' said the Colonel, 'I threw it out of the bedroom window.'

'Pa!'

'It had done a wee on my eiderdown. I threw the eiderdown after it. I'd have shot it if the gun had been handy. I'm keeping it loaded now for the Invasion. That cat knows exactly what it's doing.'

'Do be careful, dear. It's not a Nazi.'

'Cats and bees and the world, all gone mad. I tell you, there'll be no honey this year. Everything's a failure. I'm thinking of buying a cow.'

'A cow, dear?'

'There'll be no butter by Christmas. Powdered milk. No cream.'

'Why ever not?'

'It'll be rationed. Forces first. Are you a fool?'

At bedtime Eddie leaned out of his bedroom window – the bedroom now seemed altogether his own – and looked at the dark and light rows of the vegetable garden, the Colonel's obedient regiment standing to attention under a paring of moon. Silence until six o'clock tomorrow, and the factory hooter. Then the chorus of clicking feet trudging down The Goit as if nothing could ever change. Along the landing he heard the trumpet-call of the Colonel, 'Rosie – do *not* shut the window. And don't bring in that eiderdown. It stays there all night. I dare say it *will* rain. Let it rain.'

Eddie could make out the square shape of desecrated satin lying up against the house like a forlorn white flag.

Tulips

The morning after the ghastly day in London – the solicitor had muddled her diary or had had to stay at home with sick children or her mobile phone was out of order or a mixture of the three, which had meant their trip to Bantry Street had been for nothing – Filth was seated in the sun-lounge, very fierce and composing a Letter of Wishes to add to his Will. He wondered if he was quite well. A wet square of eiderdown kept floating into sight. Tiredness. He was half-dreaming. Wouldn't say anything to Betty.

The November sun blazed. It was almost warm enough to sit out of doors but Filth liked a desk before him when he was thinking. He liked a pen, or at least one of the expensive type of Biro – several because they gave out – and a block of A5 of the kind on which he had written his careful Opinions. Diligent, accurate, lucid, no jargon, all thanks to Sir, his Opinions used to be shown to Juniors as models of the form. Then they had left him for the Clerk's rooms, where they were typed. First by a single typist – Mrs Jones, who in between whiles did her knitting, often in her sealskin fur coat for there was no central heating. Later there were five typists, later still twenty. Over the years Filth had scarcely noticed the changes, from the clatter of the old black Remingtons and all the girls chain-smoking, to the hum and click of electronics, to the glare of a screen in every Barrister's room, the first fax machines, the e-mails and the mysterious Web. He was relieved not to have had to cope with all this as a Junior or a Silk, and that by the time he made Judge and lived in Hong Kong he had stepped into a world so advanced in electronics that he could hand everything over to machines but keep his pen too. His handwriting – thanks again to Sir – was much admired. He had been in Commercial Chambers. The construction industry. Bridges and dams.

And what a great stack of money I made at the Bar, he thought. It was a noble act becoming a Judge on a salary. *Letters of Wishes . . . Bequests to Friends. . . .* I've left it too long. The best friends are all dead.

And no children to leave it to. He looked across from the sun-lounge to Betty planting the tulips. She seldom spoke of children. Never to children when there were any around. She seemed – had always seemed – to have no views on their barrenness.

As it happened, had he known it, she was thinking of children now. She was wondering about yesterday, when she and Filth had made an abortive attempt to give what they had by dying. The death of Terry's child. The solicitor forgetting her job because of her children's measles. This dazzle of a morning, thirty years beyond her child-bearing years. The trees across Wiltshire were bright orange, yellow, an occasional vermilion maple – what a slow leaf fall – spreading away from the hillside garden, the sun rich and strong, the house behind her benign and English and safe, as well-loved now as her apartments and houses in the East. There would have been grandchildren by now, she thought and heard their voices. Would we have been any good with them? She could not see Filth looking at a grandchild with love.

She had never been sure about Filth and love. Something blocked him. Oh, *faithful* – oh, yes. Unswerving unto death. 'Never been anyone for Filth but Betty.' And so on.

All this time in the tulip bed, she had been on her knees and she tried now to get up. It is becoming ridiculous, this getting up. Ungainly. Not that I was ever *gainly*, but I wasn't lumberous. She lay down on her side, grinning, on the wet grass. And saw that her pearls had come off and lay in the tulip bed. They were yesterday's pearls, and for the first time in her life she had not taken them off at bedtime nor when she bathed in the morning. 'I am becoming a slut,' she told them. Her face was close against them. She said to them, 'You are not my *famous* pearls, though he never notices. You are my *guilty* pearls. What shall I do with you? Who shall have you when I am gone?'

'No one,' she said, and let them slither out of sight into one of the holes made ready for the tulips. With her fingers, she filled the hole with earth and smoothed it over.

Then she brought her firm old legs round in front of her so that they lay across the flower-beds. She noticed that each hole had a sprinkle of sharp sand in the bottom, and hoped the sand would not hurt the pearls.

Still not out of the wood, she thought. Hope Filth doesn't look up, he'd worry.

She rested, then twisted herself, heaved and crawled. The legs obeyed her at last and came round back again and she was on all fours. She leaned on her elbows, her hands huge in green and yellow gloves, and slowly brought her bottom into the air, swayed, and creakily, gleefully stood up. 'Well, I was never John Travolta,' she said. 'And it is November. Almost first frost.'

Amazed, as she never ceased to be, about how such a multi- tude of ideas and images exist alongside one another and how the brain can cope with them, layered like filo pastry in the mind, invisible as data behind the screen, Betty was again in Orange Tree Road, standing with Mrs Cleary and Mrs Hong and old friends in the warm rain, and all around the leaves falling like painted raindrops. The smell of the earth round the building-works of the new blocks of flats, the jacarandas, the polish on the banana leaves, children laughing, swimming in the private pools. The sense of being part of elastic life, unhurried, timeless, controlled. And in love. The poor little girl selling parking tickets in her white mittens against the sun. Betty's eyes filled with tears, misting her glasses. Time gone. Terry's boy gone.

Trowel in hand, a bit tottery, she turned to look up the garden at Filth.

Since yesterday he had been impossible. All night catafalque-rigid, sipping water, at breakfast senatorial and remote. The Judge's dais. He had frowned about him for toast. When she had made more toast and set the toast-rack (silver) before him he had examined it and said, 'The toast-rack needs cleaning.'

'So do the salt-cellars,' she'd said. 'I'll get you the Silvo. You've nothing else to do today.'

He had glared at her, and she wondered whether his mind, too, was layered with images. Breakfast on The Peak for eleven years at seven o'clock, misty, damp and grey, she in her silk dressing-gown making lists for the day, Filth – oh so clean, clean Filth – in his light-weight dark suit and shirt so white it seemed almost blue, his Christ Church tie, his crocodile brief-case. Outside the silently-sliding Merc, with driver waiting in dark-green uniform, the guard on the gate ready to press the button on the steel doors that would rise without creak or hesitation. And the warm, warm heavy air.

'Bye, dear.'

'Bye, Filth. Home sixish?'

'Home sixish.'

Every minute pleasantly filled. Work, play and no chores.

And the sunset always on the dot, like Filth's homecoming. The dark falling over the harbour that was never dark, the lights in their multitude, every sky-scraper with a thousand eyes. The sky-high curtains of unwinking lights, red, yellow, white, pale green, coloured rain falling through the dark. The huge noise of Hong Kong rising, the little ferries plying, the sense of a place to be proud of. We made it. We saw how to do it. A place to have been responsible for. British.

'I'll do the silver later,' said Filth. 'I shall be busy this morning with my Letter of Wishes. I shall see to my own Will.'

'I suppose I should do a Letter too,' she said. 'I'd thought the Will would be enough. But after yesterday –'

'The less said about yesterday the better. London solicitors!' and he rose from the toast-rack, still a fascinatingly tall and taking man, she thought. If it wasn't for the neck and the moles he'd look no more than sixty. People still look up and wonder who he is. Always a tie. And his shoes like glass.

'I'm going to plant tulips.'

'I'll clear up the breakfast.'

'Do you mind? It's not Mrs T's day.'

'I want to get on with the Will whilst I'm still in ferment.'

'Ferment?'

'About that woman. Solicitor. You know exactly. Lack of seriousness. Duty. Messy. The distance we travelled! Messy diary. I expect her diary's on a screen.'

'Watch your blood-pressure, Filth. You've gone purple.'

He flung about the house looking for the right pen.

'You could do it on the computer. You can make changes much quicker.'

(They both played the game that they could work the computer if they tried.)

'I shan't be making many changes.'

'The point is,' she said, 'be quick. Get everything witnessed. Locally – why not? So much cheaper. We might die at any time.'

'So you said all the way home in the train. Solicitors!'

'So you have often said.'

He glared at her, then softened as he watched her healthy, outdoor face and her eyes that had never caught her out.

'I hate making Wills,' she said. 'I've made dozens,' and looked away, not wanting to touch on inheritances since there was nobody to inherit. She didn't want to see that Filth didn't mind.

'I think,' said Filth, astonishingly, 'one day I'll write you a Letter of my Wishes. My personal wishes.'

'Have you so many left then?'

'Not many. Peace at the last, perhaps.'

And that you will never leave me, he thought.

And now, standing with the trowel, head racing a bit with the effort of being John Travolta, she closed her eyes against

64

dizziness. She opened them again, shaded them with her hand and saw him seated above her in the sun-lounge. He had some sort of wrap over his bony, parted knees. The drape of it and the long narrow face staring into the sun made him look like a Christ in Majesty over a cathedral gate. All that was needed was the raised hand in blessing. His eyes were closed. How long is he going to last? she thought. How he hates death.

However, Christ in Majesty opened his eyes and raised a hand not in blessing but holding an enormous gin.

'Gin,' he called down. 'Felt like gin.'

I won't get any nearer to him now, she thought, turning to pick up the bulb-basket, taking off her gloves. Too late now. The holes look good, but I'll do the planting tomorrow. There might be a frost. I won't risk them out all night on the grass.

The Ferment

After her funeral, Filth, now old as time, was at his desk again.

Garbutt, the odd job man, trundled a wheelbarrow stacked up with ivy between the sun-lounge and the tulip bed. Garbutt's jaw was thrust forward. He was lusting after a bonfire. The woman, Mrs Thing, arrived at Filth's shoulder with a cup of coffee, then with a Ewbank sweeper.

'Lift your feet a minute and let me get under them and then I'll leave you in peace,' she said. 'Here's more letters. Shall I come back with your ironing tonight? I could make you a salad. The way he goes at that ivy!'

'Thank you, no. Perfectly capable,' said Filth. 'I must keep at desk.'

'I liked the ivy,' she said. 'Not that my opinion. . . .'

'It's done now,' said Filth.

'I'm sorry. Well, there's plenty in the fridge and you've only to phone up. . . .'

'Letters,' he said. 'Letters. Many, many letters,' and he picked one up and waved it about to get rid of her. There were no black-bordered ones now, thank God. They had disappeared with the Empire. This one was in a pale green envelope and came from Paris. As the woman, Mrs-er, slammed the front door and Garbutt stamped past again with the empty barrow, Filth had the sensation of a command not to open this letter and looking across the garden saw Betty standing on the lawn watching him with an expression of deep annoyance.

66

'Ha!' he said, and stared her out. 'Leave me be,' he shouted. He picked up the ivory paper knife to slit the envelope and saw the name: *Ingoldby*. He stared, looked back at the now empty lawn, looked down again.

Not the Colonel or Mrs Ingoldby, long ago gone. Not Jack or Pat. No issue there. *I. Ingoldby*, it said on the envelope and so it must be Isobel. Ye gods.

Well, I'd better face it.

The year that Eddie left Sir's Outfit for his Public school, he was to spend the summer as usual at High House. Pat Ingoldby, a year older, had left Sir the year before but had written a weekly letter from the new school to Eddie and Eddie had written back. Other boys did the same with absent brothers. Sir had insisted from the start on weekly letters to parents and, although Eddie had had none back from his father, the habit had continued until Pat moved on. Then Eddie had struck, and asked to write to Mrs Ingoldby instead of his father and, as Eddie's stammer was threatening again after Pat's departure, Sir agreed, and Mrs Ingoldby did write back occasionally, in a hand like a very small spider meandering across the thick writing paper and passing out and dying off in the faintest of signatures. Years later, in a different life, Eddie found that his father had kept all his letters from Sir's Outfit, numbered carefully and filed in a steel safe against the termites. Eddie's letters to Mrs Ingoldby and to Pat did not survive.

Sir had also insisted on letters being written to Auntie May, who occasionally sent a postcard; Uncle Albert, her missionary husband, once sent the school a coconut for Christmas.

Pat's short succinct, witty letters from the new school were a great pleasure to Eddie. He absorbed everything offered for his information: accommodation, lessons, boys, games (which were more important than church), menus, lack of humour among staff. Both boys missed each other but never referred to the fact, nor to the fact that the fraternal arrangements of the holidays would of course continue. Eddie wrote to his aunts, one of about three letters in his five years with Sir, asking if he could have some of the money his father had put aside for him, to give Sir a present, and Aunt Muriel sent a ten shilling note.

'I don't accept presents,' said Sir, looking briefly at *Three Men in a Boat*. 'This is a clean school. No nonsense. But yes, I'll have this one. Send your sons here when you've got some. Present us with a silver cup for something when you're a filthy rich lawyer, I dare say? Yes. You'll be a lawyer. Magnificent memory. Sense of logic, no imagination and no brains. My favourite chap, Teddy Feathers, as a matter of fact. I dare say.'

'Thank you, Sir. I'll always keep in touch.'

'Don't go near Wales. And keep off girls for a while. Soon as girls arrive exam results go down. Passion leads to a Lower Second. Goodbye, old Feathers. On with the dance.'

High House – it was now 1936 – where Eddie now brought all his (few) possessions, was reassuringly the same and here was Pat on the railway platform, taller and spotty, with a deep voice but still talking. Talking and talking. There was to be a girl staying, he said, but not to worry as almost at once she was going off on holiday to the Lake District with his mother.

'She's here already. She's a cousin. Pa's niece. She's causing trouble.'

But up at the House there was no sign of this cousin and nobody mentioned her and she didn't show up all day.

The next day at breakfast Eddie asked the Colonel about her.

'How's your niece, Sir?'

'Done very badly in her Higher School Certificate. And she's too old to try again. I tell her nobody will ever ask her what she did and she'll forget it herself in six months. She'll find a husband. Poor fellow.'

'One can't be sure,' said Mrs Ingoldby. 'She's rather *secretive*. I've a feeling that a husband isn't on the cards. And *very* stubborn, I'm afraid. I've sent her breakfast up as she has a headache. *And* she's upset.'

The next day there was a sighting of Isobel Ingoldby pacing

68

about the garden, up and down, up and down in the rain with a haversack on her back.

'Is she going somewhere?' asked Pat.

'She talks of Spain. She has an urge to help the rebels. I thought I might telegraph her parents.'

'Let her be,' said Pat. 'She'll be in for dinner.'

'But did she have *breakfast*?'

'Well, it was all laid up for her on the sideboard.'

'I wouldn't want her going home and saying we'd given her nothing to eat. And oh dear, look! Maybe she *didn't* have breakfast.'

Isobel could be seen writhing about in her haversack and then disembowelling it on the grass. She took from it a hunk of bread, stood up, tilted back her head and began to devour it. Her eyes seemed closed. Praying perhaps.

'I think she may be a little peculiar,' said Colonel Ingoldby. 'There is some of that in the Ingoldbys. Not Pat, of course, dear, and certainly not Jack.'

Elder brother Jack, the beloved, now passed through High House only very occasionally. Sir and the family's traditional public school had seen him to Cambridge and he was there or abroad most of the time, swooping through his old home, once or twice a summer, bringing rare and various companions, playing wonderful tennis, clean and groomed, at one with his parents' world. Mrs Ingoldby, like a dog which awaits its master, seemed to know by instinct when he was on the way. 'Just a mo. Isn't that Jack?' They would listen, then continue life, and a few minutes later would come the splutter and roar of Jack's car, its silver body tied up with a classy leather strap.

Eddie had an instinct about Jack, too; that Isobel was being kept away from him and that was why she and Mrs Ingoldby were off to the Lake District. That was why Isobel was peculiar. Seeing Isobel in the garden he could tell that the Lake District and her godmother would not be sufficient for her.

'Oh, do bring her in,' said Mrs Ingoldby, 'or at any rate someone go and talk to her. . . . You, Eddie. Would you go?

You'll be new to her – she finds us boring. You could talk to her about the Spanish Civil War. I don't want any stories about our neglecting her going back to Gerard's Cross.'

So Eddie had walked rather awkwardly across the lawn and into the trees, on his fourteen-year-old lengthening legs and oval knees. His curly hair; his hands in his pockets like some of the more blasé of the Mr Smiths' had been. His feet in scruffy sand-shoes very huge; his height endearing. His voice, breaking, was surprising him all the time by sudden booms and squeaks. Yet there was grace about him. He hadn't taken in a thing about the Spanish Civil War.

The girl was standing with her back to him. The rain had stopped and it was becoming a warm and honeyed July morning and in the hills below stood the factory chimneys rising brown and mighty like Hindu temples.

'Oh, hullo,' he said.

The girl stopped munching and turned. She stared.

'I'm Edward Feathers. Pat's friend. I've been told to ask if you – well, if you might be coming in for lunch?'

The girl was gigantic; bony, golden and vast; as tall as Eddie and certainly pretty old. She could be twenty. Her face was like a lioness's – flat nose, narrow brow, wide cheekbones, long green eyes. Supreme self-command. Wow!

Her legs were bare and very long, like his own, and her sandals had little leather thongs separating the toes.

Eddie felt something happening to his anatomy and though he had no idea what it was he began to blush.

She looked him up and down and began to laugh.

'I don't go in for eating round a polished table,' she said. 'I need to be out of doors. They know that.'

'They didn't seem to. Oh, well, OK, then. I'll tell them.' And he fled.

'She says she doesn't like eating round a polished table.'

'Oh, God,' said Pat.

'That's her mother,' said the Colonel.

'I'm afraid I'm going to have a difficult time with her in the Wastwater Hotel,' said Mrs Ingoldby.

'Maybe the table won't be polished,' said Pat. 'Anyway, why take her? Jack's abroad.'

His mother gave him what in any other woman would have been a searching look. 'I *am* her godmother,' she said, 'and her mother *has* gone off with a Moroccan drummer.'

'I don't blame her,' said Pat. 'Fevvers' mother went off, and he doesn't go eating in the trees.'

'Oh, Teddy! I didn't know! I thought your mother only *died*.'

'She did only die,' said Eddie. 'She died when I was two days old.'

'She must have caught sight of you,' said Pat.

'That will do,' said his mother, and 'Damn bad luck,' said his father, 'don't suppose there were many Moroccans in Malaya.'

'There were a lot of drummers,' said Eddie and began to squeal and cackle. The Colonel and his wife looked baffled and embarrassed.

Pat had given Eddie some sort of sudden freedom. Eddie's ideal mother, whom he had always thought of as an Auntie May sort of person, became a houri, off to bed and that with a Moroccan drummer! Pat had given him confidence. Right from the very start. And crikey, he needed it, now, after that thing that had happened to him in the trees. He wondered whether to mention it to Pat; then knew that it was the first thing ever that he couldn't discuss with him.

Pat was watching him.

'Shall we go out on bikes?'

'Yes, great. Yes, please.'

'OK, Ma?'

'Yes. But what are we to do about Isobel?'

'It's out of our hands to do anything about Isobel.'

And the leopardish girl went prowling past the windows, haversack in place and reading a map.

'She's a fine looker, I'll say that,' said the Colonel.

'Jack thinks so, too,' said Pat.

*

The two of them trudged up a hill, pushing their bikes, wishing for modern three-speeds and not these childhood toys with baskets. 'And you – hein?'

Eddie said nothing.

At supper Isobel appeared and sat down at the Colonel's right hand. She leaned back in her chair and glittered her eyes.

'What a pretty dress,' said her godmother. 'Were you thinking of taking it to Spain? I'm sure it has to be dry-cleaned. It will be difficult at the frontier.'

Isobel messed with her food.

'Oh, dear. I'm afraid you've stopped liking fish-pie. You used to love. . . .'

'It's fine,' said Isobel, scraping it about with the tips of the prongs of her fork. She had picked out all the prawns and now leaned her sun-burnt shoulders towards Eddie and began to pick prawns off his plate.

'Yummie,' she said, and Eddie found himself in trouble again beneath the tablecloth. He blushed purple and Pat exploded in his glass of water.

'I think she's after you,' Pat said after dinner, playing tennis with Eddie in the dark. 'Go easy. She's a cannibal. It's going to rain. We'll have to go in. Get the net down. She'll be out there somewhere, gleaming in the bushes. Aren't you going to laugh?'

But Eddie, busy catching up tennis balls, winding up the net, said nothing. On the way back to the house he slashed at vegetation for all he was worth.

'Sorry I spoke,' said Pat. 'Only joking.'

'Oh, shut up,' said Eddie. 'I can't stand your cousin. OK? Sorry.'

But they stopped at the bench for the view from the hill. 'Can't see much, but we could maybe hear the nightingale. Then we could send a card to Sir,' said Pat.

'It's too late for the nightingale. And too far north.'

'D'you want a weed?' Pat lit up a cigarette.

'No fear.'

'It turns on the girls. Not that you seem to feel the need.'

'It's disgusting. It's all disgusting,' Eddie yelled out and pushed Pat off the seat and sat on him. Pat flailed about and then began to sing:

> 'My friend Billy
> Had a ten-foot. . . .'

'Stop it!'

> 'He showed it to the boy next door.
> 'Who thought it was a snake
> 'And hit it with a rake
> 'And now it's only. . . .'

And they rolled about, fighting as they had done for years, stopping the clocks for a minute longer.

But there was a change somewhere. He and Pat were moving on. Glaciers would soon come grinding them apart, memories would be forgotten or adapted or faked.

Eddie followed Pat heavily into the house that evening and even Pat looked thoughtful. In the drawing-room the Ingoldbys were talking their pointless evening birdsong. No sound of Isobel anywhere.

As Eddie lay in his adored High House bed the rain began to patter down again outside and he jumped out to shut the window where the moon soon disappeared behind the rain clouds. He climbed back into bed.

All the following years, the memory or dream of what happened next never quite left him. His bedroom door opened and closed again, and the goddess – lioness – girl was at the end of his bed. Standing and watching, brooding on his inability to take his eyes off her.

She then walked to the window and looked out. He knew that something was expected of him but had no idea what it was. Not long ago, he would have shouted out, 'Help! Burglars!' In time, in only a few years, he supposed, from books he'd read in the back of bookshops near Sir's, he and the girl would have merged their flesh together in some sort of way in the bed. But he didn't know what happened next. And didn't want to know.

She's old and she's evil and she only wants to hurt, he thought.

'Eddie?' the shadow whispered from the window. 'I wonder what you think of me?'

She walked back across the room and he found that he could sit up straight under the blankets and confront her, brave as – brave as *Cumberledge*. There! He'd said the word. Cumberledge. Wherever he was now. Silent Cumberledge whose spirit had never been completely broken.

Eddie would finish her, as once already in his life he had finished a woman. 'I think you're bad. A bad woman,' he said. 'Get out.'

And she was gone.

The weird dream (or whatever it was) was never quite obliterated. He had not so much kept it to himself as denied it. In a way he never understood, it both shamed and saddened him.

Why ever? Nothing had happened. He had won. He had silenced the sirens. If there had been sailors on board, they would not have had to tie this Ulysses to the mast. So sucks to sexy Isobel, the cradle-snatcher.

Yet, all his life – regret.

Isobel and Mrs Ingoldby were gone first thing next morning. And when Eddie next met Isobel it was in another world and a great many people were dead.

The Donheads

And so it was Isobel. The green letter was from Isobel. A letter of condolence for the loss of his wife.

> Dear Teddy (if I still may, Sir Edward),
> I have just seen in the *New York Times* here in Paris the very sad news of Betty's death and I am writing to say how very much I feel for you, and for all of us, come to that, who knew her and will miss her.

(*Miss* her? *Knew* her?)

> I wonder just how much you remember? I wonder how much you remember of anything before you met Betty and became the icon of the jolly old Hong Kong Bar? Before you *really* met me? We never mentioned High House, did we? Again?
> It hardly outlasted the War, you know. You and Pat were so very much together there. You and Pat were the spirit of the place, and I was a hole in the air. Did you ever know, I wonder, after you met Betty, that she and I were at school together? I went to High House after the Higher School Certificate disaster. She left St Paul's Girls in triumph. But they had me later in the War at Bletchley Park and there we met again. Bletchley Park was full of innocent, nice girls (not me) who had a very particular aptitude (crosswords) for solving cyphers and things, as you will be hearing in a year or two when ALL IS TOLD (the fifty year revelation). That is how we won the War. How we stopped the U-Boats. *So* we were told. We were schoolgirls, Teddy. I was still a schoolgirl when you met me. Do you remember my teenage sulks? I was a schoolgirl

75

five years on – no. Not five years on. Not in Peel Street. Oh, my beloved Teddy.

I was so pleased when you married Betty. I would have destroyed you, my sweet, beloved Teddy. But because of – well, I expect you have forgotten – but because of the day your great big feet came left, right, stamp, stamp down Peel Street and I was waiting for you and then –. Well, because of this I think I am allowed to write to you now. Oh, look – forget Peel Street. Kensington. Peripheral. I loved you from the moment you came walking (embarrassingly!) up to the trees at High House. I loved you and I love you.

Betty and I always exchanged Christmas cards. I expect you didn't know. You probably never noticed mine. Betty was a very untouchable woman. Nobody knew her – though I always suspected that there was a great well – *comprehension* – with someone, somewhere. She wasn't very pretty. She always sent *me* a Christmas card.

I was so very sorry to see in the NY *Times* – my word, she was a surpriser! You and I, Teddy, won't make the *NYT* – I was so very sorry to see in the obituary that there were 'no children of the marriage'. It is – in every language – a bleak little phrase. It means that you and B had a sadness, for when I last saw Betty forty years ago, she told me how much she longed for a child. We were in a park at the Hague. You were at the Court of International Justice, against Veneering. Betty and Veneering – what a saint you were, Eddie!

I have no children either, come to that. And no partner (Christ! Christ! – '*partner*'). I can no longer bear a partner, but I most desperately regret not having had a child. You guessed, Eddie. I think. There wasn't the word 'gay' then and it was something you didn't care to think about. But I believe you guessed.

I hope you still have friends about you in the south of England (NOT your place, I'd have thought?). Dear Teddy, everyone always loved you in your extraordinary never-revealed or unravelled private world. I am one of those who know that you were not really cold.

Sincerely yours, *Isobel*.

Filth picked up this letter and then its envelope and dropped both in the waste-paper basket. His face had taken upon it the iron ridges of a stage or television version of a prosecuting Counsel before he rises to the attack.

He found air-mail stationery of antique design. He addressed the envelope and attached three expensive stamps to be sure of covering the French postage. He drew the old-fashioned flimsy paper towards him, pushed aside the cheap Biros and took up his Collins gold pen (a retirement present from the lawyers of his Inn). He filled the pen from the ink bottle. Quink. Black. He wrote:

> Sir Edward Feathers thanks Miss Isobel
> Ingoldby for her kind letter of condolence.

He dated it, muffled himself into a coat, tweed hat and woollen gloves, took his walking stick and the letter, and set off down the drive and up the village hill to the post office.

He dropped the letter into the red box that still said, *V.R.* and strode inexorably home again. One or two people on the hill noticed him, and stopped what they were doing as he passed, glad to see that the old boy was going out again, ready to speak to him if he noticed them.

But he went by, the lanky, old-fashioned figure of long ago, walking painfully between the over-hanging trees of his drive. He passed Garbutt without a glance.

Isobel Ingoldby.

He sat again to his desk and wrote three more letters, replying to the formal, kind messages of condolence. Several times the telephone rang and he heard the drone and click of the answer-phone and paid no attention. Lunchtime came and went. He wrote more replies to letters including one (good heavens!!) from *Cumberledge* in Cambridge. Billy Cumberledge. What is this? What's this? I need Betty.

Mid-afternoon, and he walked into the kitchen and looked hard and long at the fridge and did not open it. He boiled up water but, when the kettle clicked off, did nothing about it. He stood at the kitchen window idly swirling water from the hot tap around in the little green teapot to warm its inside, standing until the steam began to scald his fingers. Then he poured himself a glass of milk and walked to the study where the newspaper lay ready for him by his armchair. He sat, and regarded his rows of law books, his grand old wig-box now laid out again upon the hearth. Eventually he dozed and awoke with the sun gone down behind the hills, and the room cold.

He wondered wherever the glass of milk had come from. He had not drunk milk since Ma Didds in Wales. She must be here. He heard the hated voice. 'You don't leave this cupboard until you've drunk this glass of good milk and you'd better not stir your feet because there's a hole in there beside you deep as a well and you'd never be heard of more.' The long day, and not let out till bedtime, and six years old.

He walked over to the waste-paper basket and re-read the letter. It existed. It had not been a dream. She had waited over forty years. The letter of a cruel spirit. 'Loves me' – how abhorrent. She is a lesbian. 'Not cold' – enough! Betty wanting a child. . . . How dare she! This Ingoldby, the last traitor of all the traitorous Ingoldbys.

Oh, I am too old for any of this.

He took the milk back to the kitchen and poured it down the sink, opened a cake-tin and cut himself a slice of Betty's birthday cake and ate it rather guiltily because it wasn't yet stale. Then he poured himself a whiskey and soda, walked into the sun-lounge and held the letter up towards the tulip-bed.

'Betty?'

Emptiness. Silence. And silence within the house, too. Outside a most unnatural silence. Not a car in the lane, or a plane in the sky, not a human voice calling a dog. Not the church clock on the quarters, not a breath of wind, not a bird on a bough. All darkness as usual from the empty invisible house next door. Then a fox walked tiptoe over the December grass, its brush trailing but its ears pricked. At the steps that led up to the sun-lounge it turned its head towards Filth and smiled.

He remembered the Ingoldbys' delinquent cat angrily shaking its paws at the time of the breaking of nations. 1939. The roar of the Colonel that had shattered the family's self-deception and serenity. Then that earlier shadow, three years before, of the girl. Her shadow detaching itself from the blacker shadow of the yews. The term before he went to Public school.

School

Eddie found himself very much the junior to Pat at Chilham School when he followed him there in 1936. At first they were in different Houses. Eddie, after Sir's Outfit, was able to cope easily with the new place's idiosyncrasies. He was good at getting up in the morning and untroubled by Morning Prep at 6.30 a.m. The work was easy. He was good at games. He liked the slabs of bread and jam half-way through the morning. Whenever he caught sight of Pat he sent him a salute and Pat, untroubled that he was senior to Eddie, saluted back or did his Herr Hitler imitation. They naturally continued to keep together whenever possible. After matches – they were both in good teams – they would walk unselfconsciously round and round the playing fields, talking. They were soon a famous oddity, and were spoken to about it.

'It is not as if you were brothers,' said the Headmaster when the case was at length referred to him, the highest court.

'We've been brought up as brothers,' said Pat. 'Sir.'

'But even brothers here do not go about together all the time. What do you say, Feathers?'

'I can't think of anything, Sir.'

'Do you, we wonder' (this was a trap) 'wish you were in Ingoldby's House?'

'No, not specially. I've never thought about it. I'm with the Ingoldbys all the holidays.'

'How very unusual.'

'My father knew his father in the Great War,' said Pat,

astonishing Eddie who hadn't known of it. 'We're a sort of sub-family.'

It was a mystery.

'There seems no *physicality* about it,' said the Headmaster to their Housemasters. 'They're both very bright. And very unusual, but then all boys are unusual. Put Feathers in Ingoldby's House – might be the best thing. Treat them like other brothers here.'

Pat, most ridiculously young, went up to Cambridge for several days for the university entrance exam. The phoney war was over and the Battle of Britain had begun. The journey would not be unexciting. Pat made much of taking his gas mask.

Without him that week the school felt dull and empty and for the first time Eddie realised that he had made no friends. He felt an outsider as he lay in his bed in the dormitory.

'Is Ingoldby some relation?' came a shout in the dark.

'Not of mine,' said Eddie.

'You don't look like him,' came another shout. 'Not like his brother Jack did.'

'I'm not his brother. How d'you know what his brother Jack looks like?'

'In the team-photographs. Holding cups and shields. Head boy in a *gown*. Hamlet in *Hamlet*. Just a taller Ingoldby. Good looking, not carroty.'

'I come from Malaya.'

'Do they all have red hair there?'

'Yes. Every one of them.'

'Doesn't Ingoldby's brother mind?' someone shouted far down the row of beds, made brave by the black-out curtains.

'Mind what? I'm his brother's friend, too.'

'Mind your being so important to him?'

A searchlight began to scale the walls, to pierce the black windows. It was joined by another and they danced together for a while, searching for German bombers on the way to Liverpool.

'Why ever should he? Jack's in the Air Force. He's got more important things to think about.

'I dare say,' Eddie added, like Sir.

'What do Ingoldby's parents think?'

'I've never asked them. They've always wanted me there.' (And, he thought, they're mine. Blood of my blood and bone of my bone.)

'Where's your own family then, Feathers?' shouted an up-and-coming man. 'Where's your own family?' (They were braver with Ingoldby away.)

'My father's in Malaya.'

'Was he in the Great War? Smashed up?'

'Yes.'

'Why doesn't he come and see you?'

Pat returned from Cambridge with an assured place to read physics, having decided that history was all out of date – oh joke!

'After this War,' they had said, 'you have your foot in the door by being accepted by the college now. You can be deferred if you wish. Volunteer and wait to be called. They'll give you the first year. Excellent papers.'

But on the way home from Cambridge, overnight at High House, he had managed to volunteer for the RAF at the end of the summer term.

'If I'm spared,' he said to Eddie, in a Methusaleh voice. 'Bloody raids, here every night. Why didn't they evacuate us? We're going to be clobbered.'

'They think slowly here,' said Eddie. 'Sir moved his Outfit the minute Chamberlain wagged the white paper.'

'Chamberlain saved us,' said Pat. 'Gave us a year to make more broomsticks to look like rifles. Even the carpet factory's making tents now. I don't know where they'll be using them. Africa?'

'Sir's gone to America.'

This made them unhappy.

They were lying between damp grey blankets, among rows of other boys in the school's underground shelters, water running in rills down the walls. Far away a never-ending thunder meant that somewhere was being flattened again. York? Liverpool? Even as far away as Coventry.

The same week, on a night when there had been no air-raid siren, a drenching cold and moonless night and the boys asleep in their dormitories, every alarm bell in the school had begun to ring, followed by hooters, whistles and military cries. The dormitory doors were flung open and every boy ordered to dress immediately and gather by his House front door.

'And uniform, please, if you are in the Corps.'

'What – puttees, sir?'

'Puttees, Ingoldby.'

'They take a good five minutes, sir.'

'Then die, Ingoldby. Or get moving.'

Out from all the seven Houses of the school streamed boys of several ages in various attire. Each one was handed a rifle, Officers' Training Corps or not, and five rounds of ammunition.

'Invasion. Get on there. It's the Invasion. Go!' and five hundred boys, some trailing khaki bandages on their legs, some in their pyjamas and without their dressing-gowns ('*dressing-gowns*'), were quickly lost in the midnight fields and ditches of the North Midlands. Somebody cried 'Hark!' and some of them heard the death knell: the cry of the bells from all the muffled steeples. This was later denied.

'Oh,' said Pat, still purring from the Cambridge grown-up claret, 'INVASION. Five rounds. Bang, bang, bang, bang, finish. Farewell the red, white and blue.'

Those who knew how, loaded their rifles. Those who didn't, dropped their cartridges in the mud. There was occasional unfortunate friendly fire (though the phrase had not then been invented and the one used was balls-up) and a few disagreeable misfortunes with bayonets. There was the occasional, but not serious, scream.

Then, the silence. Darkness and rain settled over the North's infant infantry who did not trouble the landscape or the night, which passed with very few prayers and still fewer orgasms or

83

unexpected desire. Little poetry was engendered. After several hours some word of command must have been passed and the great old school found itself staggering from the ditches, crossing the sodden ugly fields, falling into bed again at four a.m.

But at 6.15 a.m. it was pre-breakfast Prep, as usual.

It had been a false alarm.

'We're going to lose this war,' said Eddie. 'Am I right, Pat?'

'Can't speak,' said Ingoldby. His hair looked like black lacquer which someone had painted on his head. His face was carmine. Under the bedclothes in the dormitory he was wearing last night's Army uniform sopped through and caked with mud. At the end of his bed, purple feet stuck out. Above them, his semi-putteed legs.

''You know the whole bloody issue was nothing?' someone was saying. 'A barrage-balloon come loose over the Vale of York, for God's sake. Trailed its cable over the electric pylon and blacked out the North. Invasion, my foot!'

'Invasion, my feet,' shuddered Ingoldby, looking with interest down his body under the blankets at them. 'Sometimes there are two of them, s-s-sometimes – oh God! S-s-sometimes four.'

He was found to have pneumonia and put in the school San. There, he was scooped from all friends, and therefore of course from Eddie, and absorbed into the antiseptic of the nutcracker-faced Matron in charge. Days passed.

On one of them, in a free-period, Eddie on his ostrich legs went walking to the San and found this woman seated just inside the door knitting an immense scarf in khaki wool that curled inwards down the sides like a tube.

'May I go and see Ingoldby, Matron?'

'Certainly not. You know the rules.'

'How is he?'

'That's my business.'

'Would you give him a message?'

'You know that's not allowed, neither.'

84

'I'll ask Oils, then.'

'Ask away.'

Eddie knocked on Mr Oilseed's door and found Oils, his Housemaster, late of Ypres, France, sitting one-eyed and holding a little glass weight at the end of a silver chain, swinging the chain gently over a desk covered with mountains of unmarked essays.

'Matron says I can ask to visit Ingoldby, sir.'

'Now – where is Ingoldby? I forget.'

'He's in the San, sir. As a result of The Fiasco. The other night.'

'Fiasco? Oh, I don't think we should assume that. It was a valuable exercise.'

'It's said that Ingoldby has pneumonia.'

'"It is said",' said Oils, 'is not a phrase I ever recommend. It does not commend itself. Ingoldby's parents are coming later today.'

'But, sir. . . . I'm pretty well part of that family, you know. Since I was eight.'

Oils let the fine chain ripple and fall into a heap upon the green baize of the desk. (What *was* he doing? Sexing a child?) He continued to stare at it.

'Feathers,' he said, 'the times are moving on, but very slowly.'

'Yes, sir?'

'There is something today that is a wonder in the school. This *Victorian* and bourgeois school. This is that the unnatural closeness between you and Ingoldby has not been terminated. There are certain explanatory circumstances but, as we who were in the trenches know, emotions have to be contained. This, like your Prep school, is a school in which we endure.'

'I loved our Prep school, sir.'

'I suggest that you go back to your study and read Kipling.'

'Kipling's childhood was very like mine and he *was* queer. I should like to appeal.'

'I beg your pardon?'

'I have the right of appeal here.'

'To whom, may I ask?'

'To the Headmaster first, sir. Then to the Board of Governors. Finally in the correspondence columns of *The Times*.'

'On what grounds?'

'Slander, sir. And antediluvianism.'

He left Oils' study and made for the Headmaster's House where no foot trod unbidden except those of the old spider himself and his paddly housekeeper. Eddie stood outside, and turned the great iron ring on the tall gate. The flagstones were slimy, the windows glimpsed through tangled plants.

'Come round the side,' said a threadbare voice from behind a pane. 'Kitchen.'

'Ah, yes,' said the Head after blinking at the daylight Eddie brought in with him, 'Tussock, isn't it?'

'*Tussock*, sir? I'm Feathers.'

'Ah, Feathers, Feathers. "The life of man is plumed with death." It's part of a plea of mercy by a seaman to Queen Elizabeth the First.'

'I know, sir.'

'*Do* you? We aren't told whether it was successful. I knew your father, Feathers. He was a boy here when I was. How is he?'

'I never see him. He's in South-East Asia. I think he's gone to Singapore now.'

'Yes. Of course. And that's what we must talk about. I've been pondering the matter all week, Tussock. But first – what?'

'I want to visit my friend, Ingoldby, in the San, sir. I am told by Mr Oilseed that it is an unholy desire.'

'Yes, yes. You would be.'

'It's obscene of him, sir, to say a thing like that.'

'Yes. But it's an old obscenity. Very primitive. Age gives these flabby ideas weight. Oh yes – and *parents*. No, the reason for isolation of patients in the San is the possibility of infection.'

'But, it's pneumonia. Caught in the performance –'

'– ah, yes. The invasion by barrage-balloon. I slept through it.'

'All I want is to wish him well. Put my head round the door. You'd allow me if he were my brother. Wouldn't you, Headmaster?'

'Yes. Yes, I would. And you are a prefect. And, I understand, fairly sane. Yes.' The Head had shrunk in his chair. 'Particularly today, I would.' He pointed to a second armchair across the fireplace. 'Stick another log on the fire as you go by, would you? Will you have a cup of tea? We ought to be talking about your future. We have a bit of a worry with you – oh, nothing to do with this David and Jonathan business. We all grow out of every loyalty in the end.'

'It's called friendship, sir.'

'Yes. Yes. And you won't be seeing much more of Ingoldby. Your father has written to us to say that he wants you to leave school after Christmas. He wants you to go to Malaysia. Or Singapore. We have been giving it a lot of thought.'

'He – *what*?'

'He thinks you should be evacuated from England. To get away from the bombing. Place of safety. He was – I needn't tell you – through the last one. And he's been out of touch with British politics. We're trying to persuade him to let you take the Oxford entrance exam first.'

'But it's *children* who are evacuated. And women. I'm going on eighteen.'

'Until you *are* eighteen, your father has the say.'

'But I've his sisters. My guardians. What do they say?'

'We have written to the Misses Feathers and they replied in a very – sanguine – manner. Busy women. War work, one supposes.'

'I don't know. I've hardly seen them. Am I to leave school after *Christmas*?'

'And here is tea. Let us hope for crumpets though it will be only marge.'

'May I go now? I want to think.'

'If you feel it wise. One can of course think too much. Your father tended to think too much.'

As Eddie opened the door of the study, there came padding towards it an old lady in slippers pushing a tea-trolley. The teapot was muffled in a knitted crinoline of rose and orange frills and had an art-nouveau lady's head on top, a black painted curl against each porcelain cheek. Whenever afterwards Filth beheld such an object – at a church fête, perhaps, at the end of his life and long after the precise reason for it had been lost – he found himself near tears.

The old woman handed Eddie a silver dish full of crumpets and indicated a brass crumpet-stand on the hearth.

'Oh, good. Jam,' said the Headmaster. 'This is Ingoldby's friend, Mrs P.'

'Ingoldby's a nice boy,' said the housekeeper, 'and so was his brother, God rest him.' She left the room.

'*What's* this?' cried Eddie.

'Sit down a minute, Feathers. I was coming to it. I'm sorry. But tomorrow I shall have to give the news out in prayers. I'm glad you came over. Jack Ingoldby's plane has been reported missing over the Channel. His brother doesn't know. We're waiting until he is better. He is being taken home tomorrow. Keep it to yourself.'

Eddie ran from the penumbrous house to the nearest public phone box, on the corner of the playing fields, and dialled Trunks for a long-distance call. He asked for the High House number and was told by the operator to expect a long wait. 'Will you be ready when a line comes free? Maybe twenty or thirty minutes, dear, and you must have the right money. One shilling and a sixpence and two pennies.'

'I haven't got thirty minutes.'

'Try later, dear. And it's cheaper.' She cut him off.

He ran back to his House and began a letter to Mrs Ingoldby, but the words were senseless. I can't write formalities, I can't. I'm the family. She'll want to hear my voice. She'll be *expecting* to hear it. They'll have been trying to get me and nobody's told me. He sat, thinking, then wrote:

> Dear Mrs Ingoldby, I am thinking of you
> all the time, your loving Eddie.

Have I the right to be their loving Eddie?

The voids of his ignorance opened before him. I'm still the

foreigner. To them. And to myself, here. I've no background. I've been peeled off my background. I've been attached to another background like a cut-out. I'm only someone they've been kind to for eight years because Pat was a loner till I came along. I'm socially a bit dubious, because they know my father went barmy. And because of living in the heart of darkness and something funny going on in Wales. And the stammer.

He signed himself

Sincerely yours, E. J. Feathers

He stuck a penny-ha'penny stamp on the letter and took it to the postbox as the evening Prep bell rang. It was his night to invigilate the little boys in the House but he doubled-back to the San.

The windy restless afternoon was done and clouds covered the moon. It was damp but not viciously raining now. At the top of the San's staircase he looked into Matron's room where her coal fire blazed and the ghastly scarf lay abandoned. There was the smell of her meaty supper and a clink from her kitchen. Coals crashed, then blazed up in the grate. He walked on along the corridor expecting the San to be rows of beds, blanket-rolls, empty lockers with open doors, the smell of Dettol. But there was Pat in a small lone room with a blanket over his head.

'Hey – Pat?'

Pat sat up. His head rose out of the blanket, its folds draped around his shoulders.

'Where are you, Fevvers? Put the light on.'

'How are you? They wouldn't let me in.'

'Fine. I'm going home tomorrow. I'm ravenous. But, listen –'

Noises as of tom cats on a roof top issued from Pat's chest.

'Good God!'

'It's the Banshee. They're giving me some new weird drug. It's going to cost Pa something. I can make it sound like distant machine-guns, listen.'

'They'll fix it,' said Eddie, considerably frightened. 'I've just written to your mother.'

'Well, keep it cool. There's a scare on. Jack's missing.'

'I – don't know anything –'

'Yes, you do. If I've heard in here, you'll have heard it out there. If he's. . . .'

Silence.

'. . . . if he's gone, well then, he's gone. It's what he believed in.'

A poker was being rattled about in the grate next door.

'You'd better go, Fevvers. She'll have an orgasm if she finds you. "This is a CLEAN school."' He began wheezing.

'I'll. . . . Shouldn't I ring High House?'

Pat's black eyes became blacker. A certain hauteur. 'Nope. Leave them alone. I'll be home tomorrow. There's nothing you can do. It's family stuff.'

Eddie turned for the door, amazed at how cold he felt.

'Oh, and hey – Ed?'

'Yes?'

'Don't join the RAF. You couldn't handle it. And don't join the Navy – you've done the sea.'

'I can't see myself in the Army, not any more. I couldn't kill someone I was looking at. I mean, at his face. The point is, *you* can't join the RAF. Not now. I mean, God – for your parents' sake.'

'Oh yes I can,' said Ingoldby. 'They'll survive even if I don't. My parents. I've told you – they don't really feel much. Bye – see you sometime, Fevvers.'

A couple of days later and after no luck with the High House telephone though Eddie tried several times, a letter came to him from Pat in dithering writing.

Dear Ed, I'm fine now but staying home.

> I'll not be coming back, lad,
> When all the trees are green,
> I have to join the pack, lad,
> And drink my Ovaltine.

Take the lead soldiers we had at Sir's. Melt them down for plough shares or a sixth bullet, whatever. Will you gather up my

90

stuff? – Pa forgot it and so did Matron-La-Booze. Hang on to it till – when? The clothes-brush you always fancied, my god-father's, it's from Bond Street (he used eau-de-cologne and had a mistress in Clarges Street) you can have but it will cost you a penny.

Regards PI

A few days after the news that Jack Ingoldby was missing came the news that he was certainly killed. It was the sort of notice the Head was giving out repeatedly at assembly that term. Hundreds, maybe thousands, of people in East Kent saw the planes from the dog-fights of the Battle of Britain come spinning and flickering down to sizzle in the Channel or burst into flames in the orchards. Parachutes blossoming out would raise a cheer; but most pilots were invisible and people went on with what they were doing, like harvesters in medieval France during the Hundred Years War. Nevertheless, a certain and recorded and undeniable filmed death was a shock.

There was no further card from Pat nor response to a second letter from Eddie to High House. Half-term was coming but there was no sign that he would go as usual to the Ingoldbys. He was, it seemed, to go at last to his guardians, for a jokey invitation had been received by the Headmaster from the Bolton aunts. But still he hung about the school until the very last minute in case a call should come from Pat.

As the cab to take him to the train for Bolton was arriving, he tried once more with a thumping heart to telephone High House.

'Hullo?'

'Who's that?'

'Is that – the Ingoldbys?'

'It's Isobel.'

'Oh. Hullo. It's Eddie. Teddy Feathers.'

'Oh, hullo.'

'I just rang to see. . . . To hear. . . .'

'Yes?'

'It's half-term. Should I come over?'

'Oh no. I shouldn't do that. Pat's not here. He's gone off somewhere to volunteer again.'

'How is – Mrs Ingoldby?'

'Oh, she's fine. Very patriotic, you know.'

'I'd love to see her.'

'I'll tell her.'

'Actually, would you tell her that I won't be in England much longer?'

'Joining up?'

'Not exactly. I'm too young. My father's sent for me.'

'Whatever for?'

'Could you tell them? The Ingoldbys?'

'What?'

'Well, say goodbye. And s-s-so many many thanks. I'll be on the other side of the world.'

'So will a lot of people.'

'Say I'll write. I'll *always* write. Thank them for. . . .'

'OK. Bye.'

'I'd love to hear. . . .'

But she was gone.

So Eddie picked up Pat's belongings and shook hands with Oils, and stepped into the taxi for Bolton where, even with Pat's extras, there was not enough luggage to justify a taxi from the station, so he walked to the house, surprised that he remembered how to get there after a single visit long ago; the half-term holiday after the Didds' business in Wales. His father had come to England for the first and only time and had taken the eight-year-old Eddie to see his sisters.

It was a sleek, boastful, purple-brick house like a giant plum standing back from the road behind a semi-circle of lawn with shaven edges and Victorian (purple) edging tiles. In a round bed stood the winter sticks of roses.

Aunt Hilda appeared, flinging wide an inner vestibule door of rich cream paint and crimson and blue glass panes, and cried out, 'Muriel! He's here. It's the boy. Come in, come *in*. We should have written. You've arrived – well done! We've sorted everything out. Your passport should be here by Christmas. Excellent. *Muriel.*'

They were in the hall now and Aunt Muriel was coming down the stairs in tweeds and a hat. 'Dear old chap – how like Alistair.'

'There's a pretty important golf today,' said Hilda, 'and we're just off. Not a tournament nowadays of course, the links are so restricted. But still quite a highspot. So we'll go on ahead. You settle in, then you can join us for lunch or tea? No distance. Take the bike from the garage. We must fly. Duties on the course – so few men now. The lunch won't be at all bad. You're very thin.'

They departed, their car's rear window nearly covered by patriotic slogans. *Careless talk costs lives*, he read. He wandered through the house.

There were brass urns full of ferns and an ironwood table topped with a brass disc engraved with dancing Orientals. In a sitting-room were crowds of family photographs. Odd, he thought. He was family but they had shown no interest in him since he was eight. He wondered if photographs were substitutes for hospitality. Looking around, he saw no photographs at all of children. And nobody who could possibly have been his mother. He had no idea what she had looked like. Most of the photographs were of people a generation older than his aunts, bearded or braided, sepia, stern and sad. Beside them, were other photographs and more ferns in brass containers. On a table by themselves were golfing trophies and a silver cup engraved *Hole in One, Hilda Feathers*. There was a magnificent fireplace of wood and tiles, with a shiny clock with icicle pointers let into the chimneypiece. Instead of coals there was a pleated fan of paper, and in the hearth a miracle of barbola work covered in thonged parchment and filled with newspaper spills to save matches.

Then he saw, on the mantelpiece, a photograph of a dazzling young man in open-necked khaki shirt and shorts, arms crossed and a cigarette burning nonchalantly in one hand, and, on the other wrist, a big, beautiful, seductive gold watch. On his head, an army beret without a badge, like a Frenchman, and eyes dark, wise, amused and most beautiful. On the silver frame was engraved *Alistair, 1914*, and there was a little jug of flowers arranged beside it, as if the photograph was of a dead man, or like a funeral bunch upon a grave. Flowers for the dead. But this was his father. No doubt of it. Eddie knew.

And his father was alive enough to have sent for him, to get him out of another set-piece of butchery like the one that had all but extinguished him and his country in 1914.

Eddie picked up the photograph and felt pride. He wanted it. He'd nick it. It was his. He wished Pat could see it, or the vile Isobel. Had Colonel Ingoldby really known his father? Why hadn't he ever said anything about him? His father's wonderful face, a poet's face, he thought, and with an exciting hint in it of his own. It occurred to him that he must write again, after years, to his father.

And now. Write now.

He turned to the writing desk – brasses galore (*The Snake and His Boy*, a row of ugly monkeys) – and searched around for writing paper, found his own fountain pen, stared at the laurels outside the window, the bald lawn, the grey street. The gate flung open. *No Hawkers or Circulars* nailed to it on a plaque.

Dear Father

I am at Aunt Muriel's having left school this morning for half-term or, for all I know, for good. I only heard this week that I'm to leave school and come out to you. I *wish* you could have written *to me* about it. The Head says they've been discussing it with you for some time, and Aunt Hilda says my passport will be ready by Christmas. I'm seventeen and shall soon be eighteen. It is ten years since you saw me and I've had nothing from you of any kind except I suppose all my expenses have been paid and I'm told there is a bank-book for me some-time soon. So thank you for that.

But our last meeting was so horrible and unhappy and I wish you could have written, even once, years ago, to put that right. Nobody had told me that you have a stammer and nobody had probably told you that I had one then (Sir cured mine) and I think [the pen began to take on a most uncharacteristic volition of its own] that I tried just to forget you. The Ingoldbys were so kind. Just now I've seen a photograph of you on the mantelpiece here at the aunts – first time I've seen them since you were here when I was eight – taken in 1914, and you don't look all that much older than I am now. It made me very regretful. I felt you might be a father I could have talked to.

However, no go. So would you very kindly read the following points that will state briefly my reasons for not wanting to come and live with you in Malaya or Java or S'pore or wherever?

(1) I should at Christmas be going to Oxford for an interview at Christ Church for a place after the War.

(2) I want, after that, to volunteer for the Army.

(3) For me to be 'evacuated' out of danger now, at my age, is absolutely unheard of in England at the moment. I should have to travel with children aged between seven and twelve. Whatever would the ship's company think of me?

(4) I would lose my English friends for life. It would be a continuing stigma. I am six-foot-two and look older than my years. I am *very fit*.

and (5) and sorry to sound gung-ho, but I believe that I should be fighting for my country. I *can't* run away. You haven't heard Churchill. Even people like you, the bitter ones of '14/18, listen to him. I have lived in this country since you sent me here as almost a baby. Had there been [the pen was beginning to race and Eddie's face was red with a rage he had had no knowledge of] any friendship, any contact, between us, if you had *once* written to me not just handed me that pin-box, it might be different.

I shall argue these points with my aunts – though they seem to be very indifferent listeners. I've tried to argue with the school. All they say is that until I am eighteen you can do more or less what you like with me.

Do you *want* me with you on these autocratic and loveless terms?

Sincerely, E. J. Feathers

He read the letter through, and by the end of it was seeing not the god-like young soldier of the photograph but the father who had turned up at Sir's Outfit soon after the Ma Didds's affair, the affair that was – and still was – his closed, locked box. He saw a lank and trembling figure sitting in Sir's study, the mountain trees of the Lake District tossing blackly about in the wind through the window behind him. The figure had sat cracking his finger joints.

Sir had kindly left the two of them together ('just out here if you need me, Feathers's) and father and son, neither clear which of them Sir was referring to, had stared long and hard at the pattern on the carpet.

Eddie remembered the hands. How his father had clasped and unclasped them. How the knuckles had cracked like pistols. He remembered the thin shanks of his father's legs in the old-fashioned European suit; the bald head; the lashless eyes that looked almost blind. How the man shifted in his chair, said nothing, looked at a wrist watch far too big for the wrist. The watch that must have come through the Great War with him. The watch in the photo. Maybe it had been an amulet?

Eddie had been far too frightened to speak and reveal his stammer, especially after he heard a long staccato rattle begin in his father's throat and realised – who better? – that his father stammered, too. He became inexorably mute. His father was asking a question. If he tried to answer it, his father might think his son was mocking him.

Tears came. Eddie did not look again at his father's face. The patterns on Sir's carpet swelled and ran together into chaos and oblivion.

When Sir returned, father and son both jumped up and Sir said to Eddie, 'Away you go then,' and Eddie fled back to the classroom, to Pat Ingoldby and the lead soldiers under the desk-lid, and nobody ever mentioned this interview with his father again.

Once, only once, had Eddie met the aunts. Yet he knew that these aunts no longer talked about their brother. Not a breath in them confessed to the twitching, half-mad widower with the yellow face and strange eyes. (Once at Ma Didds one of his cousins, probably Babs, had said, 'Your pa has malaria,' and the other had said, 'No, he doesn't. My mother says it's opium.') Nor did these Bolton aunts, out on the numbing golf course, any longer ever say a word about the young, quizzical, handsome, alert spirit that had been their brother and with whom they had grown up.

Eddie went through the address book on the desk until he found his father's name. After Kotakinakulu, there were many crossings out. The current address seemed to be Singapore. It did not sound very grand. A back-street address. An instinct, some gentle gene in Eddie, made him write a P.S. before he licked the air-mail envelope:

> P.S: I should like to say, though, Father, you've been very generous to someone you clearly found it impossible to like. Now that I've really thought about it, your wanting me to come to you in order to survive the War seems [he was going to write 'very civil'] a miracle of unexpected kindness.
>
> Eddie

And so, he thought, I spoil my case.

He did not go to the golf-course lunch, but found his way below stairs to a kitchen where a diminutive old woman was folding paper spills for the grate. She looked depressed and paid him no attention, so then he lay on his bed in a room with eiderdowns and heavy flowered curtains and huge lampshades and wondered if this was all.

He stayed on, apparently invisible, for a week. And then for several weeks, while he waited to hear from school about the Oxford interview. There was no reply to his letter to his father and, though he often wondered if today there might be a cable, none came. He spent the days mugging up for the possible Oxford interview – there was a good public library in the town – and thinking unhopefully about life. From his bedroom window, steamed with delicious heat from a Victorian iron radiator, his dreams merged into other bedroom windows. One, that mystified him on the edge of sleep, was an unglazed slit with the black knives of banana plants against a black-sapphire sky. This dream always woke him.

His Bolton bedroom now was rich in Lancashire splendour, the carpet pure olive-green wool overflung with white roses. The heavy curtains, interlined for the black-out, were damask within and without. The eiderdown was of fat rose-pink blisters and beside the bed was a lamp with pink silk and bead fringes. The wallpaper could have stood by itself, thickly embossed with gold, and the blankets were snowy wool, and satin-bound. 'You are in the best spare,' said Muriel. 'The wardrobe may be a Gillow.' 'Now put the fire on if you need it,' said Hilda. 'Both bars. We have to go out now.'

Going out was their refrain. Eddie's life was beyond their interest. They dwelt like Siamese twins in each other's concerns and in the present moment. Every morning they came down to the breakfast-room talking before they saw you but telling you their plans. Their eyes were always blanks. They were always in one of a number of uniforms but always the same as each other. There was the Red Cross officer with stripes and a cockade; the WVS plum and dark green; a scarlet and grey ensemble reminiscent of the North-West Frontier; and a white and navy serge with wings on the head indicative of some variety of military nurse. They left the house every day by eight-thirty and were never home till supper. On Sundays they were up betimes for the eight o'clock Communion, and later sat knitting gloves and listening to *Forces Favourites*. There was a nice medium sherry before a heavy supper each evening. The midget maid crept about doing wonders with the chores and a muscular woman came in for the rough and a man for swilling down the yard. Each day Eddie ate his lunch alone at one end of the mahogany dining table, also a suspected Gillow, laid up with lace mats and shining silver. He received no mail and the phone never rang for him.

'Now, don't you overwork,' they shouted. 'You'll get in. It's your father's old college. There's a nice flick on at the Odeon,' and they clashed shut the vestibule door not interested in his answer.

The winter gathered. Once or twice he grew desperate to telephone the Ingoldbys but dared not because of Pat's bombshell: *It's family stuff.*

The air-raids in the North-West had for the moment stopped but the dog-fights went on in the South-East and Eddie wondered whether Pat had his pilot's wings yet. 'They're sending them up after twelve hours' instruction,' said an old soldier at the golf club. 'They're running out. Slaughter of the innocents.' 'I heard after *six* hours,' said someone else. 'Six hours' flying instruction and they're in their own Spitfire.'

According to the six o'clock news on the wireless each evening huge numbers of the Boche were being shot down, twice as many casualties as our own. But the bulletin always ended with 'a number of our own aircraft are missing.'

At last he set off for the Oxford entrance exam in a blizzard and a series of unheated trains, each one packed down every corridor with troops, all smoking, drinking, sleeping, hawking, balanced against each other or jack-knifed on their knees on the floor. Coughs, oaths, laughter, glum silence, sudden waves of idiotic singing (*Roll out the Barrel*, *Tipperary*) from the War before. The final train groaned out of a station to stop as if for ever outside Stratford-on-Avon in the dark. Planes droned above. ('Dorniers?' 'No Messerschmitts.') More soldiers sank upon their haunches, heads into their spread knees, asleep. The crumpling sound of bombs, the W.C.s surrounded by the desperate, jigging up and down. When you did get inside, heel holding the door to behind you, the lock broken, the floor awash, the smell was rank, no water in the taps. No lavatory paper. '*Roll me over in the clover*,' sang the soldiers who mostly had never seen clover. '*Roll me over, lay me down and do it again.*'

Eddie burst from the train at Oxford station and looked for someone on the gate to take his ticket and tell him how far his college was. There was no one and no taxi. No one at all. It was bitter midnight and in his head he could still hear the horrible singing.

Then, stepping out down a dark road something changed. Out from clouds sprang a great white moon and showed pavements and roads of snow, sleeping buildings, spires and domes all stroked by dappling snow. There was not a soul, not a light and not a cry.

Over some bridge he went in such dazzling moonlight he wondered there were not crowds turned out everywhere to see it. He walked exalted, his feet light and the moon came and went, and then soft flakes began to fall. He looked back and saw his footprints already softened by the snow, the snow ahead of him waiting to be imprinted. He had strayed into medieval Oxford like a ghost.

And nobody to direct him and he was growing cold. A great silent street widened. A church stood in the middle of it, its windows boarded, its glass taken into safety. He wondered whether its door might be open and then saw opposite a large building that might be a hotel where he might try to get them to answer a bell and tell him where to go. Then, behind him, he heard a sound from the black church and all at once there was a figure beside him, a muffled-up giant who was graciously inclining his head towards him, the head bound about by some sort of scarf. The man was wearing a flowing macintosh like the robe of someone in the absent stained-glass.

'May I help you? Did I frighten you? I was in the church.' The young man swung a key. He was very young indeed to be a clergyman. He, too, must be a ghost.

'I'm looking for a college called Christ Church.'

'You are going in absolutely the wrong direction. Follow me,' and the soft and boneless giant went padding away with Eddie following.

'There,' he said, in time. 'Straight ahead.'

'My train was late.'

'Bang hard for the night-porter. Are you all right now?'

The snow had stopped and the moonshine gleamed out again.

'Excuse me, are you – someone in the church?'

'No. I do fire-watching there. And praying. I'm a student.'

Eddie felt his kindliness and confidence and cheerfulness.

'Goodnight,' said the young huge fledgling. 'Good luck. I suppose you're up for the entrance exam?'

'Yes. Tomorrow.'

'I'm leaving tomorrow. I'm joining up.'

Eddie felt ridiculous regret. And then confusion. Somehow, he knew this man.

'Thanks,' he said. 'It was a mercy I met you.'

They went their different ways, but when Eddie stopped and looked back, he found that the muffled giant was doing the same thing, looking back at him.

'Feel sure I know you,' Eddie called. 'Very odd.'

Then the man waved and padded out of sight down a side street and Eddie was trying to rouse his college.

As he fell asleep in a monkish bed in a mullioned room he thought: How can I possibly leave all this for Malaya?

A few days later, 'I suggest,' said the man who might in time become his tutor after the War, if that time ever came, 'I suggest that you come up as soon as possible.'

'Does that mean I'm accepted, sir?'

'Of course. Goes without saying. You wrote excellent papers yesterday. Well taught. Were you at Sir's? I thought so. And your public school is very clever with closed scholarships, though I hear you are rich enough not to need one.'

(Am I? thought Eddie. I've ten shillings a week.)

'Now, I suggest you volunteer for the Navy. It takes them a year to process you, so you can get your Prelims done with here, before you go, and you'll have a toe in the door for when you're demobilised. You'll be reading history?'

'I'm not quite sure, sir, what. . . .'

'Your father was here. How is he? Still about, I hope?'

'He lives in Malaya. Well, I think he may be in Singapore now. I hardly know him.'

'I'm sorry. I heard shell-shock? Poor chap. But he'll be proud of you now.'

Eddie swam with guilt. Ought he to say? His father had ordered him out of the country. His father had no notion or memory of Oxford. His father had – shell-shocked or not – organised a passport and visa and made his sisters get Eddie his jabs. He was to be 'an evacuee'. Well, he would not do it. No. He would come to Oxford where he was welcome and admired and befriended and a familiar ghost had directed him to a safe haven after midnight. He would say nothing.

'May I come up next term, sir?'

'Ah, not quite so fast. But leave it to me. We'll find you a room in Meadow Buildings, where your father was.'

As he fell asleep in the beautiful ice-cold room with his coat and the hearth-rug over the blankets, and watched the moon light the snowy rooftops, he briefly wondered about money. Will my father pay my fees if I refuse to go out to him? Will my scholarship be enough? I might be poor. I've never been really poor. Well, hell, so what? And he watched the moon bowling along, lighting the sky for the bombers.

I could live and die here, he thought. They'll never destroy this. I'll stay and fight for it.

And with these noble thoughts he slept.

By morning the snow had gone as if it had been dreams and it was raining hard and the pavements soiled and splashy. From the mullioned window could be seen people hurrying, bent forward, miserable and mean along the streets, and it was not the fairy city any more. The bedroom door opened and a lugubrious man called a Scout came carrying hot water in a jug across to a washbowl and asked if he would be taking breakfast early so that his room might be cleaned? For some panic-stricken reason Eddie said, No, he would be leaving before breakfast. 'Very good, sir,' said the Scout, eyebrows raised, and Eddie wondered whether to leave him a tip and, if he didn't, whether it would be remembered next term and held against him. In the end he left a shilling on the dressing-table, took his bag and went head forward into the slushy street. As he butted along against the wet and the umbrellas, bicycles wetting his trousers as they passed him, melancholy struck. Was this place after all a delusion? It was criminally cold. Nobody had said goodbye to him. Hot water in a jug and the W.C. three flights down. Not a word about the date of his return. And he was bloody hungry.

He turned into a tea-shop because the steam on its windows promised warmth, but once inside it was cold and crowded and dark, with people sitting in buttoned-up clothes. A long and silent queue stood by the counter, each one holding a ration book in a gloved hand and hoping for an extra cake.

But yet there was a sort of warmth there in the fug and Eddie edged further in to the shop where there were tables and chairs. They were all smoking and reading newspapers or warming their hands on their coffee cups. He sat down at a table where a girl was leaning back in her chair, smoking through a cigarette-holder and watching him. Her legs were crossed and one high-heeled shoe was swinging up and down from her big toe.

'Is it all right to sit here?'

He sat, and looked around him to see what was on offer in the way of breakfast.

'I've not had breakfast,' he said. 'I'm up here for my entrance exams. I suddenly wanted to go home, so I skipped breakfast. Now I'm hungry.'

'Which college?'

'Christ Church.'

'You'd have been given a good free breakfast there. Even in the vacation. Quails' eggs and flagons of porter I shouldn't wonder. Small-talk about the Christ Church Beagles. It won't survive the War, you know, Christ Church. Thank God. You don't look *exactly* Christ Church. I'll say that for you.'

'I don't know a thing about it. I was told to apply. It could have been St Karl Marx's College for all I know about it.'

'I'll bet your father was there.'

'Yes, he was. Actually. I can't help that.'

She leaned forward to the ashtray, looking at him carefully, and he looked back into bright hazel eyes which were somehow familiar. He remembered the giant who had also been familiar.

I'm over-tired, he thought. Over-excited. 'I've not seen my father in ten years,' he told the girl. 'He's a very hard-working civil servant. Out East.'

'I've not seen mine for years, either,' she said. 'He's still bashing away in India. And I know you, you're Teddy Feathers.'

The eyes became at once the ten-year-old eyes of his cousin Babs – eyes that he had last seen pouring out tears by the fuchsia bushes in Ma Didds's garden. The long, tapping finger over the ashtray became little Babs's fierce claw which could pick out any tune without thought on the chapel harmonium. Just out of sight somewhere was the watchful pink and gold of their six-year-old cousin, Claire.

'Babs?'

'Teddy.'

Eddie ordered them both some milky bottled coffee and a Marie biscuit and Babs lit another cigarette.

'So. You live in Oxford? I'd no idea, Babs.'

'No. I'm up. At Somerville. I'm packing it in, though. It's no time to be here. I'm volunteering for the Navy. I'll be gone by next week.'

'Where's Claire?'

'Oh, I don't know. She's married. Straight from school. Didn't you hear? She's in East Anglia somewhere among all the airfields. As far away from us as possible. Well, she would be, wouldn't she?'

'I don't see why.'

'She was very passive always. And they made sure we were never to meet up again – or they tried to. Wanted us to drop each other dead. So – what's been happening to you, old Teddy-bear?'

'*Did* they? Try to stop us?'

'Well, you had some sort of crack-up, so I heard. Began to chatter like a monkey. A Welsh monkey.'

'I never cracked up. Do I stammer now?'

'No. You talk proper. You'll do for Christ Church.' When she smiled, she dazzled. There were smoker's lines already etched on her face but sunlight was still behind them.

'I've got myself into one hell of a bigger mess now,' Eddie said. 'I've nobody to tell me the answers. I find I don't know how to – proceed.'

'*Proceed*,' she said, and leaning forward stroked his wrist. 'I always loved your words. I suppose it was books. Your father sent you so many books at Didds's.'

'Did he? Nobody told me. What? Were the books from him?'

'You weren't wanting to hear anything good about your father then. *Proceed*,' she said. 'Maybe you'll be a lawyer? A Barrister, but it'd be a pity to cover that hair. *Proceed* – look, you *proceed* by yourself now. You don't need Claire or me or Auntie May. Get on with life! You can take decisions,' she said, 'if anyone can.'

They both looked down at the insides of their coffee cups.

'You were bloody wonderful,' she said, 'that day. Braver than any of us and eight years old.'

'I've not made a decision since,' he said. 'That must have been my one decisive moment.'

'Where did you go in the holidays all these years? You can't have been alone?' she asked him.

'Schoolfriend. Sort of second family to me.'

'Can't they help now? And what about your pa's sensible sisters?'

'They are psychologically deaf,' said he.

'They're just reacting against your pa,' she said. 'Don't forget they were all Raj Orphans themselves. They say it suits some. They come out fizzing and yelling, "I didn't need parents," and waving the red, white and blue. Snooty for life. But we're all touched, one way or another.'

'I don't think it suited my father,' said Eddie. 'He's gone entirely barmy.'

'Yep. I heard. You know, my lot and Claire's are still in India, and I never give them a thought. Not after ten years.'

Eddie realised that since the Ma Didds's horror he had never given a thought to either Babs or Claire. Not a thought.

'Have you a girlfriend, Eddie?'

'I never meet any girls. I just work. And play games. And read.'

'Come home with me now,' said Babs. 'To my digs. There's no one there.' She put out her cigarette. 'We'll go to bed. We have before.'

Eddie, scarlet, was aware of a drop in the background conversation at the nearby tables. Babs's voice was beautiful and old-fashioned, a penetrating voice like Royalty, clear and high and unconcerned, and he stumbled out of his chair, withdrawing his hand from beneath hers. 'Sorry. Can't. Getting a train. Might miss it.'

And she leaned back, laughing, and called across the steamy shop – the still-immobile cake-queue – 'We'll never forget each other, Teddy-bear. Never.' He fumbled at the door. 'You and I and Claire. And Cumberledge. Whatever happens to us. *Never*.'

He was on the train, sopped through with Oxford's rain. He watched the tangled hedges threaded with the dead spirals of last year's weeds. This was an empty, slow, uncertain train that trundled insolently through anonymous stations, their names painted out with coarse black brush-strokes to confuse the Germans when they eventually arrived. Station waiting-rooms stood barred; cigarette- and chocolate-machines stood empty with their metal drawers hanging out. It was not until he had changed trains in Manchester (I could still be in her bed) that he remembered that he had left Babs to pay for the coffee.

He was sitting now in another railway carriage looking, above the man sitting opposite, at a pre-War watercolour reproduction of a happy artless English family on a sunny English beach. The other picture frames below the rack held patriotic slogans and he wondered if the sandcastle country scene had been deliberately preserved. The clean-cut daddy; the Marcel-waved mummy; the innocent little one; the happy dog, Towser. Presumably in some people's memory? He closed his eyes to keep them from tears. He dozed and found himself in a richer place, a sleep-laden, dripping dell with drops on every great leaf, the clattering of banana leaves, black children dancing in foetid puddles on the earth – earth beaten hard as concrete with dancing feet but which could become in moments under the warm rain a living mud. Laughter. The smell of sweet hot skin. He was being tossed up high in someone's arms and he was looking down again upon a brown face, white teeth, gloriously loving eyes. The eyes of the man across the carriage were staring at him as Eddie woke.

'You all right, lad?'

'Yes. Sorry. Was I snoring?'

'No. You were moaning. Want to see a paper?'

'No, no. I was. . . . I think I must talk in my sleep.'

'Here. I'm reading the *Deaths*,' said the man, 'and I've discovered something quite important. See what you think. Just see what you think – no prejudice. Just look down the list of places and you can tell which deaths are from enemy action. You can tell from *The Times* exactly where the raids were, dates given. Nobody's thought of it here, I'll bet. I'm writing to the authorities. I'll bet the enemy has noticed.'

Eddie, scrambling from the tropical dream, said, 'Careless talk costs lives.'

'D'you want to see, though? Just you see what I mean. It's a bloody check-list for the enemy,' and he passed across the outer pages of *The Times*. Eddie arranged them as a barrier between himself and the man and began, automatically, as his eyes re-focused, to read in alphabetical order. He immediately read: *Ingoldby, Patrick, aged eighteen years, RAF*, a date of one week before, and *For King and Country*.

The Time of Frenzy

When Betty died suddenly, planting the tulips the day after their day in London attempting to sign their Wills, Filth's astonishment lifted his soul outside his body and he stood looking down not only at the slumped body but at his own, gazing and emptied of all its meaning now.

'It has happened,' 'It has occurred,' 'Keep your head,' said the spirit to the body. Stiffly he knelt beside her, watching himself kneel, take her hand, kiss her hand and put it to his face. There was no doubt in either soul or body that she was dead. Dead. Gone. Happened. Lost. Over.

Throughout the funeral service he silently repeated the words: Dead. Lost. Happened. Gone. A small funeral, for neither of them had much in the way of relations and Babs and Claire did not take – or so he assumed – the *Telegraph* or *The Times*. Filth, the ever-meticulous, had lapsed. He forgot (or pretended to forget) that you should telephone people. His old friends were all in Hong Kong or with their Maker. A small funeral.

Touchingly, some members of his former Chambers turned up and his magnificent old Clerk, once the Junior Clerk who had been a schoolboy with pimples, was there in the church, magisterial now in a long Harrods overcoat.

'So sorry, sir.'

'How very good of you to come, Charlie. Very kind.'

'Mr Wemyss is here, and Sir Andrew Bysshe.'

'Very kind. Very long way for you all to come.'

The dark, serious, pallid London figures in the second pew. The rest of the mourners were locals, mostly church ladies, for Betty had been on the flower rota. She had been very forceful with the flowers, banging their stalks down hard in the bottom of the green bucket, commandeering the Frobisher Window from the moment of her arrival, a position not usually offered until you'd been in the parish for several years.

Betty stood no nonsense from flowers. In Hong Kong she had once done the cathedral, and the Hong Kong iris, the Cuban bast flower, the American worm seed and the Maud's *Michellia* had all known their place there. She harangued flowers. She wanted of all things, she often said, to have a flower named after her. 'The Elizabeth Feathers. Long-leaved Greenbriar?' Filth had thought sometimes of organising such a thing for her; he'd heard that it was not really expensive. It was a birthday present always forgotten. Filth was not taken with flowers. He found them unresponsive, sometimes even hostile. It was tulips, he thought, that had got her in the end.

As he stood beside the grave and thought of his long life with Betty and his achievement in presenting to the world the full man, the completed and successful being, his hands in their lined kid gloves folded over the top of his walking stick, he was aware of something, somewhere. He looked up at the sky. Nothing, yet he was being informed, no doubt about it, that there was something in him unresolved. He was inadequate and weak. If they knew, they would all find him unlikable. Despicable. Face it.

Yet he felt nothing. Nothing at all.

They had put on a do for Betty afterwards in the church hall. Tea and anchovy sandwiches and fruit cake and the ubiquitous pale green Anglican crockery, known from the Donheads to Hong Kong to Jamaica. He took nothing, but moved among the guests magnificently, like a knight of old. He talked of the weather. Of their kind journeys to the Donheads. A nice woman, when they had all gone, offered him whiskey and he must have drunk it for he found himself looking down into an empty glass when she suggested seeing him safely home.

'Are you going to be alone here tonight, Edward?'

'Oh, I shall be perfectly all right. Perfectly.'

Outside, the tulip bed had been tactfully raked over and Filth and the woman (Chloe) stood looking carefully beyond it from the sun-lounge and over the hills. The woman smelled nostalgically of some old scent – not Betty's, he thought. It was the scent, he supposed, but suddenly (and the nice woman had long lost her waistline and her hair was grey) Filth experienced an astonishment as great as the sight of Betty dead – her untenanted body, her empty face. Filth experienced a huge, full-blown, adolescent lust.

At once, he walked away from the woman, and sat down in the sitting-room alone.

'I could sit with you for a while.'

'No thank you, Chloe, I think as a matter of fact I'd like to be by myself now.'

When she had gone he sat for a time. (Lost. Over. Gone. Finished. Happened.) She was not here. She was dead.

Not here. But, he felt, elsewhere. They had both detested the macabre Chinese funeral rites and the Oriental notions of an afterlife. They were (of course) Anglicans and liked the idea of Heaven, but whether the spirit survived the ridiculous body they had never discussed. They certainly had never considered the idea that they might meet again in another world. The notion is rubbish, now thought Filth.

'Don't you think?' he asked Betty directly for the first time, speaking to a point above the curtain rail.

There was no reply.

Yet he slept well. The lust had retreated and the next morning early, properly dressed with a purplish tie, he telephoned his two cousins.

From the first, Claire in Essex somewhere, there was no reply, not even from an answerphone. It rang on and on. The second was Babs, who lived now for no known reason somewhere on Teesside called Herringfleet. She was alone in the world and, Betty had thought, a little odd now. Babs had known Betty at school (everyone, he thought, seems to have known Betty at school). Betty and Babs had been at St Paul's Girls School and had the Paulina voice.

So that it was Betty who answered the phone. 'Hello?' she said, 'Yes? Teddy?'

(Betty must be staying up there with Babs, he thought – caught his breath and plunged into hell.)

'It *is* Babs?'

'Yes. I suppose so. Barbara.'

'Edward. Betty's husband.'

'I know.'

'I'm afraid I have bad news.'

'I know. I saw it in the paper. Poor old thing.'

'Well, I'm not exactly –'

'I mean Betty. Poor old thing.'

It was Betty talking. He longed for more.

'I thought you would want to know. . . .'

'Yes, what?'

'The funeral's over, Babs. I thought you'd be glad to know that she died instantly. She can't have known a thing about it. Wonderful for her, really.'

'Yes. That's what they say.'

Silence.

'Babs?'

Now a long silence. Then a crashing waterfall of musical notes on a piano. Filth remembered that Babs had something to do with music. Even in Herringfleet presumably.

'Babs, is that a piano?'

The scales ceased. Then Schubert began. On and on.

'Babs?'

Eventually, he put down the telephone and tried the other cousin again. Again, no answer. He thought of Chloe yesterday and then there was a shadow of someone watching him somewhere from a wood.

Again, the astounding lust. Lust. He put his face in his hands and tried to be calm. What is all this? He found himself praying as he had never prayed at all during the funeral. And very seldom during Betty's life.

'Oh Lord, we beseech thee. . . . direct our hearts and minds in the knowledge and love of God.'

He had not shared a bed with Betty for over thirty years. Double beds were for the bourgeoisie. Sex had never been a great success. They had never discussed it. They had disliked visiting friends who had not two spare bedrooms. Betty had joked for years that the marriage would never have survived had Filth not had his own dressing-room. She had meant bedroom.

Had he ever *desired* Betty? Well, yes. He had. He remembered. He had desired everything about her. Her past, her present, her future with him. Her sweet, alert, intelligent face, her famously alive eyes. He had wanted to possess every part of her for she had fitted so perfectly into his life's plan. She had made him safe and confident. She had eased old childhood nightmares.

But – this. Not ever this. Where did this lust come from? Were she alive, could he have told her about it? She who had never done a passionate act. She would have sent him to a doctor.

But yet – so very close they had been. Sometimes at night in Hong Kong, hot and restless in the swirling mists of the Peak, the case of the previous day, or worse, a judgement lingering, he had gone to her room and lain beside her and she had stretched out a hand.

'What's this?'

'Nothing.'

'Bad day?'

'I condemned a man to death.'

Silence.

She would never have taken him in her arms from pity. Never presented her body to him as a distraction. Never indicated: Here is balm. Take me. Forget it. Your job. You knew there would be this to face here. You could have stayed in England.

Instead. . . .

'Was he guilty?'

'As hell.'

They lay quiet, listening to the night sounds on the Peak.

'*Crime passionel*,' he said.

'Then probably he will be glad to die.'

He said, 'You still shock me. If you had been the Judge. . . .'

'. . . . I would have done as you did. There is not an alternative. But I would have suffered less.'

(But I would have wanted you to suffer more. I want you to make me resign because I disgust myself. I feel, truly, filth.)

'I should have stayed in Chambers at home in the Temple. Famous Feathers of the Construction Industry. Sewers and drains.'

But Betty had already fallen asleep again, peacefully against his shoulder, unconcerned, proud of him, a very nice woman. An excellent wife for a Judge. And two miles off, in a sink across the spangled city, the condemned man, like a small grey bird, his mean little head on its scant Oriental neck soon to be crushed bone, lay alone.

I got out just in time, he thought when they retired and came home to the Donheads. Couldn't take much more emotion alongside the drudgery. Still can't manage emotion. All under control. I am a professional. But why this lust? This longing?

'Babs?'

It was the following morning and he was telephoning her again, 'Babs, I want to come and see you.'

Betty's voice answered – he remembered that it had been Veneering he'd once overheard saying that Betty's voice was like Desdemona's.

'Babs?'

'Just a minute.'

A full tempest of Wagner was stilled somewhere. 'Yes? Teddy again? What?'

'Babs – may I come and see you?'

'Yes. I suppose so. All right. When?'

'Any time. This week? Next week?'

'Yes. All right.'

He heard a sob, which surprised him.

'Babs, don't cry. She died so easily. A ful-ful-ful-filled, a splendid life.'

'I'm not crying for Betty,' she said, 'or for you, you old fool,' and she crashed down the phone.

He didn't telephone again; he wrote. He would visit her the following Friday and perhaps stay the night?

There was no reply.

However, in the new, footloose and irrational way that his body was behaving, Filth made his preparations, taking the car to be checked over in Salisbury, looking out something good of Betty's as a present for Babs.

He would have liked it so much more if he had been going to Claire. He wished she would answer the phone. He searched for the address to write to in Hainault where her Christmas cards came from, but the only card he could find was very old and blurred with no postcode. Nevertheless he wrote to say that he might perhaps be passing near her next Saturday. He told her about Betty.

No reply.

As Mrs-er set down his morning cup of coffee on his desk, Filth gave the mighty roaring garrumph that had often preceded his pleadings in Court. (There was a rumour that it was the remains of some speech impediment though this seemed unlikely in such an articulate man.)

'Ah-argh. Aha! Mrs-er, I meant to tell you I'm going away. Taking a short trip. Leaving on Friday. Doing a round of the family. What?'

'I didn't say anything.'

'Travelling by car,' he said.

'Then I *will* say something. You're out of your mind, Sir Edward. Wherever do you think you're going?'

'Oh, it's up in the north somewhere.'

'You haven't driven further than Tisbury station in years. That car's welded to the garage.'

'Not at all. I've had it checked over.'

'Sir Edward, it's the motorways. You've never driven on a motorway.'

'It's an excellent car. And it's a chance for you to have a break, too. You've been very – very good these past days. Take a holiday.'

'If you insist on going, I'll not take a holiday. I'll steep them grey nets in your bathroom window.'

'You could, actually,' he said, not looking at her, 'perhaps do something about Lady Feathers's room. Get rid of her – er – the c-c-c-clothes. I believe it's usual.'

'Sir Edward.' She came round the table and leaned against the window ledge looking at him, arms folded. 'I've something to say.'

'Oh. Sorry. Yes, Mrs-er. Mrs T.'

'Look, it's too soon. You're doing it all too soon. You started in on the letters before the funeral. You ought to let them settle. I know, because of Mother. And it's too soon to go round handing out presents, you'll muddle them. I'm sorry, but you're not yourself.'

'Mrs-er, if you don't want to do Lady Feathers's room I'm sure that Chloe – the one from the church – would do it.'

'I'm sure she would, too. Let's forget all that though, I'm only interested in stopping you driving. Now then.'

His face, with the light from behind her full on it, she saw must have been wonderful once. Appealing, as he gazed at her.

She carried a mug of coffee out to Garbutt who was waiting near the house wall that stood raw and naked without its ivy.

'He's off in the car. Visiting.'

'On his own?'

'Yes. On the motorways. I've told him he's not rational yet. She'd have never let him. He doesn't know what he's doing. He's answering every letter return of post and ticking them off on a list, every one hand-done and different and she's scarcely cold. There was a green one –'

'Green what?'

'Letter. From Paris. He threw it in the bin. It upset him. He wrote out an answer and they say he was up the street with it in his hand before the postman was hardly gone.'

They both regarded the wall.

Garbutt knew she had read the letter in the waste-paper basket. He would not have read it.

'You know, he's never once called me by my name. *She* did, of course.'

Garbutt finished his coffee, upturned the mug and shook the dregs out on the grass. 'Well, I can't see we can do much about it. He's the Law. The law unto himself.'

'I tell you, we'll both be out of a job by Monday and who else is going to kill on the road? That's what I care about.'

'He might make it,' he said, handing her back the mug. 'There's quite a bit to him yet.'

Nevertheless, on the Thursday afternoon Filth found the gardener hanging about the garage doors.

'I've had her looked at,' said Filth, 'I seem to be having to tell everybody. She's a Mercedes. I'm a good driver. Why have you removed all the ivy?'

'It was her instructions. Not a fortnight since. Sir Edward, you're barmy. It's too soon. You're pushing eighty. *She*'d say it was too soon. You haven't a notion of that A1.'

'Is it the A1 now? I must look at the map. Good God, I've known the Great North Road for years. I was at school up there.'

'Well, you'll not know it now. That's all I'll say. Goodbye then, sir.'

Filth looked up the seaside town of Herringfleet where Babs hung out and was surprised. He'd thought it might be somewhere around Lincolnshire, but it was nearer to Scotland. Odd, he thought, how I could still find my way round the back streets of Hong Kong and the New Territories with my eyes shut and England now is a blur.

Whatever was Babs doing up there? Where would he stay if she couldn't put him up? There seemed to be no hostelry in

Herringfleet that the travel guides felt very happy about.

But he went on with his plans, polishing his shoes, looking out shirts. He loved packing. He packed his ivory hair-brushes, his Queen Mary cufflinks from the War and, rather surprising himself, Betty's *Book of Common Prayer*. Maybe he'd give it to Babs. Or Claire, if he ever found her. He folded two of Betty's lovely Jacqumar scarves, packaged up some recipe books and then, in a sudden fit of panache, swept a great swag of her jewellery from the dressing-table drawer and poured it into a Jiffy bag. He put the scarves and recipe books into another Jiffy bag and sealed both of them up.

On Friday morning early, Mrs-er standing on the front doorstep with a face of doom and Garbutt up his ladder at work on ivy roots and not even turning his head, he made off down the drive and headed for the future.

His eyesight was good. He had spent time on the map. The day was fair and he felt very well. He had decided that he would proceed across England from left to right, and somewhere around Birmingham take a route from South-West to North-East. Very little trouble. His visual memory of the map was excellent and he plunged out into the mêlée of Spaghetti Junction without a tremor, scarcely registering the walls of traffic that wailed and shrieked and overtook him. He admitted to a sense of tension whenever he swerved into the fast lane, but enjoyed the stimulation. Several very large vehicles passed him with a dying scream, one or two even overtaking him on the driver's side although he was in the fast lane. One of these seemed to bounce a little against the central reservation.

Filth was intrigued by the central reservation. It was a phenomenon new to him. He wondered who had thought of it. Was it the same man who had invented cat's-eyes and made millions and hadn't known what to do with them? He remembered that man. He had had three television sets all quacking on together. Poor wretched fellow. Death by cat's-eye. Well, that must be some time ago.

Lorries in strings, like moving blocks of flats, were now

hurtling along. Sometimes his old Mercedes seemed to hang between them, hardly touching the road. Seemed to be a great many foreign buggers driving the lorries, steering-wheels left-hand side where they couldn't see a thing. Matter of time no doubt when they'd be in the majority. Then everyone would be driving on the right. Vile government. Probably got all the plans drawn up already. Drive on the right, vote on the left. The so-called left, said Filth. Not Mr Attlee's left. Not Aneurin Bevan's left. All of them in suits now. Singapore still drives on the left, though they've never heard of left. Singapore's over, like Hong Kong. Empire now like Rome. Not even in the history books. Lost. Over. Finished. Dead. Happened.

Two dragons, Machiavellis, each carrying a dozen or so motor-cars on its back, like obscene, louse-laden animals, hemmed him in on either side of the middle lane. Surely the one in the fast lane was breaking the law? Both seemed impatient with him, though he was doing a steady sixty-five, quite within limits.

He could feel their hatred. One slip and I'm gone, he thought with again the stir of excitement, almost of sexual excitement, 'One toot and yer oot,' as the bishop said to the old girl with the ear-trumpet. Wherever did that come from? Too much litter in old brains.

Ah! Suddenly he was free. The lorries were gone. He had turned expertly eastwards – with some style, I may say – and into Nottinghamshire.

He found himself now on narrower two-way roads broken by enormous, complicated country roundabouts. Signs declared unlikely names. Fields began, the colour of ox-blood. (Why is ox-blood darker than cow's-blood?) Clumps of black-green trees stood on the tops of low hills. Streaming towards him, opening out before him, passing him by, were old mining towns all forlorn. Then a medieval castle on a knoll. Then came an artificial hill with a pipe sticking out of its side like a patient with nasty things within. Black stuff trickled. The last coal mine. Black stuff wavered in the wind. Never been down a coal mine, thought Filth. There's always something new. (But no. Over.

Finished. Gone. Dead.) Better stop soon. Seeing double. Need to pee. Done well. One of these cafés.

But now there were no cafés. They had all disappeared.

'Worksop,' said Filth. 'Now, there's a nasty name. Betty would be furious – *Worksop*!' She hated the North except for Harrogate. 'Why ever go to ghastly Babs? You're mad. She's mad. I met her after you did.' (Oh, finish, finish, finish.)

He came upon pale and graceful stone gates leading to some lost great estate with the National Trust's acorn on a road sign. He turned in and drove two miles down an avenue of limes. Families shrieked about. He found a Gents and then returned stiffly to the Mercedes in the car-park. People ran about taking plants from a garden shop to their cars to plant on their patios. If I had ever loved England, he thought, I would now weep for her. Sherwood Forest watched him from every side, dense and black.

On again, and into the ruthless thunder of the traffic on the A1; but he was in charge again. Bloody good car, strong as a tank, fine as a good horse. Always liked driving. Aha! Help! Spotting a café he turned across the path of a conveyor of metal pipes from the Ruhr.

A near thing. The driver's face was purple and his mouth held wide in a black roar.

Shaken a little, Filth ate toasted tea-cake at a plastic table and drank a large potful of tea. The waitress looked at his suit and tie with dislike. The man at the next table was wearing denim trousers, with his knees protruding, and a vest. Brassy rings were clipped into all visible orifices. Filth went back to the car for a quick nap but the rhythmic blast of the passing traffic caused the Mercedes to rock at three-second intervals.

'On, on,' said Filth. 'Be dark soon.'

And, two hours later, it was indeed pretty dark and he must have reached Teesside. There was no indication, however, of any towns. Only roads. Roads and roads. The traffic went swimming over them, presumably knowing where it was going. Endless, head-on, blazing head-lights. It is only an airport now, he thought. My spacious lovely North. We are living on a transporter. Up and down we go. *We shall chase you up and down*. That swine Veneering liked *Midsummer Night's Dream*. Silly stuff, but you can't help quoting it. Forest of Arden. Forest of Sherwood. Gone, gone. Finished. Dead. Like Garbutt's ivy. Betty would have been in a fury. 'You could have been in *Madeira* by now, in a nice, elderly hotel. And you go to Babs on Teesside. And here's a place called *Yarm*. What a name! *Yarm*.'

'You wouldn't think so if we were in Malaysia.'

'Don't be silly, Filth.'

'Or the dialects. Malay lacks consonants.'

'*Yarm* seems to lack everything.'

'Oh, I don't know. Rather a fine-looking town. Splendidly wide main street. Shows up the Cotswolds.'

'Well, don't stop, Filth. Not now, for goodness sake. You've only half an hour to go. *Get* there.'

Just outside Yarm he saw a signpost which amazingly, for he had not been here before, he recognised. Standing back on a grim champaign behind the swishing traffic stood the Old Judges' Lodging, now an hotel. Once the Circuit Judges would have lived there throughout the Quarter Sessions. No wives allowed. Too much port. Boring each other silly. Comforting each others' isolation with talk. Every evening, like cricket commentators between matches, discussing their profession. Finished. Gone. Dead. Hotel now, eh?

'Ha?'

Sign for Herringfleet.

Babs.

What a dire town. And not small. How to find 25 The Lindens? Here was the sea. A cemented edge of promenade. A line of glimmer that must be white sandy beach. Long, long waves curving round a great bay, and behind their swirling frills, spread into the total dark, was the heaving black skin and muscle of the ocean. Sea. How they had hated the sea in Wales. The cruel dividing sea. How could Babs ever choose this?

He had stopped the car on the promenade where, looking blank-eyed at the sea, were tall once-elegant lodging houses now near-slums, bed and breakfast places for the Nationally Assisted, i.e., the poor. No lights. The rain fell.

'The Lindens? What?' shouted a man on an old bike. He got off and came across and stuck his head through the window. The smell was chip fat and beer and no work. 'The Lindens, mate? (Grand car.) Just over to your right there. You'll not miss it, pal.'

It was a terrace of genteel and secretive houses on either side of a short street bordered by trees. The trees were bulging with round gangliae from which next year new sprouts would shoot like hairs from a mole. Revolting treatment. What would Sir say? Number 25.

At the top of steep stone steps there was a dim light above a front room and another light in a window beside it. A gate hung on one hinge. There was a sense of retreat and defeat. He remembered laughing, streetwise, positive Babs in the Oxford tea-shop. *We'll go to bed. We have before.* Laughing, wagging her cracked high-heeled shoe from her toe.

It was so quiet that Filth could hear the beat of the sea two roads away, rhythmic, unstoppable. 'Too soon,' it said. 'They were right. This is histrionic nonsense. You've arrived too soon. You're in shock. You'll make a fool of yourself. There's nothing here.'

Suddenly, at the top of the steps, the front door was wrenched open and a boy ran out. He came tearing down, missing several steps, belted along the path towards Filth at the gate. One hand held a music-case and with the other he pushed Filth hard in the stomach so that he fell back into the hedge. The boy, who was wearing old-fashioned school uniform, vanished towards the sea.

Badly winded, Filth struggled out of the hedge, dusted down his clothes, picked up the fallen parcel of presents, looked right and left and gave his furious roar. The quiet of the road then re-asserted itself. The child might never have been.

But the front door stood wide and he walked uneasily up the steps and into the passage beyond, where, as if he had stood on a switch, a torrent of Chopin was let loose in the room to his right.

'Hello?'

He stood outside its open door.

'Hello there? Babs?'

He knocked on the door, peered round it. 'It's Teddy.'

The music stopped. The room appeared to be empty.

Then he saw her by the back window, staring into the dark. She was wearing some sort of shawl and her hair was long and white. She seemed to be pressing something – a handkerchief? – into her face. Without turning towards him further, her voice came out from behind her hands, clear and controlled. And Betty's.

In one of her very occasional cynical or bitter moods which Filth had never understood, and which usually ended in her going to London for a few days (or over to Macao from Hong Kong), Betty had said, 'Look, leave me alone, Filth. I'm in the dark. Just need a break.'

'I'm in the dark, Teddy-bear,' now said Betty's voice inside this crazed old creature. 'You shouldn't have come. I should have stopped you. I couldn't find the number.'

'Oh, dear me, Babs. You're ill.'

'Ill. Do you mean *sick*? I'm sick all right. D'you want tea? I make it on my gas-ring. There's some milk somewhere. In a cupboard. But we don't take milk, do we? Not from our classy background. I'm finished, Teddy. Broken-hearted. Like Betty. You'd better go.'

(Like Betty? What rubbish – never.)

'I can't stay more than a few minutes,' said Filth, realising that this was absolutely so, for the room was not only ice-cold and dark, but there was an aroma about. Setting down his parcels on a chair piled with newspapers, he touched something unspeakable on a plate.

'Babs, I had no idea. . . .'

'You thought I was well-off, did you? Sky television and modems? Well, I am well-off, but because I am still a teacher of music. I live alone. Betty always warned me against living

alone. Said I'd get funny. But I prefer to live alone. Ever since –
well, you know. Wales. I had mother of course until last year.
Upstairs. I still hear her stick thumping on the floor for the
commode. Sometimes I start heating up her milk. But I'm glad
she's gone. In a way.'

'Then,' said Filth, prickling all over with disgust, making
stabs at various shadows to find perhaps somewhere to lean
against or sit. 'Then it can't *all* have been bad.' He had begun
to lower himself into what might have been a chair when
something in it rustled and streaked for the door.

'Ah,' he said, easing his shirt-collar. 'And you have a dog.'

'What dog? I have no dog.'

'I'm sorry.'

'I'm not sorry. Even with a dog I would be utterly alone. And
I *am* going mad.'

'*Well*' – he had sprung up from the chair and was standing to
attention – '*Well*' (half-heartedly). 'Well, I'm here now, Babs.
We must sort something out. Get something going. Betty
wouldn't want. . . .'

Babs had left the window and was fumbling about. A light
came on and an electric jug was revealed. A half-empty milk
bottle was withdrawn from an antique gramophone. Cups and
saucers were wrested from their natural home upon the hearth.

'You see, I'm quite independent. No trouble to anyone.
Sugar? No, that's not *us*, either, Teddy, is it?'

'Babs, let me take you out somewhere for a meal.'

She flung her long hair about. 'I never go out. I watch and
wait. First Flush? Do you remember?'

For a dreadful moment Filth thought that Babs was referring
to the menopause, though that, surely, must be now in the
past?

'First Flush?'

(Or maybe it was something to do with Bridge? Or the
domestic plumbing?)

'*Tea*, Teddy. First Flush is *tea*. From Darjeeling.' (She pro-
nounced it correctly. Datcherling.) 'Don't you remember?' She
seemed to be holding up a very tattered packet marked

123

Fortnum and Mason, Piccadilly. 'He gave it to me always for years. Every Christmas. In memory of our childhood. You, me, him, Claire, Betty.'

'But we weren't in India, Betty and I. I hadn't met Betty. You and I and Claire were in – Wales.'

She looked frightened.

'But he sent me tea from India. They took him back there after. . . . Year after year from India he sent me tea.'

'Who?'

'Billy Cumberledge.'

'Babs?'

'My lover.'

'Oh, I'm so sorry, Babs. And he died, too?'

'I'm not sure. I used to see him in Oxford. He was a lovely man. She could never touch his soul, never break him utterly. He and I – no, you and I, Teddy. We got into one bed that night to be near together while Claire went to get help.'

'I'd forgotten.' (A wave of relief. So that's what she'd meant in the tea-shop.)

'Yes, he was my lover. But not my last lover. My present lover you may have seen just now as he went scampering down the steps.'

'But that was a schoolboy. . . .'

'Yes, but a genius. I don't do examination work now, except for this one. He is a genius.'

'Yes. I see.'

They drank the First Flush which was not noticeably refreshing.

'This is of course a First Flush of some time ago.'

'Yes,' he said. 'Some time ago.'

The lights in the street came on and revealed a Broadwood piano by the front window and a piano stool lying on its side. He remembered the terrified boy.

'Edward,' she said, abandoning the tea to the grate, 'oh, Edward, we were so close. I have to tell someone. I am in love again.'

'Oh – Oh dear –'

'He is fourteen. You know how old I am. Way over seventy. It makes no difference.'

Something out in the passage fell with a crash to the floor and there was the sound of running water.

'It's that dog,' she said, weeping. 'Everyone's against me. I need God, not a dog.'

All that Filth, now deeply shaken, could say was, 'But you haven't got a dog.'

'Haven't I? Of course I have. I need some protection, don't I?' (And, sharply, in Betty's voice.) 'Come on now, Filth. Work it out.'

A cat ran down the hall as Filth stepped out into it, and water was still dripping from a vase of amazingly perfect lupins.

'Let me help.' Filth stood, unbending.

'It's all right. They're artificial. I always put them in water though, it seems kinder. I arrange them for *him*. The boy. My boy. I don't somehow think he'll be coming back.'

'He won't?'

'No.' She clutched the shawl around her and bent forward as if butting at a storm.

'You see – I showed my hand.'

'Your hand?' (Again, he thought hysterically of Bridge.)

'I showed my hand. I showed my heart. I showed my. . . . Oh, Eddie! I fell to my knees. I told my love.'

Filth was now on the top step. Very fast, he was on the bottom step. 'So sorry, Babs. Time to go. Sorry to leave you so. . . .'

'Don't worry about the flowers,' she said. ' It wasn't your fault.'

She was now on her knees crawling about in the water.

'So sorry, Babs. Not much help. Terribly sorry. God, I wish Betty. . . . I'll try and think what's to be done.'

He could not remember getting back into the car nor the road he took next, but in time found that he was hurtling back in the dark and then into the blinding lights of traffic coming towards Yarm. The Judges' Hotel was before him, agreeably behind its lawns like a flower in a gravel pit. He drove through its gateway with care for he was beginning to shake, and at its great studded doors he stopped. A cheerful young man, in a livery that would not have disgraced Claridges, but eating a sandwich, bounded forward and opened the driver's door.

'Good evening, sir, staying the night? Out you get, leave the key, I'll park it. Any luggage? Nasty weather!'

Filth stepped in to a black and white marble hall with a grand staircase and portraits of Judges in dubious bright oils hanging all the way down it. How very odd to be here. Yes, there was one room left. Yes, there was dinner. Yes, there was a bar.

Filth removed his coat in the bedroom and regarded the two single beds, both populous with teddy bears. A foot-massager of green plastic lay by the bedside and a globe of goldfish with instructions for feeding them ('Guests are asked to confine themselves to one pinch' – was it hemp?). There were no towels in the bathroom but a great many plastic ducks. The noble height of the room that had in the past seen scores of judicial heads on the pillow seemed another frightening joke. I suppose I don't know much about hotels now, he thought and had a flashback of the black towels and white telephones and linen sheets of Hong Kong.

For the first time in many years he did not change his shirt for dinner but stepped quickly back into the hall where the eyes of the old buggers on the staircase, in their wigs and scarlet, gave him a sense of his secure past. Glad I got out of the country though. No Circuits in Hong Kong. No getting stuck in luxury here for weeks on end with the likes of Fiscal-Smith. He wondered where the name had come from. Hadn't thought of the dear old bore for years.

Good heavens.

Fiscal-Smith was still here. He was sitting in the bar in a vast leather armchair and as usual he was without a glass in his hand, waiting for someone to buy him a drink.

'Evening, Filth,' said Fiscal-Smith. (Ye gods, thought Filth, there's something funny going on here.) 'No idea you'd be here. Thought you'd retire in Hong Kong. How's Betty?'

'We retired and came Home years ago,' said Filth, sitting down carefully in a second leather throne.

'Oh, so did I, so did I,' said Fiscal-Smith. 'I retired up here though.'

'Really.'

'Got myself a little estate. Nobody wants them now – it's the fumes. It was very cheap.'

'I see.'

'Or they *assume* there are fumes. Actually I am out on the moors. Shooting rights. Everything.'

'How is . . .?' Filth could not remember whether Fiscal-Smith had ever had a wife. It seemed unlikely.

'. . . the Bar up here these days?'

Fiscal-Smith was looking meaningfully over at the Claridges lad, who was hovering about and responded with a matey wave.

'Have a drink,' said Filth, giving in, signalling to the boy and ordering whiskeys.

'Don't be too long, sir,' said the boy. 'Dining-room closes in half an hour.'

'Yes. Yes. I must have dinner. Long drive today.' He was beginning to feel better though. Warmth, whiskey, familiar jargon. 'Are you staying the night here?' he asked Fiscal-Smith.

'I don't usually. I go home. Always a chance that someone might turn up from the old days. Very good of you. Thank you. I'd enjoy dinner.'

They munched. Conversation waned.

'Fancy sort of food nowadays,' said the ancient Judge. 'Seem to paint the sauces on the plates with a brush.'

The waitress patted his shoulder and shouted with laughter. 'You're meant to lick 'em up. Shall I keep you some tiramisu?'

'What on earth is that?'

'No idea,' said Filth, his eyelids drooping.

'Trifle,' said the waitress. 'You're nothing now, if you haven't tried tiramisu.'

'Is this usual?' asked Filth, reviving a little with coffee.

'What – trifle? Yes, it's on all the time.'

'No. I mean the – familiarity. They're very matey. I never worked the Northern Circuit.'

'It's not mateyness.'

'Well, it's not exactly respect.' Filth's mind presented him with Betty ringing for the invisible and silent maids. He suddenly yearned for that sycophantic time in his life, like a boy thinking of his birthday parties. 'They're very insensitive. And I can't understand the teddy bears. I always detested teddy bears.'

'What teddy bears?'

'The beds are covered with them. Is it a local custom?'

'I'm afraid you are ahead of me, somewhere. But of course, yes, it's different up here. Very nice people.'

'But you're not local, Fiscal-Smith. Is there anybody to talk to? On your estate?'

Fiscal-Smith took a second huge slice of cheese. 'No. Not really. Sit there alone. I like it here though.' (Old Filth's grown stuffy. Home Counties. How does Betty put up with him?) 'They're rude to your face but they boast about knowing you. House of Lords, and all that. It's a compliment, but you have to understand it. Good friends at The Judges to an old bachelor.'

All but one of the lights were now switched off in the dining-room, where they were the only diners left. The waitress looked out from a peephole.

'Yes, we've finished, Dolly. I think I'll stay the night. Too much wine for driving. "Ex-Judge drunk at wheel." Wouldn't do.'

'Yes. Keep it within closed doors,' said Dolly. 'But I don't think there's a room ready. The housekeeper's gone off.'

'Twin beds in your room, Filth?'

'Well, I'm afraid. . . .'

'Room One?' said the waitress. 'Yes. Twin beds.'

'No,' said Filth in the final and first, utterly immovable decision of the day. 'No. Sorry. I – snore.'

'Oh, then, we'll find you somewhere, Lord Fiscal-Smith. Come along. The trouble will be bath-towels. I think she hides them.'

'Shan't have a bath.' He tottered away on her arm. 'Borrow your razor in the morning, Filth.'

'We can do a *razor*,' she said. 'Did you say he was called Filth?'

She handed Fiscal-Smith over to the Claridges boy who was drinking a glass of milk in the hall.

When Filth lay down on one of his beds the room rocked gently round and round. 'Pushing myself,' he said. 'Heart-attack. I dare say. Sir? Good. Hope it's the finish. And I'm certainly not lending him my razor.'

Then, it was morning.

The goldfish were looking at his face on the pillow with inquisitive distaste. On the floor a heap of bears gave the impression of decadence. The bedside clock glared out 9.30 a.m. which filled him with shame, and he reached breakfast just in time.

'So sorry,' he said.

'That's all right, dear. You need your sleep at your age.'

Far across the bright conservatory, where breakfast was served, bacon and eggs were being carried to Fiscal-Smith whose back was turned firmly away from all comers as he perused the *Daily Telegraph*. Filth changed his chair so that his back was also turned away from Fiscal-Smith. Outside, across the grey Teesside grass, stood magnificent oaks and, above them, a deep blue autumn sky and a hint of moorland, air and light. The *Telegraph* was beside Filth's plate. He must have ordered it. Couldn't read it. Not yet. Rice-Krispies.

'Oh dear no, thank you. Nothing cooked.'

'Oh, come on. Do you good.'

She brought bacon and eggs.

Why *should* I? thought Filth, petulant, and clattered down his knife and fork.

'I'm disappointed,' said the waitress, bringing coffee.

He drank it and looked at the oak trees and the light beyond. Must get out of this wasteland. Not my sort of place at all. What was Babs doing here? What was I doing, coming to visit her? Rather frightening, what grief can uncover in you.

Don't you think so, Betty? Just as well I wasn't in the middle of a case when you went. But you'd have dealt with it. Got me through.

Remembering, then, that the cause of the grief was that she could no longer get him through anything, he gulped, shuddered, watched the oaks, as his eyes at last filled up with tears.

A hand came down on his shoulder but he did not turn. The hand was removed.

'So very sorry, old chap. So very sorry,' and Fiscal-Smith was gone.

It was some time later – breakfast still uneaten, Filth's back the only sign of anyone in the room, silence from the kitchen – that the oaks began to return to their natural steadiness. Filth, his face wet, blew his nose, mopped with his napkin, took up the newspaper, opened it, shook it about. He found himself looking straight into Betty's face.

Obituary.

Good gracious. Betty. No idea there'd be an obituary. And half a column. Second on the page. Good God: Red Cross; Barristers' Benevolent Association; Bletchley Park. Dominant personality. Wife of – yes, it was Betty, all right. Fiscal-Smith must have been reading it. Good God – *Betty*! They'll never give me half a column. I've never done anything but work. Great traveller. Ambassadress. Chinese-speaking. Married and the dates. No children of the marriage.

He sat on. On and on. They cleared the table. They did not hurry him. On and on he sat. They changed the cloth. They said not a word.

At some point he began properly to weep. He wept silently behind his hands, sitting in this unknown place, uncared about, ignorant, bewildered, past it.

Much later they brought him, unasked, a tray of tea. When at last he had packed his case and paid his bill at the desk in the marble hall and was standing bleakly on the porch as the boy brought his car, he remembered that he had invited Fiscal-

Smith to join him for last night's dinner, and that this had not been on the bill.

'Don't you worry, sir,' said the receptionist. 'He's paid it himself.'

She said no more, but both understood that this was a first. And that it was touching. It lifted Filth's desolate heart.

He drove for an hour before addressing Betty again. 'You never know where help's coming from, do you? Yes. You're right. I'm ten years older than yesterday and I look it.' ('*Fool*,' he yelled at a nervous little Volkswagen. 'Do you want to be *killed*, woman?') No more gadding about for a while.

'But stop worrying. I'll get home. I'm a bloody good driver.' The car gave a wobble.

He thought of the hotel which loomed now much larger in his consciousness than the Babs business (Babs had always been potty) and he understood the goldfish, the bears, the box of Scrabble in the wardrobe, the tapedeck and the vast television set in the room. They were an attempt to dispel the sombre judicial atmosphere of the place's past. The seams of the Judges' Lodging had exuded crime, wickedness, evil, folly and pain. All had been tossed about in conversation each night over far too much port. Jocose, over-confident Judges.

Well, they have to be. Judges live with shadows behind them. There are very good men among them. Mind you, I'd never have put Fiscal-Smith among those, the horrible old hanger-and-flogger.

'Seems we were wrong, Betty,' he said, turning the car unthinkingly Eastward in the direction of the Humber bridge.

And on it sped for three hours, when he had to stop for petrol and saw signs for Cambridge.

Cambridge?

Why Cambridge? He was making for the Midlands and home in the South-West. He must have missed his turning. He seemed to be on the way to London. This road was called the M11 and it was taking its pitiless way between the wide green fields of – where? Huntingdonshire? Rutland? – don't know anything about any of them. Claire lives somewhere about down here. Hainault. Never been. Must have the address somewhere. Hadn't intended to come. Hadn't consciously intended to come. Had quite enough. Saffron Walden? Nice name. Why are you going to see Claire? You haven't seen her since – well, since Ma Didds.

Betty knew her. Betty saw her. Why must I? Wasn't Babs enough?

He drew out in front of a Hungarian demon. Its hoot died slowly away, as at length it passed him, spitting wrath as he swayed into the slow lane. Mile after mile. Mile after mile. Fear no bigger than a child's hand squeezed at his ribcage. 'If it's a heart attack, get on with it,' commanded Filth.

But he drew off the motorway and dawdled into a lane. There were old red-brick walls and silent mansions and a church. A by-passed village, like a by-passed heart. Not a café. Not a shop. He'd perhaps go and sit in the church for a while. Here it stood.

The church appeared to be very well-kept. He pushed open an inner red-baize door. The church within echoed with insistent silence. There was the smell of incense and very highly-varnished pews. A strange church. The sense of many centuries with a brash, almost aggressive overlay. You'd be kept on your toes here. Never had much idea of these things, thought Filth.

Lists pinned up everywhere. All kinds of services. Meditations. *The lamp is lit over the Blessed Sacrament.* Vigils. *Quiet is requested.* An enormous Cross with an agonised Christ. That always upset Filth.

This terrible silence.

He sat in the south aisle and closed his eyes and when he opened them saw that winter sunshine had lit up a marble memorial to some great local family. It was immense, a giant wedding-cake in black and pink and sepia. Like an old photograph. Like a sad cry.

Filth got up and peered closer. He touched some of the

figures. They were babies. Dozens of babies. Well, cherubs, he supposed, carved among garlands of buds and flowers, nuts, leaves, insects, fat fruits. More marble babies caught at more garlands at the foot of the pyramid, all naked, and male of course. They were weeping. One piped its eye, whatever piping was. Their fat lips pouted with sorrow. They stood, however, on very sturdy legs with creases across the backs of their knees, and their bottoms shone. There was a notice saying that the memorial had three stars and was thought to have been designed by Gibbons.

Well, I don't know about that, thought Filth. What would Gibbons be doing here? And he gave one of the bottoms a slap.

The air of the church came alive for a moment as the baize door opened and shut, and a curly boy came springing down the aisle. He wore a clerical collar and jeans. 'Good afternoon,' he cried. 'So sorry I'm rather late. You're wanting me to hear your confession.'

'Confession?'

'Saturday afternoons. Confessions. St Trebizond's. Half a mo while I put my cassock on.'

He ran past the weeping pile and disappeared into a vestry, emerging at once struggling into a cassock. He hurried into something like a varnished sedan chair which stood beside the rood screen, and clicked shut its door. The silence resumed.

Filth at once turned and made to walk out of the church, clearing his throat with the judicial roar.

He looked back. The sedan chair watched him. There was a grille of little holes at waist level and he imagined the boy priest resting his head near it on the inside.

It would be rather discourteous just to leave the church. Filth might go over and say, 'Very low-church, I'm afraid. Not used to this particular practice though my wife was interested. . . .'

He walked back to the sedan chair, leaned down and said, 'Hullo? Vicar?'

A crackling noise. Like eating potato crisps.

'Vicar? I beg your pardon?'

No reply. All was hermetically sealed within except for the grille. Really quite dangerous.

He creaked down to his knees to a hassock and put his face to the grille. Nothing happened. The boy must have fallen asleep.

'Excuse me, Vicar. I'm afraid I don't go in for this. I have nothing to confess.'

'A very rash statement,' snarled a horrendous voice – there must be some amplifier.

Filth jumped as if he'd put his ear to an electric fence.

'How long, my son, since your last confession?'

'I've –' (his son!) '– I've never made a confession in my life. I've heard plenty. I'm a Q.C.'

There was a snuffling sound.

'But you are in some trouble?'

Filth bowed his head.

'Begin. Go on. "Father I have sinned." Don't be afraid.'

Filth's ragged old logical mind was not used to commands.

'I'm afraid I don't at the moment feel sinful at all. I am more sinned against than sinning. I am able to think only of my dear dead wife. She was in the *Telegraph* this morning. Her obituary.' Then he thought: I am not telling the truth. 'And I am unable to understand the strange games my loss of her play with my behaviour.'

Why tell this baby? Can't be much over thirty. Well, same age as Christ, I suppose. If Christ were inside this box. . . . A great and astounding longing fell upon Filth, the longing of a poet, the deep perfect adoring longing of a lover of Christ. How did he come on to this? This medieval, well of course, very primitive, love of Christ you read about? Not my sort of thing at all.

'My son, were there any children of the marriage?'

'No. We didn't seem to need any.'

'That's never the full answer. I have to say that I saw you touching the anatomy of the cherubs on the Tytchley tomb.'

'You *what*?'

'Reveal all to me, my son. I can understand and help you.'

'Young man,' roared Filth through the grille. 'Go home. Look to your calling. I am one of Her Majesty's Counsellors and was once a Judge.'

'There is only one Judge in the end,' said the voice, but Filth was in the car again and belting on past Saffron Walden.

He drove very fast indeed now, as the roads grew less equipped for him. I am a coelacanth. Yes. I dare say. I have lived too long. Certainly, I cannot cope – cope with a mind such as I have. The bloody little twerp. Wouldn't have him in my Chambers. I *can* drive, though. That's one thing I can do. My reactions are perfect, and here is a motorway again.

And hullo – what's this? Lights? Sirens? Police? 'Good afternoon. Yes?'

'You have been behaving oddly on the road, sir. It has been reported.'

'I have been stopping sometimes. Resting. Once in a church. In my view, essential. No, no need for a breath test. Oh well, very well.'

'You see. Perfectly clear,' said Filth.

'Could we help you in any way?'

'No. I don't think so.'

'Your licence is in order?'

'Yes, of course. I am a lawyer.'

'It doesn't follow, sir. I see that you are eighty-one?'

'With no convictions,' said Filth.

'No, sir. Well, goodbye, sir.'

'There is one thing,' said Filth, strapping himself back in his seat with some languor. 'I do seem to be rather lost.'

'Ah.'

'I don't suppose you know this address. Hainault?'

'We do, sir. But it's not Hainault. That is in Essex. It's High Light. Not High Note. A house called *High Light*. And we know who it belongs to. We know her. It's five miles away. Shall we go ahead of you?'

'She is my cousin. She can never have had any Christmas

cards. Thank you. And thank you for your courtesy and proper behaviour. A great surprise.'

'You oughtn't to believe the television, sir.'

'Who the hell was he?' one policeman asked the other. 'He's like out of some Channel Four play.'

A Light House

Claire in her house all alone sat in her shadowless kitchen and down came her beautiful little hands slap-bang across the *Daily Telegraph*. She closed her eyes and sat for a full minute, 'No,' she said, 'Of course it's not Betty. Someone would have told me.'

She opened her eyes, removed her hands and stared down at Betty Feathers' eyes which looked back at her with sharp but pleasant intelligence. 'Well,' she said, 'an obituary for Betty.' She smoothed the paper, read Elizabeth Feathers, MBE, and then the whole thing.

The phone rang. She folded the paper and turned it on its back. She walked to the phone.

'Hullo?'

'Beware. The Ice Man Cometh.'

Claire sat down quickly. The quiet life she had diligently followed over years was the rent she paid to a weak heart. Her control, balance, yoga, good sense, none of it natural to her, had been necessary if she was to see her husband out. She had told the doctor that it was essential she outlive him, and the doctor had thought her wonderful and her husband a weak old bore. Now, as a widow, Claire found that creeping about and being careful was a habit she could not drop. She would have liked a lover, but the heart battering about inside her made the practice impossible. Today, it was beating like an angry butterfly under a jam jar.

'Claire? Claire? Are you there? It's Babs.'

'Oh yes,' she said. '*Babs*. Yes, of course. You always did sound like Betty.'

'Can't help it. I suppose you were at the funeral. In at the kill.'

'I've just this minute seen the *Telegraph*. An utter shock.'

'Well, it would be the hush-hush Bletchley Park thing. She wasn't there for long. I never thought she was very clever. She's had a pretty good life with him. You might have told me about the funeral. She had some wonderful rocks.'

'Rocks?'

'Jewellery.'

'Oh. Had she? I didn't know she was dead until now.'

Claire had been wild about Filth since she was four, but as inscrutable then as now she sat prettily in her pink dressing-gown with her hand firmly against the butterfly.

'He turned up here yesterday. He only stayed ten minutes. He brought me some recipe books but I can't find them. He'll be en-route to you now. At a guess.'

'He would have telephoned. Though I suppose I do tend to switch it off.'

'He's not himself, I warn you. He never told me when he was arriving. Then ten minutes later he was gone. Actually I wasn't very well. I'm not a very well woman.'

'But why did he come? We haven't seen either of them in years. All that way! Dorset! She can't have died more than. . . .' She glanced at the folded paper. She would look properly later.

'Just over a fortnight. He was bringing us keepsakes. I'd rather hoped she'd made a Will. I think he thought better of giving me the recipe books. I expect he'll offer them to you.'

'But I'm diabetic.'

'Yes, well, I don't suppose he remembers that. Just at the moment.'

'No,' said Claire.

'He was very strange. He fled the house. I seemed to horrify him. I can't think why. My ways are not everybody's ways, of course, but knowing what we three have been through together. . . .'

138

'Your ways were not everybody's ways then.'

'Neither were yours.'

'Why not?'

'All that *perfection*, Claire. *Nauseating* perfection. From the start.'

Silence.

'Claire?'

'Yes?'

'Sorry. I only meant that it's a bit chilling.'

'It seems,' said Claire, 'that Betty's death removes barriers. It's bringing corpses to the surface. I can honestly say I never had anything to hide.'

'Oh, no?'

Claire was watching through the huge window an immaculate Mercedes nosing about in the lane. It paused, considered, started off again and cruised out of sight.

'You'd better ring me if he turns up,' said Babs. 'He looked to me as if he was in need of special care, like they used to say of drawn-thread work on laundry lists. Get him to see someone.'

Elgar's *Enigma Variations* began to boom in Babs's background.

'Laundry lists? Hello? I can't hear you.'

Claire put down the phone.

The car must have turned somewhere down the road, for here it was nosing slowly back again. 'He won't come here,' she said aloud. 'He doesn't need me. He never did and we won't be able to look each other in the eye. "It was Betty who made him," Isobel Ingoldby used to say. I never believed her. He's made himself. Made his impeccable, astringent self.'

The phone rang again.

'Well, all I can say, Claire, he was shaking all over and grey in the face and terrified of my poor animals under his feet. *Gob-smacked*, outraged by my little lover with his little music-case.'

'What are you talking about, Babs? I wish you wouldn't say "gob-smacked". It doesn't become you. You're not a teenager.'

139

'Yes, I am. At heart I am fourteen.'

The car had now stopped at Claire's gate and Filth's stony face, with the Plantagenet cheek-bones and thick ungreying curly hair, could be observed, peering out.

'When old women say that,' said Claire, '"I'm just a girl inside", I. . . .' The butterfly was hammering now on iron wings. Filth's long right leg, like the leg of a flamingo but in Harris tweed, was feeling for the pavement. 'I,' said Claire, 'cease to find them interesting.'

'I may not be interesting, but it was me he turned to at Ma Didds, when you went running down the village.'

Claire let her fingers stray about over the glass table-top, feeling for her butterfly-subduing pills. And here came the old flamingo, the old crane, lean as a cowboy still. What? Six-foot-three, and still melting my heart.

Well, he seemed to be carrying the parcel of recipe books.

'I must go now, Babs. The laundry man's here. And Babs – you're drinking too much. Goodbye.'

'Have you any luggage? I hope you'll be staying the night?' she asked at once.

Filth jack-knifed himself into a small, gold-sprayed Lloyd-loom chair and his knees were nearly up to his chin. Light fell upon him like a greeting as in fact it always did upon everybody inside the rambling bungalow which Claire had moved into a few years ago for that very reason, and because it was sensible for someone with A Heart. The building followed an easy circuit. Sitting-room led into kitchen, kitchen led into bathroom, bathroom led into Claire's bedroom and out to the hallway again. Off the hall was a second bedroom and bathroom, the bedroom narrower and full of hat-boxes and tissue paper and old letters and Christmas lists spread permanently over the bed. In each room she kept a supply of pills and on the bathroom mirror she had stuck a list, written in her beautiful calligraphy, of all the pills she took, and when. 'You make poetry of every word you write,' the Vicar had said, but Claire had passed the compliment by.

'I have a spare room, Teddy.'

'I could take you out to dinner,' he said, without enthusiasm.

'I don't go out for meals. I hardly go out at all. I watch the Boy Scouts doing my gardening outside my windows. That is my fresh air.'

'You have a beautiful complexion, nevertheless,' he said. 'And you have the figure of a – of an angel.'

He saw Betty's jolly old rump above the tulip bed. Her weather-beaten face. 'A hundred in and a hundred more to go,' she had called. 'I don't want a gin. Could we miss lunch?' Then over she fell.

He looked now long and piercingly – but unseeingly – at Claire's open and beautiful face. She'd been a sunlit, lovely child who'd grown plain (or so Betty had told him). A stodgy bride in horn-rims. Then pretty again, and now beautiful. He remembered being told that she had ruled her children by a mysterious silence, her adoration of them never expressed. Betty said the children had felt guilty about it, knowing they could never deserve her; they had become conventional, monosyllabic members of society. Her nice husband, Betty said, had taken to drink. Claire (Betty said) believed that marriage and motherhood meant pain. Betty had agreed with her about children, and thought that Claire lived for the moment when they fled the nest and she was peacefully widowed. And here she sat now, gentle, shoulderless as a courtesan on her linen-covered sofa, smiling. (Filth turned to Betty on his interior telephone to ask what she thought about it, but Betty had left the phone off the hook.)

'Of course!' he said. 'I remember. You have diabetes. You can't come out to dinner. Let me. . . .' he had never gone shopping in his life. 'Let me go and forage for us.'

'So you *will* stay?'

'I'd be – delighted.'

'Teddy, there's no need to forage. The girl gets me what I want. There's a freezer. And there's whiskey.'

'Whiskey?'

'Oh, just for anyone who drifts in. The police – very nice people, out of hours. They come here when I fall over. The Vicar.

The woman down the road with one eye. The window-cleaner. I'm fond of the window-cleaner. I have him once a week, though "have" alas is not any longer the word. I "have" a weak heart.'

Filth's eyes were startled as a dog's. This silvery, powdery woman.

'Oh, Teddy,' she said. 'So easily shocked.'

'Well, Claire, really. We are way over . . . seventy.'

'Yes. And I have a weak heart.'

She poured him an immense whiskey and sat on, smiling beyond him out through the gleaming clean window.

Soon Filth eased himself down in the chair, tilted his head back on the curved rim and looked up at the ceiling which was studded with dozens of trendy spotlights, like an office. He took another deep swig of whiskey and sighed.

'Our mutual cousin, or whatever she is, Babs, exists in perpetual darkness and you in perpetual light.'

'Yes,' she said. 'It's odd. I can't get enough of it. Maybe my eyesight's going. I'd love a cataract operation, wouldn't you?'

'I'm lucky there,' said Filth. 'I brought you a present, by the way. Betty wanted you to have them.'

'Oh, yes?' She looked canny. She examined his face for lies.

'Nothing much. Family stuff mostly. Some from way back. She wanted you to have them. She was insistent. If she departed first – only you.'

'What about Babs?'

'She'd put something else aside for Babs. As a matter of fact we were in the m-m-m-middle of our, what's called "Letters of Wishes".'

'I see. She had other friends?'

'Yes. Don't know how well she kept them, though. Not exactly friends. At the funeral. . . .'

'Ah yes. The funeral.'

'Didn't bother you with the funeral. Sorry now. Thought I'd spare you. Never get this sort of thing right. And a big journey. Our time of life, it's a funeral a week in the winter. They don't do anyone any good.'

'I hope mine will be private. On the Ganges on a pyre.'

'I never read obituaries. No idea Betty was getting one.'

'Did nobody turn up at the funeral, Teddy?'

'No idea.'

'Teddy –?'

'Didn't look around. Eyes front. Usual hymns. Discipline and all that.'

'Of course,' said Claire. (Oh, where was the boy, the blazing young friend in Wales?) 'Of course. You were with the Glorious Gloucesters in the War.'

He gave her a look.

'I believe there was a pack of church ladies,' he said. 'From the flower committee. Coffee rota. One of them walked me home and made herself rather too friendly. I'm told you have to watch this.'

'Was there a wake?'

'Bun-fight in the church hall.'

'Nobody from Chambers?'

'Oh, yes. Yes. My Clerk. Retired now. Very civil of him.'

'Well, you made him a packet.'

Again the look.

'And there were a few from the Inn. Hardly knew them. Can't think why they came, trains being what they are.'

'But, Teddy, they may have wanted to come. They were fond of Betty. Maybe it helped them to wear a dark suit, make an effort on your behalf. Respecting you. Helping you.'

'Helping me?' He looked at his glass. 'Nonsense, Claire. Whenever did I need help?' He seemed outraged. 'We all come to an end.'

'Teddy, you must grieve for her. You will soon. It hasn't hit you yet, but listen, there may be a very bad time coming. You were married nearly half a century and you never – I'd guess – strayed?'

'Strayed?'

'You were never unfaithful to Betty with another woman?'

'Good God, no.'

Yet his eyes were dazzling, hungry eyes. Claire thought how Betty had underestimated him. And fooled him.

143

'Then, Teddy, you are in trouble. You are in shock.' ('She should have seen you on the motorway,' said Betty to Filth on her mobile.) 'Why else would you have come charging round the country after Babs and me?'

'How did you know about Babs?'

'She rang.'

'Was she drunk? She was drunk yesterday. On tea from Fortnum's, or worse. Very squalid.'

'You can be a cruel man, Teddy. More whiskey? Hello, who's this?'

Outside in the road a motor-bike came clattering up to the gate and a young man in a medieval black helmet with belligerent lip got off and stood looking at the Merc.

'Oh, Lord, it's the Vicar. I'll get rid of him. Unless of course. . . .'

'No thanks,' said Filth as the Vicar removed his disguise and emerged as the cherub of the sedan chair. 'I'll find your spare bedroom and lie down,' and he seized his bag from the hall and made off.

'Ah, I see you are not ready for each other at the moment,' called Claire.

The young man in the road, having walked round the car and examined the number plate, climbed back on his bike and roared away.

'He saw I had a visitor,' said Claire, and went to the kitchen to look in the freezer. Fish fingers. Oven chips, but she kept these for Oliver so she and Teddy mustn't eat them all. A square of mild cheddar in plastic. Flora margarine and frozen peas. Splendid. Though Teddy never noticed what he ate.

'Or anything else,' she said, sadly, and mistakenly.

Wandsworth

Parents' weekend, thought Claire's younger son, Oliver, in Wandsworth on Friday, flinging a few crumpled things into a sports bag. Wonder if I need petrol. Trip to the bank machine. No need for condoms, anyway, all by myself. Might step out and buy some real flowers for Ma, not petrol station ones. Saturday morning.

He was happy to be going to see his mother and trying not to face the fact that he was happier because he was going alone. Vanessa, at present snarling and snapping incisively into the sitting-room phone, was off in a moment to her own parents in Bournemouth. They arranged these filial visits every other month, Oliver ringing his mother every week to check up on her diabetes, Vanessa ringing hers, who was hale and hearty, every three. When Vanessa was not about, Oliver sometimes rang Claire in-between-times from station platforms, airports, or the forecourt of the Wandsworth supermarket. He had premonitions about his vague and undemonstrative mother and found it hard to look at the advertisements in the papers showing resigned old women with bells round their necks like Swiss cattle lying waiting for rescue, or for the end. He knew that, should his mother fall over, she would never ring for help, but would lie there, thinking. Thus she would be avenged for his believing her immortal. Another part of him said that his mother was a cynic, even a torturer. Then he thought: And I am a swine, and don't believe in selflessness. He adored her.

Vanessa was brisker. The three-weekly call to Bournemouth

was always made at 6 p.m. sharp on a Friday, and she set aside half an hour. She was a Barrister in Shipping Chambers, a prestigious area and rare for a woman. She had had to swim enjoyably hard to keep up with the tide. She was respected in the Chambers and held in awe in Bournemouth where her parents knew nothing of the Bar except what they saw on television. She regaled them, third Fridays, with accounts of her daily round – from the 7 a.m. orange juice in the super-nova kitchen, to her reading Briefs last thing at night. ('A case you'll be seeing in the papers.') Her Opinions were not usually complete before midnight.

'Well, I'm sure I don't know how you fit it all in,' her mother said. 'How do you do your housework and shopping and cooking? And laundry?' (And where are the children?)

Vanessa ignored her. Work first. No philosophising.

'Whenever do you see your *friends*?' asked her mother. (Or us?)

'Oliver and I have it all under control. We eat out. Friends at weekends. We probably see more friends than you do.'

'I miss your friends, Vanessa,' said her mother. 'Every weekend we saw your friends, all through school and Cambridge, they used to come. I miss your friends.' (And I miss you, too. I don't know this sharp-faced, black-suited, almost bald-headed, lap-top sprite.)

'I ring you every three weeks.'

'Yes.'

'Last time I couldn't get through. You were engaged.'

'Yes. We do occasionally have another phone-call.'

'And what about *this*?' Vanessa said now, marching into the hall as Oliver picked up his sports bag en-route for a work-out. 'They're not going to be there.'

'What? Your parents?'

'My consistent and saintly parents say they'd no idea I was coming down this weekend. They're going to a Fortieth Wedding Anniversary on the Isle of Wight. They said they told me. They're going senile. Parents of some of my *primary-school* friends I've not seen for twenty years. They said why don't I go, too, for goodness sake!!'

'Well, why don't you?' Oliver saw, and his spirits fell, the way things would now develop. 'Better come with me and visit my Ma,' he said, not looking at her.

'Half-way to Scotland? On a Saturday morning? And there's only a single bed. No thanks.'

'We could go to a hotel. Stay in Cambridge if you like.'

She wavered while he kept his balance. He loved her. They would have a nice time. It was just that alone, with his mother, he could slop about with his shoes and socks off. Read the tabloids. Pick his nose.

'And what do I do there to pass the time?'

'In Cambridge?'

'No, fool. In your mother's house looking out at nothing and nothing looking in. All that silence as she sits and smiles.'

'At least she never asks when we're getting married.'

'Well, neither does mine.'

'Your father does.'

'Oh – does he? I'm surprised.'

'Because he doesn't like me? You're right. He asks in order to smirk when I say not yet. You're too close to your aged P, dear, it's unhealthy.'

She frowned and began to bustle about. He thought her tiny waist and neck miraculously beautiful. He'd have liked her in a silk kimono and little silk shoes. They'd been together six years and she was thirty-two and as rich as he was. She could stop work tomorrow and. . . .

'Come on,' she said. 'We're at it again. I'm sorry. It's just – the bloody *Isle of Wight*. They could have said. I'll come with you.

'And it's all right,' she said, 'I'll behave. I won't sulk. I won't go and lie down with a headache. I won't say "Thanks, I'm fine" when she offers me another fish finger.'

'I'll ring and tell her,' said Oliver. 'And I'll book a hotel for tomorrow night. Or you could go in the spare bed and I could have the sofa? OK, OK, I didn't mean it.'

'Fine,' he said ten minutes later. 'I've booked the George at Stamford and I've told Ma. Turns out we couldn't have stayed with her anyway. She's got an old chum there.'

'Oh no! She's going the same way as mine.'

'No, he's all right. Sort of cousin. She fancies him. Family solicitor or something down in the West Country. Nice.'

'*Solicitor*? Oh well then, we can't go. He'll be all over me. Oliver, let's get the Eurostar to Paris.'

But he had had enough. 'If you don't want to come, stay here. That's it. I shan't come back here if you won't come with me now.'

She looked hard at him, thinking things over. He was big. And good. He was clever. He was loyal. He could be as ruthless as his mother. I don't like his mother, but I do like him.

'Coming then?' he asked on Saturday morning – he had slept on the sofa bed in the study. 'Coming for a spin to see the Mater in the motor?'

'OK,' she said. 'Agreed. Can't wait to meet the family solicitor.'

A Light House

Filth lay in the light, pale bedroom after a very long night's sleep, and opened his eyes upon the hat-boxes stacked now on top of a 1930s wardrobe with varnished panels of marquetry fruit and flowers and an Arts and Crafts iron latch. One hat-box, labelled *Marshal and Snelgrove*, and another *Peter Robinson*, engaged him. He had known them somewhere else. A child's voice inside him cried out for someone to come and help him in some way. To come and love him. Explain some fear. Only she could help.

The name would not come. He tried to scream, but the scream wouldn't come. Terror took hold. He could not move. They were the wrong hat-boxes. The right hat-boxes had been battered and mouldy. He could hear the sea, the vile sea. He could hear Ma Didds coming. After breakfast she would beat him because he'd wet the bed. They all wet their beds.

There was a gentle tapping at the door and Filth felt about himself and he was dry. Oh, salvation, thank you God. Wonderful relief. Let her come. Let her come and look. She'd get him for something else today, but not for that. As she got Cumberledge almost every morning. Boiling the sheets in the copper, putting them on the line for all to see.

'Eight years old,' she'd say.

'She's a bit afraid of me though,' said eight-year-old Teddy Feathers. 'Because I can pierce her with my gimlet eyes. One day I shall blind her,' and he practised the look on the bedroom door. Claire came through it in her rose-pink dressing-gown.

She was carrying a huge cup and saucer painted with brown

flowers and a primrose-coloured inside. In the other hand she carried a tipping silver sugar-basin with some silver sugar-tongs sticking out.

'I can't do trays,' she said. 'And I can't remember about sugar. I do remember no milk.'

She put the cup down on the bedside table. 'Are you awake, Teddy? You look glazed.' She moved some old dress-boxes from a chair and sat down. 'I'm glad I insisted on a house with decent-sized bedrooms.'

'A danger, I'd have thought,' he said, relaxing, drinking the hot tea. 'Open invitation. People arriving and demanding beds. Thinking you're a boarding-house. We keep – I keep – our spare bedrooms quiet.'

'Oh? Why? I like company. I like open doors.'

'Well, watch out for the window-cleaner.' He was pleased to find yesterday's conversation totally in place, like yesterday's Court-hearing used to be.

'And the Vicar,' he added.

'Oh, the Vicar is perfectly safe. He's slightly charismatic, or working at it, but he's sound on the *Gospels*. And I love women priests, too, don't you?'

'Not altogether,' said Filth, 'but there they are.'

'No. I keep the spare bedroom at the ready, dear Teddy, not for the window-cleaner, despite his lovely hairy chest, nor for the fifty-thousand to one chance that the beloved of my childhood should turn up after twenty years in need of a bit of peace. No – I keep it for Oliver. And of course I have to have somewhere to do up my Christmas presents.'

'Oliver?'

'Not that I send many now. Only about three apart from your handkerchiefs. But I like to be able to spread the wrapping-paper out. And then there is the ironing. . . .'

'Who is Oliver?'

She paused to regard with pity someone who did not know Oliver. When it comes to people's children, she thought, Teddy looks at emptiness.

'Oliver is my younger son. Your second cousin twice removed, or something of the sort. He has your eyes, and your height but he's beginning to run to fat. He's almost as clever and as handsome as you were.' (And I hope you've left him some money, she thought.)

'Oh,' said Filth, unconvincingly. 'Yes, yes. Of course. A nice little chap. I remember.'

'You haven't ever met him. He's nearly forty.'

'Oh. Yes. I see. Betty and I were hopeless at all that.'

'All what?'

'Genealogy.'

'Yes. You were ahead of your time. Genealogy's over. It's a wise child now all right that knows its own father. You know, Teddy, the withering of the family tree is one of the saddest things ever. Who else can you turn to when you're old and sick without having to feel grateful?'

Filth, lying like a knight on a slab, holding his cup to his chest, swivelled his eyes at her.

'They don't marry any more,' she said. 'Surely you've noticed? It's over. Their children are unbaptised so there'll be no baptismal record. Our times will become dark as Romano-Britain.'

'Genes not genealogy?'

'Exactly. I know you don't care for children. . . .'

He drank the tea and waved the empty cup for her to take, sat up in bed and looked uneasily at the hat-boxes.

'The hat-boxes were your mother's,' said Claire, 'I've no idea how they got here.

'*Anyway*,' she then said. 'You will have to meet a thirty-six-year-old child today. Oliver's coming for the weekend with Vanessa.'

'Vanessa?' (Which one was this?)

'Yes, Vanessa. She's his partner. She's at the Bar.'

'Is Oliver at the Bar?'

'No, he's an accountant. *Vanessa*'s at the Bar. His partner.'

Filth was about to say that at the Bar there are no partners, but lost confidence.

'They live together, Eddie dear. They "co-habit". They have "co-habited" in Wandsworth for six years.'

'In *Wandsworth*! They're not doing too well, then?'

'Wandsworth, dear Eddie, is now the crème-de-la of the Euro-chicks.'

'Rubbish. It's where all the taxi-drivers live.'

'Not now. It's full of rich thirty-year-olds who owe thousands on their credit cards and go to Tuscany for their holidays but have never heard of Raphael.'

'They sound particularly unattractive.'

'Yes, they are. But they seem to have a very good time.'

'And two of them are coming here? Look here, Claire, I'll be off. Can't have your boy arriving with nowhere to sleep.'

'He's staying with Vanessa at the George at Stamford, so don't fuss. I've told them you will be here. They'd be mortified if they thought they'd pushed you out.'

'I very much wonder if they would?'

'Don't wonder, Teddy, *learn*. You'll like Vanessa. You'll have so much to talk about. She's Inner Temple, like you. And nobody –' she said, taking the empty cup towards the door, looking kindly back at him, speaking of the only area in which she had been blinded for life, '– nobody, if I dare say so, could possibly dislike Oliver.

'And what they do all have nowadays – this isn't the sixties (I must give all these old things in the dress-boxes to Vanessa) – what they *do* have now, Eddie, when they come here, is perfect manners.'

And so they bloody should, thought Eddie.

And it was afternoon and Filth was drinking tea again and Vanessa sat near his hammock on the wide, shaven lawn in front of the house, adding more hot water to the teapot from a silver thermos jug. There were small sandwiches. It was a warm late November and Claire's dahlias glowed and dripped with sunlight. The exposed garden, on a corner – High Light was an end-of-terrace site on a rise, like a Roman villa built over a hill fort – looked down and across at a shiny shallow lake where boats were moving about and children shouted. Beyond, straggled the town and, beyond that, droned the invisible motorway like bees in the warm afternoon.

Oliver had taken his mother out in his car for tea in Saffron Walden, a suggestion she had greeted with the luminous silence which was always followed by refusal.

'I've not been into the town for –'

'Oh, come on. You'll be fine.'

(The black butterfly opened its wings.)

'It's no distance and we'll have the top down. It's a lovely day.'

'*Not* on the motorway, Oliver.'

'Of course not.'

'I can't take the motorway. Not until I'm dead.'

'What are you talking about?'

'The crem is on the motorway. I really don't care for it.'

'Ma, would I take you to the crem?'

'Though I dare say you can get a cup of tea there,' she said. 'Darling, what if the doctor saw me as we pass the surgery?'

'We won't pass the surgery.'

'I think we have to.'

'Then we'll disguise ourselves.'

'Oh, Oliver – what as?'

'Barristers. We'll borrow Vanessa's and old funny-face's wigs.'

'I don't think they travel with their wigs.'

'Well, get a big hat out of the spare room, and some dark glasses.'

'I haven't enjoyed anything like this for years.'

'Hold on to your hat.'

'I will. I wore it at poor Babs's wedding. It must be thirty years old.'

'Is Babs still alive?'

'What? Can't hear. Are you *sure* this isn't the motorway? *Oliver*! How dare you! This is Cambridge. It *was* the motorway.'

They sat by the Cam and the low sun shone through the straps of the willows. Students called to each other and splashed

153

about, or glided along. King's College Chapel reared up like a white cruise-liner on a grassy sea. 'I've organised tea for us,' he said. 'Come on. It's not far.'

She walked lightly beside him on the tow-path and over a bridge. Fat common people in tight clothes licked ice creams and ate oozing buns and shouted. Some, despite the season, had bare midriffs. Some looked at Claire's hat. She was enchanted.

'It's a shame so many young people are bald now,' she said. 'I wonder why? Is it Aids or this awful chemotherapy? I'm sure we never had either.'

'It's the fashion, Ma.'

'Oh, it can't be. That's dreadlocks.'

'No, they're out. Or at any rate localised.'

'Do they go over their pates every day like their chins? Will you be doing it, Oliver?'

'Ma, I'm nearly forty and I'm a chartered accountant.'

'Yes, and you have lovely hair, Oliver. What is Vanessa's hair like – I mean, when she lets it grow?'

But they had reached Oliver's old, undistinguished college; a door and a staircase of someone of distinction; a huge, gentle old man. Claire did not catch his name. He was expecting Oliver and was pleased to see them and he nodded at Claire and looked affectionately at her hat. They sat in a room with a tall window that seemed to let in little light and where mountains of books and furniture were deep in dust. They ate cinnamon scones. Other crumby plates lay about the room among the books and balled-up garments that suggested socks and what Claire thought of as woollies. What a peaceful quiet place. What a nice man. How nice for him to know Oliver.

'We thought we'd make for Evensong at King's,' said Oliver. 'Have we missed it, d'you think?'

'Oh, no. Still the same programme,' and the old man began to talk about politics. 'I am very fond of Oliver,' he said as he stumbled along with them to the door of the chapel. They all said goodbye.

'Tired?' asked Oliver as they sat down in the choir stalls.

'Not in the least. Did he put on that performance just for us? I didn't know there were any left.'

'Any what?'

'Eccentrics. Had you told him we were coming?'

'Yes, I rang him up. At the petrol station.'

'From a call box?'

'From my handset.'

'You keep his number?'

'No. I dialled directory enquiries.'

'You are wonderful, Oliver.'

'I am.'

'The world is full of miracles,' she said, 'but I think you set it all up. There were computers and internets and e-mails hidden in all those books, and he was an actor who does E. M. Forster parts. I really loved him. Who was he?'

'Who's E. M. Forster? Anyway, he liked your hat. He was the Dean.' Delighted with the day, the music, the chapel, he said, 'You're a cynic, Ma. Go on – he fancied you. Have him over.'

They stood for the *Nunc Dimittis*, and Oliver wondered what havoc Vanessa was wreaking on poor old Uncle Eddie.

'Have you always practised in Dorset?' asked Vanessa from her canvas chair.

'No, no. I returned there. Travelled a lot.'

'That was rather good luck.'

'Very good luck.'

'You found some ex-pat clients? Over the years?'

'Not exactly ex-pats,' he said. 'The locals.'

'I often think,' she said (Vanessa was magnanimous to people who were no threat), 'that to be a family solicitor, in any country, is to be the most useful person in the world. You have to be so subtle. And cleverer than any Barrister. Anyone can be a Barrister. The Bar finals are a joke, you know. Solicitors' finals,' she said, 'are a marathon by comparison.'

'I believe so. So they always said. But it is so long ago.'

She thought: He is quite unaware of me. He is Methuselah. Why do I care? He is so mysterious. I hadn't expected to be drawn to someone as old as this. Sad silence. He's so old he's almost gone, yet he's sharp – sharper than Oliver. I like his eyes. I wish he'd open them again.

The striped canvas hammock had come from Harrods – a present from Oliver to his mother, last birthday, like the huge, navy-blue sun-umbrella worked by rope pulleys, as for a yacht, supposed to be supported by a dollop of concrete that the window-cleaner and the gardener and the Vicar together had not been able to budge from where the van-man had dropped it by the gate. Claire had begun to grow trailing plants over this base and the umbrella, unwrapped but in cobwebs, was still propped in a corner of the car-less garage. Today Oliver had made an effort and had fixed up the hammock, just before lunch. It hung inside an outer wooden cradle, rather like a horse-jump at a gymkhana. There were no trees in Claire's garden and the hammock stood out in high display. Passers by along the avenue looked curiously at the old long person stretched out in it, fine nose pointed at the winter sky.

A rope hung beside the hammock ending in a baroque blue tassel.

'I could swing you if you like,' Vanessa suggested, wondering at herself. She had refused Filth's offer of the hammock for herself as firmly as she always refused a seat from a man on the Underground. She often offered her own seat on the Underground to an older woman. Sometimes these older women refused, too, not feeling older. Great games are played on the Underground, she thought, the premier sport being that everyone avoids everyone else's eyes. Oh, how happy I am to have enough to think about. Work to do. How pleased I am to have mastered the pleasure – never acknowledged – when scanned, leaned against, breathed upon in the Underground by a man. I've got rid of that.

'Do you mind being stuck up here in the hammock in full view of Saffron Walden, Eddie?'

They had called him Eddie. And sometimes Teddy. They had not properly introduced him. They behaved as if she must know him. 'Shall I give you a swing with the rope?'

'You sound like Mr Pierrepoint,' he said, without opening his eyes. 'I don't feel exposed. No, not at all, thank you. No, I don't need to be rocked.'

'Who is Mr Pierrepoint?'

'I'm glad you can't remember. He was the hangman. His last hanging was of a woman, Ruth Ellis, who shot her unfaithful lover a few weeks after losing his baby and whilst her mind was disturbed.'

'Oh yes, well, of course, I know about that. They buried her in quick-lime at Wormwood Scrubs prison, didn't they?'

'They did. Before you were born, but not long before, I think.'

'I think,' she said, pouring tea through Claire's Edwardian tea-strainer, 'we have to forgive history a very great deal.'

'I think,' he said, 'that we should forgive history almost nothing.

'I met the government hangman of Hong Kong,' he said soon, a breeze over the dahlias, a breeze over the lake, the hammock gently moving. Hot, hot November. 'Had a long talk with him. An Englishman. Not a bad man. Not at all sadistic. Just unimaginative and conformist. Common, ugly English man. A good husband, I believe.'

'Hadn't two wives left Pierrepoint though?'

'Yes. Yes, there was that. I am glad of that.'

'And he resigned after Ruth Ellis didn't he?'

'Yes. That was interesting.'

'You've had a varied practice then, down in Dorset?'

'I told you, young woman, I *retired* to Dorset long ago. Away from the cut and thrust. The heat and dust.'

At heat and dust something flickered in Vanessa's head. A novel? A film? Something to do with lawyers abroad?

'Have you Oriental blood?' Filth asked.

'Certainly not, I come from Bournemouth.'

'You remind me of someone with kind hands. You are very beautiful. How old are you?'

'I'm thirty-two.'

'Did you have children? When you were young? You *must* have Oriental blood. Your age is not obvious.'

'Well thanks, I'm sure. You'll be saying "younger than she are married mothers made" next.'

'Oh, I'm not interested in your past life.'

'Well, I'm glad of that. You're not like my parents.'

'What about Oliver?'

'Oh, he doesn't think about it. Never has. Marriage, kids. Good God, no!'

'Then he'll leave you,' said Filth, closing his eyes.

'Let him. He'd miss me.'

Filth said nothing.

'It's the way of the world now,' she said. 'It must be incomprehensible to your generation.'

'Not entirely.'

'It won't change back, you know. We meet, we part. Life is pretty long nowadays to be satisfied by a single sexual partner.'

'And my lot will soon all be dead?' said Filth.

'Oh, of course I don't mean that – that your generation is without influence. No. *Personally*, I respect your generation. I respect your attachment to duty and the Law, your lifetime dedication. But we live so long now that there's time for three or four professions and partnerships. And we all have aides –'

'Yes, you have Aids,' said Filth. 'I don't know much of the technicalities of "Aids" with small or upper case "A".'

'You see us, though – don't you – as negative?' she said. 'Selfish? Everyone under, say, forty?'

'At the moment I feel it about everyone under a century but I dare say this will pass. My wife would have no patience with me.'

'I'm sorry you've lost your wife. Was it long ago? I'd have enjoyed meeting her,' said Vanessa kindly to the imagined Betty: the marmalade-maker, Bridge-player, no doubt church-flower arranger, and the grandchildren in the holidays. 'Did you have many children?'

'We had no children.'

Should she say she was sorry? Then she knew she was sorry. Sorry for him. The wife was probably –

'Sorry,' she said.

'It was deliberate. Think carefully before you bring children into the world. Betty and I were what is called "Empire orphans". We were handed over to foster parents at four or five and didn't see our parents for at least four years. We had bad luck. Betty's foster parents didn't like her and mine – my father hadn't taken advice – were chosen because they were cheap. If you've not been loved as a child, you don't know how to love a child. You need prior knowledge. You can inflict pain through ignorance. I was not loved after the age of four and a half. Think of being a parent like that.'

'Yes. I suppose.'

'A parent like you, for instance, young woman. What child would want a parent like you?'

She was furious. '*I* was loved,' she said. 'I'm still loved by my parents, thank you very much. And I love them. We have – difficulties, but it's normal family life.'

'Then I made a mistake,' he said, still not looking at her. 'Maybe it's your hair. It is so thin. I'm sorry.'

'My hair is a Sassoon cut and it cost one hundred pounds.' She flung about with the cups and tea-tray and made to go off into the house.

'I have my career,' she said. 'I know it's what all women say, but it's true. It matters to me and to Oliver and to the economy of the country. I make a lot of money. I can have a child when I'm fifty.'

'See if you do,' he said. 'I hope you don't. Children are cruel. They are wreckers of the soul. I hate children. I am a paedo-phobe. Betty knew we must not have a child because of the child I was myself. I would have damaged a child. I don't mean physically, of course.'

(The old thing's deranged, she thought in the brightness of Claire's kitchen, washing up the lunch and the tea-cups. Whoever is he? Some sort of hypnotist? Thinks he's the Oracle. Why is he attractive? He scares me. And I damn well will have some children. When it suits me. *And* with Oliver. Or some-one.)

She wrung out the dishcloth (no washing-up machine) and

159

hung up the tea-towel. God, I'm behaving like a daughter-in-law. Oh Lord, here's Oliver and his Ma and Claire will say, Thank you dear, you shouldn't.

'Thank you dear, you shouldn't,' said Claire thinking how fierce and snappish Vanessa looked. She's like a little black fox, she thought. What has Eddie been saying to her?

'Has it been very dull?' she asked.

'Not at all. I think he's asleep.'

'Now we must think about supper. We have eight beautiful eggs.'

Oliver saw Vanessa's face.

'No, Ma. Thanks a lot but Vanessa and I have booked a table at the George. You've enough on your hands with Eddie and, anyway, I want to put some flowers on Dad's grave on the way. OK? We'll be back after breakfast. I'll bring us all some lunch.'

'Are you sure?' (Relief!)

'It's been quite a day for you.'

'I suppose it has.'

'OK, then. Off, Vanessa. Say goodbye to the Great Man for us, Ma, and don't let him keep you up half the night with sophistry.'

'All he does is sleep,' said Claire. 'And I'm glad. It means he feels he knows us well. He just turned up,' she told Vanessa. 'After hundreds of years. His wife was a friend from way back. She died less than three weeks ago.'

'Oh, *no*! Not three weeks!'

'Such a shock. She seemed set to live for ever.'

'Oh, Oliver!'

'What?'

'You should have told me. I've been chatting on about – about marriage and how interminable it must seem!'

At the churchyard she was still angry. They walked up the path together, Oliver carrying flowers, Vanessa her laptop.

'Makes me look so *gauche*,' she said. 'So *insensitive*. You are the strangest family. You tell people *nothing*. No, I'm not

160

helping to put flowers on your father's grave, I never met him.'

'Go on into the church then. There's the famous marble Gibbons.'

'The what? I hate Culture.'

'Three-stars in all the guide-books. Known locally as The Four Brass Monkeys.'

'What is it?'

'Memorial to some great family, can't remember who. Nobody can. Sort of marble pyramid of fruits and flowers and cherubs weeping. Mum knew it when she was a child, too.'

'How ghastly. Why monkeys?'

'Gibbons, sweetie. Surname of Grinling. They think he did the drawings for it. Worth seeing. You can't help stroking it. Bite the peaches. Pat the bottoms. It's never been vandalised. It was our job to wash it when we were kids. Get in the cracks. Took hours. Saturday mornings.'

'You had a sensational childhood.'

She pranced into the church through the self-sealing door and Oliver fished about for a green tin vase with a spike that his subconscious remembered would be behind the dead-flower bin near the tap. He pushed the spike into the grass above his father's head, arranged the flowers, stood up and leaned against the headstone and took note of his father's name and the space left for Claire's. He thought how much he'd like to have a talk with his father. On the other hand he knew every word of it.

'How d'you think your mother's looking?'

'Very well, Pa. You mustn't worry.'

'Can't say I think she's looking well. I led her a dance, you know.'

'I know.'

'Not coming home till dawn. She was always out looking for me. As far as Stamford. Found me once hiding behind some dustbins. I thought she was the police. Old Contemptibles' Dinner, or something. Not the behaviour for a bank-manager. Marvellous woman.'

'I'll bet she never cross-questioned?'

'No. Never.'

'Mine grumbles. Cross-questions. Very cross questions!'

'What, this new one?'

'Well – we've been together six years. She's not new.'

'Grumbles all the time, does she?'

'Well, criticises mostly. It's her job. Analysis of motives, then development and execution.'

'Sounds like Eddie, dry old stick.'

'Yes. A lawyer. And a "new woman".'

'Ah, your mother couldn't be labelled. Result of that childhood.'

'Ma's pretty much all right,' he said. 'You *can* bury your childhood. Not that I want to.'

God, but I miss him, he thought, and watched Vanessa marching forward from the church, hopping the graves, laptop tight-clutched.

'There's a boy in there dressed up as a Vicar and he came up and asked if I wanted him to hear my confession. And I swear – I *swear* – he looked me over to see if I was pregnant.'

At the George they went straight in to dinner, Vanessa first twirling off her shirt to reveal a black silk camisole beneath, the size of a handkerchief. Her sloping white shoulders and tiny white neck against the panelling turned heads. Claret. Roast beef carved from the silver dome. Vanessa shone and talked, oblivious. The waiters admired. She nattered on about the Vicar and the marble babies crying and holding shields against their private parts. It hadn't seemed a Christian monument to her, three-stars or not.

'Did you say so?'

'Yes, I did. And I told him I had nothing to confess and *he* said, "My child, then you are in a bad way." I nearly socked him. What are these people *doing* in the church now, Oliver?'

'He sounds a bit of a throw-back to me. You don't see them now in the church at all. It's a rare sighting, a clergyman in a church, out of hours.'

'I think he hides in there all day, and then he pounces. He sees guilt all the time. He's a monster.'

'He's a friend of Ma. She likes him.'

'Oh no! Then that's it.'

'That's what?'

'She'll want him to marry us.'

'*What* did you say?' They were in their grand bedroom after the coffee and the crème brûlée, both of them happy with wine. '*Marry* us?'

But she was somewhere else now. 'Oliver, *what* room is this? It's the bridal suite. Look at the hangings, and the drapes. It's obscene. And whatever is it costing us?'

'A hundred and fifty pounds – so what? It was all they had left.'

'But we could have gone to a B&B. We're supposed to be going to Thailand.'

'We can afford it.'

'Well, you might have asked me first. Oh, well. Never mind,' and she took off her handkerchief top and cast off the rest of her clothes. She lifted her legs high in the air. 'Haven't I wonderful feet?' she said.

(God, Oliver remembered, I forgot to bring any condoms.)

'OK,' she said. 'Pass my purse.'

'Why?'

'I'll give you my half of the hundred and fifty pounds.'

'No. Let me do this one,' he said. 'I let you in for it. Only young once.'

Remembering the old fossil who'd thought she was past the age of child-bearing, she said, 'Why are you still in your clothes?'

When they went back to Oliver's mother the following morning Vanessa was surprised to find how disappointed she was that the old chap was no longer there. The hammock, which had stood out all night in the dew, now hung empty and Claire, still in her dressing-gown, was standing looking at it.

'Yes,' she said. 'He's gone. I couldn't keep him, although it's Sunday and he'll have a terrible journey. He asked me to say goodbye to you. Now I do hope' (untruthfully) 'that you'll stay for lunch?'

'Yes, we've brought it,' said Oliver, smiling about. 'Supermarket.'

'We'll have to stay, anyway,' said Vanessa, 'until Oliver's taken the hammock down. And what about that umbrella business in the garage? I said it was too big when he bought it. Shall we get it changed for you?'

Claire blinked. 'How very kind of you. As a matter of fact the church could do with it. For fêtes.'

(Oh, Ma – oh, Ma! Don't push her.) Oliver started to fling things out of bags and into the microwave. (Keep it cool. Keep off the Vicar!)

'I met your Vicar yesterday,' said Vanessa.

'I'm afraid he's all over the place,' said Claire.

They eyed each other.

'Oh, and by the way,' said Claire, when they began to go. 'Would you take this parcel with you? I think it's only recipe books. Eddie wanted me to have them. His wife's. She never used them. I don't want them. They were meant for someone else. Betty was a dreadful cook, so they won't be thrilling, but they'd be her mother's. Quite historic. Old Raj puddings from Shanghai. Tapioca.'

'Ma, I'll put them in the bin.'

'No,' said Vanessa, 'I'd like them. Thanks.'

And back again in Wandsworth where it was dark and the velvet curtains shrouded the windows with Interior Designer bobbles – I'm not sure I like Victorian stuff any more, thought Oliver – rain had begun to fall. 'I think we're getting stuck in the nineties,' he called through to the kitchen where Vanessa was scuffling about. 'You know, we could get a manor house in Yorkshire for this. Commute from York. What's happening?'

'The recipe books,' she called back. 'But it's not recipe

books, it's a box. It has gold clasps on it, and a drawer in it and – oh, good God.'

Out of the box showered jewels. Gold chains, brooches, earrings. They glimmered on the kitchen table.

'Look!' she said. 'Look at the jade! Look at these blue things. Look – look at *this*!' Out of a plush bag fell a magnificent rope of pearls. 'Oliver! These aren't recipe books. Here's a note.'

> Dear Claire [it said], I've given the recipe books to Babs. Betty wanted you to have the trinkets. They'll need cleaning and restringing and so on. Some of them she hadn't worn for years. But they're very much the real thing. The pearls were given to me long ago. Eddie.

'But I can't have these. I can't possibly keep them. There's thousands of pounds here. Thousands! Look – Aspreys 1940! Look at this jade ring – it's like an egg! Oliver!'

'I'll ring mother.'

'She's delighted,' he came back saying, 'and you're to keep them.'

'Did she say singular or plural "you"?'

'Shall I ask her?'

'Not yet. Let me think. No – I don't have to think. I won't have them. They'll think that's why I married you.'

'Come on,' he said. 'It's not going to be in the papers. Nobody's to know we've got them but me.'

'I never wear jewellery.' She stroked the gold adoringly, the jade ring.

'You could change.'

'I *never* change. Was that old Eddie out in the East a lot, Ollie? *Oh* – Ollie!' She had seen the signature on the note and the letter-heading, for frugal Filth was still using up his old Chambers writing paper. 'It says here, *Sir Edward Feathers*.'

'Yes. That's him. Cousin Ed. Ridiculous name.'

'But Oliver, Edward Feathers is Old Filth.'

'I hope not.'

'Oliver, *Old Filth* is a legend. At the Bar. I thought he'd died years ago. He was a *wonderful* advocate. He had a stammer.'

'A stammer? Yes, well, Eddie does sometimes make odd noises.'

'Oliver – it was *Old Filth*. Of Hong Kong. And he became a wonderful Judge,' and she began to moan.

'What's so dreadful?'

'I told him all about the Bar. And how easy it was to pass the Bar exams. And I asked him if he'd always practised in Dorset. Oh, Oliver!'

'Vannie, I have never seen you so discomposed.'

'I want to die.'

'Will you marry me?'

'Yes, of course. But, oh, *Oliver*!'

Filth was invited to the wedding six months later but could not remember Vanessa and could not think whom he knew in Bournemouth. The groom's name rang no bell. Some relative? Was he Claire's? But he refused the invitation. Claire, true to form (and because she had not been told of Betty's funeral), did not get in touch. She attended the wedding, the Vicar driving her. He did not officiate but enjoyed the fun and talked about sin to Vanessa's mother. Babs turned up with her hair short and blood-red. She and the Vicar got on famously and danced the night away.

And Claire waved the pair off to Thailand, hoping the baby wouldn't be born there, though they can do wonders with premature babies now.

Vanessa gave Claire the rope of pearls she'd worn to the altar to look after until she returned.

Claire took care of her heart to be sure of seeing the grandchild.

She wrote to tell Filth of the birth three months later. Edward, they were calling him. Edward George.

Thus is the world peopled.

PART TWO

Scene: Inner Temple

The smoking-room of the Inner Temple, almost deserted. It is much re-furbished: easy chairs stand about. Portraits of distinguished former Benchers on the walls, the one of Mr Attlee – gaunt and glazed – seeming to be wringing his hands. One wing chair has its back to the rest and Mr Attlee seems to be looking down at it. Filth is in the chair half-asleep. Post-prandial. No one can see him. Enter the Queen's Remembrancer and the Purveyor of Seals and Ordinances.

The Queen's Remembrancer: He must have gone.
The Purveyor of Seals and Ordinances: To get his hair cut?
QR: Possibly. Very great surprise to see him again.
PS&O: Looks well. Amazing physique still. Nothing ever been wrong with him.
QR: Nothing ever did go wrong for him.
PS&O: Nothing much ever happened to him. Except success.
QR: There's talk of a rather mysterious War, you know. Didn't fight.
PS&O: A conchie?
QR: Good God, no. Some crack-up. He had a stammer.
PS&O: Pretty brave to go on to the Bar then.
QR: Remarkable. He joined a good regiment. It's in *Who's Who*. The Gloucesters. He had something to do with the Royal family.
PS&O: *Had* he indeed!
QR: And there was something else. Someone gave him a

push upstairs somewhere. Or out East. There's always something a bit dicey about that circuit. A lot of people you can't really know socially but you have to pretend to.

PS&O: Betty was very O.K. though. Don't you think? Don't you think? There was of course Veneering. Veneering and Betty. Aha!

QR: What do the likes of us know, creeping round the Woolsack at Home and round the Inns of Court?

PS&O: 'What should they know of England
Who only England know.'

QR: Kipling. You know Kipling had a start like Filth? Torn from his family at five. Raj Orphan.

PS&O: Kipling didn't do too badly either.

QR: Kipling had a crack-up.

PS&O: Did he stammer?

QR: He went blind. Half blind at seven. Hated the Empire, you know. Psychological blindness.

PS&O: Are you having coffee?

QR: No. I just came in looking for Filth. Just missed him.

PS&O: Did we imagine him?

QR: I expect he was having his last look round.

Exeunt. Room apparently empty.

Filth rises from the chair and takes a long last look at Mr Attlee.

Filth: Have I the courage to write my Memoirs?

Attlee: Churchill had. But on the whole, better not. Keep your secrets.

The Watch

In that train of 1941, after the Oxford interview, Eddie had pushed *The Times* back into the hands of the man opposite, left the compartment and walked down the corridor where he stood holding tight the brass rail along the middle of the window. The train stopped very often, filled up. The corridor became crammed with people mostly silently enduring, shoulder to shoulder. Even so it was cold. Water from somewhere trickled about his feet. Troops started to climb in – maybe around Birmingham. These troops were morose and quiet. Still and silent. Everyone squashed up tighter. It grew dark. Only the blue pin-lights on all the death-mask faces.

And Eddie stood on.

At some point he left the train and waited for another one that would take him to the nearest station to High House, and there he jumped down upon an empty, late-night platform. After an unknown space of time he found that he was travelling in a newspaper-van that must have stopped to give him a lift. It dropped him outside the gates of the avenue which were closed and guarded by two sentries with rifles. He walked off down the lane, then doubled back through a hedge, then across in the darkness to the graceful iron railings of what he felt to be his home.

The house stood there with lightless, blindless windows and the dark glass flashed black. The place was empty. But there were army vehicles everywhere in the drive and a complex of army huts where the land began to drop away above the chimneys of the old carpet factory. Eddie walked round the resting, deserted house and met nobody. He began to try the familiar door-handles: the side door from the passage into the garden with its dimpled brass knob; the door to the stables; the kitchens. All were locked. He grew bolder and stood beneath a bedroom window and called, 'Mrs Ingoldby? Is anyone there? It's Eddie.' He rattled the door of the bothy where the gardener had lived. Nothing. No dog barked. In the garage, there was no old car, the car in which you had to put up an umbrella in the back seat when it rained. The Colonel's vegetables stood scant and scruffy, Brussels sprouts like Passchendaele. The beehives had disappeared.

He set off on foot back to the railway station; slept the rest of the night on a bench along the wall of the waiting-room with its empty grate; reached his aunts' warm house by the following lunchtime.

There was no car outside it and so 'Les Girls', as they liked to be known, were not at home, but Eddie had his key and planted his bag and his icy feet on the rug in the hall. He stood.

He heard Alice, the midget maid, creeping up from the kitchen. She gave a chirp of surprise, touching her fingers to her lips, and Eddie remembered he'd slept in his clothes, wet through since Oxford, and was unshaven. He found – with the old terror – that he couldn't speak.

'Mr Eddie. Come, come, come,' she said and led him down to her kitchen and gave him tea and porridge which he could not eat. 'Oh dear, oh dear, oh dear,' she said. 'Have you failed your exams?' She had been sitting beneath her calendar of the King and Queen and the photograph of Mr Churchill in his siren-suit, making more paper spills for the upstairs fireplace. Vegetables were prepared on the draining-board, the kitchen clean, alive and shining. 'Oh dear, oh dear. I expect you have heard the news.'

'Yes. I read it in the paper.'

She seemed puzzled, and he remembered that nobody in this house cared a fig about the Ingoldbys.

'I'm meaning their news, Mr Eddie. Miss Hilda's and Miss Muriel's. I don't know what's to become of us all now. Or this house. Or you and me, Mr Eddie. Mind, I'd seen it coming. There's been talk for years. They think I'm deaf. They never told me a thing, never warned me. I've been here nearly twenty years. It was little to expect.'

'They've never sacked you, Alice?'

'In a sense, yes, Mr Eddie.'

The slam of the front door above. The clash of the vestibule glass. The shriek of Hilda spotting the bag in the hall. 'He's back. See? Now for it – Eddie? Where are you?'

'Yes. I'm back.' His head rose up from Alice's cellar rabbit-hole, and he saw that the eyes of the girls were particularly wild. He thought: They must have won a cup. 'Have you been on the course?' Then he saw they were wearing Air-Force blue with several stripes. Not golf.

'We have some news for you,' said Muriel. 'Better get it over and tell you right off. We're getting married.'

For a dizzy moment Eddie thought they were marrying each other.

'You'll easily guess who,' said Hilda, and mentioned two names from among the red faces at the golf club.

'Married!'

He thought: Whatever for? Old women. Over forty. And this great house full of their stuff. And Alice.

'Go and wash, Eddie dear. Then come and have some champagne. It's been on the cards for years but of course we couldn't split up and leave you until we'd got you off our hands.'

He looked at their untouchable hands.

'But you mean you'll be living apart now?'

'Oh, quite near each other. And near Royal St Andrews. In Scotland. All four of us.'

'Does my father know?'

'We've written. He's known for several years that we – well, we put off our plans. For you. That's why he's been so generous to us while you've been living here all these years.'

173

'*Living here?*'

'Yes. Ever since you were a tiny.'

When he came downstairs again Alice was anxiously laying up the dining-table. The silver and glasses shone. When she saw him she scuttled out of sight.

'What about Alice?'

'Oh, she's much too old to move in with either of us. Someone else will probably take her. She's got her Girls' Friendly Society. And she's over seventy and pretty well' (Hilda whispered like a whistle) '*past it*. She *ought* to retire. So it all fits in.'

'*Fits in?*'

'Alice retiring. You going out to Alistair as an evacuee. And this tragedy of the Ingoldbys.'

'Yes,' he said. 'I know. I saw it in *The Times*. I'm surprised you did. Or that you even remembered – their name.' (Tears, tears, stop. And, bugger it, my voice is going.)

'Of course we remembered. They used to have you over there. Very kind to help us out. Anyway, someone rang up.'

'Someone? Who? Please, *who?*'

'I'm afraid I didn't ask. It was a girl. Quite a young voice. Yes, Isobel. Isobel Ingoldby. That would be a sister? Rather snooty we thought. La-di-da.'

'Did she leave a number?'

'No, no. Very quick she was. Now dear, no brooding. Let's talk about you. And Singapore.'

'It's Singapore you're going to,' said Hilda. 'Alistair'll meet you there. Safest place in the world.'

'Did you pass your exams?' asked Muriel.

'Yes.'

'Jolly good. Something to look forward to after the War. Your tickets are all fixed up and you leave next week.'

'And bottoms up,' said Muriel, with the champagne. 'Here's to all of us.'

'And we have a present for you,' said Hilda. 'He said you were to have it when you left school. We've kept it for you. It's your father's watch.'

To Colombo

After a torrid and joyless Christmas with the brides- and grooms-to-be – gravy and turkey from somewhere and gin galore – Eddie was ready for the voyage to his father. He'd given ten pounds to Alice and promised her a postcard. He would have given wedding presents to Les Girls, but would have had to ask them for the money. He had only the money for the journey to Londonderry to pick up his ship; that and his Post Office Book with fifteen shillings in it and a new cheque book he didn't know how to use.

The day dawned. The vestibule door slammed behind him and his luggage was in the car, the watch on his wrist.

Both brides had *genuinely* (they said) intended to see him off from Liverpool – the journey from Bolton was short – and had dressed for it in excellent pre-War mufti of tweed and diamond-pin brooches, uniforms set aside; but at the last minute Hilda was called away by her beau to discuss some marital arrangement, and Muriel drove Eddie to the dock alone. There they got out of the car, she landed him a smacking kiss, said how she envied him a wonderful voyage into the sunshine and out of the War –

'Aunt Muriel –?'

– and how they would *miss* him, and how she was looking forward to seeing him in Oxford after the War –

'Aunt Muriel, I'm sorry –'

'Yes?'

'It's just that I have no money.'

'Dear boy, you're going to have plenty of money. You'll have all that we are having to give up, now that you're gone. Your allowance.'

'Yes. But I mean for now. I've only about a pound.'

'You won't need money on board ship.'

'Something might go wrong. We might be stuck half-way.'

'Oh, Eddie – what a fuss-pot. Alistair's meeting you.'

'I'm not sure how long –'

'Well, *I* don't know. I don't know that I've much with me. Would five pounds –?'

'I think I shall need perhaps a bit more.'

She scratched in her purse and came up with seven pounds, twelve shillings and sixpence.

'There,' she said, 'you've cleaned me out.'

Then she was gone, dropping from his life unlamented and unloved. He felt shaken and depressed, as if another boy, a sunny, golfing chap, would have done better.

She tooted her horn at the harbour barrier. The clashing and hooting, the crowd at the ferry. He saw her big amiable face as she turned the corner.

The ferry was no trouble. The sea, hatefully grey, was thank God calm. He stood at the rail watching the submarines of the English Navy busy in the Irish Sea practising the sinking of U-Boats. The West coast of England dwindled behind him.

There were tickets in code on his suitcase, and someone beside him watching the U-Boat exercises said, 'You'll find plenty of them things if you's away over the water. Stiff with U-Boats.'

On the train towards Londonderry – blank scenery – the idea occurred to him that he should have roused himself to take an interest in what lay ahead. He did not even know the length of the journey. Then it all slid away. He wondered languidly if he'd even find his ship.

But somehow here he was at the dock of a huge bay and some sort of official had his name on a list.

'Travelling alone? No group? Don't think we'll tie a label on you' (Eddie towered over him). 'All plain sailing up to now?'

'Yes thanks.'

'But no more plain sailing for a while. The convoy's not ready. She'll be in harbour at least three weeks.'

'Three *weeks*?'

'Yes. Here's your billet address. Don't worry, we won't forget you. Can you get there by yourself or do you want a school bus?'

'I'll find it. I've left school.'

The man looked at him curiously as he turned away.

'What's the bus fare?' he called, but the man was gone.

He found the bus, and the journey was not very expensive and he got out in green mild country to the West of the city and saw that he was to be on a farm where a maidservant greeted him and brought him a glass of buttermilk. He was at present the only lodger.

'Evacuees comes and goes,' she said. 'Poor little souls, crying and that, and hung with tickets. See *me* letting a bairn go where there's none it knows. Who's sending yous off, then? You's old for an evacuee. Or is yous home abroad then? Or is yous not for fighting?'

He hated her.

He walked in the fields, helped on the farm. The empty days followed each other. Time stood still. When the servant girl – she smelled of earth and corn and her eyes were aching and knowing – passed behind his chair at dinner with the tatey stew and the heavy suet puddings she leaned very close over him. Sometimes she ran her warm hands through his hair. One night she came to his room and tried to get into his bed, but he was terrified and threw her out.

Then, after a week and still no ship, he found himself looking for her and when she came over the fields with the buttermilk his heart began to beat so loud he blushed.

'Is there no letters you should be writing? Is there nobody should know?'

He felt her kindness and that night wrote, on scented paper

she gave him from her bedroom drawer, to his school. He told them about Oxford and that his aunts had despatched him to Singapore. He thanked old Oils who'd taught him history and asked him to tell Oxford how he'd been powerless to stay and would be back as soon as ever he could. He could not write to Oxford himself. He was too wretched. He felt weak, guilty, a schoolboy, a pathetic child again. And he couldn't tell Oxford where to reply.

Then he wrote to Sir, but could find nothing to say that mattered. In neither of his letters did he mention Pat Ingoldby.

His weakness and self-loathing numbed him. He began to stammer again, and so stopped talking. When he woke one night in his white clean bed, the room full of moonlight, the old closet, the bare floor, the ewer and wash-basin and soap dish on the marble washstand, the pure whiteness of his towel for morning, he turned to the girl and let her do what she wanted.

Which he found was what he wanted. And she made it easy.

The next night he was waiting for her and took control. 'You's wonderful,' she said and he said, 'Well, I'm good at games,' and she laughed into the pillow. He had a feeling that the farmer and his wife knew. The next night she didn't come. He was desolate. Desperate. 'Where were you?' he said next day, but she stared and went out to do the dairy. She was in his room that night again but he did not enjoy it. As she washed in the soft soapy water in his bowl she said, 'How much money is yous going to give me?' and when he said he only had a few pounds she didn't believe him. 'All right then – you can give us yous watch.'

He said, 'Never. It was my father's.'

At breakfast there was a message brought by a farm boy that his ship was near to sailing. He packed and was at the bus stop without breakfast, leaving a shilling on his bedroom mantel-piece. The leaving of the shilling pleased him. A man who knows the rules. A Christ Church man. A man of the world. The buttermilk girl had disappeared.

And when he reached the dock this time, he felt jaunty and no longer worried that he'd be herded into a group of small children and weeping parents. He presented his papers to an office on the quay. A whole fleet now lay at anchor. A mammoth fish tank of troop-ships, battle-cruisers, destroyers, freighters, cargo boats, awaiting release.

An old-time tar spat over the rail of his own ship.

'Is this the *Breath o'Dunoon*?'

'It is, so. Step aboard.'

'Am I the only one? – the only evacuee?'

'Not at all, there's one other. He's below.'

Eddie clambered with his case down three metal ladders into smelly darkness and walked along a narrow passage that dipped towards the middle. It was way below the water line. Les Girls had not been interested in classes of cabin on the *Breath o'Dunoon*.

Nobody was to be seen. The sound of the sea slopped about. There was a dry, clicking noise coming from behind a cabin door.

He opened the door and found two bunks at right angles to each other, so narrow that they looked like shelves, each covered with a grey blanket. On the better bunk, seated cross-legged, was a boy, busy with a pack of cards. One of his very small hands he held high in the air above his head, the other cupped in his lap, and between the two, arrested in mid-air, hung an arc of coloured playing-cards, held beautifully in space. As Eddie watched, the arc collapsed with lovely precision and became a solid pack again in the cupped hand.

'OK, how's that?' said the boy. 'Find the lady.'

He was an Oriental and appeared to be about ten-years-old. His body, however, seemed to have been borrowed to fit the cabin and was that of a child of six. The crossed legs looked very short, the feet dainty. The features, when you looked carefully, were interesting for they were not Chinese though the eyes were narrow and tilted. He was not Indian and certainly not Malay. After thirteen years, Eddie still knew a Malay. The boy's skin was not ivory or the so-called 'yellow' but robust and ruddy red.

'OK then,' said the boy, '*don't* find the lady. Just pick a card. Any card. OK?'

'I have to settle in.'

'You'll have months for that. We're in this rat-hole for twelve weeks.'

'*What*! I hope not. I'm only going to Singapore.'

'Me too. Via Sierra Leone. Didn't you know? We change ship at Freetown, if one turns up. Choose a card.'

Eddie sat on the other end of the bunk.

'Go on. Pick a card. No, don't show me. Very good. Nine of diamonds. Right?'

It was the nine of diamonds.

'Are you some sort of professional?'

'Professional what?'

'Card-sharp.'

'Yes,' said the boy. 'You could look at it that way. I'm Albert Loss. I'd be Albert Ross – I have Scottish blood – but I can't say my Rs, being also Hakka Chinese. Right?'

'Why can't *other* people call you Albert Ross?'

'You can, if you want. They did at school. And they called me Coleridge. "Albat Ross". Right? *Ancient Mariner*. They like having me on board ships, sailors. Albatrosses bring them luck.'

'Are you a professional sailor, too?'

'I've been around,' said Loss. 'D'you play Crib?'

'No.'

'I'll teach you Crib.'

'Are there going to be some more of us on the ship?'

'More what?'

'Well –' (with shame) '– evacuees.'

'No idea. I think it's just the pair of us. OK? Pick another card.'

'I'm going back on deck,' said Eddie.

'OK. I'll come with you. Watch them loading. It's corned beef. We unload at Freetown and she'll sail full of bananas.'

'Bananas? To the Far East?'

'Don't be stupid. *We* change ship at Freetown, hang about.

The *bananas* get taken Home by the *Breath o'Dunoon* for the Black Market and the Commandos.'

'I've not seen any bananas in three years.'

'Well, you're not in the know. You can eat plenty in Freetown. Flat on your back. Nothing moves in Freetown. There's RAF there, and they've all gone mad. Talking to monkeys. Mating with monkeys.'

'How do you know all this?'

'Common knowledge. I've done this trip before. Often.'

'How old are you?'

The boy looked outraged. Eddie saw the long eyes go cold. Then soft and sad. 'That's a question I don't often answer, but I'll tell you. I'm fourteen,' and he took from his pocket a black cigarette with a gold tip, and lit it.

Thirty-six hours later there were signs that the huge herd of ships might be thinking of sailing. Eddie asked again if they were the only passengers.

'Four months. Just you and I.'

'I suppose so.' Loss spat black shag at the seagulls. 'Shag to shags,' he said. 'I am also rather witty. I'm a master of languages as well. I could teach you Malay.'

'I speak Malay,' said Eddie. 'I was born there.'

'Mandarin, then? Hindi. All one. Nice watch.'

'It was my father's.'

Days, it seemed, later they saw the last of Ireland sink into the sea. The prow of the ship seemed to be seeking the sunset, such as it was, rainy and pale. Great grey sea-coloured ships like lead pencils stood about the ocean and smaller brisker ships nosed about them. The *Breath o'Dunoon* looked like a tramp at a ball. The Atlantic lay still beneath its skin.

'We're in a convoy.'

'Well, of course, we're in a convoy,' said Loss. 'We can't go sailing off to Africa alone. We're not a fishing boat. It's a widespread War.

'Mind you,' he added, 'we'd probably get there faster if we

were a fishing boat. The convoy always goes the speed of the slowest ship. And we're headed out to the West for days on end, to get clear of the U-Boats. Nearly to America, zig-zagging all the way.

'Am I right?' he condescendingly enquired of the Captain at whose none too clean table they were dining. The Captain ignored him and spooned up treacle pudding.

'Is that all we're going to do all the time? I've brought no books. I thought it would be just a few days.'

'You can do the cooking if you like,' said the Engineer Officer. 'You couldn't do worse than this duff. It's made of lead shot. Can you cook, Mr Feathers?'

'No, not at all.'

'I can cook,' said Loss, 'but only French cuisine.'

'You can both peel spuds,' said the Captain, 'but remember to take that watch off, Feathers.'

'And keep it away from *him*,' said the Engineer Officer, pointing at Loss. 'Ask me, he's escaped from a reformatory school for delinquents.'

'It was Eton,' said Loss. 'I was about to go to Eton. Do you play Crib?'

'Not now,' said the Sparks, 'but I'll thrash you when I do.'

They left the rickety *Breath o'Dunoon* at Freetown for a blazing beach where the air throbbed like petrol fumes. The jungle hung black. Black people were immobile under palm trees. Nobody seemed to know what should happen next. After a shabby attempt at examination by the customs, where interest was taken in the watch, the two of them stood about, waiting for instructions. There were none. The crew of the *Breath o'Dunoon* were taking their ease before the unloading of the cans of meat, and the Captain had disappeared. There was a suggestion that they should give up their passports which they ignored.

Heat such as Eddie had never known blasted land and sea. The smell of Africa was like chloroform. Inland from the port were dancing-hot tin sheds, one with a red cross on it, asphalt, some apologies for shops, and RAF personnel in vests and shorts. More black people stood about in the shadows beneath the trees.

Beyond the white strip of beach the mango forests began and Albert Loss sat down neatly under a palm tree and ate one, first peeling off the skin with a little knife from his pocket, then sucking. He took out a notebook and began to make calculations. Eddie ate bananas and thought about the buttermilk girl, with some satisfaction.

He watched the rollers of the Atlantic. 'I think I'll bathe,' he said. 'Get rid of the banana juice.' He licked his fingers and ran down to the sea and was immediately flung back on the beach. He tried again and was again spat out. He lay with a ricked back and a badly grazed knee as the waves slopped over him with contempt.

'The sun's dangerous,' Loss announced from the edge of the jungle.

But Eddie, exalted to be free, warm, deflowered and full of bananas, lay on in the sand. The dangerous part of the journey was over. They had seen no U-Boats, and there would be none on the next ship for they were out of range now. They were taking the Long Route down Africa to the Cape, and out to Colombo to refuel. Then Singapore and safety. And the next ship might be better. Even comfortable. A Sunderland flying boat suddenly roared from beyond the mangoes and came towards him along the sea, bouncing like a loose parcel chucked from hand-to-hand. It blundered to an uncertain lop-sided stop some way out. Bloody planes, thought Eddie. I want to sleep. He was sated, different – happy.

'How many bananas have you eaten?' asked Loss.

'Thirty-six.'

'You are intemperate. I wouldn't have thought it.'

'They're miniature bananas. They're nothing.'

'They're very over-ripe. Where did you get them?'

'Off a heap. Under a tree. Any objection?'

Loss watched him.

'No. I am glad you have some powers of enjoyment. D'you want a game of Patience?'

'It's about a hundred and five degrees. I want a beer.'

Eddie stumbled up the beach, to a stall under the trees where a massive lady in orange appeared to be in a trance but took his English money into her pink palm.

'You've left your watch lying on the sand,' called Loss.

'Look after it,' Eddie shouted. 'D'you want a beer?'

'Certainly not. Not that stuff. And don't touch the bottled water. I've been here before.'

Eddie lay back in the sand and went to sleep.

Waking he felt about him, sat up and began to swig from a dark bottle. His head began to swim deliciously. He lifted his legs in the air. Loss observed him.

'You are behaving quite out of character,' he said. 'I have known you six weeks, but I know this to be out of character.'

'I like this character.'

'I am amazed. You have a rational mind.'

'I've slept with a woman,' said Eddie. 'Yippee.'

Loss chose not to comment.

After a pause for thought Eddie said, '*Have* you been here before?'

'Somewhere like it. Down the coast.'

'Oh, I've been somewhere *like* it. Plenty of this. Worse.'

'When?'

'When I was five. When I came over to England with a missionary. Auntie May, she was called. To live in England on my own.'

'On your own?'

'No. With a woman called Ma Didds. Professional foster mother. Me and two vague cousins I'd never heard of. It wasn't safe for Raj brats to stay in Malaya. We died off after five. And before five in hundreds. I felt pretty well in the East but I hadn't a say in the matter. "Terrible for the parents," everyone says but I hadn't a mother and my father lived in a world of his own. Anyway, all Raj Orphans forgot their parents. Some of them attached themselves to the foster parents for life.'

'Not you?'

'No.'

'Where did you go?'

'Wales. It was Wales or Norfolk. Wales was cheaper.' Suddenly he knew that it must have been his aunts who had chosen it. 'What about you, Loss?'

'Something of a mystery, my parents. They didn't send me to England until I was ten. And they didn't call it "Home". They weren't Raj.'

'What did you do in the holidays?'

'Oh, I always went to Singapore.'

'You couldn't have done. There wasn't time.'

Loss continued to play Patience with a cloth over his head.

'Well,' he said vaguely. 'I got humped about. I am a natural traveller. We are of Hakkar stock.'

'So you keep telling me. Were there many Hakkars going to Eton?'

'I beseech you, Feathers. You may have found your tongue at last and it is all very interesting, but do not drink any more of the beer. And leave off the bananas.'

'Why?'

'I shall have to look after you. I can see the fruit moving. It will be a humiliation.'

'For me or for you?' shouted Eddie, tight as a tick, flat on his back, feet in the air, peeling a thirty-seventh banana.

'Both of us,' said Loss. 'Here. Cover yourself. Here is your shirt. You are calling attention to us.'

'Not true,' yelled Eddie. 'They're all drunk here. Look at the beer cans everywhere. Or they're drugged – look at them all just standing staring. All des-o-late. All the best ones dead. We're going to lose this War so we may as well drink and die.'

Another flying boat split the air with sound. 'Bundle of spare parts,' shouted Eddie. 'Won't make it back. Torpedo boats bang bang – down. England won't last six months against Germany. Churchill's a buffoon. Ham actor. Country's finished. Europe's finished. Thank God I'm going away.'

Someone from the Red Cross hut came down the beach and took him off, Loss walking thoughtfully behind.

*

Eddie, put to bed, raved for three days. Loss moved into the Missions to Seamen and watched a scorpion hanging from a rafter, ate mangoes and played cards with anyone who would give him a game.

The Missions to Seamen medical man was troubled by Eddie. 'How old is he?' he asked Loss. 'Your friend. The other evacuee – a schoolfriend?'

'I am not an evacuee,' said Loss. 'I am travelling home to pursue my life. Feathers is a young friend of mine, no; for I only met him on the *Breath o'Dunoon*. He is an unwilling evacuee. His father sent for him to return to Malaya. He wanted to stay and Do His Bit.'

'Did he? Well, now he's yelling and ranting about dead pilots and the Battle of Britain.'

'That's over,' said Loss. 'I expect he's lost best friends. There are those with best friends. I avoid such. He'll be OK. He needed to blow up.'

The doctor looked dubious.

But by the time the Portuguese freighter arrived a fortnight later to carry them on, a gaunt, monosyllabic (but not stammering) Feathers was allowed to continue his journey.

'He's strong,' said the Purser. 'There's those get malaria soon as they get to Freetown. He's not had that. There's blackwater fever if you so much as look at the swamp. He's not had that. Just the guts. The guts and the brains. He'll recover.'

'He drank palm-beer from a bad bottle,' said Loss, tight-lipped as a Methodist.

'Maybe, lad, it saved his life.' The Purser was the only Englishman on the new ship, and spoke Portuguese. He had avoided the call-up, he said, because of flat feet. 'I dare say the bugger'll live,' he said. 'He's walking.'

But as they sailed – their neutral flag flying or rather hanging limp on the mast – down the bulge of Africa and at last out upon the hot-plate of the Indian Ocean, day after day, day after day, Eddie lay prone in the sick bay, hardly eating, drinking only lime juice, not talking but muttering and yelling in his sleep. Loss, three flights down in the noisome, sweaty bilges, sat on his bunk and wrote up his log book. He also sat with Eddie several hours a day thinking his Hakkar thoughts. In the night he went on deck and sat about learning Portuguese from the crew. He watched each morning the raising of the neutral flag to ensure that the sea and the sky and the sea-birds (there were few now) and the enemy submarines (there were none) knew that this was a craft on peaceful business.

In time, Eddie got up and began to wander on deck, sit against the davits, lean over the rails. He felt so alien and remote from anything that had happened to him before that tears of weakness filled his eyes and reflected the tremendous starlight. He was hollow, a shell on a beach – but safe at last. I could be OK now, he thought, if I could stay here for my life on the circle of the sea.

Loss watched him and considered the ranting he'd heard in the sick bay and risked saying, once, when they were sitting on the creaking deck under the moon, 'Tell me about Ma Didds. Go on. You'll have to tell somebody, some day.'

But Eddie froze to stone.

Breezily on another occasion, the crew eating fish stew, Eddie crumbling bread, Loss said, 'I suppose you know that there are those who believe that endurance of cruelty as a child can feed genius?'

'I have no genius,' said Eddie, 'and never would have had.'

'Bad luck,' said Loss. 'It is perhaps a pity that *I* wasn't sent to Ma Didds.'

'She would have broken even you.'

But this conversation was a turning point, and Eddie seemed to relax. As the heat grew ever stronger, the sea a shimmering disc wherever you looked, and the two boys shrunk into any patch of shadow under the life-boats; and as the engines chuntered on, and the wake behind them curdled the water, and the sea beneath held its mysteries, and as time ceased, Eddie began to sleep again at night and exist, and often sleep peacefully again in the day. Once or twice his old self broke through. He wondered about his father and whatever the two of them would do in Kotakinakulu – or Singapore or Penang, or wherever his father was now – but soon he dismissed all thoughts of the future and the past, and lazily watched Loss dealing out the cards.

'Do you smell something?' asked Loss. 'Do you smell land?'

Eddie sniffed.

'We're still too far out.'

'Lanka,' said Loss, 'was said by the poet to be the Scented Isle, the Aromatic Eden, the last outpost of civilisation. We've half a day's sailing ahead. We should be sensing it now.'

'What – flowers? Wafted over the sea?'

'Yes. You can always smell them. It gives a lift to the heart.'

After a time Eddie said, 'I do smell something. Not flowers. Something rather vile. I was wondering if there was engine-trouble.'

'I have noted it, too,' said Loss, and went to the rail and stared hard into the Eastern dazzle on the sea.

'It's smeary,' said Eddie, joining him. 'The sky's smeary.'

In half an hour the smears had turned to clouds black as oil and soot, lying all along and high above the curved horizon. The ship's engines were slowing down.

Then they stopped and fell silent, the wake hushed, and the crew called to each other, gathered along the rail to stare.

Then a torrent of excited Portuguese splattered out from the tannoy on the bridge.

'I'll find the Purser,' said Loss. 'But I know what it is.' He listened. 'There's been a signal. There has been a signal from Colombo. Singapore has fallen to the Japanese!'

'The *Japanese*? What have they to do with us?'

'We have seen no newspapers. We have heard no news since Christmas. We have been nearly four months aboard.'

'Singapore is impregnable.'

'It seems not.'

After dark, very slowly, the ship began to move on towards Colombo, though whether, said the Purser, they would get their refuelling slot was uncertain. Black smoke covered all the hills. The rubber plantations were all on fire. The dawn seemed never to come as they sailed nearer and nearer the murk.

And they were all at once one of a great fleet of battered craft, most of them limping towards harbour, a macabre regatta, their decks packed with the bandaged and the lame.

'They're wearing red flowers in their hats,' said Eddie. 'Most of them.'

'It's blood,' said Loss.

Some of the bandaged waved weakly and uncertainly put up their thumbs and, as the boats reached harbour, there came feeble cheering and scraps of patriotic songs. 'They're singing,' said Eddie. But *There'll always be an England* trailed away when the refugees on board were near enough to see the whole port of Colombo crammed with other English trying to get away.

'They look numb,' said Loss.

'They look withered,' said Eddie. 'Like they've been days in water. Shrivelled. Hey – you don't think Singapore can *really* have gone?'

Loss said nothing.

Then, 'Look ashore,' he said, and pointed at the thousand fluttering Japanese flags that were flaming on every harbour-side roof and window.

'I don't think that they will be any safer here,' said Eddie.

'Nor will any of us,' said Loss.

All at once, high above the Fragrant Isle and to the South, there was a startling scatter of light. Several groups of tiny daylight stars, triangles of silver and scarlet that the sun caught for a moment before they were lost in the smoke. Aeroplanes.

'Like pen-nibs,' said Eddie. 'Dipped in red ink.'

'Japs,' said Loss.

The British Army was everywhere on the quays, top brass

striding, the Governor with his little cane, the refugees being welcomed but too dazed to understand. A procession of stretchers. Eddie saw one old woman on a crutch asking courteously if anyone had seen her sister, Vera; then collapsing.

Crowds hung over the rails of the Customs and Excise who were unhurriedly examining credentials even of the stretcher-cases.

'What will happen to us?' said Eddie. 'We'll vanish in all that. The bombing here will start any time.'

'We're to refuel and turn round,' said Loss – he had found the Chief Engineer. 'It'll be quite a time before we're refuelled though, and we'll be taking on refugees.'

'Turn *back*?' said Eddie. 'To Sierra Leone again?'

'No. Back to England. All the way. Probably via Cadiz.'

'I must get a message to my father.'

'If you send a message, it will have to be in Japanese.'

The ship somehow sidled into the madhouse harbour, the engines shuddered loudly, then stopped, and they were tied up and the first gangplank let down. Loss and Eddie stood above it, side by side, like lamp-post and bollard. Loss, now that Eddie looked down, had with him his suitcase and haversack.

'Feathers, I'm staying.'

'You're *what*?'

'I'm staying here. D'you want to come with me?'

'You can't stay. You've no money. You'll be on your own.'

'I've a bit of money and I won't be alone. I've a couple of uncles. Attorneys. Everyone's an attorney in Colombo. I shall be an attorney one day. So will you, I can tell. I'll be safe from the Japanese. I'm not British. Not white. Come with me. My relatives are resourceful.'

'What about the customs?'

'Oh, I am adept at slithering through.'

'Loss, you'll disappear. The Japs'll be here in a week. After they've bombed Colombo into the sea. If you don't get killed by a bomb, they'll dispose of you and no one will know.'

'I tell you, Feathers, I am lucky. I am The Albat Ross. I'll give you my pack of cards. An Albat Ross feather. A feather to

Feathers. Here you are. Oh, could you give me your watch? For emergencies?'

'It's my father's.'

'I may need it.'

The masked face. The humourless, cunning, dwarf's eyes. . . .

'Yes, of course.' Eddie took it off and put it in Loss's out-stretched hand.

'See,' said Loss. 'You'll be safe. Just look –' and he pointed up behind Eddie at the mast-head '– an albatross. You don't often get them this far South.'

Eddie looked and saw nothing. He turned back and Loss had gone.

The Donheads

Cracks like shots and a roar followed by heavy black smoke emerged from the region of the bonfire, just off-stage from Filth's sun-lounge, and Garbutt, looking older now, went rebelliously by with yet another load of leaves.

I don't know what's the matter with the man. He knows how I feel. It's too soon to burn. The stuff hasn't died down. He's not normal.

Garbutt came back, past him again, a fork over the barrow for the next load. Each time he passed his jaw was thrust out further, his eyes more determinedly set full ahead.

He's a pyro – pyro. Pyro-technic? Pyrocanthus? Pyro-whatever (words keep leaving me). He's destructive as old Queen Mary. Pyro – pyro? How can I get on here?

And to whom could he complain now old Veneering was gone?

He was amazed at his regret for Veneering. It was genuine grief. Veneering the arch-enemy had become the familiar and close friend. The twice-a-week chess had become the comforting note in an empty diary. There had been visits to the White Hart for lunch, once even for dinner, in Salisbury. Once they had taken a car to Wilton to look at the Van Dycks. Veneering turned out to be keen on painting and music and Old Filth, trying to hide his total ignorance of both, had accompanied him. Veneering read books. Filth had not been a reader. Veneering had introduced him to various writers. 'Only of the higher-journalism,' he'd said. 'We won't tax our addled brains.

Patrick O'Brian. You were a sea-faring man, Filth, weren't you? In the War?'

'I hate the sea,' said Filth, putting down O'Brian.

'I'd quite like a cruise,' said Veneering, but saw Filth look aghast. 'I'd not have even thought of a cruise once,' said Veneering. 'I was beyond cruising before you came round that Christmas Day.'

'Yes,' said Filth with some pride. 'You were in dry dock.'

Muffled up, the two of them walked sometimes round the lanes, Filth instructing Veneering in ornithology.

'You are full of surprises,' said Veneering.

'My prep school Headmaster,' said Filth. 'He went off to America in the War and I suppose he died there. He didn't keep up with any of us. He'd done his duty by us.'

'Very wise.'

'I tried to find him when I came back from my abortive attempt at being an evacuee. We had to turn for Home, you know. Took three months. Four months, going out. Singapore fell before we got there. My father was there. He died in Changi.'

'I'd heard something of the sort.'

'I used to make a joke of it. Dinner parties. All the way to Singapore, and about turn, back again.'

'It can't have been a great joke.'

'No. The journey home was worse than going out. We were stacked with casualties. They kept dying. There was none of the Prayer Book and committal to the deep and *Abide with Me* and so forth. They were just shovelled over. I hung on. I kept imagining Sir – my Headmaster – would be waiting for me at Cadiz. Or my Auntie May.'

'I had not thought you the type for an Auntie May.'

'Missionary. Wonderful woman. There was another missionary on the boat. A Miss Robertson. She died of gangrene and they shovelled her off, too.'

'Have you written about all this?'

'Certainly not. Old Barrister's memoirs are all deadly. Don't you think?'

'Yes. But maybe you'd have surprised us.'

'I've grown my image, Veneering. Took some doing. I'm not going to upset it now.'

'You mean upset *yourself*?'

'Yes. Probably. Have some more hock.'

But Veneering gone – ridiculous to have taken a cruise at his age – Filth's loneliness for the old enemy was extraordinary, his mourning for him entirely different and sharper than his mourning for Betty. He'd told Veneering more than he'd ever told Betty – though never about Ma Didds. He'd even told Veneering about the buttermilk girl. Veneering had cackled. He'd told him about Loss. 'Did you tell me about that before?' asked Veneering. 'It rings a bell. Did I know him?'

'You're wandering,' said Filth. They were playing chess.

'Not far,' said Veneering, taking his queen.

I suppose Memoirs might be in the order of things, he thought, with Veneering dead and his house next door torn apart, windows flung wide, a family with children shouting, crying, laughing, breaking through his hedge; the parents growing vegetables and offering him lettuces. Once a child from Veneering's house had landed at his feet like a football as he sat in the garden reading the Minutes of a new Temple Bench-table. He wanted to throw the child back over the hedge. 'Sorry,' the child said.

'I suppose you want your ball back.'

'I haven't got a ball.'

'Well, what's that in your hand?'

'Just some old beads.'

Giggles from the bushes.

'I found them in that flower-bed.'

He vanished.

Bloody self-confident, thought Filth. I don't understand children now. Sir would have flayed him. Then: What am I talking about? Acting the Blimp. Sir wouldn't have flayed him. He'd have lectured him on birds.

But, too late for that, he thought.

He sat to his desk and attempted a Memoir, but found it impossible. Opinions, Judgements had made him famous, but how to write without opinion or judgement? Statement of facts – easy. But how to decide which were the facts? He shrank from the tremendous, essential burden of seeing himself through other people's eyes. Only God could do it. It seemed blasphemous even to try. Such a multitude of impressions, such a magnitude of emotion. Where was truth to be found?

'Why did you become an advocate, Filth?' Veneering used to ask. 'Don't tell me you wanted to promote the truth.'

'Justice. It interested me.'

'And we know that justice is not the truth.'

'Certainly not.'

'But it's some sort of step towards it?'

'Not even that. Do you agree?'

'I agree,' Veneering had said, busy with his ghastly jigsaw. 'The Law is nevertheless an instinct. A good instinct. A framework for behaviour. And a safeguard (good – bit of the church roof) in time of trouble. *Parlement of Foules* – Chaucer.'

'Rooks have a parliament,' said Filth, keeping his end up.

But though his Memoirs went on endlessly, and rather impressively as he thought them through in the small hours of the night, sometimes to the accompaniment of his beating heart and too much whiskey, when it came to getting them upon paper they would not come. They made him feel so foolish. He felt Betty looking over his shoulder and saying kindly, 'Jolly good.' He sat in the sun-lounge each morning, defeated, and Garbutt went tramping by. Oh, how could one concentrate? And, oh great heaven! Here came that Chloe in lacy mauve and a perm, round the back of the house and waving a cake. To think he had once. . . .

He deliberately arose, holding his tartan blanket round him and shuffled to the other side of the table to sit with his back to her, facing the door to the sitting-room which immediately opened and in came the cleaning lady, Mrs-er, with a cup of tea.

Decisions came fast to Filth, all decisions except what to include in his Memoirs. Mrs-er put down the cup and saucer, talking the while, saying that that Chloe from the church was wanting to give him another sponge.

'Mrs-er,' he said, 'I've been meaning to tell you. I am going away.'

'Away? Oh, yes?'

'Yes. I am going to Malmesbury.'

'*Malmesbury*? Down Gloucester?'

'Yes. I was there in the Army during the War. Just for a look round.'

'If it's hotels, be careful. There'll be steps and stairs you don't know. Remember poor Judge Veneering.'

'It is not a ship. I'll leave my address.'

'I'll pack for you.'

'Thank you, I'm sure I can manage. And I'll be hiring a car.'

Two minutes later he saw her outside, furiously conferring with Garbutt, the mauve woman having disappeared. Their excitement maddened him.

The next day, she came in to tell him that if it was a hotel he ought to have new pyjamas.

He said, 'Oh, and Mrs-er, when I come back I intend to manage here alone.'

'*Alone*?'

'I think I am becoming too dependent on you all. I'm going to employ the Social Services. The Meals on Wheels. I'm sorry, Mrs-er.'

'After all these years you still don't know my name,' she said. 'That's it, then. I'll go now. Get yourself to Malmesbury.'

He saw her clacking at Garbutt on the lawn and marching away, and felt gleefully cruel. He opened the glass doors and waited till Garbutt went by.

'I know what you're going to say,' said Garbutt. 'I'll just see the fire's out, then I'm off. You know where to find me if you change your mind. Her name's Katey, by the way. You've gutted her.'

*

In the hotel at Malmesbury, journey safely accomplished, splendid room looking across at the Abbey, smell of a good dinner floating up, his unrepentant euphoria remained. Their blank faces, ha! Their disbelief. They'd see he was his own master yet. And here in Malmesbury not a soul knew him. He stumbled on the stairs and limped into the dining-room, rather wishing he'd brought his walking-stick for his explorations tomorrow.

The ankle next morning was the size of a small balloon and he telephoned the Desk for assistance. They suggested bringing him breakfast in bed which outraged him. Staggering down a steep flight of stairs between two waiters, he somehow made the breakfast-room. Outside it was pouring with rain and people went by behind umbrellas at a forty-five degree angle against the wind. Unable to walk from the table, he enquired whether there was a doctor who could come and see him and was told the way to a surgery. It was not far, they said, but Old Filth couldn't even reach the hotel's front door and sank upon an oak bench. People passed by. A whole coachload of tourists streamed past, chattering about the disappointing weather. He asked if the Desk would ring for a doctor to call to examine him.

'You'd have to go to the hospital for that. For an x-ray.'

'I only need a GP's opinion.'

The Desk stared. 'You'd have to go round to the surgery. They don't do home visits now unless it's serious.'

He asked the Desk to call a taxi.

The paving stones between the taxi and surgery door shone slippery and menacing. He hesitated. The umbrellas continued to go by. At last he was helped in, and found a room crowded and silent like a church and one girl at a screen with her back to the audience.

'I need to see a doctor.'

'Yes.' She handed him a disc saying '21'.

'Do I wait here?'

She looked surprised. 'Where else?'

'This means that there are twenty people ahead of me?'

'Yes.'

'What sort of wait will that be?'

'A long one.'

'An hour?'

'Oh, nearer two.'

He rang the Desk and asked for his luggage to be collected and brought down to the hotel foyer. And would they kindly ring the car-hire company to come and take him from the surgery, then back to the hotel and then home to the Donheads.

'It wasn't even Malmesbury I really wanted to go to, it was Badminton. Just down the road,' he told this driver.

'It is. Just as it ever was. Down the road and down the hill.'

'I was there in the War. Wanted to have another look. I was in the Army.' (His ankle was hell.)

'There's a good hotel near there where you could keep your foot up. They might get you a doctor. Were you there with the Royals? They'll be pleased to see you if you were. Still the same sort of place.'

(Anything better than creeping home to shame and emptiness.)

'I might give it a try. Thank you.'

They swooped from the hill to the plain. Through the rain he saw the great house again, the broad quiet streets of the village, the stretch of woodland, the wide fields.

'Terrible weather for sight-seeing,' said the taxi man. 'I'll take you right home when the time comes, if you like. I'll just look in here and see if there's a room. It'll cost you, mind.'

Exhausted, he sat in the foyer of the new hotel which was calm and gracious. Someone brought him a stool for his foot. Someone else said they were going to get a doctor. The rain eased and Filth was brought lunch on a tray alone in the lounge. He was tired, humiliated and – something else – what? Good God! frightened. I have been frightened! He sank into himself, dozed, was helped to a big ground-floor bedroom with a view across the parkland, and very cautiously, a snip at a time, allowed himself the past.

'Would you very kindly put my name and address in your address book, young man?' said the ragged skeleton beside him on the boat-deck as they left Cadiz. 'I fully intend to reach Home, but, if not, I would like to be sure that Vera knows what happened to me. That's to say, of course, if she gets Home herself, which I doubt. She was always rather feeble without me to get her anywhere. I am Miss Robertson. Miss Meg. She is Miss Vera. We're daughters of the late Colonel Robertson. Teachers. This is our only address in England now. It belongs to some old chums from school who've always paid us a little rent. I hope we'll get on together now that I shall have to live with them. Well, school's a long time ago, you know.'

Her skin was pale and glazed with fever and her eyes far too bright. Her wooden crutches lay beside her and she tried all the time to clutch their handles. 'Have you a pen, young man? Turn to "R" in your address book.' Eddie lay immobile. Someone crept up to Miss Robertson and wiped her face with a cloth. Other people muttered together that she should have been detained at Cadiz. She had been formidably against it, even in fever. She had to get Home.

'If *any* of us gets Home,' she had said. 'I hear that there's one ship a day being sunk just now in the Channel.'

As it grew dark, one night, he heard Miss Robertson whisper, 'Look in my little bag. There's some trinkets. Take them, young man, and give them to your sweetheart.' The little bag lay pushed up under the life-boat blocks and the crutches near it. There was a cold clean breeze. When daylight came, where Miss Robertson had been there was a stain.

The smell beneath the life-boat where she had lain had gone too.

She had been complaining of the rotting smell on the ship. Eddie had not cared about it, hardly noticed. 'Gangrene,' he heard someone say. 'The stink was from herself. The boy don't look much better. He's filth all through.'

A crewman went away for a bucket of water and scrubbing brush, and Eddie, eyes closed, stretched to touch Miss Robertson's walking aids and found his hand on the bag. He took it and pushed it beneath him, later found a corner for it in his own suitcase with his father's photograph and Pat Ingoldby's clothes-brush. Through his headache and fever, and through the now endless vomiting, he found himself thinking that he was becoming like Loss. A scavenger. Survival. Take anything. Old lady. Couldn't see her own doom. Her isolation. Talking about address books.

The ship sailed on like some faery invisible barge. The sea shone, still and blue. No planes. No U-Boats. Other craft nowhere near. Way out, towards the West, fishing boats. A wonderful calmness.

A kind of whisper went round at last among the humped and now many fewer passengers; a sibilant, urgent word. 'Yes. Yes. it is. It's land. Yes. Yes. It is.'

And cold now. Eddie was unwrapped first from his life-jacket then put inside a tarpaulin. Someone washed his face as he vomited. Cleaned him when he shat his clothes. 'Here's another going, if you ask me.'

Now he was left alone.

The odd thing, said the speck of the rational in Eddie within him – he guarded it like his life – the odd thing is that I did once have an address book. Alice gave it to me. In the kitchen. Leather. Small. Red. Someone had given it to her, but, she said, 'I don't need it. I never had any addresses to write to.' One day, at the billet in Londonderry, Eddie had written in it, for comfort, all the addresses he knew. School. Oxford, the Ingoldbys (hopelessly), Sir, Auntie May, one or two schoolfriends even though he'd never write to them. Not Les Girls. Not the buttermilk girl. As his temperature soared now he began to wonder if he'd ever again find the addresses of his cousins. If the old address in Kotakinakulu would ever find his father. He had had no address for Loss. By now there was probably no Loss to write to.

Then he remembered that he had not seen his address book for a very long time. He felt about in his bag and it was not there and he knew, without any question, that Loss had stolen it. God knows why, except he was a natural crook. A delinquent. The bastard. Vanished, and with my watch. And no Loss. No loss. But such a monstrous act! Cutting Eddie off from every hope of contact.

Loss's defection was the metaphor for Eddie's life. It was Eddie's fate always to be left. Always to be left and forgotten. Everyone gone, now. Out of his reach. For the first time, Eddie was utterly on his own.

He had his passport – yes, he felt that in the bag. He had Pat's brush. He had Miss Robertson's pouch. He felt fat beads inside it and pulled them out. A great string of pearls. Thank goodness Loss wasn't there. They'd be gone in five minutes. Lightness almost mirth filled Eddie as the ship, charmed, blessed, unhindered, sailed slowly, slowly, up the Irish Sea and such as could gathered at the rail and gazed unbelieving at the peaceful green Welsh hills. Over the Styx, thought Eddie. Crossing the bar.

Aeons passed and Eddie, wrapped in blankets, shaking with fever but ice cold, a structure of bones, was dumped on a stretcher and carried through customs unhindered, and ashore. At the ambulance station in his fever he looked for a car like a bread-bin but found instead a man playing with a yo-yo. He was familiar. He was old Oils, his Housemaster. Standing alongside him was Isobel Ingoldby.

Diagonally falling drops alighting on the windowpanes of Gloucestershire, and Old Filth awoke in the new, ever-silent hotel to see a girl smiling down at him, holding a tray of tea. He thought: Oh God – the buttermilk girl! Then, seeing the sweet open smile, thought: No.

And I am an old man, he thought.

'I am an old man,' he said.

'I've brought you a cup of tea. Is it true you were a soldier here, sir?'

It took him some time to remember where he was. Near Badminton.

'I was stationed at Badminton,' he said. 'In the War.'

'My gran was at Badminton then. In the War. Queen Mary was here but we all kept it quiet. They said nobody would want to kidnap her but my gran said – she was parlour maid at the house – that she had three bags ready packed to take her to America. In the attics.'

'That was probably true. Though she might not have gone herself.'

'One was full of jewels.'

'Oh, I'm sure that was true. That would have gone into safety.'

'Did you know her, sir?'

'Yes, I did.'

'Is it true she was always cutting down trees?'

'Yes, it is.'

'Especially ivy. She hated ivy. She had half a platoon chopping down ivy. They say the first year she didn't realise it would grow back again.

'I expect it was the way she'd been brought up,' said the girl. 'My gran says she was kept in a band-box as a girl. Never opened her mouth – well, her mother never stopped talking – and what a bottom! Her mother's, that is. Lovely woman. Real old England, her mother. Queen Mary was brought up in Teck, which is German, and she didn't like Germans. My gran said she'd been brought up to gravel paths and never seen a field of hay. And my gran says it was all psychological, the ivy.'

'Your gran sounds a very perceptive woman.'

'She is. My mother sang for Queen Mary, you know.'

'Sang?'

'In the village school. Queen Mary used to turn up there unexpected and sit at the back. She had a turned-up nose.'

'Oh. I never noticed that.'

'Yes. Look at the stamps. She was embarrassed by it, my

gran thinks. She had never been thought a beauty. But she *was* a beauty, my gran says. And all that about being a klepto-maniac was wicked lies. And she never forgot a birthday.'

'That's true.'

'And she fancied some of the subalterns. She liked them with a stammer, did you know that? My uncle had a stammer. He was one of her four motorbike bodyguards and she chose him for his stammer. She said, "I have a son like you." She meant the King.'

'D'you know, I never knew that,' said Filth. 'I didn't make the connection.'

'Won't you go out now and sit in the sun? I'll help you. My gran has a terrible leg. I wouldn't be surprised if it was gangrene. What's the matter? Have I upset you? Now then, you know the doctor said yours is but a bad sprain. You'll be fit in a week. Shall I ask my gran to come up here? She'd love a talk.'

'Do you want to talk with my gran?' the girl asked the next day, bringing him a breakfast tray and no refusals. 'It'd be a breath of life to her. Maybe she'd remember you.'

'I hardly remember myself.'

'She said there was one always reading. Law books. She got them for him, Queen Mary. And chocolate. He used to hold her wool for her. He'd been through it, she said. Very good looking. Oh yes, and *he* had a stammer. She found him – now what was it? – very *personable*. That's what we heard her tell her lady-in-waiting. "The Captain's very personable, isn't he?" She took up very close to him after her son got killed, the Duke of Kent. He was nearest to her, that one, they said. She never cried though. She and this soldier – he was a junior Platoon Commander – I asked gran when I got home last night – this soldier used to sit with her by the hour. She even used to pass through the library when he was reading in there, not looking up. Deep in his books. He was invited to stay in the house you know. Dine with them all. The Duke and Duchess – and my, there were some sparks flying there – them being kicked

203

upstairs in their own home and all the best rooms taken over by Queen Mary *and* her fifty servants.'

'This all sounds very credible.'

'He refused though, the young Captain. He said he had to be with his men in the billets in the stables and Queen Mary couldn't but say he was right. I believe now and then she was poking about the stables too, searching out ivy. And maybe –' she had his tie straight now and his socks on and his polished shoes ready for him. 'He was very good-looking, my gran said.' She thoughtfully looked Filth over. 'And very young and nice.'

'I was young but far from nice,' said Filth. 'I don't think I'd better meet your gran.'

'I'd like a look round the stables, though,' he said, the next day. 'When I'm walking again.'

'I can get you a wheelchair.'

'No. No thanks.'

'Queen Mary used to go round in a horse and cart to save petrol. No side to her. They used to put a couple of basket chairs in the cart and hoist her and the lady's maid up into it and one of the bike boys shouted up, "You look as if you're in a tumbril, Ma'am," and she said, "Well, it *might* come to that." So she can't have been *altogether* no fun.'

'I think she wasn't *much* fun. She hadn't had *much* fun,' said Filth.

'Oh that terrible King!' said the girl. 'All those pheasants. All he ever thought about, my gran said. Where the children came from, we'll never know, my gran said.'

'Yes, that's often a puzzle,' said Filth.

He was in a private room. It might be a cabin of some sort. Outside the window there were trees but trees do not grow in the sea and the sea still moved beneath him, up and down, up and down, lift and drop. Seven months at sea. But the clouds above the window sailed along without the elf-light from the sea beneath them. And these tree tops? A woman ran by him and her hat was a plume of white starch. Her dress was navy blue but she, too, had nothing to do with ships. She had a face of wrath and across her broad front hung a watch and chain. She did not speak. He floated away.

Later he opened his eyes on a member of the Ku Klux Klan seated at the end of his bed playing cat's cradle with some bed-tape.

'Hello?' Eddie said and the dreadful figure looked up with surprise. It was Oils again.

'Hello, sir.'

'Hello, Feathers. Well done. Awake?'

'What for, sir? Why well done?'

'Getting home.'

'Not in my hands, sir.'

Adrift again. He was remembering the image at the end of the bed when it was suddenly present again.

'Hello, sir. Why are you in those clothes?'

'They're antiseptic, Feathers. You're infectious.'

'What have I got?'

'A variety of things.'

'Will I recover?'

'Yes. Of course. In time. Then you can come back to school until it's time to go to Oxford.'

Away he floated. Nurses came and went and put needles in different parts of him, and tubes. Did unspeakable things to him. They wore masks. An unpleasant one told him he'd no right to be there. 'You should be in the Hospital for Tropical Diseases,' she said, 'but it's too far off. They're doing tests on you there. We're not equipped here. We've had to ask for volunteers.'

'What for?'

'To nurse you.'

'Thanks.'

Here was the Ku Klux Klan again, now back with the yo-yo.

'The Headmaster sends his good wishes. He says you must convalesce at school.'

'Thanks. You mean in the San?'

'I suppose so, Feathers, but we've not planned anything yet.'

'I won't go in the San.'

'The Headmaster has offered you a room in his house.'

Remembering the tea-cosy, Eddie flinched.

'My aunts have gone to Scotland somewhere,' he said. 'I don't know where. If you find out, don't tell them. But I'd like to know about my father. If you can find out somehow.'

'I have to go now,' said Oils. 'Ten minutes at a time.'

A nurse came in one day with mail which lay by the bed for several days.

'Shall I read it?' asked another nurse. 'Well, this is nice, it's from your aunts. It says: "*Bad luck, Eddie dear, what a hoot.*"'

'The police found them,' said Oils on his next visit, embarrassed. 'Your aunts.'

'Can they be lost again?'

'I'd think so,' said Oils.

'This visiting card's been stuck to your locker since the first day you came in here,' said the Red Cross hospital librarian, pushing round her trolley. She always stopped by his bed though he read nothing. Masks had been abandoned now. 'You're not ready to read yet, are you?'

'I don't think so.'

'I don't blame you. These are all awful old trashy paperbacks. They have to be burnt in case they get into the general library and spread infection. They can't get librarians for this ward. I wipe all the books in Dettol – not a nice job. Shall I read you this visiting card, it says *Isobel Ingoldby*, that will be the girl that brought you in, her and the schoolmaster – he's a funny one.'

'Has she been back?'

'Yes. Several times. When you were not with us.'

'Where does she live?'

'The card has her address. It's in London.'

'However did she find me here?'

'How did you find me, Mr Oilseed? I'm glad you're out of your overalls, sir.'

'You're not infectious any more. You're to sit up at the window tomorrow.'

'But how did you know I'd be on that particular ship?'

'There were signals sent of some sort. From Colombo. To me and to Ingoldby's sister and maybe to others but we haven't heard. The Admiralty tracked the ship. Ingoldby's sister has some underground job there somewhere. Something to do with the Admiralty.'

'*Underground* in the Admiralty? Was it signed? What was it – a telegram?'

'It was a cable. Unsigned. I gather it came by way of a place called Bletchley Park. Where Isobel Ingoldby was.'

'Could it have been from my father?'

'No,' said Oils. 'No. Sorry. I don't think so. Singapore isn't in touch. Some prisoners have got letters out, somehow . . . but no. . . .'

'D'you think someone in Colombo got a message to him?'

'I'd not think so. Not unless someone knew every single one of our addresses.'

They moved him by ambulance to the South of England and Oils said goodbye, with some relief, Eddie thought. 'By the way, we've informed Christ Church. You are not forgotten. As soon as you're released.'

'Thanks. Thank the Headmaster for me, sir.'

'Yes. Of course. And well done again. You're fit now.'

'But I'm going to another isolation ward. The Plymouth Naval Hospital. Whatever for?'

'The ways of medical men are very strange.'

'Sir – thanks for being so brave.'

'Nothing brave about me,' said Oils. 'Matter of fact you've cheered me up. Glad you're better.'

In Plymouth, in the isolation wing, he kept apart from the rest who were thoroughly dispirited, most of them gnarled old salts who swore considerably and talked of past delights. One of them had been at Gallipoli, and he talked on through the night of the horrors of the deep. 'There was one sailor,' he said, 'looked ninety. Homeless. Living miracle. He was so riddled with corruption – look, one day on deck he coughed up something with legs and a backbone.

'A *backbone*,' he said. 'I've never forgotten it. What's the matter with the lad? Squeamish?'

Slowly they let Eddie walk about outside along the old stone terraces. It was autumn. The air was sweet.

Then one afternoon came Isobel, striding along.

'They wouldn't let me in before,' she said. 'They didn't tell me what you'd caught, either. Whatever have you been doing? You never left the ship, did you?'

'I a-a-ate bananas in Freetown.'

'Your stammer's come back.'

'Only i-i-in-intermittently.'

'You're keeping something to yourself.'

'I suppose so but I don't quite know what.'

She leant towards him and stroked his arm. 'You look like a grub,' she said. 'One of those things you can see through.'

He was in tears. 'Sorry. I'll be OK in a minute. Don't go.'

'I have to get the train back. I've come two hundred miles.'

'Isobel.'

'You've got my card and number.'

'Come next leave.'

'My next leave maybe I'll go to Scotland to flay your aunts.'

'*Don't*,' he said. 'I'm nothing to do with them now. Just get me near to you. Somehow. For ever.'

'Child,' she said, and was gone.

And – six full months later – 'You are passed and fit, Feathers,' said the Surgeon Commander, RN, with a facial tic and a foghorn voice who ran the hospital like a cruiser, each patient to attention each at the end of his bed. 'I suppose you will now depart to Oxford?'

'No, sir. I've decided not.'

'Yes?'

'I'm going to join up, sir.'

'We've just got you shipshape. You may prove we've been wasting our time. A very expensive case. Expensive and unsavoury. But good show.'

'I'm sorry, sir.'

'You will want to join the Navy, I suppose? Return to the source of the trouble?'

'No, sir. The Army. My father was in the Army. I'd like to join his old regiment.'

'No accounting for taste,' said the Commander. 'Foolish of you. The sea is pretty well ours now. The going is easier. The Army's just about to move to the thick of the last long shove. It will be slow and bloody, and you don't look like a soldier.'

'I think I might be, sir. Given the chance.'

He felt naked on the hospital forecourt. He travelled to Gloucestershire alone. It was as terrifying as the journey to a first school, as horrible as his first walk with Babs and Claire to the Welsh baby school when he was five. He'd been feeling ill with the Welsh winter then. There had been a pain in his chest – but every time he had turned to look back at the farmhouse, Ma Didds, as usual clutching her stomach, holding her little stick, had waved him furiously on.

He missed the safety of the hospital.

Now it was a ride in a train again into a different world, the West Country, Eastward from Plymouth, across a beautiful river, soil the red of sunset, a change of trains; and into Gloucestershire. Someone had given him a bed and breakfast address and a warm soft-voiced old couple saw that he had a hot water bottle. There was a boiled egg for breakfast. An egg! 'Joining up?' they said. 'Make the most of the egg, now.' He borrowed a bike and turned up at the recruiting office, in Gloucester; where he was expected.

There were three of them behind the desk and they looked at him with considerable interest. They spoke of his health. He had been cleared one hundred per cent fit and he was brown from the air and sea off Plymouth and he looked every bit of his nearly nineteen years. His hair was curly again and auburn. His weight was now normal. His eyes were alive.

'Your father's regiment?' they said. 'The Gloucesters?'

'Yes, sir.'

'I know your father.'

'I'm afraid I hardly do, sir. I was on my way –'

'So we understand. There is, I suppose, no news from Changi?'

'No, sir.'

'I hope very much that we'll hear something and that he will hear of you. We'll do what we can.'

The middle one nodded at the other two who got up and went out.

'We have a proposal to make to you, Feathers. You were a member of your school's OTC, I understand, and have done some basic training – can march and so forth?'

'Well, I could, sir.'

'It doesn't leave you. We have decided to send you to the platoon that is guarding Queen Mary.'

Eddie stared. 'But she's well-guarded, sir. And she's in the Pacific Ocean or somewhere.'

'Not the ship. The Queen. The mother of our Monarch. She is down here in the West Country. We have one hundred and fifty men in her defence and four particular bodyguards. What's the matter?'

'It is not s-s-soldiering, sir.'

Instead of darkening with rage, the Colonel's blue eyes shut and opened again quickly.

'Only a run-in, Feathers. Not for the rest of the War. It is to finish your restoration. I notice you have a stammer and I have heard that it can be chronic. You would find it hard to give orders. The stammer must be removed.'

'It is only i-in-int-int-ermittent, sir. It re-t-urns when it is comm-comm-ented on.'

'You will report to Badminton barracks tomorrow at fourteen hundred hours. Understood?'

'Yes, sir.'

'But there is one more thing. Your health.'

'I'm a hundred per cent, sir.'

'I wonder if you know what has been the matter with you, Feathers?'

'Fever, sir. A bug from Sierra Leone. Pretty lethal, I suppose. They never told me.'

'You have been infected, Feathers, with three different types of parasitic worm. And certainly from Sierra Leone.'

'Sir?'

'But that has not troubled us. The worms are gone. We know how to treat these things. But the other thing was more serious. You have been suffering from a venereal disease.'

'What is that, sir?'

The Colonel looked at him warily.

'You have been in close contact with a woman.'

'She died of gangrene, sir, on the ship after Cadiz. I only did what I could. Miss Robertson. She was over seventy –'

'I doubt that she was the source of the infection. What I am saying, Feathers, is that you have acquired sexual knowledge through a most unpalatable source. Isn't this true?'

A long and thoughtful silence.

'It was dark, sir. I never really looked at her. I never thought of her as palatable or unpalatable. She just climbed in. I'd no idea how to do it, and she had. She gave me buttermilk, sir. It was in Northern Ireland, sir.'

The Colonel paced hurriedly across to the window and stood looking out intently.

'Were you taught *nothing* at school, Feathers?'

'I have won a scholarship to Oxford, sir.'

A sort of sob from the window. A pause for recovery.

'Feathers, I have decided that this disreputable episode should not be passed on to Badminton. Primarily because of Queen Mary. I hope I am not being unwise.'

'Thank you. Yes, sir. I can't think that Queen Mary would be in any danger from me.'

'Go! Enough!' roared the Colonel. 'You're dismissed, Feathers. Go.'

Afterwards the Colonel wondered if he'd been made fun of. Beaten in argument. Run rings round.

Feathers wasn't certain, either.

And so, this October, Filth was in a wheelchair being pushed round the Badminton meadows around Badminton House by the nice girl and her grandmother, their feet crunching on the crystalline grass. They stood at a distance from the great house.

'The cedar's gone,' said Filth. 'Well, well.'

'Oh, the cedar's gone,' said the grandmother. 'Not so very long after Queen Mary. The sixties. She'd be pleased. It was what might be called a running sore, that tree. "Have it down," she told the Duchess (and her hardly moved in!). "It's in the wrong place. It blocks the light." "Lord Raglan used to climb in it," says her Grace. "It's not to be touched." "*Over my dead body*," the Duchess said. I heard the very words.'

'The tree was still the issue when I arrived,' said Filth.

He had not seen Queen Mary his first month at Badminton, after a three-week OCTU course in another camp. Once he saw a silvery pillar above him on a terrace. Once again he seemed to see something moving slowly inside a long glass gallery. Then one day, reading in the vegetable garden – he had begun to order Law books from London – there she was, watching him from over the hedge. It was a hot day but she was dressed in full rig – a long coat and skirt, pearls and brooches, and a rucked hat like a turban with a sweep to it. He stood up at once and she gave a strange half-bow and turned away. There was an attendant nearby who was knitting on four-peg needles. Knitting steadily, she turned about and followed the Queen. The next week he was invited to the house to tea.

It was served in the large salon where new acquaintances were tried out. If they made the grade there would be a future invitation to Her Majesty's private sitting-room upstairs. Big test. The Queen sat doing needlework, her lady-in-waiting sat picking over some scraps of cloth, and a fat noisy woman was shouting.

'*Over my dead body*,' she was saying, 'will you cut down my tree. Cut down my spinneys, my ivy, my woodlands, my bramble bushes. Cut down my *house*, but not the tree.'

Queen Mary continued with her blanket stitch. The lady-in-waiting looked exhausted and the fat woman came up alongside Eddie Feathers as the twelve-foot high doors to the salon were being held open by footmen in scarlet.

'She's impossible. I'm the Duchess of Beaufort. I know I look like somebody's cook, but that's who I am, and this is my house. She's only an evacuee,' she spat as she blew past, the doors being silently closed behind her.

Queen Mary looked across at Eddie and smiled.

After the tray had been put down (margarine on the bread, pineapple jam but really made from turnips, a terrible seed cake and some oatcakes) Queen Mary passed him an almost transparent cup half-full of pale water.

'Cream?' she asked.

'No, thank you.'

She nodded. There was no cream, anyway, and the milk looked blue.

The lady-in-waiting brought out a box of pills and dropped one in the Queen's cup and one in her own. 'Saccharine?' she said.

'Oh, no, thank you.'

'It is quite true. What my niece says is perfectly true. I am only an evacuee. A very unwilling evacuee.'

Eddie wondered what to say. 'I was once an evacuee,' he said. 'And very unwilling. And far too old.'

'I am far too old,' said the Queen. 'How old were you?'

'Eighteen.'

'Good gracious. How humiliating for you.'

'Yes. It was. My father sent for me to Malaya, to escape the War.'

'How disgraceful of him.'

'He had had a very bad time in 1914.'

'Yes. I see. But you escaped? To tell you the truth I don't altogether feel ashamed to have escaped. It was the Government's decision I should come here. They told me I would be much more trouble in London. In case of kidnap. Personally I think that a plane might come and bundle me off more easily from here. That of course is why you're all here. A hundred and fifty of you. Quite ridiculous.'

'Yes, your Maj –'

'Call me Ma'am.'

'You must miss being at the heart of things – Ma'am?'

'I don't, now. I'll tell you more another time.'

She looked pointedly at the lady-in-waiting who gathered up a skein of mud-coloured wool and passed it to Eddie who was having trouble with the turnip jam. 'Hold Her Majesty's wool, please.'

Eddie held out his hands and the wool was arranged upon them in a figure of eight. The lady-in-waiting began to roll it up into a ball. He felt a ninny.

'Do you think you will enjoy soldiering?' asked the Queen, looking hard at him.

He blushed and began to stammer.

'Ah yes. I see. You'll get over it. I know a boy like you.'

He walked in the park with her through the next hard winter. The ground was black, the trees sticks of opaline ice.

'We shall just walk up and down,' said Queen Mary. 'For an hour or so. We must get exercise at all costs. D'you see how the wretched ivy is coming back?'

'Did you walk like this, Ma'am, before you came here?'

'I've always tried to walk a great deal. You see my family runs to fat. They eat too much. My dear mother would eat half a bird and then a great sirloin for dinner, and she loved cream. And the Duchess – I used to walk in Teck but only round and round the box-beds. Sandringham was the place to walk, but somehow one didn't. One went about in little carts to watch them shooting. And one didn't walk in London of course. I luckily have magnificent Guelph health.'

'I have never been to London.'

She stood still with amazement. 'You have never been to London? Everybody has been to London.'

'Most of Badminton village has never been to London.'

'Oh, I don't mean the village. I mean that a gentleman, surely, has always been to London?'

'No, Ma'am. I've been in Wales and in the North –'

'You haven't seen the galleries? The museums? The theatre?'

'No, Ma'am.'

'That is a personable young man,' she said that evening, hard at work arranging family photographs in an album before getting down to the red despatch boxes the King sent her daily. She read them in private, and nobody was quite sure how many, but probably all.

'Very good-looking indeed,' said Mary Beaufort. 'He'll be useful at dinner parties.'

'We don't give dinner parties,' said the Queen. 'It would be out of kilter with the War effort. But we could ask a few of the Subalterns.'

'We could.'

'In fact it seems quite ridiculous that a boy like that should be billeted down in the stables. Why can't he come and live in the house, Mary? Do you know, he has never been to London?'

Eddie refused to live in Badminton House. He said he must stay with his platoon. He began to find the tea parties rather trying. The mud-coloured wool had been overtaken by a cloud of unravelled powder-blue which clung to his uniform in tufts. He let it be known that he had to work hard, and he settled to his Law in the stables.

But the tall shadow would fall across his book and he would have to find a garden chair and she would sit with him among the dying dahlias in the remains of the cutting garden – every foot of land, she had instructed, to be used for vegetables. The Duchess fumed, and one day came thumping down to look for Eddie and complain.

'She brought fifty-five servants,' she said. 'She's stopped them wearing livery because of the War and Churchill in that awful siren-suit. Six of them are leaving. They've worn scarlet since they were under-footmen and they're old and say they can't change. Can you do nothing with her?'

'What – me? No, your Grace. Couldn't; c-c-couldn't.'

'Well, you'll have to think of something. Distract her.'

'I've stopped the tree. Well, I hope s-s-so.'

'Oh, good boy. But listen, she's determined to take you to London. Her chauffeur, old Humphries, is half-blind and not safe. Once he lost Her Majesty for over an hour in Ashdown Forest. She won't sack him. And she makes him stop and pick up any member of the forces walking on the road. Once she picked up a couple who were walking the other way and once it was an onion seller. She'll be murdered, and then we'll all be blamed.'

'Eddie,' said the Queen, a little later. 'I am determined to get you to London. When I first came here I went back every week, you know, on the train. Then it became painful because of the bombing. The Guildhall. The City churches. All gone. And of course the antique shops are all closed or gone to Bath (you and I might perhaps go to Bath one day). But I have a great desire to see London again. It might not be patriotic to insist that the Royal coach be put back on the train, but I have plenty of my petrol ration untouched, and you could do the driving, on the main roads, Eddie, if it is too much for Humphries. We shall of course need two outriders.'

'I'm sorry, but I can't drive, Ma'am.'

The expedition was put off until Eddie had learned to drive, instruction being given in a tank on the estate.

'I can only drive a tank, Ma'am,' he said when a London visit was again suggested.

'The principle must be the same,' said the Queen.

'We must clear it with Security.'

She looked imperious. The ex-Empress of India. 'Well, we'll go out wooding, Eddie. Get my bodyguards and my axe. No, I'll keep my hat on. I'm determined to take you to London.'

It was fixed at last that Queen Mary should make the journey to London by the train, the Royal coach still being rested in a siding near Gloucester. Some of the Badminton staff were sent to wash it down and the stationmaster of Badminton railway station had to look out the white gloves he had worn to haul the Queen aboard the 6.15 a.m. in 1939 at the beginning of her evacuee life.

'Good luck, Ma'am.'

The lady-in-waiting followed her in, and Eddie and a couple of Other Ranks with rifles took up their posts.

'Hope you don't meet Jerry, Ma'am,' said the stationmaster. 'Everyone stand back from the lawns.'

'Oh, the bombing is totally over,' said Queen Mary. 'I shall go to the Palace and have a look at the ruins of Marlborough House. And there is a little shopping –'

He blew the whistle and waved the flag. The Queen's progress had cheered him up. She'd be back on the 5.15 from Paddington. She wasn't dead yet.

'She's got some spirit,' he told the empty platform. Even at Badminton there were no porters. 'We're better off than Poland. Or Stalingrad.'

Just before Paddington, Eddie in a different side-carriage alone, the Queen sent for him and handed him a slip of paper.

'Here are the things you ought to see. I haven't given you too many. It is not only a first visit but you will find it confusing without signposts, and all the bomb-damage. You ought to have time for the Abbey and take a glance at St James's Park and No.10. And Big Ben. Here we are. It's a pity you don't know anyone who could show you about. Have a splendid time. Now, lunch – I really don't know what to suggest.'

'I'll miss lunch, Ma'am. It's going to be a tight schedule.'

She stepped from the train. There was a bit of rather old red carpet down for her and she stood in silver grey with doves' feathers in her toque, grey kid gloves, ebony stick. A whisper began – 'It's Queen Mary. Hey look – Queen Mary' – and a crowd gathered up like blown leaves. There were feeble hurrahs and some clapping, growing stronger, and the little crowd closed round Her Majesty and the lady-in-waiting. The two bodyguards melted away.

Eddie, all alone, made at once for the taxi-rank and the bed-sit in Kensington of Isobel Ingoldby.

'I'm not sure how far it is,' he told the taxi-driver, after waiting in a long queue, tapping his leg with his military stick. His uniform helped him not at all for everyone seemed to be in uniform. 'It's Kensington. Off Church Street.'

'Twenty minutes,' he said, 'unless we're unlucky.'

'You mean an air raid?' Eddie was looking round the Paddington streets disappointedly. This was London: sandbags, shuffling people, greyness, walls hanging in space.

'Nah – air raids ain't a trouble now. We've licked all that. We have him on the run, unless he starts with his secret weapon, he talks about. Not that we believe he's got one.'

(They really do talk like the films, Eddie thought.)

'You're here. D'you want to borrer a tin 'at?'

He was set down at the end of a narrow curving street of shabby cottages with gardens. There was no paint anywhere and grime everywhere. Nobody much about, and most windows boarded up. Isobel Ingoldby's number must almost certainly be a mistake for it had Walt Disney lattice windows, and a shaggy evergreen plant trailing over it which would have sent Queen Mary into action before she'd even knocked at the front door. There was a squirrel made of plaster on the doorstep and a tin case full of empty milk bottles with a note saying *None Today. Do not ring.*

It's somebody's who's out. This couldn't be hers, he thought, at the gate, as the door opened and she was standing there.

His first thought was a blankness.

She was ordinary.

She was big and ordinary and bored.

She had a cigarette in her hand and leaned back against the door saying, 'Come on in then,' as if he had come to read a gas meter.

Her hair was untidy and too long. Her feet were bare and she wore a shapeless sort of dressing-gown.

'Ciao,' she said, closing the door behind him. He saw how tired she was, and sad.

And maybe disillusioned? Was she disillusioned about him, too? She'd last seen him in hospital, pale and almost dying, the centre of attention. But she had made no effort of any kind though she'd known he'd be coming. He'd written a fortnight ago. She looked as if she'd just turned out of bed. She was even yawning.

'You're tired?' he said.

'No. Well, yes. I'm always tired. Ghastly job.'

'I thought you were some sort of egghead hush-hush type?'

'I am. Of a cryptic variety.'

'What d'you mean?'

'Secret. D'you want –?'

She vaguely gestured towards the kitchen.

'Tea or something? A wee?'

'No. I thought of taking you out to lunch. To the Savoy, or somewhere?' He'd heard of the Savoy. He looked anxiously at her night clothes.

'I was there yesterday.'

'Isobel – what is it?'

'What's what?'

'What have I done? Have I changed or something? You said to come.'

She put out the cigarette on the hall table ashtray, caught sight of herself in the mirror and said, 'Oh my God! I forgot to comb my hair.' She turned to him and grinned and it was as if the sun had come out. The sloped cat's eyes were alive again. Her long arms went up behind her head to gather up her hair into a bundle and she pinned it there. A piece of it fell down, a lion-coloured tress. Slowly, she pinned it back again, her fingers long, and lovely, and her fingernails painted the most unflinching vermilion. The dressing-gown fell open when she dropped her hands and stretched them out to him.

'Oh Eddie. You are golden brown like a field of corn.'

Her fingertips were at his collar. When he took off his British warm, then his officer's jacket, he saw that she had loosened and then removed his tie. She draped it over a wall-light and then was in his arms.

On the kitchen floor, naked, he thought the taxi must still be outside. He had got out of it only a minute ago. Then he forgot all that; where he had come from, where in the world he had landed, which was upon a kitchen floor, the filthy lino torn and stuck up with some sort of thick paper tape. There was an old fridge on tall legs. It was gas. Lying on the floor beside her, then above her, he could see the fridge's blue flame. It must be the oldest fridge in the world – oh, my God, Isobel. Isobel.

Later, oh much, much later, they rolled apart.

'I don't like this lino,' he said. 'It's disgusting.'

'You're spoiled. Living in palaces.'

'I was not living in palaces when you last saw me.'

'You were hardly living at all.'

They had moved on to a tiny sitting-room which was in darkness. It smelled of booze and dust. They felt their way to a divan that stank of nicotine.

'Why is there no light?'

'Do we need it?'

'Oh, Isobel.'

'It's blacked-out. Permanently. Convenient. We've never taken down the shutters since the Blitz.'

'*We*?'

'The other girl and I.'

'Is she likely to come in?' His head was on her stomach. His tongue licked her skin. She was warm and alive and smelled of sweat and spice and he went mad for her again.

Later, 'Who is she?'

'No one you know. She's Bletchley Park. Like me.'

'It's a man, isn't it?'

'No. No, certainly not. Shall we go upstairs?'

The bedroom was lighter. It had a sloping ceiling and the windows looked country as if there had once been fields outside. It had the feel of a country place; a cottage. So here's London.

'It is a cottage,' she said. 'London's full of cottages. And of villages. This bed is a country bed. We found it here.'

The bed was high and made of loops of metal. Its springs creaked and groaned beneath them.

'Please never get rid of it. Keep it forever.'

The hours passed. Wrapped, coiled, melded together they slept. They woke. Eddie laughed, stretched out to her again.

'You are like a jungle creature,' he said. 'In an undiscovered country.'

'Eddie,' she said at last, winding herself into the sheets, 'I have something very important to say. How much time have we got? When's your train?'

'Five fifteen.'

'It's nearly five o'clock already.'

He fled the bed, he ran for the stairs, he limped and hopped into scattered garments, he yelled with terror.

She laughed and laughed.

He found one shoe, but the other was gone.

'This will finish me,' he said. 'This will be the end of the Army for me.'

She howled with laughter from the bedroom; came laughing down the stairs wrapped in the sheet, lighting a new cigarette.

'Don't laugh at me.'

'I am in love with you, Eddie.'

'I have a bad reputation already. With my Colonel. And I am in charge of Queen Mary. Oh God – there's my shoe!'

He was in his jacket, in his British warm, had found his cap as she wrapped herself around him.

'Eddie, Eddie. You look still the boy in the trees at High House.'

'What time is it? Oh God. I've fifteen minutes. There won't be a taxi.'

But there was a taxi. God has sent me a taxi, he thought. It was standing outside the door. 'Paddington,' he said. 'In ten minutes.

I'll give you ten pounds.' He did not look back to see whether she was watching.

'Ten pounds, sir.'

'Thank you. Thank you very much.' (It's only what I'd have spent at the Savoy. God but I'm hungry.)

'Yes. Platform one. Where's the bit of carpet? Is it gone?'

It was there. And word had gone round. Somehow a crowd had gathered beside the Royal coach and the top of the toque with its doves' feathers could be seen passing between the clapping avenue of loyal subjects. The lady-in-waiting was invisible, a small woman to begin with, and no doubt weighted down now with more wool. The bodyguards were already on the train. Eddie gave a brief nod to the guard and jumped into his private cabin, slammed the door and fell on the banquette.

I'll go along in a minute. Just get my breath.

The train began to steam slowly, powerfully, inexorably away from London.

Go along in a minute, he thought and fell asleep.

He woke to a crash and shriek of brakes. The whole train jolted, shuddered and stopped. Outside it was now dark and he jumped from his long blue velvet couch and made for the corridor, to meet one of the bodyguards coming to find him.

'Emergency, sir. Probably unexploded bomb on the line. Queen Mary's sent for you.'

The lady-in-waiting was trembling. From outside came a series of shouts. The train began to shunt backwards, squealing and complaining.

'It's the Invasion,' said the lady-in-waiting.

'Don't be ridiculous, Margaret,' said the Queen. 'Eddie, take her along to your compartment and find her an aspirin. She needs a rest. Then come back again and we can talk. I want to hear every single thing you've done today.'

'So *tiresome*,' she said an hour later. 'The carriage so dark. These blue spot-lights are very clever but they're just not bright enough to read by.' She fell silent. 'But it's nice to look out at the moonlight.'

'Yes, Ma'am.' (And he realised she was afraid. He'd heard that though she never showed it by a tremor she was terrified of kidnap.)

'And you did no more than that, Captain Feathers?' (Captain Feathers? What's this?) 'No more than go about in taxis? You didn't even go to the Savoy for luncheon as you'd so wished?'

'I'm afraid not. I found London – overwhelming. Kensington seemed quite like an unknown vil-vill-vill-village.'

'A *village*? How very odd. I was born there. In Kensington Palace. I never felt it a village.'

'I – couldn't find Kensington Palace.'

'Oh dear,' she said.

The train at last jerked forward, stopped, jerked again and then began to steam sweetly along towards the West.

'That *is* a pity,' said Her Majesty. 'By the way' (looking out at the moonlight) 'whatever has become of your tie?'

On the way home from their walk about the meadows around Badminton House, Old Filth asked the girl and her grandmother if they would stop the wheelchair at the post office for him to buy postcards. 'No, no,' he said. 'Let me get out and walk. Do me good,' and he hopped into the shop and back again, carrying three postcards of the village, all ready and stamped. He was able to hop around the car, and hold open the door for the grandmother as the girl put the folding chair back in the boot.

'So extremely kind of you,' he said. 'A splendid afternoon.'

Sitting by the reception desk he thought he would write the postcards at once though it was too late for the post, for a cloud no bigger than a man's hand had gathered around the recollection of his departure from home. He would write to Mrs-er – to *Kate* – and to Garbutt. Perhaps he would write to lacy Chloe, too, and make her day.

Then he found that he had never had Mrs-er's (Kate's) address. It was somewhere in the next village. It would be offensive to send it c/o Garbutt, for she had preceded Garbutt in his employment by years. He addressed one card to Garbutt at the house down the hill from his own, well known to him. Peep o'Day. Easy to remember. So was Chloe's: The Manor House, Privilege Lane. On Garbutt's card he wrote, 'Please say I'm sorry to Kate.'

He had one card left over now and wrote it to Claire, mentioning that he had sprained something but was otherwise having a very good holiday by himself in Gloucestershire at this beautiful hotel. He was exalted. His optimistic self, he felt, was just around the corner.

But in the early hours of the next morning he woke with a chilling certainty that all was not well. He switched on his bedside lamp, hopped from the bed, opened a window upon the night. He shivered, and then flushed and sweated. He went for a pee, then drank a glass of water, hopped back, hot and cold by turns, clambered between the sheets. He knew that he was ill.

He knew that he was very ill. He had no idea what it was, but he knew that he was not in control. He lay and waited.

He stretched his hand out to the bedside table drawer and felt about for the never-failing *Gideon's Bible* that had seen him through many a sleepless hotel night during his legal life. In skyscrapers in Hong Kong, in the Shangri-la in Singapore, the dear old Intercon in Dacca. Lonely places, until he'd been married and able to take Betty along with him. He thought he needed a *Gospel* tonight, and turned up one of Christ's ding-dongs with the lawyers.

He wondered, the pages shaking as he turned them, why Christ had so hated lawyers when He'd have been such a brilliant one Himself. Christ, when you considered it, was simply putting a Case. He may well have been enjoying the lawyers' examinations of him. Pilate's was his most respectable interrogation. Pilate had not been a lawyer, but another excellent lawyer manqué. Pilate and Christ had understood each other.

'We still use a little Roman Law, here,' he told Christ

tonight. 'The Law can always do with a going-over as you pointed out then. Execution should be entirely out. Execution leads only to victory for the corpse. You proved that,' he informed the Holy Ghost.

He dreamed for a little, drifted, read the Sermon on the Mount, remembered hearing that no child nowadays has heard of the Sermon on the Mount and most guess it is a book or a film. He thought benevolently how he should like to be upon another Bench listening to Christ going for the defence in a Case to do with, say, a land-reclamation.

A fist grabbed him in the chest and pain shot through him. He could not breathe. He stretched for the bell and kept his right hand on it as the pain sank down, then surged up again. It's the Hand of God, he thought. And nobody but God knows where the hell I am.

Garbutt's house was empty when the phone began to ring the next morning. He had gone to Privilege Road to help the tedious Chloe with her asparagus bed and they were both down in the garden when her phone began to ring, too.

'I'll leave it,' she said. 'It won't be anything.'

But it rang on.

She caught it as the other end was about to put it down.

'I'm very sorry to hear it,' she said. 'Yes. He's a neighbour but not a *close* friend. No – I don't think there are any relations. Well, he's over eighty. He's never had anything wrong with him in his life. The time comes. He's not very popular here in the village, I'm afraid. He treats his servants badly. Very difficult for you. I think there are some cousins in Essex. Oh, I see, you've tried them. Well, I can't help you. Goodbye.'

'Sir Edward's had a heart attack,' she said, returning to the asparagus bed. 'I said last week it was blood-pressure, the way he was behaving.'

'What? Where?' said Garbutt.

'Well, around his heart.'

'Where was the call from?'

'I didn't ask.'

Garbutt blundered her out of the way, ran through her French doors and across her pastel Chinese carpet, dialled 1471, then pressed three.

'He's in hospital,' said the hotel. 'The ambulance came very quickly. We were surprised. He'd been so much better. He'd been out in the afternoon and eaten an excellent dinner.'

'Had he been ill already, then?'

'Yes, he arrived with a sprained ankle. Do you want the name of the hospital? I hope you will excuse us asking but will there be funds to pay his account?'

'Funds have never been a trouble to him.'

'Thank you. We were beginning to grow very fond of him.'

'People do,' said Garbutt, and phoned Kate, and then his wife.

Garbutt found Filth, looped up to drips and scans, trying to shut out the quack of the television sets and the clatter of the public ward where male and female lay alongside each other in various stages of ill health. Like Pompeii.

It was an old hospital. The windows were too high to see anything except the wires and concrete of unexciting buildings and the sky. The light was not the pearly light of yesterday in the meadows of Badminton, which Filth was trying to remember and decide when and where it had been and whom he had been with. Memory, he thought. Memory. My memory has always been so reliable. Perhaps too reliable. It has never spared me. *Memory and desire*, he thought. Who said that? *Without memory and desire life is pointless*? I long ago lost any sort of desire. Now memory.

Suddenly he knew that this was what had been the matter with him for years. He had lost desire. Not sexual desire, that had been a poor part of his nature always. He had been furtive about the poverty of his sexual past. Dear Betty – she had been very undemanding. He had never told her about the buttermilk business and had skimmed over Isobel Ingoldby. Whatever would the young make of him today? It seemed they were all like rabbits and started haphazardly as soon as they reached double figures. He found them repellent.

And homosexuals repellent, if he were honest. And divorce repellent. Blacks – here he was disturbed by a cluster of different coloured people surrounding his bed. These are not the black people of the Empire, he thought, and then realised that that was exactly what most of them were. 'Any of you chaps Malays?' he asked. 'Malaya's my country. *Malaysia* now, of course. And Ceylon's Sri Lanka, Lanka's what my friend Loss called it, and he should know. It was full of his uncles. That's what he said before he went down the trough. Bombed by the bloody Japanese, I expect. Oh, sorry.' The lead figure in the performance around his bed was Japanese. 'Didn't realise. It's your West Country accent.'

'OK, grandpa,' said the Japanese. 'Take it easy.'

Filth's days passed. Various bits of equipment were detached from him. Once he thought that Garbutt was sitting at the end of the bed and gave a feeble wave. 'Very sorry about this. How's Mrs-er? Very sorry to have upset Mrs-er. Feeling better. I'd like to see a priest, though.' Then he slept, and woke in the night trying to ring a bell for a priest.

'It's not Sunday,' said a nurse. 'Or are you a Catholic? You're getting better. Talk to them in the morning. Go to sleep, old gramps. Think positive.'

Times have been worse than this, he thought. Much worse. It's just there's no chance of many more of them, of times of any sort, now. That's absolutely rationally true, a serious, even beautiful equation. Life ends. You're tired of it anyway. No memory. No desire. Yet you don't want it to be over. Not quite yet.

Bloody memory.

'I was very happy round here, you know, in the War,' he said to a passing Sikh. 'I was a friend of Queen Mary. She remembered my birthday. She sent me chocolate.'

'Who's Queen Mary?' asked the Sikh in an Estuary accent. 'The Queen Mum?'

'While I lived here in Gloucestershire,' said drowsing Filth, 'I rather buried my head.'

'Bury it now,' said the Sikh, 'and get to sleep.'

'Before I go,' said Filth, 'I really do want to see a priest.'

But when they found him a priest next day, he was feeling much better, was loosed from his bonds, was sent to a terrible place to wash, was given cornflakes and a type of meat which smelled of onions and was laced with a fluid called 'brown sauce', and was told that he would later on be going home.

Moreover, the priest, when he arrived, was wearing jeans and a T-shirt and Filth did not believe in him. He would have preferred a female to this one, and that was saying something. His confession would have to be postponed. He sat and read the *Daily Telegraph* in a small, contained cubicle, his carrier bag at his feet. He sat there all morning, and at some point dozed off, thinking of other occasions in his life of total reversion, of failure.

After six months he had been posted away from Badminton. The War had changed. We were now on the winning side and there was a new jauntiness. Queen Mary's staff unpacked her three suitcases in the attics and he was sent to the War Office on the mistaken premise that he was a linguist and well-connected. He experienced the Mall on VE Day and was released to Oxford much more quickly than his War record deserved. He took a First in Law after only two years and was called to the Bar and set about the much harder matter of finding a seat in somebody's Chambers.

It was the winter still talked of, half a century on: 1947.

Memory and desire, he thought.

Chambers

The January rain of 1947 slopped down upon dilapidated Lincoln's Inn Fields, puckering the stagnant surfaces of the static-water tanks implanted in its grass. Eddie Feathers observed it from the passage in a small set of undistinguished Chambers in New Square. He kept the door open between the passage and the Senior Barrister's empty room on the front of the building, otherwise he had no view except the dustbins at the back. On days like this and on days of smog which were getting more frequent though coal was rationed to a bag a week, he could look through the door to what he might look forward to if the old fellow stopped coming in altogether. A good old room with magnificent carved Elizabethan fireplace and a large portrait of the Silk's unhappy-looking wife: the sort of wartime bridal face that wished it had waited.

In an adjoining, equally historic, equally dusty room but lacking an uxorial photograph sat the only other member of Chambers, usually asleep. These rooms had been built as legal Chambers hundreds of years ago and had housed a multitude of lawyers from before the Commonwealth. Wigs in these rooms had been worn naturally, like hats. Then even hats around Chambers had gone – bowler hats had also just about disappeared by 1947, though Eddie Feathers had bought one for five excessive pounds, and it hung, laughably, on a hook inside the Chambers' street door.

The passage was bitterly cold. There were no carpets, no curtaining, a small spluttering heater. He sat before a splintered table where transcripts of a dispute stood two feet high – almost indecipherable blueprints concerning the installation of new water-closets throughout a bombed government building, his annotation of which went down at about a sixteenth of an inch per hour.

Sir, his school, his college, Queen Mary, all pointed stern fingers at Eddie. Habit dictated. There had been black hours before. Diligence gets you through. Keep going. Oh God – why?

Gloucestershire and Oxford kept breaking in on him. Christ Church meadow, the bells stumbling and tumbling, calling down the High. The wallflowers – the smell of the velvet wallflowers outside his set of rooms. The emptiness of his Quad, returning home at night. Hardly a soul about. Music from the open windows. And the spring there, and the politics and the friends. Too much work. Too much work to go to parties, even to attend the Union, meet any girls, too many men just up from school drinking themselves silly, schoolchildren who had missed the War. Leaving Oxford had surprised him by its finality.

The rain fell. In the far room with the door shut he heard the comatose, under-employed Head of Chambers fart and yawn. The fart was an elderly fart – lengthy, unmusical and resigned.

Eddie found that he was crying, and mopped his face. He thought he might as well go home for the day.

But, no. Better not. Another quarter-inch of notes. No point in going out in the rain. It was a longish walk to the Aldwych tube station and he had no macintosh. There were a couple of changes on his tube (everyone wheezing and smelling of no soap) to get back to his bed-sit in sleazy Notting Hill. Then out again for something to eat at an ABC café: sausage and mash, stewed apple and custard, keep within a shilling. There was still no sign of his inheritance. He'd been told it might take years to prove the death, let alone the Will. He was still unable to put his mind to the imagining of his father's end. No friend of his father, no official notification from the Foreign Office. Eddie pushed down the guilt that he had made no enquiries. There had been no communication from the aunts. 'I shall learn one day,' was all he allowed himself.

He must get a bike. Save the fares. He was earning a hundred pounds a year devilling for the absent Silk with the difficult wife. Three hundred a year in all, with the very odd Brief. He had one good suit, kept his shoes soled and heeled, washed his new-fangled nylon shirt every evening and hung it round the geyser in the communal bathroom at his lodgings, to dry for the morning. To keep up appearances before solicitors and clients. Not that there were any clients. Not for him. Not for years yet. Maybe never. Nobody knew him. Along the passage the old Silk farted again.

It had been nearly a year ago that Eddie, walking round the once-beautiful London squares one evening – without money there was nothing else to do, he was putting the hours in until bedtime – had thought of the building and engineering aspect of the Law. The War was over. One day – look at Germany – rebuilding of the ruins must surely occur in this country. Building disputes, he thought. There'll be hundreds of them. Enquiring about, he had found a set of engineering Chambers that had been bombed and moved into this backwater of Lincoln's Inn.

There was not even space for a Clerk's room. This had had to be rented across a yard. The Senior Clerk, who looked like an unsuccessful butler and spent much time in rumination, left early after lunch for South Wimbledon. The clever Junior Clerk, Tom, hideously unemployed, worked like mad around the pubs at lunchtime among the Clerks of other Chambers, trying to get leads on coming Cases and plotting where he would move to next. He liked Eddie and was sorry for him. 'I should pack it in, sir,' he said one day. 'You're worth better than this – First from Oxford. I can't sell you here. Go to New Zealand.'

I might, thought Eddie today, looking through the door to the grander room and then beyond it out of the old, absent Silk's window to the rain falling. Between the building and the Inn garden where stood a great tree which had survived other wars, a white Rolls-Royce was parked. He could see the chauffeur inside it in a green uniform. Not usual. Eddie sighed, and lifted the next pages of transcript off the pile.

The street door of the Chambers now banged open against the wall and feet came running towards Eddie's alley. The Junior Clerk, macintosh flapping – he'd been waiting to go home – flung open his door and shouted, 'Come on, sir. Quick. Quick, sir! Get up. Leave those papers. Get into that front room. Behind the desk. You've got a client.'

'Client?'

'New solicitor. Get the dust off those sets of papers. Smarten your clothing. Where's that classy clothes-brush of yours? Here. I'll put his wife's photo out of sight. Wrong image. You're young and free to travel. I think you're on the move.'

'Move?'

'I've got you a Brief. It's a big one. Four hundred on the Brief and forty a day. Likely to last two weeks.'

'Whoever –?'

'Don't ask me. It's Hong Kong. It's a Chinese dwarf.'

'You've gone insane, Tom. It's a hoax.'

'Turned up in that Rolls. I've had him sitting in the Clerk's room twenty minutes. I'll bring him over.'

'WAIT!'

'Wait? Wait? Look, it's a pipeline failure in Hong Kong. You're on your way.'

'A *Chinese dwarf*?'

'Come back. Where you going, sir? I bring him over here to you, you don't go running after him.'

'Where is he now?' Eddie shouted from the courtyard.

'He's still in the Clerks' room. I told him I was coming to see *if* you were free. I bring him to *you*. *Gravitas*, sir.'

But Eddie was gone, over the courtyard, under the lime tree, running in the rain. The chauffeur in the Rolls turned to look, raising an eyebrow.

Eddie ran into the Clerks' room, where Albert Loss was seated on the sagging purple sofa playing Patience.

'*Coleridge!*'

'Spot the lady. Kill the ace of spades.'

'*Coleridge*! God in heaven, Coleridge. But you're dead. The Japanese killed you.'

'Colombo didn't fall. You are an amnesiac. There were initial raids. And then they left us alone. You should have stayed. I found my uncle. Several of them. All attorneys. And so I became one too.'

'This is the most wonderful. . . . How ever did you find me?'

'Law Lists, my dear old chum. Top of the Law Lists. Thanks to me. I directed you, you will remember, towards the Law. And now I am Briefing you. My practice is largely in Hong Kong. I hope you have no serious family ties?'

'Not a tie. Not a thread. Not a cobweb – *Coleridge!*'

'Good. Then you can fly to Hong Kong next week? First class, of course. We must not lose face before the clients. We'll put you up in the Peninsular.'

'I'll have to read the papers.'

'Nonsense, Fevvers. You'll do it all in your head. On the plane. Open and shut Case, and I taught you Poker. You can *think*. I'm flying back myself tomorrow.'

'This is a dream. You're exactly the same. You haven't aged. By the way, what happened to my watch?'

'Ah, that had to be sacrificed in the avuncular search. But *you* have aged, Fevvers. You have been aged by your Wartime experiences, no doubt?'

'You could say that. *Coleridge*, come on! Let's go out. Where are you staying?'

'The Dorchester, of course. But there is no time for social punishment. I fly tomorrow and I must see my builders. I'm buying a house in the Nash Terraces of Regent's Park. All in ruins. Practically free at present. If you want it to rent, after the pipeline, it's yours. By the way, were you met?'

'Met?'

'At Liverpool? Off the old Portuguese tub?'

'Yes. Yes, I was –'

'I was forced to borrow your address book. I'm afraid it has fallen by the way. My uncles were very close to the Corps of Signals. And of course I have a phenomenal memory.'

'You should be a spy.'

'Thank you, but I am in gainful employment. It's very good to see you, Feathers. Very nice clothes-brush. Do you want it?'

'Yes. *Coleridge*!'

'And by the way,' Albert Loss said at the car, the chauffeur towering above him, holding a brolly, 'while I'm away in Hong Kong, do make use of the Royce.'

Last Rites

'Indigestion,' said the hotel to Claire over the telephone. 'A very bad case of indigestion.'

'He said on the postcard a sprained ankle.'

'The indigestion followed. It was the prawns. Looked identical to a heart attack. He's been in hospital. He's back here again now recovering from the hospital. Can we get him for you? He's out in the sun, well wrapped up. Who shall we say?'

'Will you say Claire? And that I had his postcard.'

'We were very glad of those postcards.'

'Hello,' said Filth, tottering in. 'I was wondering if someone could find me a priest.'

The bar listened. The nice girl came and sat him in a chair. Dialling the number for him, handing him the phone, she said, 'Sir Edward, the priest business was last week.'

'What? Hello? Claire? There are things I want to get off my chest. This episode was rather alarming. Some unfinished business. You know what I'm talking about.'

'I have no idea.'

'You and I and Babs.'

'What about us?'

'And Cumberledge?'

There was silence.

'Oh, long, long ago,' she said.

'But I need to tell someone, even so. What happened to your priest? The one in the church with all the marble babies?'

'Do you mean Father Tansy? I thought he was anathema to you.'

'Well, yes. He was. But I keep remembering him. Can you find him for me?'

'But you're in Gloucestershire. And I hear you can't walk and have had a suspected heart attack.'

'False alarm. Got over-excited reading the *Gospels*.'

'Say goodbye to her now, Sir Edward. We'll bring you your lunch in the lounge. You still have to take care.'

'Goodbye, Claire. Thank you for ringing. I'll ring again.'

The day wore on. He sat in remote reveries. They brought him tea.

Bloody good of them to have me back here, he thought. All thanks to Loss I can pay for it. Set me on my path. But I've worked for it myself, too. I've worked for my millions. Survived them too. Loss didn't.

He began to doze and was woken by the nice girl and her grandmother with a bunch of asters. 'You should keep off prawns,' said the grandmother. 'After seventy you should keep off prawns. You never saw Queen Mary even look at a prawn.'

'It may have been the banana split,' said her granddaughter.

'I don't eat bananas,' said Filth.

Next day came a letter from Claire in her trailing bright blue handwriting.

Dear Teddy,

It so happens that Father Tansy is coming to your part of the world to visit his Boys' Club in Falmouth. Babs will be with him. It all seems prophetic. I have told them where you are.

As to the matter of our rotten childhood, old cousin, you should forget it. I have never let what we did trouble me, even in dreams. I had no difficulty with it at the time and I've never felt the need to speak about it since. Oliver, for instance, does not know, and neither did my late-lamented husband. What would now be called 'The Authorities' spirited us all away so fast after the death that it didn't get much into the papers. Now, it would have dominated the telly for a month.

D'you know that I met Cumberledge again? It was only a few years ago. As a matter of fact, it was the day you were staying with us, when Oliver took me to Cambridge for tea with some grandee from his old college, a Dean who's still in residence. Someone who was kind to Oliver when he was up. Well, all the time we were in the old boy's rooms I felt puzzled, as if I knew him. He seemed quite unaware of me. My surname has changed and it was three-quarters of a century on and Oliver had never mentioned that I'd been a Raj Orphan. Oliver told me his name on the way home and after you'd all gone I sat down here in High Light and wrote him a letter, hoping I wasn't stirring up something best forgotten. We struck up a thoroughly boring correspondence.

I'm not sure whether I'm pleased or not that he never referred to the murder. Well yes, of course I'm sure. I was *not* pleased. I should have liked to hear what he thought we'd all been at. I often think, when I'm reading in the papers about a murder, that the murderer is the last person to be aware of the crime. Sometimes he is not aware of it for years, I'd guess. Well, you'll know all about that. Murderers are the possessed.

I'm not saying there's no such thing as guilt. And wickedness. I'm saying there is confusion and derangement in the mature murderer. What is so interesting about our murder is that there was neither. No confusion. No derangement. We three – not Cumberledge – were absorbed in the process of handing over responsibility to the powers of darkness whom we had met as children, and who had met us. We were thoroughly engaged, us three. Still untamed. We were of the jungle.

Poor Babs – she's probably the best of us – went mad. She's maddish most of the time. But she's still Babs. Ma Didds was cruellest of all to her. Stopped her singing. Gagged her mouth. Babs became castrated. Ugly in mind, body and estate. Grows uglier now. And yet I remember her dazzling for a while when she was in the War.

You, dear Teddy, Ma Didds feared because of your height

237

and strength and prodigious good looks. Oh, how unfair are our looks! Didds knew she could never make you ugly. She worked on your stammer. She was afraid of your silences. You were not like a child then. You are more of a child now. Betty came and stripped the years away from you in what looked like the perfect marriage. She never asked for more than you could give. Others gave her passion. You were a saint about Veneering. You were a wall of alabaster. You saved each other. You and Betty. I'd guess, neither of you ever spoke of it.

But nobody ever loved you like I did, Teddy.

Yet I was the coldest of us. I was the harshest. I was the actress. I was the little pretty one who never did wrong. I was the one who suggested the murder.

Cumberledge never made a decision in his quiet life (I don't know how he got so high up in the Army before he was wafted into Cambridge). He was utterly passive – all his weeping and screaming as she approached him with the whip (I am writing down what I have never before even been able to think about). But something deep in him remained untouched by her. I bet he became amiable and soppy. A man always falling in love.

You, Teddy, were horribly touched by her. You became no good at love. I don't think you ever had many friends at school. I'm the same, if I'm honest. I can't love. I'm all charm. Babs needs love. Needs it as her daily bread. Will try for it anywhere. But she repels, the poor old thing. Doesn't wash now – that's a bad sign. It won't help her with Father Tansy. She says she once had an *affaire* with Cumberledge. All fantasy.

D'you know, the one who needed love most was Ma Didds. All the hatred was love gone wrong. What did she ever get from old Pa Didds and all that chapel?

Not that as children we could have been expected to know, but I had an inkling when she took me on her smelly old lap and crooned over me and gave me buttered bread. I knew already where *my* bread was buttered. I'd been sent away younger than any of you, and my parents were faceless; but I was, and am, the toughest. I'm very glad I thought of the murder. I thoroughly enjoyed it. So don't fret. It was you who struck the blow, dear Teddy, but they can't hang you now.

Love from Claire

He tore the letter up.

I am old at last, he thought. I should be cold too. But I am casting off the coldness of youth and putting on the maudlin armour of dotage. I am not a religious man. Claire does not shock me, as she would most people. *Why* do I want a priest? Rites? Ceremonies? I despise myself. It's all superstition. Yet I know that I must tell someone that when I was eight years old I killed a woman in cold blood.

The West wind of the equinox bashed suddenly against the conservatory glass of the hotel lounge where Filth sat, now alone. Then the wind stopped and he slept. In his sleep he heard the steady beating of a drum, and started awake, thinking that it was his heart. They helped him back to his bedroom where the grandmother's asters shone on the window-sill.

'I am so undeservedly lucky,' he said to the chambermaid later, beginning the repair of his damaged image. (Claire's terrifying letter.) He smiled his lovely smile.

'Lucky in material things anyway,' he said when he was alone again, curtains closed, lying in the sweet dark. 'Their kindness is only because they've found out that I'm rich. There'll be no trouble with the bill.' Considering other people's pragmatism, he found that Claire's beastly letter receded.

But, dropping into sleep, a great face flooded across his dream landscape, filled the screen of his sleeping consciousness, loomed at him – disappeared. 'Go away, Veneering,' Filth shouted after it. 'I'm not ready to talk. Not yet.'

A few days later, Father Tansy turned up at the delectable hotel, with a woman in a wavy nylon skirt and grey nun's head-gear who turned out to be Babs.

Filth was in bed again. He had been advised to stay there for a day or two and not trouble himself with visitors, and his curtains were pulled across the daylight when the manager of the hotel knocked and eventually put his head around his door, and switched on the light, and Babs and the priest beheld the catafalque figure of Filth under the sheet, his ivory nose pointed upwards, the nose of a very old man.

'Perhaps not long?' said the manager. 'Don't stay too long.'

Babs said she would go out now and take her dog for a walk. Then Father Tansy shut the door behind him, opened the curtains and switched off the light. He picked up the bedside phone and ordered room-service luncheon in an hour's time. Then he ran round the bedroom removing drooping asters and opening all the windows. He found Filth's dressing-gown and manoeuvred him into it, heaved the old bones off the bed, slid the ivory fans of Filth's feet into his Harrods leather bedroom-slippers, sat Filth on an upright chair and set a table in front of him.

'Have I shaved?' asked Filth. 'Oh dear, I do hope so.'

'Never mind that,' said Tansy. 'Wake up. You have sent for me at last. I have been waiting patiently.'

'You have a great idea of your own importance,' said Filth. 'I remember you, awash in that great marble church.'

'Not my *own* importance,' said Tansy. 'I follow Another's importance. I try to follow the personality of Christ, and am directed by it.'

'I don't believe in all that,' said Filth. 'But there's something, somewhere, that's urging me to talk to a – well, I suppose, to a priest. You are the only priest I know. How you got here, I don't know. What I'm doing here, I don't know. I've been dreaming lately. About Queen Mary.'

'Queen Mary?'

'Yes. And my father. And a – murder. And other loose ends.'

Father Tansy waited with bright eyes, like a squirrel. 'Carry on.'

'I suppose it's going to be a confession,' said Filth. 'I'm glad you're not hidden in one of those boxes. I'm not up to that.'

'I know.'

'I can't start until Babs comes back. She's part of it. And I've been seriously ill.'

240

'Sir Edward, you can begin by telling me what's the matter with you. And I don't want to hear about prawns and strained ligaments.'

After a time Filth said, 'All my life, Tansy, from my early childhood, I have been left, or dumped, or separated by death, from everyone I loved or who cared for me. I want to know why.'

'You are a hero in your profession, Sir Edward.'

'That's an utterly different matter. And in fact I don't believe you. Nobody remembers me now at the Bar. My work is quite forgotten. I was once famous for some Pollution Law. All out-of-date now. I want to tell you something. When my Chambers were moved to a newly built office block, like a government department, costing millions which by then we could all afford – there were thirty-six members of Chambers when I decided to go permanently to Hong Kong – the old Clerk, who was retiring, took me down into the basement under the Elizabethan building where I began, and there was a sea of Briefs there, three feet deep, bundled up with pink tape. "We don't know what to do with it," he said. "We've decided to get a firm in to throw it on a dump." That was years of my life. Years and years.'

'It's not often,' said the priest, 'made as clear to us as that. I see it in my empty pews.'

'It has all been void. I am old, forgotten and dying alone. My last friend, Veneering, has died. I miss him but I never quite trusted him. My most valuable friend was a card-sharp and my wife hated him though he made our fortunes at the Far Eastern Bar. He was killed on Nine-Eleven. A passenger in one of the planes. Still playing cards, I imagine. Hadn't heard from him for years.'

Babs came back in and made the dog lie down. It immediately climbed on Filth's bed and lay looking across at him as if he'd seen him somewhere before.

'The point is,' said Filth, seated at his table, recovering a little of his former authority when addressing the Court, 'the point is, I have begun to wonder whether my life of loneliness –

241

always basically I have felt quite alone – is because of what I did when I was eight years old, living with Babs and Claire in Wales, fostered by a woman called Mrs Didds.'

Babs scratched her leg in its thick grey stocking and looked out of the window. 'Go on then, Teddy,' she said. 'Spit it out.'

Father Tansy, no trace now of the prancing comic of his parish church, his Office completely dominating him, sat still, and nodded once.

When Filth was obviously unable to begin, Babs said, 'Oh, I'll do it, then.'

There was a silence.

'She hurt us,' Babs said. 'She had that sort of smiling face, plump and round, that when you look closer is cruel. Nobody had noticed. Probably, when she first fostered children she was different. Pa Didds was a nice old man but he just sat about. Then he died. They'd had no children of their own. By the time the three of us arrived, she'd begun to hate children, but she had to keep on fostering because there was nothing else. They went on sending her children. From all over the Empire. When the children complained. . . . Most never did, they thought she was normal. Anyway the children couldn't complain until they'd got away, somewhere else. And there wasn't anywhere else. We were all sent to her for four or five years. You know, longer than we'd been *alive*. The complaining ones were thought to be cowards. We had to copy the Spartans in those days. You should have seen the illustrations in children's books of the Raj then. Pictures of children beating *each other* with canes at school. The prefectorial system. Now it would be thought porn. It was Cumberledge, of course, she hated most.'

'He was there when we arrived,' said Filth. 'In bed. Not speaking. He was pale and fat and sobbing and he didn't come down to tea. "What's the matter with the other boy?" Babs asked. "He's wet his bed again," Ma Didds said, and she laid one of her long whips over the table. "And he'll have to wash his own sheets."'

'I shared a room with him,' said Filth, eventually. 'He smelled and I hated him. He slept on the floor to save the sheets, but then he'd wet his pyjamas. He used to take them off and lie on the boards, but then she'd beat him a second time for removing his pyjamas. We had to watch.'

'How long did it last?'

'Years,' said Babs. 'They merged, the years. It seemed our whole lives. We forgot there had been anything different. Anything before.'

'Not altogether,' said Filth. 'Claire – by the way, she never hurt Claire – Claire was younger and very pretty and she used to sit her on her knee and comb her hair. Before Pa Didds went off into hospital and died, he used to be nice to me and Babs. There were several good moments.'

'He liked you,' said Babs. 'Took you for walks. He never took me for walks. I used to sing hymns very, very loud. She hated my singing. She bandaged my mouth.'

'And the end of the story?' asked the priest.

'Claire decided on the end of the story one day while we were gathering the hens' eggs in the hen-house. It was our job. We liked it – all the fluster and the commotion and the rooster crowing. It was a day when Cumberledge had been flogged and flung back to his bed and was crying again. It was almost as if Ma Didds loved Cumberledge in some horrible cruel way, especially after Pa Didds died. As if she hated herself. She used to sit rocking herself and holding her stomach after we'd all gone to bed. We peeped over the stairs and saw her. As if she had a baby inside her.'

'She shut me in cupboards,' said Filth. 'I began to stammer even worse than I did already. Then she would shout at me to answer her politely, and when I couldn't get any words out she'd bang my face against the wall or box my ears, and shout at me again to answer her.'

'She fed us well,' said Babs. 'Great plates of food. Big stews and home-made bread. "You should see the food they eat," she told them at the chapel. "Fat as pigs." She stuffed us. Except for Claire. Claire left half of hers and smiled at Ma Didds like an angel. She never punished Claire.'

'Claire is the cleverest of us,' said Babs.

243

'And so –?' said Tansy.

'And so, this evening in the hen-house, Cumberledge indoors, inarticulate as ever, Claire, she was only six, said, "I think we should kill her."'

'We all three knew how to do it. We'd had ayahs. And Eddie had his amah.'

'I used to watch her and the whole village in the compound,' said Filth. 'They would kill a cockerel as a sacrifice and then they'd beat a drum. The incantations went on for hours. They burnt things that belonged to the one they wanted dead. Hair. A button. And feathers from the cockerel. Then the person died.'

'You believed it?'

'Oh yes. It was true. It happened. Always.'

'I knew how to kill a cockerel,' said Filth. 'Ada could do it. I used to watch. But when I tried to catch Ma Didds's rooster, it was too strong for me, so I caught a hen and killed it instead. It's very easy. Ada used to tie the legs together and then break the neck by twirling it hard, upside down, round and round, in the dry mud. I did it on the floor of the hen-house. Ma Didds was at chapel. We were always alone on Sunday nights. I cut off its head with the bread knife and took it inside. Claire had taken some of Ma Didds's hair out of her comb. We took the matches and lit the hair and the hen's head in the hearth, and Babs sang.'

'I sang *There's a friend for little children*,' said Babs, '*Above the bright blue sky*, and Eddie banged saucepan lids together. We hadn't expected the hen's head to smell so bad or to be so difficult to burn. Then we heard her coming and we all ran upstairs.'

'We'd forgotten to shut the hen-house door,' said Filth, 'and that was the first thing she saw, and one or two hens roosting on the roof. She came thundering in and took up a cane and then she smelt the feathers. She shouted, "Cumberledge!" and started up the stairs. When she went upstairs, she always had to hold her stomach up. It hung down. It was repulsive. So she came up the stairs holding her stomach in one hand, and her other arm raised holding the cane. "This time I'll *break* you, Cumberledge!"'

'But at the top,' said Babs, when Filth could not continue, 'Eddie stepped forward from the room he shared with Cumberledge. Claire and I had come out of our room and were standing near. Cumberledge did not move from under his bed. He didn't see it. But we saw. We saw Eddie catch hold of her wrist, the wrist holding the cane high. He was above her on the stairs and taller than her already. And he just stood there, holding her wrist above her head. And she said, "Let go my wrist. I am going to see to Cumberledge." And she had to clutch her stomach with her other hand.'

'And so,' said Filth, 'I let go of her very suddenly so that she fell backwards down the stairs. And lay still at the bottom of them. Before she lay still, there was a – crack. Like a snapped tree.'

'I ran to clear up the burnt head,' said Babs, 'and Eddie went to look after Cumberledge. Claire put on her coat and went down to the village to get help. But she was a very long time because it was a dark night and she got lost. She's always hated the dark. So Teddy and I got into bed together to be close. We couldn't make Cumberledge get in with us. In the end Teddy and I went to sleep and we only woke up when they were clearing Ma Didds away. She wasn't dead, as it turned out, but she died the next day. They had to do an emergency operation on her for cancer of the stomach. That's what she died of, they said. She'd have died in a few days, anyway.'

'*What*?' said Filth. 'Nobody ever told me that.'

'And the other boy? Cumberledge?'

'Cumberledge's so-called guardians took him away at once. There was a scandal about his condition and he vanished from us. We were kept down in the village until Auntie May could come, and Eddie's Sir.'

'Were questions asked?'

'So far as I know, none. There had been rumours for a long time. But Welsh villages stick together against foreigners, and we were all very foreign children there. Wales was more secretive in those days and the language defeated us. But nobody suggested anything criminal about us.'

'Nobody,' said Babs. 'Claire even got some presents. Everyone always loves Claire.'

In this expensive and benign hotel in the English late autumn light, they sat, all three, in silence.

'You have come to me asking for absolution?' asked Father Tansy. 'You repent?'

Eddie Feathers, Old Filth, the Judge, Fevvers, a Master of the Inner Temple, Teddy – pillar of justice, arbitrator of truth – said nothing.

'No,' he said at last. 'I don't. I can't.'

'No, I don't either,' said Babs. 'And I know Claire doesn't.'

'Did Cumberledge survive? Is he sane?'

'Very much so,' said Filth. 'I next met him in the dark in Oxford. During the War when I was lost in the snow. I didn't realise who it was. Between eight and eighteen we all change utterly. Yet years later I somehow realised. He was coming out of a blacked-out church. He had a calmness and a kindness. He was Army. He wrote when Betty died. His essence was unharmed.'

'He became a grandee,' said Babs. 'He's retired to Cambridge. A grandee.'

'There are those who are given Grace,' said Tansy. 'But you yourself wanted to make some sort of confession, Sir Edward?'

'I wanted to express my pity,' said Filth. 'My pity for her. For Ma Didds. I've tried hundreds of Cases, many more wicked than anything here. Some I still cannot bear to think about. I don't mean I cannot bear to think about my Judgements – you have to be thick-skinned about that – I cannot bear to think about the cruelty at the core of this foul world. Or the vengeance dormant even in children. All there, ready, waiting for use. Without love. Cumberledge was given Grace. That's all I can say. We were not.'

They still sat on.

The dog stretched on the bed and yawned and jumped down, bent over and rested its head on Babs's knobbly knee.

'We'll say the General Confession,' said Tansy. 'Together.'

They did, Filth remembering it being hammered into him by Sir.

Tansy then said, 'Let us pray. Remember these Thy children, oh merciful Lord. Heal them and keep them in Thine everlasting arms.'

The Revelation

His house was clean and polished, his garden neat. A note on the kitchen table said, *Butter, cheese, milk in fridge. Eggs. Bread in crock. Bacon, etc. Welcome home. Kate.* Through the windows, looking towards the Downs, he saw movement in his apple tree and a next-door child dropped out of it, eating fruit, and wandered nonchalantly over the lawn as if he owned it. The hedge must have a hole in it, he thought. It might as well stay. His mail had been neatly stacked on his desk, the fire laid ready to light. She'd stuck some shop flowers in a vase.

It had been a good drive home. Most enjoyable. Christmas coming.

Very pleasant seeing poor Babs again. And the parson chap. Holiday full of events. And tomorrow he must see the doctor.

His ankle was very much better, and he had no trace of trouble with his heart – or digestion. All that was the matter with him now was the onset of winter aches and pains. His arthritis was remarkably mild for his age, they always said, especially considering the age of his damp old house.

'I am about to make another journey,' he said the next day after his visit to the surgery in Shaftesbury. 'Good morning, Mrs – Kate. How very good to see you. Thank you for the provisions. The house looks very well. I've brought you a keepsake from Gloucester. Where's Garbutt?'

*

'Garbutt,' he said. 'Good morning. Did I imagine it? Yes, of course I did. You didn't by any chance visit me in wherever it was I've been? I had some sort of dream. There were some very odd doctors. They thought I'd had a heart attack. Perfect nonsense.'

'Thanks for the postcard,' said Garbutt.

'Now then, you haven't got rid of me yet, either of you. I've made a decision. I'm flying to the East for the New Year.'

'You'd never get the Insurance,' said Kate.

'You've not flown in years. It's knees on your nose now,' said Garbutt.

'I shall be flying First. I always did. I always shall. I can afford it. Judge Veneering left me his set of Law Reports and I shall sell them for six thousand pounds.'

'You won't get Insurance.'

'You can't go alone.'

The two of them were closing on him like assassins.

'I have never felt so well. My little holiday has set me right. The doctor says that there is no need for the more lethal injections against diseases now. And I have the right clothes already in my wardrobe. No shopping.'

They muttered off, to confer.

'Flying's not safe any more,' said Kate. 'Not since the Twin Towers. New Year's just the time for the next attack. And you'll be flying to a Muslim country, like as not.'

He paid no attention but asked Garbutt if he would go up in the roof and look for the suitcase he and Lady Feathers had brought back from Bangladesh on their last trip.

Kate said, 'Madeira's nice. Why not settle for nearer?'

'No. Bangladesh. I must see Bangladesh – or maybe Lanka again. And I might just continue. On into Malaysia, then up to Borneo. Kotakinakulu. Where I was born.'

'Then I despair,' said Garbutt.

'Bangladesh is where the brasses come from.'

He had given Kate the beaten copper bowls of his heyday, after Betty died, to stop her from cleaning them twice a week at his expense.

She said, 'If I understand the nine o'clock news, Bangladesh is the place half the time under water and no good for arthritis. I'm sorry, but that doctor's notorious. He's never been beyond the golf course. He's never even been to Grand Canary where we go – nice and near and no chance of Economy-class thrombosis.'

'He's told you. He's not going Economy-class,' said Garbutt. 'He says it's full of children joining their families out East for the school holidays. Makes him angry. Says in his day it took six weeks and you went once in five years. Says they're all spoilt now, and playing music in their ears.'

'It's the luggage that really bothers me,' said Garbutt.

The suitcase was immense. He got it out of the roof like a difficult birth. Its label called it a *Revelation*.

'*Revelation* was once the very best luggage,' said Filth. 'They were "revelations" because they expanded.'

'They were them heavy things that went out with porters,' said Kate. 'Can't we get you one borrowed? From that Chloe?'

'Absolutely not,' said Filth.

'No way,' said Garbutt.

'Get something on wheels with a handle, then,' she said; and 'What's this, there's something written on it in brass studs?'

'ISLAM,' Filth said.

'Well that settles it. You can't carry that. You'll be thought a terrorist.'

'Islam was the name of a distinguished lawyer in Brunei. A friend. He gave me the suitcase to bring back our presents. We bought a great many – they have so little there. It was the least we could do. Buy and buy.'

'Let's get it open then,' said Garbutt.

Inside were lurid hessian table mats, cross-stitched sacking table cloths, wilting saris and some indestructible straw matting. There was also a heavy little bundle of amethysts. He had sometimes suspected Betty of light-hearted smuggling. He sent all the other stuff to a church sale and asked Garbutt to scrub the case and polish it. It came up a treat.

'You can tell Class, I'll say that,' said Kate. 'But I wish you'd reconsider, Sir Edward. We're hardly over your last.'

He stared her out.

And so into the Revelation went Filth's impeccable underwear; his singlets and what he still called his knickers; his yellow cotton socks from Harrods, twenty years old; some silk pyjamas; two light-weight suits and a dinner jacket (because one can never be quite sure where one will be invited). He added two sponge (antique phrase) bags, one for shaving things and bars of coal-tar soap, the other for his pills. Separate pills for use on the journey would go into his passport case. There was ample room in the Revelation for more.

'You could get all your things in here, too,' he called out to Betty over his shoulder – then felt a pang in the upper chest. He was doing it again. Talking to her. And as if she would ever have dreamed of sharing his suitcase! So strange that, since his extraordinary peregrination to the West Country, Betty was back in his life again. Brief pains, real pains of longing for her now. Guilty pains. He had been neglecting her memory. *Memory and desire* – I must keep track of them. Mustn't lose hold.

On Christmas Day he attended church at ten. He preferred the eight o'clock in a silent church, heady with greenery and winter-scented flowers, but eight was getting early for him now. The ten o'clock was restless with children and everyone shaking hands with each other and the Vicar was called Lucy. Never mind. He prayed for Father Tansy, and for Babs and Claire. He prayed for the souls of Ma Didds and Sir and Oils and Miss Robertson and Auntie May. This set up other candidates. He prayed for Loss, of course, as he often did, and for Jack and for Pat Ingoldby as he did every day, and for poor old Isobel who'd turned out to be a lesbian all the time. So stupid of him. And most unpleasant. He should have guessed he could never be everything to her.

He prayed – *what, will the line ne'er be done?* – for the nice girl and her grandmother, and for the aunts' little maid Alice, and for Garbutt and Kate. He prayed for the souls of his father and mother. And then he prayed for Ada, the shadow who leaned to him over water which he now was not sure was a memory or the memory of a memory. He prayed for podgy Cumberledge who had come out strong as a lion. How unaccountable it all is. How various and wonderful. He kept on and on praying through the rest of the service. For Veneering, for that unattractive Barrister girl who'd had a baby she'd called after him, for. . . . He struggled hard against praying for Chloe and the souls of his aunts – but in the end, he managed it. He didn't pray for Betty. He knew she didn't need it.

He had his usual Christmas dinner at the White Hart in Salisbury and over the next few days put his desk in order, adding a codicil to his Will that left Mrs-er – Kate (her name was *Toms*, Katherine Toms) the amethysts. He left Garbutt a cheque, then tore it up and left him a much larger one. He topped up his bequests to the National Trust and the Barristers' Benevolent. And so the last dead days of December passed.

On the thirty-first, he was waiting for the car in the hall, seated upon Betty's rose and gold throne, alone, since Kate had her family to think about at New Year, and the car drove him without incident in pouring rain the hundred miles to Heathrow.

The airport was almost empty. There had been 'an alert'. How ridiculous, he thought. We are letting these people win. Security was meticulous. He was made to step three times under the scaffold before anyone realised that the alarm signal he gave off came from his old-world eyeglass. The suitcase with its emblazoned studs and Muslim appearance was passed through without a glance. ISLAM. There was a little hesitation about the X-ray picture of Pat Ingoldby's clothes-brush which looked like a gun.

And, then, the plane.

How stewardesses do smile these days, thought Filth. How cold their eyes.

He wondered what it would be like to be hi-jacked? He wondered once again, an hour or so later, when the plane plunged like a stone for a thousand feet over the Alps.

'Just a bit of turbulence.' The pilot came strolling through, presumably to give confidence, and Filth was pleased with himself for continuing to drink his soup.

'Are you comfortable, sir?'

He was pleased that the fellow was English. Pilots nowadays tended not to be.

'What route are we taking, Captain? Round the edges?'

'Oh, sure. Well to the South. Not a missile in sight. It'll be dark over Afghanistan. Singapore for a cup of tea and then up to Dacca.'

Filth said, 'When I first used to come out here, it was Vietnam we had to avoid. Had to refuel twice then. The Gulf. Then Bombay. Bombay's called something else now, I gather. There used to be half a marble staircase on Bombay airport. Gold and cream. Lovely thing. It stopped in mid-air. Symbolic.'

'Time marches on.'

'Not so sure it marches anywhere in particular though.'

He slept. Once, jerking awake from a dream, he yelled out, thinking he was being put into a body-bag. An air stewardess with tendril arms was tucking a blanket around him.

The black night shuddered all around the plane. When he next woke there was a pencilled line of gold drawn round each oval blind.

Dawn already.

'We are in tomorrow,' said the girl. 'It's the sunrise. A happy New Year.'

(You'd think I'd never flown before.)

He watched the dawn.

Later he looked down upon a fat carpet of clouds and saw something he had never seen in his life before. Two suns stood side by side in the sky. A parhelion. A formidable and ancient omen of something or other, he forgot what. He looked about the cabin, but the other two or three First-class passengers were asleep under their blankets and the stewards out of sight.

The whiteness outside the plane became terrible. The plane was a glass splinter, a pin. It was being flipped into eternity, into dissolution. They were beyond speed now, and in infinity – travelling towards what he understood astronomers call 'The Singularity'.

But they were bringing the orange-juice and hot cloths.

And soon it was evening again.

At Singapore a wheelchair had been provided for him. (Very old gentleman with limp.) It stood waiting at the mouth of the wrinkled tube that joined the aeroplane to the earth (and that certainly had not been there in the seventies; they had had to climb down steep stepladders). He disregarded the chair and walked stiffly along the bouncing tunnel and into the air-cooled glitter of the shops, and eventually to the shadowy First-class lounge. Two hours, and a long sleep, later – and he walked easily all the way back.

The seat next to his was now occupied by a young man in an open-necked collarless white shirt and jeans who was already at work upon a laptop. Filth read across a white laminated folder 'Instructions to Counsel'.

Filth felt garrulous.

'You a lawyer? So was I. I used to work on the flight out, too. All the way out, all the way back. Don't know how I did it now. Straight into Chambers from the airport. We all got used to working through the night, even in London. Mind you, I never went straight from a plane into Court. Never did that. Too dangerous.'

'We do now,' said the boy. 'No time to hang about.'

'Dangerous for the client. Dangerous for Counsel. Going into Court not feeling tip-top.'

'I always feel tip-top. I say – you're not by any chance . . .?'

'Yes. Old Filth. Long forgotten.'

'Well, you're still remembered out here.'

'Yes. Well, I dare say. I hope so. Ha. Did you ever come across a chap called Loss?'

'No. I don't think so.'

'Or Islam?'

'They're all called Islam.'

'He's probably dead. Certainly retired. I've got one of his suitcases. Called a Revelation.'

A new stewardess, a Malay, browner, silkier, gentler, with more rounded arms and in a sari, came along with potted prawns. 'Shall we pull down the blinds for you, sir?'

'No thanks,' said the young Silk. 'Less than two hours left. Let's watch the stars.'

'You married?' asked Filth after a long rumination looking at but not eating the prawns.

'Sure.'

'I used to take mine along,' said Filth. 'Always.'

'Mine's in banking. And I don't think she actually would describe herself as "mine". We're landing. Good. And we weren't hi-jacked.'

As he made to leave the plane, a black misery suddenly came upon Filth like the eye bandage slapped around the face before it is presented to a firing squad. Then he wondered if, in fact, on this journey, he had really hoped only for death. . . . Had wanted the knife slipped out of the shoe. The gun in the sleeve. The 'Nobody move!' The spatter of bullets and blood. One blessed, releasing explosion. Lived long enough. Get the thing over.

He had been waiting.

For what was there left for him in the Donheads?

Stuck in that wet woodland place with Garbutt and Mrs-er, and lacy Chloe?

Well, there was still hope for obliteration on the return journey. Might achieve it.

And if I don't – what?

I'll move. I'll take a flat in The Temple. Don't know anyone now. Ghastly lot of new Judges. Still, they are one's own.

Bleak, uncertain, nodding thanks to the pretty girl, Filth made gingerly for the door.

From the top of the gangway, the East hit him full in the face. The thick, glorious heat washed on to him and around him, lapped his swollen old hands and his tired feet, bathed his old skull and sinewy neck, soaked into his every pore and fibre. Life stirred. The resting plane was vibrating with heat, the air around it vibrating, the airport vibrating and dancing in the soft dark. High glares and electrics together shone along the low parapet where people were waiting to meet the plane, clustered like dark flies, like frenzied butterflies.

The tremendous chatter of talk, the excitement. The toots and hoots and wails and the drumming. The prayers and the prostrated pray-ers and the prayer mats. The old, old beloved smell.

Betty seemed to be beside him, grinning away, waving back at all the people. Just at his shoulder.

'Watch it, sir. Let me help you. Is something wrong?'

'Nothing is wrong,' said Filth. The kind arms stretched. 'Nothing at all is wrong.'

For he was Home.

Scene: The Inner Temple Garden

Scene: The Inner Temple Garden.
Two Judges standing beside the monument that is inscribed, *Lawyers, I suppose, were children once*. The bell of the Temple Church is tolling on and on, as it does, once for every year of a dead Bencher's life.

The Queen's Remembrancer: That'll be for Filth.
A Lord of Appeal: There'll be ninety of them then.
QR: Not quite. Nearly. Did you read the obituaries?
L of A: Yes. Short. So difficult to say exactly what he'd done. When it came to it. Not a *great* lawyer. Never changed anything. Very old-fashioned delivery. Laughable, I expect, now. Good Judge, of course.
QR: He'd just got off a plane. Did you know? Going back to his roots.
L of A: Game of him. About the most imaginative thing he ever did, I suspect. In his long and uneventful life. Was he travelling alone, d'you know?
QR: Oh, yes. Travelling alone. Quite alone.

Acknowledgements

As will be obvious, I am very much indebted to Rudyard Kipling's *Autobiography* and to his story *Baa Baa Black Sheep*. Also to Christopher Hudson's fine novel, *Colombo Heat*, about the last days of the Raj in Ceylon (Sri Lanka); I have even taken the liberty of borrowing one of his characters and giving her a walk-on part with a crutch. Sir was suggested by Geoffrey Grigson's autobiography, *The Crest on the Silver*.

I am also very grateful to friends, dead and alive, who were once Raj Orphans, and to Peter Leyland, K.S. Chung and my husband David Gardam, all of whom set off in Wartime convoys to the East and two of whom returned.

I am very grateful to the late Michael Underhill, QC, who was for a few months Junior Platoon Commander in the Royal Gloucestershire regiment which guarded Queen Mary at Badminton House. He talked to me about it, as did his wife, Rosalie Beaumont, who showed me a charming, innocent correspondence between her husband and Queen Mary. Thanks also to Mrs Nettles, one-time housekeeper at Badminton, and her sister. I drew on *Queen Mary* by James Pope-Hennessy (1959) and *HRH Princess Adelaide, Duchess of Teck* (1900), a mighty work by C. Kinloch Cooke, Barrister-at-Law. John Saumarez Smith of the Heywood Hill bookshop in Curzon Street kindly introduced me to Osbert Sitwell's hilarious *Queen Mary and Others* (1974).

To the Benchers of the Inner Temple, the Clerks and members of Atkin Chambers I am particularly grateful for many things over fifty years; especially to Stewart Goldsmith who often got me to foreign parts and home again.

Those who believe that they recognise any of my characters are mistaken, for they are all from my imagination except for Queen Mary; her lady-in-waiting; the Duchess of Beaufort; the stationmaster of Badminton (who, it appears, really did wear white gloves and call the platforms 'lawns'); and my husband who in only one instance resembles Filth: he ate thirty-seven bananas on Freetown beach. (There were no ill-effects.) His friend at Oundle School, 'the best I ever had', was called Pat Ingoldby; he was lost at sea in 1942 and I have made use of his name in his memory.

Any historical mistakes are my own.

Jane Gardam,
Sandwich,
Kent
2004